*Your Brother
in Arms*

Shades of Blue and Gray Series
Edited by Herman Hattaway, Jon L. Wakelyn, and Clayton E. Jewett

The Shades of Blue and Gray Series offers Civil War studies for the modern reader—Civil War buff and scholar alike. Military history today addresses the relationship between society and warfare. Thus biographies and thematic studies that deal with civilians, soldiers, and political leaders are increasingly important to a larger public. This series includes books that will appeal to Civil War Roundtable groups, individuals, libraries, and academics with a special interest in this era of American history.

Robert C. Plumb

Your Brother in Arms

A UNION SOLDIER'S ODYSSEY

University of Missouri Press   Columbia and London

Copyright © 2011 by
The Curators of the University of Missouri
University of Missouri Press, Columbia, Missouri 65201
Printed and bound in the United States of America
All rights reserved
5 4 3 2 1   15 14 13 12 11

Cataloging-in-Publication data available from the Library of Congress
ISBN 978-0-8262-1920-6

♾™ This paper meets the requirements of the
American National Standard for Permanence of Paper
for Printed Library Materials, Z39.48, 1984.

Designer: Susan Ferber
Typesetter: Jennifer Cropp
Printer and binder: Thomson-Shore, Inc.
Typefaces: Minon, Jefferson, and Warnock

To Preston and Peggy Ewing, who acquired and preserved the George P. McClelland letters, and to the Civil War Trust and the battlefield preservation groups that preceded it, for making it possible today to walk the ground on which McClelland and thousands of his comrades in arms fought.

Contents

Preface

In late May 1865, soldiers of the Fifth Corps of the Army of the Potomac were encamped on Arlington Heights outside the nation's capital in anticipation of being mustered out of army service. The war was over, victory won, and at twilight one breezeless evening, the men began an impromptu candlelight march.[1] Soldiers placed candles, issued to them earlier in the day, into the sockets of their bayonets. Others from the corps soon joined the rally until it involved thousands of men. They organized themselves into lines of march, holding their lighted bayonet candlesticks before them. The procession slowly wound its way through the camp, gathering more participants along the route. A formal Grand Review of the Army of the Potomac had taken place along Pennsylvania Avenue two days earlier, but for the men, this spontaneous twilight march was not a display of martial pomp but an expression of their realization that a profound experience in their lives had come to an end, and the emotions they felt were better suited to a candlelight procession than a military parade.

The group made its way to the quarters of General Charles Griffin—commander of the Fifth Corps of the Army of the Potomac. The general came forward to acknowledge the men gathered before him, their faces illuminated by the candlelight. "Speech! Speech! Speech!" they called out to their commander. Griffin, a fearless leader on the battlefield, loathed public speaking. Instead, he asked one of his most respected division commanders to speak on his behalf. General Joshua Lawrence Chamberlain—a former college professor from Maine and hero of Little Round Top at Gettysburg—stepped forward. Acknowledging General Griffin, he began to speak to the hushed crowd: "The pageant has passed. The day is over. But we linger, loath to think we shall see them no more together—these men, these horses, these colors afield . . . This army will live, and live on, so long as soul shall answer soul, so long as that flag watches with its stars over fields of mighty memory. . . ."[2]

When he was finished addressing the men, Chamberlain saluted them and then stepped back into the darkness. The group stood in silence following the general's remarks until, one by one, their candles burned out, and the soldiers returned to their respective regiments.

One soldier who had served alongside these men from August 1862 to April 1865 was not among the assembled Fifth Corps that evening. Instead, he lay in a hospital bed in Washington City recovering from a grievous wound that had threatened to end his young life and that kept him away from the celebrations of victory, such as the grand review down Pennsylvania Avenue. George Pressly McClelland had fought with the 155th Pennsylvania Infantry, Fifth Corps, Army of the Potomac for two years and eight months in some of the most significant battles of the war.

McClelland recorded his wartime experiences in letters to his brothers and sisters. Together these letters form a perceptive and articulate chronicle of his experience as a frontline soldier who passed through "the fiery trial," as Abraham Lincoln described the war in an 1862 letter to Congress. More than battlefield reports from a young soldier, McClelland's letters reflect the social, cultural, and political currents of the war that transcend the fighting. For McClelland, letters became a crucial connection to his family and their civilian life beyond the brutality and rigors that he faced as an infantryman in the Army of the Potomac. He was an exuberant, untested teenager when he enlisted in August 1862 and a sober, battle-seasoned young man when he mustered out of the army in June 1865. His experience can be conveyed in the names of the places where he served: Antietam, Fredericksburg, Chancellorsville, Gettysburg, the Wilderness, Spotsylvania Court House, the North Anna River, Petersburg, and Five Forks.

At the beginning of his service, McClelland was filled with a young man's braggadocio:

> McClellan's strategy is played out. Pope doesn't appear to do much better. Stonewall Jackson is a match for the whole of them. Granny Lincoln has again forgot the dignity of the President of a great republic. . . . Ye fathers and statesmen, who are asleep, arouse ye from your lethargy and show yourselves in the hour of your Country's greatest distress. (August 1862)

Toward the end of his service, McClelland changed his opinion of Lincoln:

> I am glad to know my oldest brother is prospering. Tell him to vote for Lincoln and not the tool of unprincipled anti-Republican-liberty man [McClellan]. Three-fourths of the Army will vote for Uncle Abe. (September 1864)

I desire you not to decry our President. Any man who could cope successfully with the lamented Douglas is not "common" or "coarse." (October 1864)

McClelland, the battle-weary soldier, recognized that the hard-fought Union victory was in sight by early spring of 1865:

> Four deserters came in on my line and they confirmed the status told by others that Lee's army is in a desperate condition, almost open mutiny, mutterings—not loud, but deep and widespread—of a hopeless cause. . . . The final crush of the Confederacy is at hand—God Save the Republic. (March 1865)

The McClelland letters, in addition to being literate and informative, are a tribute to the discipline of a young man who was writing them under the most trying of circumstances: combat, severe weather, grueling forced marches, and harsh living conditions provided a constant backdrop. George McClelland's letters from the front line of the American Civil War kept his family informed on a continuing basis. Today, one hundred and fifty years later, they are a gift to those of us who seek to better understand this bloody, transformative period in American history from a soldier's perspective.

To help readers put McClelland's letters in context, each set of correspondence is prefaced by narratives on the activities of the Army of the Potomac and the 155th Pennsylvania Regiment and on McClelland's role as a soldier in Company F. Brief explanatory notes on people, places, and phrases follow each letter to help facilitate readers' understanding. The introductory sections provide a historical framework, but it is McClelland's own letters that breathe life into the cold pages of history.

The "Army of the Potomac" sections draw on the rich body of secondary sources available on the Civil War. For the "Regiment" sections, the author has relied on two key sources: *Under the Maltese Cross—Antietam to Appomattox*, a regimental history completed by the 155th's surviving veterans in 1910; and *Company "K" the 155th PA Volunteer Zouaves*, the published diary of D. P. Marshall, who served in the regiment. The "Soldier" sections are based on both primary and secondary sources available to the author. The "In His Own Words" sections are the letters, reproduced exactly as McClelland wrote them during the war except for minor changes in punctuation to help the twenty-first-century reader. Explanatory notes follow each letter, assisting readers with interpretations of nineteenth-century phrases and references.

Through some of man's most ancient of communications tools—pen, ink, and paper—we are able to join the soldier as he marches the roads, wades the streams, fights the battles, suffers, and, ultimately, feels the exhilaration of victory in a war that slips further into the recesses of American history with each passing day. George Pressly McClelland invites us back to share with him—if only briefly—his Civil War journey.

Acknowledgments

During the preparation of *Your Brother in Arms* there were scores of persons who helped me ferret out facts, understand the battles of the Army of the Potomac, explore the ground where George McClelland and his comrades fought, learn about the regimen of a Civil War soldier, and appreciate the limitations of medicine as practiced in the mid-nineteenth century.

I was fortunate to launch my research efforts with the guidance of Ed Bearss, National Park Service Historian Emeritus, who provided welcome encouragement and identified the fundamental resources required to begin the process. A lecture on Civil War records research by Timothy Duskin, Archive Technician at the National Archives in Washington, D.C., was invaluable in helping me set priorities at the start of my archival research. I am also indebted to the guidance provided by the late Charles Jacobs of Rockville, Maryland, at the start of my project. What began as a promised half-hour interview in his home turned into a two-hour discussion and tour of his extensive Civil War library. It was Jacobs who confirmed that George McClelland and the rest of the 155th Pennsylvania passed within a few miles of my home on their march from Washington to Frederick, Maryland, in the late summer of 1862.

Staff at the Carnegie Library and the Heinz History Center in Pittsburgh helped bring McClelland's prewar life into sharper focus. Likewise, the professional and volunteer staffs at the Davenport Library were gracious and efficient as they helped me flesh out McClelland's postwar life in Iowa. The staff of the Richardson–Sloane Special Collections Center at the Davenport Library, led by Amy Groskopf, was particularly helpful to one who always had "just one more question" or an information request that often occurred at the end of the work day.

Deb Williams at Oakdale Memorial Gardens in Davenport, Iowa, helped me locate McClelland's grave site and provided important information regarding the internment dates of McClelland's wife, Juliet, and their infant son, Charles.

At the U.S. Army Military History Institute in Carlisle, Pennsylvania, I was treated as a respected colleague from the very start of my research. Richard Sommers and his associate Arthur Bergeron provided a level of diligent investigative inquiry and sage advice that was unmatched during the research phase of my project.

An important part of McClelland's experience was his medical history. Michael Rhode at the National Medical Museum and Library in Washington helped me sort through volumes of medical information on Civil War wounds and their treatment to find the relevant facts about McClelland's injuries. Terry Hambrecht, M.D., read an early draft of *Your Brother in Arms* and provided his valuable insights on both McClelland's wounds and his probable medical condition leading up to his death in 1898. Dr. Hambrecht is a respected physician and consultant to the National Museum of Civil War Medicine in Frederick, Maryland.

I am also greatly indebted to those Civil War historians who helped me understand the relevant details of the 155th Pennsylvania's involvement in the battles of the Army of the Potomac stretching from Gettysburg to Petersburg and numerous places in between. Ed Bearss provided vivid and compelling insights into battles, including Gettysburg, the Overland Campaign and Petersburg. I was also guided by Chris Calkins and Terry Chernault of the National Park Service (NPS) at Petersburg and Five Forks, Virginia; Frank O'Reilly of the NPS at Fredericksburg; and Gordon Rhea for the Battle of the Wilderness. Gordon, a practicing attorney, author, and recognized expert on the Overland Campaign, also read and critiqued early chapters of my manuscript. Chris Calkins read the chapters dealing with Petersburg and Five Forks and gave me a candid assessment of my approach and cleared up inconsistencies in my manuscript. Clark Hall added greatly to my understanding of the winter encampment of the Union army in Virginia 1863/1864. He also reviewed an early draft for accuracy.

Also reading early drafts of the manuscript was John Hennessy of the NPS. John, author and historian, was incisive in his critique of the work and of invaluable help in streamlining the narrative. In addition to his help in my research at the U.S. Army Military History Institute previously mentioned, Richard Sommers read preliminary chapters dealing with the siege of Petersburg and later read the entire manuscript, providing his perspective on the letters, the preceding contextual narrative, and the literary approach. His critique was an invaluable "shakedown cruise" that resulted in a far better manuscript.

Another remarkable battlefield guide and invaluable source of information, including his personal insights, with whom I was privileged to spend time was

James McPherson. Never was the term *gentleman and scholar* more appropriately applied than to McPherson, Professor Emeritus, Princeton University.

Early on, the Tawani Foundation in Chicago saw the value of telling the story of citizen-soldier George McClelland. I am deeply appreciative of the foundation's willingness to fund the research required to tell the McClelland story and to fund the McClelland Legacy Grants given to the battlefields at Fredericksburg, Chancellorsville, and Five Forks; and the grant given to the Richardson–Sloan Special Collections Center at the Davenport Public Library. Colonel Jim Pritzker and Ed Tracy of Tawani were instrumental in turning the dream of telling George McClelland's story into a reality.

My colleagues in executing the Tawani Foundation grant at the Civil War Trust were a pleasure to work with throughout the project. Ron Cogswell, Doug Brouder (now at Gettysburg College), and Nicole Osier were the ideal project partners–professional, patient, and positive. Without preservation efforts in the past, I would not have been able to walk virtually all the ground on which George McClelland fought from1862 to 1865. Today, the effort to preserve land is even more critical as high-stakes development competes with land-preservation efforts at many Civil War sites. As Civil War preservationists so succinctly put it: "Once the land's gone, it's gone forever."

The work of the trust deserves the support of all who have an interest in American history and want to save important Civil War sites for future generations.

No manuscript ever survives the journey to becoming a book without discerning editorial support. Clair Willcox and his colleague Sara Davis of the University of Missouri Press gave me their unqualified support and encouragement during the publishing process. They set the bar high for editorial quality, and I am thankful that George McClelland's story was in such capable hands.

Your Brother in Arms would not have been possible without the acquisition of the McClelland letters by Preston Ewing, a past president of the New York City Civil War Roundtable and my wife's uncle. His wife, Peggy Ewing, retained the letters after Preston's death and gave them to me in the hope that I would continue to preserve what she believed to be an important chronicle of Civil War history. My lasting regret is that the Ewings did not live to see the letters published.

I owe profound thanks to my wife, Louise, who endured numerous requests to help discern words in the handwritten letters as I transcribed them, listened to many Civil War stories, critiqued drafts, and underwent a prolonged period when our dining room table was stacked with books, drafts of manuscripts, maps, letters, and other source materials, thereby making it virtually impossible to have dinner guests without a major household upheaval. Louise is indeed a patient woman, but most of all, she is a dedicated believer that the story of George McClelland needed to be told.

And, finally, I am indebted to the person whose presence permeated this project from the beginning. George Pressly McClelland, who wrote these literate and evocative letters, makes *Your Brother in Arms* a compelling personal narrative. I salute this gallant young soldier who served his country with bravery and distinction.

Years hence of these scenes, of these furious passions, these
    chances,
Of unsurpass'd heroes, (was one side so brave? The other was
    equally brave;)
Now be witness again, paint the mightiest armies of earth,
Of those armies so rapid so wondrous what saw you to tell us?
What stays with you latest and deepest? of curious panics,
Of hard-fought engagements or sieges tremendous what
    deepest remains?

—Walt Whitman, "The Wound-Dresser"

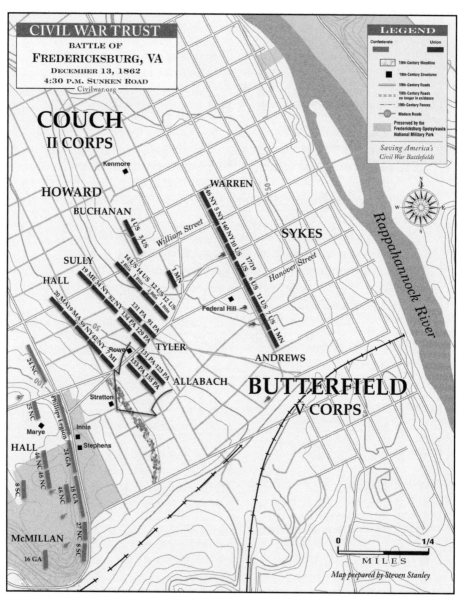

All maps used by permission of The Civil War Trust.

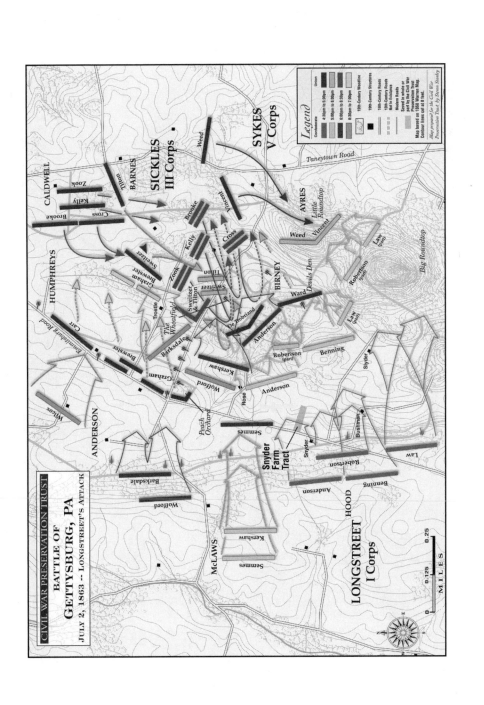

CIVIL WAR PRESERVATION TRUST

BATTLE OF
GETTYSBURG, PA
JULY 2, 1863 -- LONGSTREET'S ATTACK

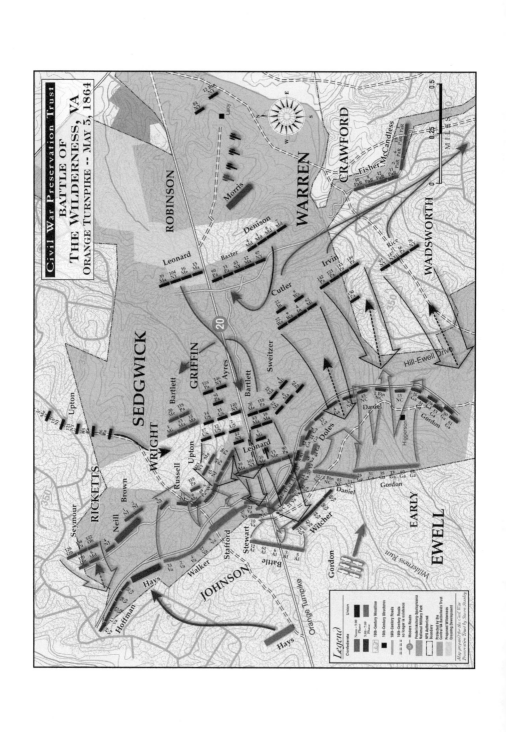

Civil War Preservation Trust
BATTLE OF
THE WILDERNESS, VA
ORANGE TURNPIKE -- MAY 5, 1864

Legend

Confederate
Union

19th-Century Structures
19th-Century Roads
19th-Century Roads
no longer in existence
Modern Roads
Fredericksburg-Spotsylvania
National Military Park
NPS Authorized
Boundary
Protected by the
Central Va. Battlefields Trust
Proposed Wilderness
Crossing Development

Map prepared for the Civil War
Preservation Trust by Steven Stanley

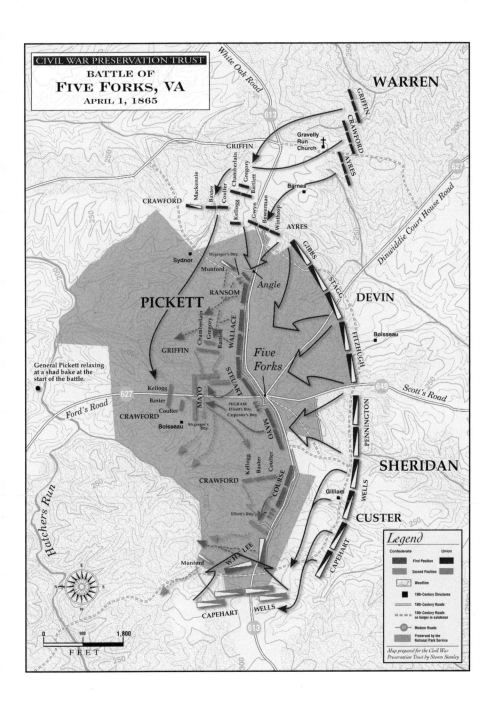

BATTLE OF
FIVE FORKS, VA
APRIL 1, 1865

WARREN

GRIFFIN

CRAWFORD

AYRES

White Oak Road

613

GRIFFIN

Gravelly
Run
Church

Mackenzie

Chamberlain

Gregory

Bartlett

Baxter

Coulter

CRAWFORD

Kellogg

Gwyn

Bowerman

Barnes

Winthrop

AYRES

627

Dinwiddie Court House Road

Sydnor

McGregor's Bty.

Munford

RANSOM

Angle

GIBBS

STAGG

DEVIN

PICKETT

Chamberlain

Gregory

Bartlett

WALLACE

Five
Forks

Boisseau

FITZHUGH

GRIFFIN

STEUART

General Pickett relaxing
at a shad bake at the
start of the battle.

Kellogg

Baxter

Coulter

CRAWFORD

Boisseau

MAYO

McGregor's
Bty.

PEGRAM
Elliott's Bty.
Carpenter's Bty.

649

Scott's Road

627

Ford's Road

MAYO

PENNINGTON

SHERIDAN

Kellogg

Baxter

Coulter

COURSE

Hatcher's Run

CRAWFORD

Elliott's Bty.

Gilliam

WELLS

CUSTER

N

S

W

E

WM. H. F. LEE

Munford

CAPEHART

Legend

Confederate   Union

First Position

Second Position

Woodline

19th-Century Structures

19th-Century Roads

19th-Century Roads
no longer in existence

Modern Roads

Preserved by the
National Park Service

CAPEHART

WELLS

613

0   900   1,800

FEET

*Map prepared for the Civil War
Preservation Trust by Steven Stanley*

Your Brother in Arms

Chapter One

The Volunteer

National War Climate, Recruitment, and War Preparations, August—September 1862

The War

Now we are in a state of war which will yield for nothing.

—Robert E. Lee, letter to his sister, April 20, 1861

The election of 1860—when Abraham Lincoln, under the Republican Party banner, carried every free state except New Jersey—was the spark that set off the tinderbox of secession. During the preceding campaign, Southern leaders had threatened secession if the Republicans won the election. Such threats had been raised in the South since 1850, but none was taken seriously. Now, with the sweep of free states in the North bringing Lincoln to the White House, the South was done with empty threats and poised to take action.

It was the South's contention that individual states had joined the Union as sovereign units, able to sever their connection to this "association of sovereign states" whenever they wished and on any substantial grounds. Secession was, to be sure, a drastic measure, but, in the minds of Southern political leaders, it was a lawful act.

South Carolina led, withdrawing from the Union in December 1860. Six other states quickly followed: Alabama, Florida, Georgia, Louisiana, Mississippi, and Texas. The group of seven was joined by Virginia, Arkansas, North Carolina, and Tennessee after the fall of Fort Sumter in April 1861.

The residents of the North observed the process of secession with almost uniform feelings of shock and disbelief. Most Northern free-state citizens and politicians were too stunned by the abrupt unraveling of the Union to consider what policies and strategies were required to meet the crisis head on. Reaction in the North was slow, but momentum was building.

"Keep a Sharp Lookout for Traitors"
—Rallying cry of Pittsburgh's Committee of Public Safety, 1861

From 1860 on, the well of pro-Union sentiment ran deep in Pittsburgh, Pennsylvania. During the closing days of 1860, Secretary of War John B. Floyd had directed the shipment of heavy ordnance (cannons) from the Allegheny Arsenal in Pittsburgh to Southern military posts. Residents of Pittsburgh, already suspicious of Southern intentions, organized a rally at the Pittsburgh courthouse to protest the action. Angry citizens pushed for retraction of the order at the highest level. A formal protest was sent by telegram over the names of four prominent Pittsburgh residents to President Buchanan requesting that the transfer of ordnance be "immediately countermanded." The president took notice of these outraged constituents and promptly asked his secretary of war to cancel the order for the removal of ordnance to military posts in the South. The cannons remained in Pittsburgh.

The following January, President-elect Lincoln stopped in Pittsburgh en route from Springfield, Illinois, to Washington, D.C., where he was to be inaugurated. On his way to the Monongahela House to spend the night, he found the crush of Pittsburgh citizens so large that the military was asked to clear a way for the travel-weary president-elect and his small party. The friendly pro-Union crowd begged Lincoln to address them. Climbing onto a chair in the hotel lobby, Lincoln implored the assembled admirers to come back in the morning, when he would have a "few words" for them. The next morning ten thousand eager Pittsburgh residents assembled in front of the Monongahela House to hear their next president deliver a fifteen-minute speech. At the conclusion of his talk, twenty thousand hands came together in a rousing applause of approval.

Some pro-Union sentiment was less benign. Right after the news of the fall of Fort Sumter reached Pittsburgh, reports tell of hangman's nooses appearing on lampposts throughout the city attached to signs that read "Death to Traitors."

Despite the bad news from the battlefields, the growing list of casualties and the seeming disarray in the Union's general officer leadership throughout 1861, the people of Pittsburgh did not waver in their strong Union support. The favorable results of several waves of recruiting in the Pittsburgh area are compelling evidence of the breadth and depth of support for the Union cause in both the city and surrounding Allegheny County.

"Young Men, Your Country Demands Your Service!"
—1861 recruiting poster in Pittsburgh

Realizing that the regular army strength of 16,000 troops was inadequate to suppress the "rebellion" that was quickly unfolding after the fall of Fort Sumter on April 13, 1861, Lincoln issued his first call for 75,000 state militia to serve ninety days. The quota set for Pennsylvania—drawing heavily from Pittsburgh and its surrounding towns—was 12,500 troops. Charged with post-Fort Sumter patriotic enthusiasm, the state exceeded the quota, providing 20,000 troops that were drawn in large part from volunteers in Pittsburgh and Allegheny County. Between April 14 and April 24, 2,000 volunteers from Allegheny County—including Pittsburgh—were recruited, outfitted, and sent to the front.

Two days after the fall of Fort Sumter, a mass meeting was held at city hall in Pittsburgh to rally citizens with an appeal to save the Union. Hundreds had to be turned away because the building would not accommodate all the citizens who wanted to express their anxiety over the secessionist threat to the Union. Prominent citizens and civic leaders spoke eloquently about the need to snuff out the rebellion in its early stages and defend the Constitution. Appeals were made to support the new president—regardless of party affiliation—and to be especially vigilant by keeping "a sharp eye out for traitors."

A Committee of Public Safety was quickly formed in Pittsburgh, and General Thomas M. Howe, a prominent Pittsburgh businessman, was chosen to lead the group.

The Board of Bank Presidents of Pittsburgh, during this same period, committed to the governor that their banks would help fund the war effort. The Pennsylvania Railroad Company president stepped forward to promise his company's cooperation with any military use required of the railroad. He also made it possible for the bright young man who was his superintendent of the railroad's Pittsburgh division—Andrew Carnegie—to leave his post to take on the responsibility of launching the U.S. Military Telegraph Corps. Carnegie organized the corps and ran it successfully before he was called back to the Pennsylvania Railroad. The organizational genius he exhibited in starting the U.S. Telegraph Corps and providing the operational framework for this vital communication service was an early display of the entrepreneurial talents that would propel him into national prominence in post-Civil War America.

As the secession continued to gain momentum in the late spring and early summer of 1861, Lincoln responded by taking bold steps to bolster troop strength that, in several ways, went beyond his constitutional powers as commander in chief. He called for 42,000 volunteers for three years of service. In addition, Lincoln called for an extra 23,000 men in the Regular Army. Sensing the urgency of the situation and putting aside separation-of-powers issues, Congress met in July and backed the president by authorizing his actions and—at his urging—providing for the enlistment of 500,000 volunteers to serve for three years.

Despite the longer terms of service and news of Union losses at Bull Run in Virginia and casualties at Wilson's Creek in Missouri, recruitment fervor continued to run high in Pittsburgh. Senior officers had little difficulty recruiting companies and regiments within Allegheny County. By the autumn of 1861, the county had recruited eleven infantry regiments, two cavalry regiments, and three artillery companies.

In October 1861 one of the final brigades to be recruited in Allegheny County before the end of the year was to leave for duty in Louisville, Kentucky, but not until a full parade and review could be held for Pennsylvania Governor Andrew Curtin at West Common in Allegheny. The governor, accompanied by his staff and decked out in full uniform, presented regimental colors to the troops. Then, in a speech called "eloquent and soul-stirring" by one observer, the charismatic governor bid the troops farewell. No doubt many in the crowd on that clear, crisp fall day thought sending out this latest round of fresh, eager volunteers meant the end of the national nightmare of secession and that the dissolution of the Union would soon be over. But it was only the beginning.

Governor Curtin returned to West Common nine months later to address a large crowd assembled to hear a group of notable political, business, and religious leaders. This time the tone was grim. Curtin began his speech to the crowd with a startling admission: "The Peninsula campaign is a failure! The Union armies have not been victorious! They have been driven to the gates of Washington!"

The Regiment—The 155th Pennsylvania Infantry

> Come forward to crush out treason!
> —Headline from an 1861 recruiting poster in Pittsburgh.

Summer's languid days of 1862 in Pittsburgh brought with them more bad news from the front lines of the war. On the eastern front, the Seven Days'

Battles between June 25 and July 1 resulted in nearly 16,000 Federal casualties and the end of the Peninsula campaign. It was small consolation that Confederate losses were even higher (20,000 casualties). Coming close on the heels of the battle of Shiloh on the western front in April where 13,000 Union soldiers died—20 percent of the total Union forces on the field of battle—and "Stonewall" Jackson's drubbing of Union troops in the Shenandoah Valley in May, the Seven Days' Battles dashed any hopes for a swift conclusion to the eighteen-month-old secession. The memory of the Union humiliation at Bull Run was still bitter even after a year. These battlefield disappointments, coupled with the ongoing shuffle of commanding generals through leadership positions within the Union army, rounded out the glum war picture for the residents of "Smoky City."

On July 2, 1862, President Lincoln issued his third call for volunteers to fill the growing needs of the Union army. Within days, the adjutant general of the U.S. Army requested that Governor Curtin raise twenty-one new regiments of volunteers in Pennsylvania as soon as possible.

Curtin, in issuing a proclamation, appealed to the patriotic sentiment of the people of Pennsylvania:

> To sustain Government in times of common peril by all his energies, his means and his life, if need be, is the duty of every loyal citizen . . . The existence of the present emergency is well understood. I call on the inhabitants of the counties, cities, boroughs and townships throughout our borders to meet and take active measures for the immediate furnishings of the quota of our state.

A "Great War Meeting" was convened in Pittsburgh on July 24, 1862, to kick off an intensive effort to fill the ranks of the twenty-one desired regiments. At this meeting Curtin made his shocking "The Peninsula campaign is a failure" statement. Scores of local and state dignitaries implored young men to "fall in" and join the companies being formed. Singers and instrumentalists filled the air with patriotic music. Upwards of twenty thousand people heard the governor, a former governor, numerous judges, professors, clergy, and prominent businessmen urge the young men to rally for the Union.

Judge William Wilken, eighty-seven, with a head of snow-white hair, standing six feet tall, and bearing a passing resemblance to Andrew Jackson, seemed to one observer in the audience "like a voice from the Revolutionary period in which he was born." Wilken appealed to the supremacy of law and the preservation of the Union. Samuel Wilson, a professor at Western Theological Seminary, asked of the assembled crowd: "What is gold—what is silver—as compared with the honor of the Nation? It is offal when thrown into the balance against the liberties of our country!"

Speakers took up positions on four corners of the West Common to literally surround the crowd with rhetoric. All the stops had been pulled out to ensure that the citizens of Pittsburgh—especially the young men who were candidates for recruitment in the Union army—heard the very best motivational speakers of the day and were inspired by the most rousing patriotic music that the participating bands and singers had to offer.

In addition to the appeals by political and civic leaders, the clergy of all denominations in Pittsburgh played an active role by urging enlistments among those in their congregations and parishes. Methodists, Presbyterians, Lutherans, and Roman Catholics set aside doctrinal differences to rally around the preservation of the Union and to encourage enlistments to bolster Union ranks. At this stage in the war, there was little public discussion among clergy in western Pennsylvania about slavery and abolition. Unlike the feeling among their counterparts in New England, the prevailing motivation for urging enlistment among the clergy in Pittsburgh was the preservation of the Union, not an end to slavery.

It was in this highly charged atmosphere of Union fervor and patriotic sentiment from all quarters of influence in Pittsburgh that the 155th Pennsylvania Volunteer Regiment was formed. From the nucleus of Companies A and B of the Kier Rifles, named for S. M. Kier, a major financial contributor to the Union cause, came the other eight companies that would form the 155th.

Recruited from the City of Pittsburgh and the surrounding countryside, the majority of members of the 155th were processed in Pittsburgh recruiting centers, with the rest being handled in the surrounding counties of Armstrong and Clarion. Outside the conventional recruiting venues of public buildings and hastily built recruiting shacks, Company G was organized at the home of Dr. Charles Klotz, a physician, who was made captain of the company after it was fully manned.

Once the men had been examined by the U.S. Army surgeons assigned to recruiting, they were formally mustered into U.S. service by the mustering officer of the 17th U.S. Infantry. Physical examinations were perfunctory at best or, at worst, not performed at all. Since the majority of the 155th's recruits were boys between the ages of sixteen and twenty, the presumption of the examining surgeons was that this youthful group was healthy. The surgeons, under intense pressure to accept all volunteers, viewed the overall group of recruits as "sturdy, healthy, athletic boys" based on their observed vitality during the cursory physical "exams."

The price for these lackadaisical physical exams was paid later, when scores of soldiers proved to be physically unfit for the rigorous demands of service. Those who did not die of illness were quickly mustered out on certificates of disability by army surgeons.

Congress had set a bounty for volunteers of $100 (about $2,000 in current dollars).[1] One quarter of the amount was to be paid at the time of enlistment and the balance paid at the end of the enlistment period. Furthermore, Congress had permitted the payment of one month's pay in advance, resulting in a total enlistment bounty of up to $38 to start. While some governors in Northern states added bonuses of $50 or more to sweeten the enlistment appeal, Governor Curtin—perhaps confident that Pennsylvania would draw the necessary number of recruits based on past successes without additional incentives—scotched any idea of a state bonus for recruits.

> The first assemblage and residence of the Companies in Camp Howe was marked with great spirit and gayety.
> *Under the Maltese Cross*

Once mustered in, the companies that would form the 155th Regiment were ordered to report to Camp Howe, a fifty-acre tract of land close to Pittsburgh with ample, comfortable barracks and a parade ground for conducting drills and reviews. The first step in turning raw recruits into soldiers was to issue uniforms. Ill-fitting coats and trousers, oafish leather brogues, and coarse woolen underwear were distributed to the men. Only camp guards were provided muskets for guard duty; the rest of the recruits remained unarmed—for the time being.

Behaving more as if they were at summer camp than in a military operation, recruits at Camp Howe formed glee clubs, played flutes, guitars, and violins they had brought with them or took part in card games. During the day, the men entertained young ladies and civilian friends from Pittsburgh and the surrounding area. In the evenings, spirited "hoedowns" filled the barracks with music and dancing. The only negative aspect of life at Camp Howe was the "deplorable" food that was served. But not all suffered. Recruits from the city were able to slip out of camp for meals. Those who came from the distant countryside could not get away for a home-cooked meal and were doomed to eat "food of the most abominable character."

The lack of order and discipline at Camp Howe was due largely to the lack of assigned commissioned officers. The available pool of potential officers was small, and even when likely candidates were identified, commissions were slow in being awarded by the state. One promising soldier, Sergeant James Collord, was to join the regiment as a company commander. Collord was already serving in the Ninth Pennsylvania Reserves stationed in northern Virginia. The sergeant was granted leave to join the 155th at Camp Howe to take command of Company F, which had been recruited in his honor by friends in Pittsburgh. When Collord learned that fighting was imminent at the second battle of Bull Run, he declined the furlough so that he could stay at the front and serve with his unit. During the battle, Sergeant Collord was seriously wounded and taken to Washington to receive medical attention. Governor Curtin, recognizing Collord's heroic efforts at Bull Run, issued a commission to Collord as a lieutenant colonel of the 155th Regiment. Collord never served with his new unit. His wounds were disabling, and he resigned from the army in late 1862.

> How you sprang—how you threw off the costumes of peace
> with indifferent hand,
> How your soft opera-music changed, and the drum and fife
> were heard in their stead,
> How you led to the war . . .
>   —Walt Whitman, "Drum Taps"

With news of the Union disaster at the second battle of Bull Run—located a mere twenty-six miles southwest of Washington—on August 29 and 30 and growing rumors that Stonewall Jackson was leading a unit across the Potomac River into Georgetown to attack the nation's capital, there was a mounting concern in the Union army about troop deployment. These developments, and the intelligence that General Robert E. Lee was moving his Army of Northern Virginia into Maryland, put an abrupt end to the frivolity in Camp Howe. Three regiments (the 123rd, 136th and 139th) and several cavalry and artillery units were ordered to report to Washington as quickly as the Pennsylvania Railroad trains could transport them.

On September 2, orders were received for the 155th to leave Camp Howe, march to Union Station on Pittsburgh's Liberty Street and proceed without delay by rail to Washington. Rumors of the impending invasion of the capital by the Confederates quickly created an atmosphere of seriousness and a sense of urgency as the 155th packed up their musical instruments, put their playing cards away, and quickly forgot about cotillions and hoedowns. The ugly beast of war was coming out of the shadows for the 155th.

Reveille was sounded at five in the morning on September 3 to rouse the 155th. Departure time for the troop train was set for 7:00 p.m. at Union Station—a short three miles from Camp Howe. Army leadership was taking no chances on their raw recruits missing the train so the predawn reveille was ordered. Despite the early start to their day, the regiment was not able to get organized and packed until three o'clock that afternoon.

Loaded down with their military gear, gifts, and goods from home, the regiment lumbered toward the station, knapsacks bulging with cups, forks, brushes of every kind, shirts, vests, mirrors, extra caps, and umbrellas. Absent strong officer leadership, the nine hundred men of the 155th made numerous rest stops, arriving at the station after 9:00 p.m. Wise railroad authorities, recognizing the lack of officers and the rawness of the recruits, had decided earlier in the day to hold the train until 9:30.

The march was made at the snail's pace of a mile every three hours. The only time that the pace picked up, according to some witnesses, was when the townspeople, notably the young ladies, came out to the streets to cheer the men on. Finally, at 9:30 p.m., the last goodbyes were said to family and friends, farewell embraces shared, and good-bye kisses given to loved ones. The freight and cattle cars of the Pennsylvania Railroad, loaded to capacity with the new members of the 155th Regiment, rolled out of Union Station to keep an appointment with history. For many, this would be a one-way trip. They would never return.

The train traveled east, its freight cars, without lights of any kind, rumbled across the Pennsylvania landscape and around the mountains—Laurel Hill, the Alleghenies, and the Tuscaroras. Past the whistle-stops—Greensburg, Johnstown, and Huntingdon. Along the Juniata River at Lewistown, eventually crossing the Susquehanna River to reach Harrisburg, the state capital, early on the morning of September 4.

An important order of regimental business while at Harrisburg was to outfit the men with firearms. Members of the 155th were issued Belgian rifles, ponderous weapons of dubious accuracy. The guns, along with their accompanying cartridge boxes, added a weighty burden to each soldier's equipment responsibilities. Once armed, the 155th was back on the train to Washington with an intermediate stop in Baltimore. There the regiment left their freight-car accommodations to bivouac near Eutaw Street where they ate pork and hardtack washed down with strong, black coffee.

Early in the morning of September 5, the regiment arrived in Washington, D.C., ending a two-day journey from Pittsburgh in cramped, fetid freight cars. After breakfast and a brief time to shake the kinks out of their travel-weary bodies, the soldiers were assembled and began a march across the Potomac River on Long Bridge to Camp Chase on Arlington Heights. The camp, named for Salmon P. Chase, Lincoln's ambitious treasury secretary, was situated on land that had been owned by Robert E. Lee's family before being seized, along with Lee's home, by the federal government. Once on Arlington Heights some of the men were issued new tents. Others had to improvise, but any shelter was better than that of freight cars!

Acculturation into the Union army began immediately. Training included guard-and picket-duty procedures, personal appearance and uniform requirements, and how to respond quickly to a call to arms. To test the men, the regimental commander, Colonel Edward Allen, ordered a call to arms—a "long roll" of drums—at midnight during one of the first days on Arlington Heights. It was only after the men had assembled that Colonel Allen told them that he was testing their ability to respond quickly and that an attack was not imminent. He praised the officers and men for their rapid response to the call.

At Camp Chase, the regiment's order of battle within the Army of the Potomac began to take shape. The 155th became part of the newly formed brigade of Pennsylvania regiments under Colonel Peter H. Allabach, a Mexican War veteran. This brigade became part of a new division commanded by Brigadier General Andrew A. Humphreys, former chief of topographical engineers on General McClellan's staff. Unfortunately for Humphreys, his division was assigned to the Fifth Army Corps under the command of the hapless General Fitz-John Porter. It was at Porter's feet that blame was laid for the recent Union defeat at the second battle of Bull Run.

The Soldier—George P. McClelland

> Writing, the art of communicating thoughts to the mind through the eye, is the great invention of the world . . . enabling us to converse with the dead, the absent and the unborn, at all distances of time and space.
> —Abraham Lincoln, 1860

The young man standing before the recruiting officer was three months shy of his twentieth birthday—a teenager in the company of other teenage males who were flooding into recruiting offices throughout Pittsburgh. This young man had fair skin and was well dressed and groomed with neatly cut chestnut brown hair. His intense gray eyes met those of the recruiter straight on with confidence. He was slightly above average in height and slender, unlike the robust, muscular farm boys the recruiter had signed up from the countryside.

The articulate way the young man expressed himself and answered questions gave the recruiter every reason to believe that George Pressly McClelland was an educated, urban gentleman who was more familiar with books than with the tools of physical labor. The recruiter was surprised when the response to his question "Occupation?" was "Carpenter" from McClelland.

McClelland was, in fact, one of the "city boys," a group whose youthful confidence bordered on arrogance. They laughed and boasted about their patriotism and the courage they expected to bring to any confrontation with the "Rebels." Ignorance of the everyday duties of a common soldier in no way tempered their enthusiasm or self-assurance that they could handle any military situation that might arise.

George McClelland, like many of his contemporaries, was motivated to enlist by the fervent speeches of political leaders, prominent citizens, and even his Presbyterian clergyman. On the one hand, George was running to the promise of glory and valor in military service to his country in its time of utmost need. On the other hand, he was running from the dead-end occupational future that faced him in Pittsburgh.

The youngest of six children of widower Archibald McClelland, George had adopted his father's profession as a carpenter. Archibald had brought his woodworking skills to the United States from Belfast, Ireland, and he had built a moderately successful business as a highly skilled finishing carpenter. He was able to support his six children, educate them (girls as well as boys were all literate), and even employ two live-in maids to help with raising his four boys and two girls. George, the youngest child, had all the advantages associated with being the youngest sibling, including the motherlike love and attention from his eldest sister, Annie, who was six years his senior.

George loved reading books and attending school, but education beyond secondary school was a financial impossibility for his father. George's occupational future was *fait accompli*—to join his father as a carpenter in the family business. When George was ten, his eldest brother, Thomas, had left Pittsburgh, setting out to establish himself in the West, where prospects seemed unlimited for a man with skills and ambition. Thomas had both. He settled in Davenport, Iowa, in 1852, just six years after that state entered the Union. Thomas's pioneer spirit was undoubtedly an inspiration to young George, who had bigger dreams than could be confined to a carpentry shop in Pittsburgh.

George's next eldest brother, Henry, may have been another strong incentive to enlist. Henry had moved west to Kansas where, in May 1861, he enlisted in the First Regiment of the Kansas Volunteers as an infantryman. A brief ten weeks after he entered the service, he was wounded in action at the battle of Wilson's Creek, Missouri. In May 1862, Corporal Henry S. McClelland was discharged on disability due to a loss of hearing that may have resulted from his wound at Wilson's Creek.

The "city boys" who filed into the recruiting office in August with George McClelland included a group of sixteen teenagers from Bayardstown (Pittsburgh's fifth and ninth wards.) The youngest was fifteen-year-old Harry Curry. They were a spirited and fun-loving group who called themselves the "Luny Crowd" for their lunatic attitude and antics. All were recruited as members of Company F, 155th Pennsylvania Infantry.

Experience on the battlefield would temper their youthful exuberance over time, but it would not dim their élan and high spirits. They proved, over the course of the war, to be remarkably brave and dedicated soldiers. (By the end of the war, four of the "Lunies" had been killed in action, one had died of fever, and five had been seriously wounded on the field of battle.)

While some recruits argued over the amount of bounty and bonus they would be paid, most would have signed up without much of a monetary premium, so filled were they with patriotic slogans, fantasies of glory in serving the Union cause, and inspiring music that money was no serious impediment to enlisting. McClelland was similarly motivated. After a brief dispute over the amount of bonus he might receive, George P. McClelland signed up for three years of service, beginning immediately. He received a $25 bounty and a $2 premium in addition to a promise of a one-month advance on his pay as a private.

George settled quickly into military life at Camp Howe, albeit in a regiment not yet completely organized, staffed by officers, disciplined, or equipped. He was now officially a member of Company F, 155th Regiment of the Pennsylvania Infantry. Quickly spotting McClelland's leadership potential and responding to a vacuum in the noncommissioned officer ranks, higher-ups promoted him to Third Sergeant a mere nine days after his enlistment.

In His Own Words—The Letters of George P. McClelland

The letters of George P. McClelland provide articulate and insightful glimpses into the life of a citizen-soldier in one of America's most cataclysmic conflicts. Sometimes colorfully descriptive and detailed, other times vague and curiously oblique about enemy engagements, his letters run the gamut of topics from chronicling camp life and food to vividly describing battlefield action and critiquing the competence of his superiors from generals to the commander in chief. McClelland is a loyal letter writer to his family, especially his sisters, Annie and Lizzie. Seldom does he write a letter without chiding his siblings about keeping up the flow of letters to him. He is ever the demanding youngest brother when it comes to correspondence.

Camp Howe near Pittsburgh
August, 1862

Dear Brother,
Your letter, which I received some considerable time ago, I now considerate to reply to. You will not think hard of me for not answering sooner when I tell you that I did not want to write to you until I was somewhat settled, because, as concerns myself, I had nothing reliable to write about.

I was played off on by a certain recruiting officer here, but as it is all over now, the least said about it the better.

I now belong to Company F Kier Rifles, a company that was raised by the friends of James Collord, a corporal who is now serving in the 9th Regiment Pennsylvania Reserves. A good man highly spoken of by everybody who is acquainted with him. He had been expected here for the last 2 weeks, but has not yet arrived. In the meantime, the Company was raised in a day and was so popular that Company B was started and recruited to the maximum in three days. Both companies are now in camp.

Enjoy myself fully and have prayer meeting every evening. Camp is about 3 miles from the City. Come in nearly every day.

Uniform I have not yet got. Water scarce in camp. Have to go ¾ of a mile for it. Consequently [I] get a pass or furlough, if not [I] run the guard. Go to town where water is plenty.

Lizzie came home from the Alleghenies a day or two ago. Gives me good advice which I shall endeavor to profit by.

An agent of the Tract Society has flooded our quarters with religious books, tracts, etc. I read them when I get an opportunity.

All the folks here are in good health. Business is good so [there is] great demand for manual labor in some branches. A regiment and half of another left last week for the seat of active operations. Another regiment goes tomorrow. We will not go away for a couple of weeks yet.

McClellan's strategy is played out. Pope doesn't appear to do much better. Stonewall Jackson is a match for the whole of them. Granny Lincoln has again forgot the dignity of the President of a great republic by opening a correspondence with a newspaper. Once before he forgot himself in addressing a political meeting in Washington. Ye fathers and statesmen, who are asleep, arouse ye from your lethargy and show yourselves in the hour of your Country's greatest distress. Arise and be doing as the Republic, that is now tottering and reeling like a drunken man, will sink forever in hopeless ruin.

I will endeavor to keep you posted in regard to my whereabouts. Write soon and tell me what you are doing. And I now bid you farewell.

George McClelland, Esquire

Notes on the August 1862 Letter

Based on his reference to James Collord, his August letter to his brother Thomas was written before the outcome of second Bull Run and Collord's fate were known. (The battle of Bull Run was fought August 29 and 30, 1862.)

McClelland is one of the "city boys" who can slip out of camp to go home to Pittsburgh "nearly every day." He is one of the few soldiers who has not yet received his uniform (no doubt making his frequent trips in and out of camp to his home less problematic.)

"Lizzie" is the youngest sister in the McClelland family, two years George's senior. She lives with the family in Pittsburgh.

He reports the departure of several Pennsylvania units to the front lines, but his estimate that the 155th "will not go away for a couple weeks yet" is not correct. The situation changes dramatically after the second battle of Bull Run. By September 2, the 155th will be on its way to Washington to protect the threatened Capital.

McClelland critiques his general officers: "McClellan's strategy" is indeed "played out" with the collapse of the Peninsula campaign in July. His reference to General Pope is prescient. At the second battle of Bull Run (which McClelland does not know about when he is writing the August letter), Pope is soundly defeated.

His remarks chastising "Granny Lincoln" may well reflect the prevailing attitude in the North regarding Lincoln's competence at this stage of the war. At this point in the conflict, the president's own cabinet frequently questioned his competence—often publicly.

Camp Chase on Arlington Heights
September 8, 1862

Dear Sister Lizzie,

I should have written you long ago, but I did not want to until I could give something reliable. Nineveh was the second stopping place on our ride from Pittsburgh.

I saw the Alleghenies by moonlight and still I did not. I only got occasional glimpses when at times I gathered up courage to look out the window and get my eyes filled with black cinders for my daring. The only resource was to button up our coats, throw the capes over our heads and let it rain.

The blue Juniata first attracted my attention as the day broke, dimly at first, but as the mist rolled off, the scene was magnificent. The most beautiful scenery I ever beheld. Around Harrisburg, or rather 2 miles this side of it, [we] marched to Camp Curtin, then to the capital. Had to stay overnight in the ancient town. Thought we were never to get out of it. Did get off at last in time. (Pretty long though.) Got to Baltimore. Had a splendid reception. From the Monumental, you know, to Washington; passed the Sabbath there—some reading the Bible, some writing to dear ones at home, others sleeping and some singing hymns.

I had a nice ride of 5 miles in a baggage wagon full [of] guns, bayonets, sack naps and [it] did not jolt a bit for anything. Got this far after several delays from other trains. I don't know how long we will be here. Liable to be ordered off in half an hour's notice.

I do not know when I can get this off. This regiment is not yet [staffed with] officers. Our colonel is not here. Lieutenant Colonel James Collord is lying at Willard's wounded. He has buckshot in his eye. One entered his nose, another the mouth and 2 in the neck. He will recover, but will lose his eye. In our company we have but one commissioned officer. Lieutenant Markle, commanding; Lieutenant Clapp is acting quartermaster. We are all to be brigaded in old brigades.

I am lying on the ground writing this, a knapsack for a table. The "Lunies" in lieu of regular have improvised tents with poles stuck in the ground and covered with our blankets to protect us from the heat of sun. Our camp is on an open field about half a mile from General Lee's White House. I supposed there is 10,000 men occupying what was formerly his property.

I have just written to Arch and am about tired. I owe you more than thanks for the many kindnesses conferred.

I now bid you goodbye. Write to me soon and confer another favor on—

Your Brother
George P. McClelland
Company F, 155th Regiment
Washington, DC
To Miss Lizzie McClelland Pittsburgh, PA

Notes on the September 8, 1862, Letter

At this point, the 155th and McClelland have been out of Pittsburgh for nearly a week. His letter reflects the difficulty of the cattle car/freight car transportation from Pittsburgh to Washington.

Glimpses of the Allegheny Mountains, the "blue Juniata" (river), and "most beautiful scenery I ever beheld" were some consolation for the cramped conditions he and his fellow soldiers experienced en route to Harrisburg.

His reference to a "splendid reception" in Baltimore contrasts sharply with the reception given the 6th Massachusetts bound for Washington on April 19, 1861, when that regiment was set upon by outraged Southern sympathizers (possibly including the mayor) as they attempted to switch trains in Baltimore. The "Baltimore Riot" was quickly put down and order restored. This marked contrast in reception for the 155th a year later in Baltimore was worth reporting to his sister, who, no doubt, had concerns about her youngest brother's safety.

McClelland's mention of the "monumental" in Baltimore refers to the Battle Monument commemorating the War of 1812 and erected in 1825 and the Washington Monument completed in 1829 in Baltimore.

This letter acknowledges the fate of young James Collord, whose severe wounds have him recuperating at the Willard Hotel in Washington. Lieutenant Colonel Collord did recover, but the extent of his wounds forced him to resign from the army before the close of 1862, never to serve with the 155th or any other unit during the war. (James Collord returned to Pittsburgh where he lived until his death in 1900.)

He reports writing to his brother Archibald, who is four years older than he. Archibald enlisted in the 22nd Pennsylvania Cavalry in September.

McClelland has less than a week after writing this letter to adjust to camp life at Camp Chase and the outskirts of Washington, D.C. General Lee is on the offensive, having crossed the Potomac River into Maryland on September 4. Soon the 155th, with about a month of military experience under its belt, will be ordered to proceed into Maryland posthaste to take a position as reinforcements to General McClellan's main body of troops. The Army of the Potomac will be moving north then west through the Maryland highlands to take a position near the town of Sharpsburg, Maryland, along Antietam Creek.

Chapter Two

Into the Fray

Antietam, Sharpsburg Area, September—October 1862

The Army of the Potomac

> The President informed me . . . that there were thirty thousand stragglers on the roads; that the army was entirely defeated and falling back to Washington in confusion. He then said that he regarded Washington as lost, and asked me if I would, under the circumstances, consent to accept command of all the forces.
>
> —General George McClellan, September 2, 1862

The opening days of September 1862 were times of rampant uncertainty in the Northern states and bickering in the high command of the Union army. The Army of the Potomac was removed from George McClellan's command in late August by general in chief Henry Halleck because of McClellan's lack of cooperation—some said insubordination—in not supporting General John Pope at the second battle of Bull Run. The president found McClellan's behavior "unpardonable."

Yet, within forty-eight hours, McClellan was back in command of the Army of the Potomac with orders to defend Washington. The threat of Robert E. Lee, accompanied by the much-feared and nearly mythical Stonewall Jackson, invading the capital was sufficient reason to overlook McClellan's past transgressions. General Halleck had doubts about McClellan, but President

Lincoln saw McClellan as a glass half-full. "There is no man in the Army who can lick these troops of ours into shape half as well as he," Lincoln reasoned. "If he can't fight himself, he excels in making others ready to fight."[1] "Little Mac" was back.

By September 3, it was clear to the freshly reinstated McClellan, based on reports from reliable sources in the field, that Confederate forces were on the move with the intention of invading Maryland and perhaps continuing on into Pennsylvania.

McClellan ordered three of his corps to the Maryland side of the Potomac River. He sent each of them on a separate route in order to maintain flexibility to thwart Lee's advancement and used the rationale—at least for the record—that the troop movements were being made in defense of Washington. McClellan stretched his narrow mandate of defending Washington much to General Halleck's displeasure. In Halleck's mind McClellan's command was defensive in objective; he was not to take any offensive steps with the troops under his command.

Halleck and McClellan also had widely different opinions on the Federal troops stationed at Harper's Ferry. Halleck saw the old arsenal town as critical and wanted it held. McClellan made the case both to Halleck and Secretary of State William H. Steward that Harper's Ferry should be abandoned and the troops assigned to more effective use elsewhere. General in chief Halleck prevailed, and Union troops remained in Harper's Ferry (until Stonewall Jackson captured the garrison and turned all twelve thousand of its defenders into prisoners of war.)

> . . . I leave in a couple of hours to take command of the army in the field. I shall go to Rockville tonight & start out after the rebels tomorrow . . . I think we shall win for the men are now in good spirits—confident in their General & all united in sentiment . . . if I defeat the rebels I shall be master of the situation.
> —George B. McClellan, to his wife, Mary Ellen, September 7, 1862

By September 7, the three corps on the Maryland side of the Potomac had been joined by two additional corps and two divisions. Meanwhile, no decision had been made as to who would command the "active army." McClellan's orders remained: "command of the fortifications of Washington and of all the troops for the defense of the Capital." Ambitious generals abhor a vacuum, and one of the Civil War's most ambitious generals, George B. McClellan, stepped into the command vacuum with the Army of the Potomac.

McClellan reasoned that the time to move that army was at hand. "As the time had now arrived for the army to advance, and I had received no orders to take command of it, but had been told that the assignment of a commander had not been decided, I determined to solve the question for myself. . . ."[2]

To his wife, Mary Ellen, he wrote from his camp in Rockville, Maryland, fifteen miles outside Washington, "I expect to fight a great battle and to do my best at it."[3]

McClellan's reconnaissance of Confederate troop movements in Maryland was generally sound, but his information on Lee's troop strength was wildly inaccurate. By September 11, McClellan was reporting to Halleck that the Rebel army in the vicinity of Frederick, Maryland, was "not less than 120,000 men." In fact, Lee had 50,000 compared to McClellan's force of 70,000, and Union numbers would soon rise to 80,000 with the arrival of reinforcements.

Beyond numerical superiority, McClellan also possessed a remarkable piece of intelligence. In what must be considered one of the most extraordinary instances of good luck in the annals of military intelligence, on September 13 a private from an Indiana unit found three cigars wrapped in a piece of paper in a field near Frederick, Maryland. The paper was a copy of Lee's Special Order Number 191 detailing the directions for the movement of the Army of Northern Virginia in the coming days. The document was rushed to McClellan's headquarters, and within an hour the Army of the Potomac was on the move to intercept Lee's men. The Union army was on the march west from Frederick toward South Mountain with two powerful advantages: half again as many troops and detailed information about the opposing army's tactical plans.

Lee, through a pro-Confederate Marylander, learned that McClellan had found the lost order and took quick corrective action. He immediately ordered troops to block the several passes through South Mountain. Along the mountain ridge that stretches forty miles, from Pennsylvania in the north to the Potomac River in the south, battles raged at Fox's, Turner's and Crampton's Gaps. Having stalled the Union army at South Mountain, Lee pulled his forces back toward Sharpsburg, Maryland, to regroup, form up, and confront the approaching Army of the Potomac.

> Are you acquainted with General McClellan? He is an able general but a very cautious one . . . His army is in a very demoralized and chaotic condition, and will not be prepared for offensive operations—or he will not think so—for three or four weeks. Before that time I hope to be on the Susquehanna.
> —Robert E. Lee, September 1862

Emboldened by Stonewall Jackson's success in taking the Union garrison at nearby Harper's Ferry, Lee gathered his forces and arrayed them in an advantageous position in the fields surrounding the sleepy village of Sharpsburg, which lay a mile from the Potomac River. Here, Lee reasoned, he would take a stand against what he considered was a hesitant, indecisive George McClellan and a demoralized Army of the Potomac. Furthermore, the political stakes were high. A retreat by Lee's forces could threaten European recognition of the government in Richmond.

As the sun rose on September 17, most of Lee's Army of Northern Virginia was in place on the ridges to the north and east of Sharpsburg. They were lying in wait for Little Mac and the Army of the Potomac. At 5:30 a.m., the Federals launched their first attack. Twelve hours later, as the sun set, the fighting was over: 6,000 men were dead or dying; 17,000 were wounded. Twice as many Americans were killed in a single day at Sharpsburg as died in the War of 1812, the Mexican War, and the Spanish-American War in total.[4] Lee's plans to invade Pennsylvania were in shambles.

Yet, despite Lee's precarious state of readiness following the battle, McClellan refused to press his advantage by following up with a decisive blow to smash Lee's weakened army. A fresh Union division with two brigades reached the battlefield early in the morning of the 18th, but McClellan refused to commit them to battle or to an aggressive pursuit of Lee. Among those reserve units arriving were the green troops of the 155th Pennsylvania.

The Regiment—155th Pennsylvania Infantry

The nation is rapidly sinking just now . . . Stonewall Jackson (our national bugaboo) about to invade Maryland, 40,000 strong.
—George Templeton Strong

At the highest levels of the Union army, generals were wrestling with command issues in early September. Meanwhile, the soldiers of the 155th were adjusting to their new lives in the military. Fulfilling their initial role as defenders of the Federal capital, the troops of the 155th were moved from the heights at Arlington to a position near Fairfax Seminary, a location five miles from Arlington's Camp Chase on the outskirts of Alexandria, Virginia.

It was becoming increasingly evident to senior officers of the Union army by the second week in September that the Confederate threat was shifting from a possible invasion of Washington to the danger posed by Lee's move to Maryland and, potentially, on to Pennsylvania. Accordingly, the 155th was ordered to leave Northern Virginia, cross the Potomac River on Aqueduct Bridge to Georgetown, and be ready to march north to Maryland. After crossing the Potomac, the regiment halted in Washington. There, thanks to the resourcefulness of their regimental commander, Colonel Allen, they were able to feast on fresh oysters.

Colonel Allen arranged with noted Washington caterer and restaurateur Tom Harvey to provide a wagonload of oysters for the men of the 155th. Harvey responded positively and promptly to Colonel Allen's request, even offering to provide a second wagon of oysters if necessary, all at no cost. (Later that evening, well after the delivery of the oysters, Army supply wagons showed up with the routine hardtack and coffee.)

While bivouacked in Washington there was other good news besides oyster feasts. The regiment was able to trade in its clumsy Belgian firearms for Springfield muskets. Along with the new muzzle loaders, the troops were issued ammunition consisting of cartridges containing three buckshot and a bullet. Called "buck and ball," the ammunition was especially lethal at close range.

By September 14, the need for additional Union troops in Maryland was becoming clear and urgent. The eight new regiments of Pennsylvania Volunteers —including the 155th—that had been marking time in Washington were now needed quickly to support McClellan's efforts to intercept Lee before he used Maryland as a springboard to invade Pennsylvania.

On the morning of Sunday, September 14, to the sound of Washington's church bells, the 155th set out on a march of fifteen miles north and west to set up camp just outside Rockville, Maryland (where General McClellan had had his headquarters two days before). As the green troops marched the route from Washington to Rockville, the ringing of church bells faded and was replaced by the rumble of cannons firing, which was coming from the north in the direction of South Mountain, where the main body of the Army of the Potomac was making its assaults on Fox's and Turner's Gaps.

Amid the serene, rural setting on the outskirts of Rockville, the troops were able to rest and prepare themselves for the next leg of the march in the morning—all except one soldier: Robert A. Hill of Company F. Private Hill had the dubious distinction of being the first casualty of the 155th Regiment. While on a personal foraging expedition in a nearby peach orchard, Hill was shot in the foot by a guard for trespassing on civilian property. Later the hapless Hill would lose his leg to infection because of the wound and be discharged by surgeon's certificate in June 1863.

> If the march has just begun, you hear the sound of voices everywhere with roars of laughter . . . later on, when the weight of knapsack and musket begins to tell, the sounds die out; a sense of weariness and labor arises from the toiling masses streaming by, voiced only by the shuffle of a multitude of feet, the rubbing and straining of innumerable straps, and the flop of full canteens.
> —David L. Thompson, Company G, 9th New York Volunteers

Early the next morning, the regiment began the march to Frederick, Maryland, thirty-one miles to the north. Marching along the Frederick Pike from

Rockville over rolling hills and ridges on a warm September day while loaded down with clothing and equipment soon took its toll on the inexperienced recruits. Heavy overcoats, blankets, knapsacks, and other gear judged nonessential (or at least nonessential at the moment) by the weary soldiers were discarded. Army teamsters following the infantry in supply wagons stopped to pick up the gear abandoned by the pike and often sold the "found" items to civilians along the way.

During the march north, enterprising members of the 155th found shelter at nightfall wherever they could be comfortable. About one hundred members of the regiment took shelter in an abandoned girl's seminary building near Urbana, Maryland. Vacated only two days before by Longstreet's corps, the building had Rebel anti-Union graffiti on the white, plastered walls. Members of the 155th drew their own pro-Union graffiti using charred sticks, including a profile of Abraham Lincoln.

The entire division resumed marching the next morning, September 17. Meanwhile, some thirty miles away, on the west side of South Mountain, the battle of Antietam was beginning. Aware that his division could play a key role in supporting McClellan, Humphreys demanded that the pace of the forced march be accelerated.

As they crossed the Monocacy River on their way to Frederick, Maryland, members of the 155th were beginning to see, for the first time, the impact of the conflict. At the Monocacy River crossing the railroad bridge had been blown up by the Confederates several days before. There, among the timbers and debris of the destroyed bridge, was the corpse of an African American man who had been employed by the Confederates to handle the explosives used to demolish the bridge.

In the same area, the regiment saw some twelve thousand Union prisoners captured at Harper's Ferry and paroled by Stonewall Jackson under the promise that these troops would not take up arms until formally exchanged.[5] As a 155th regimental historian wrote years later: "The incident was certainly one which tended to chill the ardor of the most enthusiastic patriot at that time."[6]

Compensating in part for the negative impact of seeing twelve thousand Union prisoners, Humphreys's division received a warm welcome as it marched through Frederick, Maryland. Townspeople thronged the streets waving U.S. flags, cheering and applauding the troops as they marched by. After the frosty reception given the troops in the small towns along the pike, the men basked in the pro-Union sentiment as they passed through Frederick.

Headquarters, Fifth Army Corps, September 17, 1862, 2:30 PM
General Humphreys, in bivouac near Frederick
We are in the midst of the most important extended battle of the war. The reb-

els are desperate. We have driven them some distance, but it is a vital importance to get up all our troops. Come as soon as possible, and hurry up with all
haste. Do not render the command unfit for service, but force your march.
    —Alex S. Webb, Brig. General Chief of Staff, 5th Corps

By late afternoon on the 17th, the 155th Pennsylvania, along with the rest
of Humphreys's division, began its forced march to meet up with McClellan's forces at Sharpsburg. Heading northwest, the troops marched along the
National Road, which begins rising outside the city of Frederick. Crossing
numerous streams that flow out of the Catoctin Mountains, they began the
steep climb to Middletown, Maryland. Five miles past Middletown, the 155th
crossed South Mountain at Turner's Gap and began their downward course.

As the sun set on their forced march, Humphreys's men could see evidence
of the battle of South Mountain fought only days before. Most of the buildings adjacent to the road had been converted to hospitals and were filled with
the wounded. At Boonsboro, on the National Road, the streets were jammed
with ambulances carrying the wounded from Antietam to hospitals in the
rear. Among those being transported were men of the 9th Pennsylvania Regiment from Pittsburgh who had been wounded at the cornfield at Antietam.
Members of the 155th knew many of these fellow Pittsburgh soldiers.

After passing through Boonsboro, Humphreys's division turned onto the
Sharpsburg-Boonsboro Pike on their way to the Antietam battlefield that lay
seven miles to the west. At 7:00 a.m. on September 18, after fourteen hours
of forced marching from Frederick—most accomplished at night—the 155th
and the rest of Humphreys's division officially reported in to McClellan. By
11:00 a.m., the division had been assigned to relieve General Morell's division
and held in reserve.

Despite the Confederates' vulnerability after the battle and the Union's superiority in number of troops, Little Mac took no immediate action to press
his advantage. His nemesis, Lee, slipped across the Potomac on the morning
of September 19, and the gray fox was once again back in Virginia.

The main body of McClellan's army closed in on the Potomac at Sharpsburg. A reconnaissance foray was ordered for the 118th Pennsylvania Volunteers, the "Corn Exchange" Regiment, to cross the Potomac. They quickly fell
into the arms of the enemy, who had dug in across the river from Sharpsburg.
The unfortunate 118th was easily repulsed. Many from the regiment were
captured; casualties were high, and a number of retreating troops drowned
during their attempts to flee back to Union lines across the Potomac. It was a
humiliating footnote to a campaign that Lincoln had hoped would "destroy
the rebel army."

Having arrived too late to participate in the battle and not assigned to pursue Lee's Army of Northern Virginia, the 155th Pennsylvania settled into a

regimen of picket duty along the Potomac River near Sharpsburg. The immediate threat of enemy action was lifting from what became known as Camp
McAuley, but it was replaced by a threat that was—at times—even more deadly:
dysentery.

As reported by D. P. Marshall of K Company of the 155th: "Cramp is becoming quite common and a number have it. Simon Schrecengost had a very
severe attack today. . . . In a few days he was sent to the general hospital near
Frederick, Maryland where he died."[7]

Prolonged periods of physical exhaustion following forced marches, coupled
with erratic diet and dehydration during the days leading up to Antietam,
were beginning to take their toll on the Army of the Potomac, particularly the
new recruits in Humphreys's Third Division.

The Soldier—George P. McClelland

> As he gazed around him the youth felt a flash of astonishment at the blue,
> pure sky and the sun gleaming on the trees and fields. It was surprising that
> Nature had gone tranquilly on with her golden process in the midst of so much
> devilment.
> —Stephen Crane, *The Red Badge of Courage*

Within three weeks George P. McClelland had gone from the closeness
of family, friends, and familiar neighborhoods in Pittsburgh to an encampment adjacent to the site of the bloodiest day of the Civil War. The aftermath
of that day was gruesomely apparent: the unburied dead of both sides; the
wounded warehoused in every available building; and fetid dead horses everywhere. When McClelland first arrived with his regiment, the smoke had
barely cleared from the fighting fields at Antietam, and the devastation left
behind could only shock and repulse those who came upon the scene. What
teenager could ever be prepared to experience such a frightful place or ever
clear his head of the nightmares that would result from the images seen there?
Yet, in the coming months, equally horrendous scenes would play out around
McClelland. And they would occur with a disturbing regularity.

In His Own Words—The Letters of George McClelland

Battlefield near Sharpsburg
Saturday, September 20th, 1862

Dear Lizzie,

I now write again to you hoping and praying that this will provoke a reply. It is almost 3 weeks since I left home and nothing from my friends—everybody else getting letters and papers and I get—nothing. It is discouraging, very.

Well, Lizzie, we have not yet been in an engagement, but I have been where several battles have taken place. We are now a mile from the Potomac and it is said that the "Rebs" are nearly all across with batteries planted on the other side. This is a horrible place. Men, both Union and Rebel, the latter 3 to one, are lying all around us; unburied horses in dozens everyplace you go creating an intolerable stench. Yesterday I went down to an orchard to get some apples and, before I was aware of it, I was among dozens of dead Rebels lying all through it. But worst of all were the poor fellows lying in sheds and barns unable to move who have had no surgical aid; no one to tend to them

I will have to stop now as the Brigade is getting ready to move. I don't know where . . .

Stopped again half a mile from the Potomac. The river here is not more than 100 feet wide. The "Rebs" are very quiet. Want to draw us on. A Brigade crossed this morning when they were attacked by 50,000 Rebels. Nearly all the 118th Pennsylvania Volunteers were taken prisoners and the Colonel wounded. We are in a dangerous position now. If they knew our whereabouts they could soon shell us out. I am now more sensible of the Scriptural injunction: "You know not what a day may bring forth."

Yesterday I made my first obeisance to Rebel power. I was going for water about a mile away from camp and near a battery which was shelling the Rebels when I heard a whizzing noise. Down I went flat on the ground which was no sooner done then a long "whiffler" shell went over my head exploding about a 100 feet from me.

The Artillery is still thundering and our sharp shooters are stationed along the banks of the river which rises into steep bluffs on either side.

General McClellan and staff passed just now. The boys gave him a hearty cheer. A great many think he is no man for Jackson.

We are now getting a little rest at last. Marching 18 and 20 miles a day is no fun for green men. It nearly used me up, but I always manage to keep up with the rest.

When you see Reverend John G. Brown, tell him that I had not time to see him before I left and if I had, I could not have given him any satisfactory information in regard to the Regiment. I should have written to him, but we have been continually on the move since we got to Washington.

I had better close this desultory writing. Do tell me something quick. Tell everybody to write. It's about all the way I can spend spare time, reading the Bible and . . . . . . Yes, that's all. Tell me how all the children are: Emma, Ellie, Maggie, Joe & Bob. Give my respects to Pennie Bradley, Eliza Wright, Emma Dunn. Tell them all to write. Don't forget Aunt Chess and all the folks in Birmingham. Tell Father & Arch & Annie to write. I can't name all my friends. God bless you.

Good bye,
George P. McClelland
Company F 155th Regiment Pennsylvania Volunteers
Colonel E. J. Allen
Washington, DC

Excuse lead pencil and punctuation. I have no opportunity to write with ink.

Notes on the September 20, 1862, Letter

McClelland wrote to his sister Lizzie two days after arriving in Antietam. His regiment was encamped near the Potomac with the meandering river separating the Union troops from Lee's forces.

At this stage in the war, General George McClellan was held in high regard almost universally by his troops, but soldier George McClelland seemed to have his doubts about his commanding officer. He reflected the grudging admiration and respect that Union soldiers had for the legendary Stonewall.

Potomac River near Shepardstown, Maryland
Thursday, September 25th, 1862

My Dear Sister,

For the first time since I commenced writing at all, I now use a pen. Whether this writing will be any more legible remains to be seen.

I received your letter on last Sabbath while on picket, together with a side from Henry. There is no use talking about it. If I had stain [sic] in Old Pitt, as I could have done, I could have seen him, but I had no notice of his coming.

I will try to draw a good bead, but not on Stonewall. That is impossible. If the young Napoleon had not let slip the opportunity, the like of which he may never again get, the whole Rebel Army would have either been cut to pieces or captured. As it is he has retreated without the loss of a single man, gun, wagon or anything else. And the war, which might have been ended by one stroke, is now put forward 6 months or more.

They did not stop on the other side of the river and plant batteries as reported. It was a regular rout on their side. Our forces moved stealthily and, two days after they crossed, commence shelling the woods on the other side when only a few stragglers were there.

For about a week we have been moving around within a radius of 5 miles. One night in camp here, the next night there, and back to the same place again. The Brigade is now doing picket duty. Our regiment going first last Sabbath and today, Thursday we are on again.

I had command of a squad of 10 men last night and was aroused twice by false alarms. The first time by the greenness of a picket. The relief was one man for one hour, the rest sleeping. The countersign had been given and the picket was on his post when the Colonel and a stranger passed along. The Colonel was commanded to halt when the following words ensued: Colonel: "Are you the guard of this beat?" Answer: "I am." Colonel: "Did the officer of the guard give you the countersign?" "He did." "What is it?" "Allegheny" was the answer. He was severely reprimanded and I had to waken the whole squad to have it impressed upon them to challenge General McClellan or any other man. Poor fellow. He is now the butt of the whole Regiment. We are only on duty at night.

Today I drilled my squad for an hour. The rest of the time I have been reading a little and making mush and frying it. This is the process: We go to an adjacent corn field, get some corn. Next got a tin plate, punched holes in it with a fork, then grind our corn into meal, boil it and, for a change, fry it. The mush put me in mind of the big sauce pan full of mush last winter.

If you would see me now, you would see a curious specimen of the genus homo. When in full uniform, knapsack weighing about 15 or 20 pounds, a belt on which is strung a cartridge box containing 60 rounds, a cap box and bayonet scabbard, a canteen, and dirty haversack containing generally nothing, sometimes meat and crackers, corn & apples. I captured a coffee pot which I carry on all occasions. A tin cup and plate dangling by my side and a musket on my shoulder closes the picture.

You need not be afraid of me falling a victim to evil passions or strong drink. I am not exposed to any temptations like I would be in a city like Pittsburgh. And as for strong drink, it cannot be had for love or money, so those say who lust after it.

I know it was a joyous meeting, that of my dear brother Henry and you all, I need not say. I would [if] I had been there. It was decreed otherwise, however, and I do not demur. It is good you tell me of Arch in one sense. It depends on who goes with him, however. Annie need not pout because I did not mention her name in your letter. I think of you all alike. I wrote to her the same day I wrote to you, I think. I have now written to Father twice, receiving no answer. I would like to hear from him, how he is getting along, and the old shop, whether there is any work going on in it. Old Mr. Macklin talks as much over the bench.

You would like to know how I spend the Sabbaths. The Army knows no Sabbath. Last Sabbath was the first day of rest to me. The Sabbath previous was consumed in a march of 20 miles in a boiling sun. I read some in my Bible and then cooked my breakfast after which made preparations for dinner. Had to kill a couple of hogs and dress them. That is for the Company. I, in company with 3 others, went down to a house and bought a couple of chickens, got some potatoes and corn, borrowed a sauce pan, built a fire and had a nice chicken pie. All we wanted was a little flour & butter. We had no sooner put it out of the way then, unexpectedly, I was handed a—what?—a letter.

I sat myself down under a tree and pondered over it. Yes, it was a letter and the right kind too. Send them on. I can devour anything. I was told by Johnnie Macken [Mackin] who has just joined the Regiment, that there are 3 bushels of letters remaining in Washington for this Regiment. That accounts, I suppose, for the milk in the cocoanut. About a dozen I'll bet are for me.

Our Regiment is the only one in the Brigade in which the public worship of God is not performed. Our Company started it in Camp Howe, but since we left Pittsburgh, for some reason or other, it is not done. Clark's Regiment of our Brigade, after a toilsome march of 18 or 20 miles, you would hear at night singing the praises of God and calling upon Him in fervent prayer.

You have had an awful explosion at the Arsenal. It must have been a heart rending calamity. I saw some of the names of the killed, but none that I knew.

We took a prisoner about an hour ago. He had secreted in a house since the battle last week. I saw a beautiful young man in the hospital yesterday. He was from Louisiana. A private in the Rebel ranks worth $250. His leg was shattered. I saw them amputate it and throw it out on the road. It was the smallest and prettiest foot I have ever seen on male or female grown.

Remember me to all my friends and relatives.

Yours affectionately,
George P. McClelland
Company F, 155th Regiment
To Miss Lizzie McClelland
Pittsburgh, Pennsylvania

Notes on the September 25, 1862, Letter

George's brother Henry visited the family home in Pittsburgh, but George's deployment and Henry's lack of communication about the timing of his visit resulted in the brothers missing each other.

Sharing the frustration that official Washington felt, George believed "young Napoleon" (George McClellan) missed an opportunity to crush the Confederate army. Instead, the Rebels escaped "without the loss of a single man, gun, wagon or anything else." While his opinion that the war could have ended "by one stroke" if only McClellan had pursued Lee might have been wishful thinking, his conclusion that the war would end in six months was wildly optimistic, even for a raw recruit.

Despite the seriousness of their assignment, there was time to enjoy the humor of a green recruit picket in the regiment blurting out the countersign to a senior officer. McClelland had to drum the need for strict security into the heads of his men.

Finding an entire regiment outfitted as George McClelland described himself would have been an unforgettable visual and auditory experience: haversacks, canteens, coffee pots and eating utensils swinging to and fro; the sound of metal on metal and canvas on leather keeping time to the thump of marching feet. Infantry on the march—as the 155th was for most of September 1862—was a sight that few civilian observers would forget or envy.

The mention of "an awful explosion at the Arsenal" was a reference to the tragedy that occurred at the Allegheny Arsenal on September 17, 1862. At 2:00 p.m., three separate explosions leveled two buildings and killed seventy-eight workers—primarily females between the ages of ten and twelve—at the arsenal located in the Lawrenceville section of Pittsburgh. The magnitude of the explosion shook buildings throughout the city's downtown area. Cause of the explosion was attributed to gunpowder leaking from barrels that were being moved. The arsenal hired preteen children, especially females, to assemble cartridges because of the advantage their small hands provided in munitions assembly.

Camp near Sharpsburg
September 30th, 1862

Dear Sister Lizzie,

"As cold water is to a thirsty soul, so is good news from a far country." I received your number 1 letter on Saturday the 27th for which I am obliged. I also received, at the same time, a literary paper from a young lady. I can appreciate her thoughtfulness. It would have amused you to have seen the different expressions of the boys when the mail arrived.

We have no shelter from the weather except what we form ourselves such as stretching our blankets on the guns from one stack to another. We are lying on the ground, some sleeping, some reading. When we are aroused from our lethargy by the cry: "The mail has come," we all crowd around expectant, waiting for the names to be called. Some got half a dozen, others none. Then was to be seen the smile of satisfaction contrasted with the look of disappointment. Some, however, took it good naturedly. Johnnie Ralston, who has not received a letter yet, said he felt like whaling the whole Company.

The letters you mention, Lizzie, to have been mailed to me I have no doubt are lying in Washington. As Lieutenant Clapp says, when he left there were 3 bushels [of] letters and other mail matter there for us. You need not be afraid of any letters not reaching me if you direct them right. Always, no matter where we are, direct [them] to Washington, DC.

I am sorry about Henry. To think of him coming all the way from the far west to New York only to be disappointed. I would like to hear from him, although I cannot reply appropriately. He's too well versed in Shakespeare, still I would do my best . . .

I can't complain much of this life. It is dirty, of course. Hard for one to keep himself clean, but now we have had a good rest and all we want are tents of some kind to protect us from the weather.

There are a great many sick both in our Regiment and the rest of the Brigade, but I hold out first rate. There are no winter quarters for the Army this season. The Government can't stand the cost of supporting 1,000,000 men lying idle this winter. I now see why the routed army of the Rebels was not pursued. No blame rests on our gallant General McClellan whatever. On the contrary, he deserves the thanks of the whole country for the victories achieved over an army flushed with success. They gnashed their teeth with rage on being compelled to relinquish the rich country they had commenced to ravage. Now a grand forward movement of our Army is being made as the decimated divisions are being filled up.

Humanity itself cried out after the battle of Antietam for the relief of our suffering thousands. I have conversed with men in nearly every division of the Army engaged who say had it not been for McClellan, we would have been defeated. He would ride up in the hottest fire, see the whole aspect in one glance of a field stretching for four miles of a line of battle, and plant 100 guns in the most splendid positions.

You need not think of sending boxes, etc. It's entirely out of the question. I've too much to carry now.

It's all nonsense about the "Rebs" treating their men so well, etc. Our men are as well taken care of as circumstances will admit. It is only those grumblers that you find everyplace that are never satisfied who start such fabrications.

The war is now going to be pushed into Africa and you need not be a bit surprised to see me home in the spring of 1864, the time I predict for the conclusion of the war, proclamations of emancipation, etc. to the contrary notwithstanding.

I wish, Lizzie, Arch had not changed his mind. Nothing would please me better than that he would join the Army of the US. Try and persuade him to go. Hurrah for the Militia and good for the Miller establishment. I wish they had been sent near where we are to bury the dead. It would have made them hold their noses.

The last Sabbath was the most quiet one I have seen yet. We had divine service in the woods, the Reverend Wallace from Pittsburgh officiating. The Reverend Colonel J. B. Clark also preached to his Regiment. I wish he was our Colonel. It does one good to hear him giving command: "Forward, my brave boys." He mingles freely with the men and they dote on him.

We are in Humphries' [Humphreys's] Division, the Brigade under command of Colonel Allabaugh [Allabach], Acting Brigadier; no man at all. Fitz-John Porter is our Corps Commander.

We had an order read us the other evening on dress parade. All officers' baggage to be sent to Frederick and stored there. The number of wagons to a Regiment to be cut down which betokens a forward movement. Also a strict order concerning stragglers who are to be arrested at once. This will teach some of our Company a lesson who have been hanging back in Washington. Every man now is needed in the ranks.

The Kier Rifles are being thinned somewhat. Several have been detached. John Ralston is Quartermaster Sergeant and W. B. Glass Commissary Sergeant. Will Dickson is the Colonel's Orderly. T.H. Dickson [is] Adjutant's Clerk. While I stay in the ranks as 4th Corporal and believe it's best place to be.

I saw Peter Wilkinson yesterday. He says, "Tell Arch to remember his promise." Pete is a changed boy.

I think, Lizzie, before I get an answer to this, I will be down in "Ole Virginny." How the "Secesh" are going to live there this winter is ahead of my time. There is not a bit of vegetation from one end to the other. Men who have been through it describe it as a barren waste.

The Sutlers around this camp are making a fortune. They charge outrageously. Small pies are 25 and 30 cents apiece. Small loaf of bread 25 cents and everything else in proportion. I never get anything except what I cannot do without from them. I bought a tiny bottle of ink for 10 cents. They ought to be drummed out of this altogether or else be compelled to sell reasonable.

Well, Lizzie, to use a vulgar phrase, I had better dry up. Tell Annie this is the last of the month, to get her letter ready. I want Father to write me. I suppose he has though, and it's lying in Washington, DC. There's a hitch there.

It seems I've been away from home about a year instead of a month. Farewell all. That loved ones at home are all in good health & circumstances is the fervent wish of your bro.

George P. McClelland

Don't forget to send paper & envelopes as I don't want to patronize cheats of Sutlers for same.

Notes on the September 30, 1862, Letter

Writing letters and reading those from home occupied a large part of a Civil War soldier's free time. McClelland was no exception. He wrote to his father, sister, and brothers and expected them to reciprocate with the same frequency and diligence. Often, however, even faithful letter writers from home were hindered by the sporadic army mail delivery system.

Union soldiers were expected to put a stamp on their letters sent home, but wet weather that turned stamps into a "welded mass" and lack of funds to buy stamps frequently frustrated regular mailing routines. Later in the war, the postmaster-general of the U.S. allowed soldiers to send a letter without payment if "soldiers letter" was written on the envelope. The Christian Commission also provided envelopes with stamps for soldiers.

George McClelland took a more conciliatory position regarding General McClellan in this letter. The general is not the "young Napoleon" of the prior letter but rather "our gallant General McClellan." This idea of General Mc-Clellan fighting against a numerically superior Army of Northern Virginia fresh from several key victories was shared by many of the officers and men of the Army of the Potomac at this point in the war. The general's personal bravery, demonstrated as he rode up "in the hottest fire" to make bold tactical commands, went a long way to elevate his reputation among his soldiers.

The reference to the war being "pushed to Africa" was based on a figure of speech—"carrying the war into Africa"—that dates back to the Punic Wars. It reflected the strategy of some in the Roman military that the way to defeat Carthage was to invade its home territory—Africa.

Young George McClelland's prediction that the war would conclude in the spring of 1864 did not take into account the fierce tenacity of the Confederate army and its leader, Robert E. Lee.

Several of McClelland's friends and fellow "Lunies" were given staff positions, but he was satisfied to stay in his line position in Company F of the 155th. His friends who accepted staff roles served unscathed throughout the war. McClelland, in his role of growing frontline leadership responsibility in Company F, would not be so fortunate.

The reference to his brother Arch's "promise" along with related references in other letters lead to the conclusion that George's brother had taken a temperance pledge. Peter Wilkinson, mentioned in the letter, became a "changed boy" in McClelland's view by swearing off alcohol.

McClelland reflected the outrage many soldiers felt when they dealt with the "Sutlers" who were seen as notorious price gougers.

Camp Macaulay near Sharpsburg
October 9, 1862

My Dear Sister,

Yours of the 25th did follow the Regiment, as you desired, and I hope the others will be considerate enough to do the same, especially the one with the 2nd D C/5. [2nd Division, 5th Corps] It will be along after awhile. I had rather he had not sent so much, as I don't like to carry a great deal at a time. I would rather send home for it as I need it.

As for what you speak about Arch, it's the best thing he has done in a great while. People labor under a delusion in regard to the Army. Of course my experience is limited, but I have seen representatives of 150,000 men and in 9 cases out of ten, there is a great change. I have seen men, outcasts from Pittsburgh, from whose lips with every sentence issued an oath, now quick, sensible and moral. I can tell by their language.

The picture you draw in regard to the Union is gloomy, entirely too despondent. Nil desperandum[8] as long as there are willing hands and willing hearts to do battle against the foul traitors. Looking above for the victory and to Him be all the glory ascribed. I hardly know what more to write.

In lieu of tents we have put up quarters of brush and rail. Our mess got a little ahead. In place of brush on top, we put our gum blankets for the roof, filled around the sides with green boughs and then put a nice green carpet of spruce underneath. Place our woolen blankets on this and we have a regular mattress bed. We fixed our Captain's next door up in the same style.

Once in a while we have a nice meal such as we had yesterday. Some nice fried beefsteak, fried onions, boiled rice, fried over in granary sauce and seasonings, and good apple pie for desert. It was a regular Christmas dinner for us. Two of our boys you know are in Commissary and we get some choice bits occasionally.

This is a beautiful day. Just such a day we have in Pennsylvania in the latter end of June. A trace can hardly be discerned of autumn as yet. Nights are cool and days sometimes hot. The leaves are yet green in the trees. In fact, were it not for the spoliation, everything would be lovely. We go on picket tonight for 24 hours. Have to march 3–4 miles.

Lizzie, this is the 3rd letter I have written today being on guard for 24 hours. I have today to myself—was relieved this morning.

Being drowsy and facilities not in good working order, you must excuse this letter. Now, Lizzie, there is one thing I almost forgot and that is to pick me out a nice little wife again I come back.

Give my love to all and kind respects to friends. Tell me in your next of the whereabouts of Miss Pennie Bradley and the rest of the girls.

Yours forever, GPM

Notes on the October 9, 1862, Letter

George applauded the news that his brother Arch had joined the army. The wayward brother had taken a temperance pledge *and* joined the army, to his youngest brother's delight. George was convinced that the vast majority of men benefited from army service—even the "outcasts from Pittsburgh."

Conspicuously absent from this letter is any mention of President Lincoln's visit to the troops at Sharpsburg in early October. D. P. Marshall, of Company K in the 155th, described the visit of the president along with Generals McClellan and Fitz-John Porter, commander of the 5th Corps. Marshall reported: "McClellan is very much like his picture, only he is of a very fair complexion. He has a bright eye. Lincoln looks like some old farmer, no foppishness, but all honesty and sincerity."[9]

In camp 1 ½ miles from Sharpsburg
Tuesday, October 14, 1862

Dear Sister,

Without waiting for a letter and not having anything to do, I thought I could not employ the time better than by writing to my own dear sister, Lizzie.

The right wing of our Regiment is on picket duty and I would have been along had I not been indisposed. It was only last Thursday we were on the same duty. I will give some notes taken then, viz:

"On this day, Thursday the 10th of October, we are picketed on the Maryland banks of the classic Potomac, the Baltimore and Chesapeake canal on our flank. The canal is in some places from thirty to 40 feet above the surface of the river. I slept last night on the tow path with my head almost overhanging a precipice while my feet were almost in the canal.

For about three miles the bank of the canal is composed of a mountain of solid rock here and there broken in large openings which serve to scale it.

In some places it is one solid perpendicular mass at least 100 feet high (the ground rising above it 150 feet higher with a gradual slope) While in others it shoots up like an iceberg in sharp and rugged points, here and there with crevices and fissures out of which sprout shrubs and bushes. At one point it takes a rough pyramidical shape until near the top out of which extends a large sycamore (where it receives its sustenance is inexplicable to me) which projects high over the canal looking as though it would come down every moment with a crash. . Altogether it presents an appearance at once sublime and imposing.

Turning the eye from this to the Potomac—which here is not more than 300 or 400 feet wide—and we have a striking contrast. Gentle undulating fields and beautiful sloping meadows, here and there interspersed with groves of trees, meet your gaze as far as the eye can reach. All under cultivation and bearing no indications of ravage or spoliation. Naught mars the beauty of the scene but the few wretched looking hovels and large but dilapidated barns which are here and there discerned."

John Ralston and I took the opportunity while washing our clothes to swim the river and stood on the Virginia side while the minnows nibbled our toes.

The "Lunie" mess dined on fresh fish—caught with pin hooks—and fried mush. It was a hunky meal.

The mail came along, but nothing for me. I am getting anxious about that letter from Arch.

It commenced raining and has rained ever since. No shelter and it is enough to kill every man in the Regiment. About half are on the sick list now and no hospital accommodations. Friday night it rained all night and I lay in it 'till morning, soaking wet and a cold wind blowing. About one half the Regiment spoiled the boundary lines of sundry fields, commonly called worm fences, made some big fires and stood shivering around them nearly all day. On Sunday we were inspected by our new Brigadier General Briggs. Rained all that night. Monday cloudy and sprinkling all day. Passed a pretty comfortable night.

This Tuesday morn got some tea from the Commissary and had toast and tea for breakfast. Mixed up the prescription that, by [the] Army's forethought, was put in my trash bag. The sun has at length made his welcome appearance.

Lizzie, I think that monied letter has been stolen as all our mail has arrived. I don't know what to do about it.

My love to all and remember me, as ever, your loving brother,
George P.

Send a pair of mits, if you have them, in the box along with my boots as I lost my best gloves.
GPMC

Notes on the October 14, 1862, Letter

From his notes taken on a prior picket duty, McClelland described the area near the Potomac River and Baltimore and Chesapeake Canal with the discernment and eloquence of a practiced travel writer.

The proximity of the Potomac provided an opportunity for washing clothes, swimming, and catching fish, but this vacation-like experience was soon replaced with rain, cold winds, and pervasive illness throughout the regiment. Rails from local "worm fences" were used to provide heat as the weather began to become more autumn-like and the lack of tents as suitable means of shelter was taking its toll on the members of the 155th, who were not quite two months into their military experience.

Chapter Three

On the March

Maryland, Harper's Ferry, and Virginia, November—December 1862

The Army of the Potomac

I have just read your dispatch about sore-tongued and fatigued horses. Will you pardon me for asking what the horses of your army have done since the battle of Antietam that fatigues anything?
—Abraham Lincoln, telegram to General McClellan, October 24, 1862

Union euphoria in the aftermath of the battle of Antietam was brief, but two watershed events resulted. European leadership—especially that of the British—cooled to the idea of recognizing the Rebel government in Richmond. Attempts by Britain's chancellor of the exchequer, William Gladstone, and the foreign minister, Lord John Russell, to gain cabinet support for recognizing the Confederate states were voted down following the outcome at Antietam. France proposed a six-month armistice—along with dropping the trade blockade against the Confederates—that would be backed by France, Britain, and Russia. The armistice would clearly be of greater advantage to the Confederates and their trade interests with Europe. Britain and Russia both turned down France's proposal. Increasingly, British leadership was equating the Confederate cause with the perpetuation of slavery. This moral position, coupled with the growing recognition, post-Antietam, that positive military momentum was building on the Union side, took official recognition of the Confederate states off the table for the British.

The other watershed event following Antietam was the abolition of slavery in America through the Emancipation Proclamation. The Union advantage following Antietam gave Lincoln the glimmer of victory he needed to issue the proclamation.

McClellan kept his negative opinion about the proclamation to himself. A number of powerful Democratic friends in New York pleaded with the general to accept the proclamation and not contradict his commander in chief. But members of McClellan's staff were less temperate. Fitz-John Porter called the Emancipation Proclamation an "absurd proclamation of a political coward."

Another McClellan staff officer said that the reason Lee's army had not been "bagged" at Antietam was because the purpose was to let neither army get much advantage over the other. In this way, a compromise could be made to save the institution of slavery. When Lincoln learned of the officer's public remarks he had him cashiered.

Responding to grumbling in the staff officer ranks, McClellan issued a general order to all of the Army of the Potomac reminding the army of the need to subordinate military opinions to civilian authority.

> There is an immobility here that exceeds all that any man can conceive of. It requires the lever of Archimedes to move this inert mass.
> —General Henry W. Halleck, October 1862

Despite strong showings at Antietam in mid-September and Corinth, Mississippi, and Perryville, Kentucky, in early October, these were not clear-cut, unambiguous Union victories. Lincoln and general in chief Halleck were growing impatient with the lack of aggressiveness at the top of the Army of the Potomac and with the Union army at the western front. Their dissatisfaction focused on the two responsible generals: George B. McClellan and Don Carlos Buell.

As he reflected on his role at Antietam, McClellan became increasingly pleased with his performance. Yet this growing confidence was not sufficient to embolden him to take an aggressive stance. Thinking that Lee's forces significantly outnumbered his own, McClellan instead chose to hunker down in a defensive posture along the Potomac River near Sharpsburg.

Lincoln's patience with Generals McClellan and Buell was reaching its breaking point. Lincoln removed Buell from command in the west in September because of his inaction in Kentucky, brought him back briefly, and then sent Buell packing in late October, putting Major General William S. Rosecrans in command.

The president's growing dissatisfaction with both men was over lack of aggressiveness. (He said of McClellan, "He has got the slows . . . An auger too dull to take hold.") Yet Lincoln was not blind to McClellan's powerful relations with northern Democrats—the president's own political adversaries. During the national elections of 1862 was not the time to throw the gunpowder of a McClellan dismissal on the political fire.

While Washington leadership was fuming over McClellan's lack of action, the general ordered the army to pack up and break camp on October 26. At last the Army of the Potomac was on the move after considerable prodding by Lincoln and Halleck. Once again, the elusive objective was to take Richmond. Strike at the heart of the Confederacy, went the rationale, and the insurrection could be brought to a swift end.

Moving an army the size of the Army of the Potomac was a slow process, even under a general who might display a greater sense of urgency than George McClellan. The Union army lumbered out of camp near Sharpsburg, giving Lee ample opportunity to take the steps necessary to blunt the Union offensive. Lee quickly moved Longstreet's corps between the Army of the Potomac and Richmond. Furthermore, Stonewall Jackson's position in the Shenandoah Valley essentially flanked McClellan's right.

On November 5, Lincoln's patience ran out, and he replaced McClellan with General Ambrose Burnside. The order replacing McClellan reached the Army of Potomac encampment as the season's first snow storm covered the ground and Union tents near the small Virginia town of White Plains.

There were fiery emotions and discontent among members of McClellan's staff about how their general was treated by the bureaucrats in Washington. Yet, uncharacteristically self-effacing, McClellan willingly stepped aside and gave his full support to Burnside. "Stand by General Burnside as you have stood by me, and all will be well," he said. Tears were reported to have filled the eyes of officers and men alike as Little Mac made his gracious exit. As historian James McPherson has succinctly expressed the change in command: "[N]othing in McClellan's tenure of command became him like his leaving of it."[1]

Burnside, sensing the mood in Washington, moved the Army of the Potomac with a speed that must have startled those accustomed to McClellan's sluggish pace. Within ten days, Burnside had positioned his 100,000-plus troops at Falmouth across the Rappahannock River from Fredericksburg, Virginia. His plan was to cross the river and strike Richmond to the south after rolling through Fredericksburg.

Key to striking boldly was dependence on a critical engineering device: the pontoon. The large, unwieldy structures that had been linked together to cross the Potomac and Shenandoah earlier in the march would be essential to crossing the Rappahannock at Fredericksburg. Simply put: no pontoons, no crossing.

Burnside and his Army of the Potomac sat stalled for a week waiting on the banks of the river across from Fredericksburg for the pontoons to be transported. By the time they arrived, Robert E. Lee was able to fortify Fredericksburg and dig into the hills surrounding the town. Burnside had superior numbers of men and, finally, the required pontoons. What he didn't have was the element of surprise or the momentum of an energized army. Instead, he had 75,000 pairs of Confederate eyes watching his every move; an enemy possessing an impregnable front; and a swift-flowing, wide river between the two opposing forces. Now once again, as at Antietam, the two armies were facing each other, and a battle of monumental fury was about to begin.

The Regiment—155th Pennsylvania Infantry

> With its cloud of skirmishers in advance,
> With now the sound of a single shot snapping like a whip,
>   And now an irregular volley,
> The swarming ranks press on and on, the dense brigades
>   press on,
> Glittering dimly, toiling under the sun—the dust-cover'd men,
> In columns rise and fall to the undulations of the ground,
> With artillery interspers'd—the wheels rumble, the horses sweat,
> As the army corps advances.
>   —Walt Whitman, "An Army Corps on the March"

During the period of inactivity following the battle of Antietam, the 155th Regiment was able to use the time effectively in camp by honing their martial skills. The raw recruits were drilled, educated in military discipline, inspected regularly, and assigned to picket duty, reconnaissance duty, and other activities that helped turn boy recruits into skilled fighting men.

The military schedule: reveille at 5:00 a.m., followed by roll call; breakfast at 6:00; squad drill at 7:00; company drill at 8:00; battalion drill at 9:00; at 11:00, noncommissioned officer drill; 12 noon, dinner; 2:00 p.m., company drill repeated; 3:00, battalion drill; squad drill at 4:00; 5:00, dress parade; at 5:30, supper; and at 9:00, lights out. Repeat the next day . . . and the next . . . and the next.

Regimental Colonel E. Jay Allen, with a deft mix of preparedness and imperious whimsy, passed the word among the regiment one Sunday evening in October that the troops needed to be prepared to march on two minutes notice in order to meet the Rebels should they cross the river to invade the camp. Waiting a sufficient time to ensure all the men were fast asleep, Allen had the drummer sound a roll to awaken and mobilize the troops. Within five minutes, each man in the regiment had rolled up his overcoat and blanket, put on his cartridge box, knapsack, haversack, and canteen and was ready to march. Once the troops were ready to proceed, the colonel made his way through the regiment to tell the officers to have the men count off. According to a contemporary report, after the count was completed and Allen was satisfied that all of his regiment had turned out, he said: "Well done. I only wanted to see how many and how quick they could get into line. All can now go back to bed." [2]

Most members of the 155th Regiment remembered a similar drill initiated by Colonel Allen while they were encamped on Arlington Heights in early September. The commanding general of the Army of the Potomac may have had "the slows," but the 155th was clearly ready to respond to a call to arms within five minutes. This was the last recorded drill initiated by Colonel Allen. The military challenges to come in the months ahead would be sufficient tests of the men's responsiveness without further surprise drills from Colonel Allen.

While the regiment waited for marching orders from their commanding officers, a small, invasive enemy entered their camp: *Pediculus vestimenti*. The infestation of body lice caused even the most fastidious soldiers to take measures to reduce their persistent numbers from uniforms.

"Like death, it [the louse] was no respecter of persons. It preyed alike on the just and unjust. It inserted its bill as confidently into the body of the major-general as of the lowest private."[3]

Some felt that lapses in good hygiene caused the plague of lice. "It was soon evident that they were not visitors, but had come to stay, because they were already raising large families and had lots of eggs deposited about the seams and secret recesses of our undergarments, and in all their numerous hiding places. Perhaps we had unwittingly given them an invitation to come because when we first went into the service, we were more careless in our habits of cleanliness than we would have been at home. . . . Soldiers have many things to learn. . . . We had now become well acquainted with that small insect generally called a 'grayback,' which kept us on the move continually, when their namesakes over the line didn't."[4]

On October 30, the 155th received orders to pack up and break camp at Sharpsburg. Marching from Sharpsburg across Maryland Heights to the east and then south through Pleasant Valley to Sandy Hook, Maryland, the 155th crossed the Potomac River at Harper's Ferry on pontoons. Running bank to bank over the river, the 540 feet of pontoons were crucial military engineering structures that would play an important role for the regiment in the next thirty 30 days at Fredericksburg.

Troops of the 155th passed by the remains of the U. S. arsenal that had been blown up the year before. Rusted gun barrels, bayonets, and shell casings lay in heaps on the arsenal grounds. As the 155th made its way through Harper's Ferry, they also passed the engine house where John Brown and his followers had made their stand three years earlier (October 17, 1859). Some of the members of the regiment sang, "John Brown's body is a mouldering in the grave" as they passed the site.

At Harper's Ferry the troops crossed the Shenandoah River on pontoons, marched approximately four miles and encamped on what some sarcastically called "the sacred soil of Old Virginia." The 155th—indeed the entire Army of the Potomac—was now in enemy territory.

Whether is was a hunger for food more savory than army rations or they felt they had license to appropriate food now that they were in Rebel country, the 155th and their counterparts in the Army of the Potomac went on a foraging and raiding binge. Chickens, ducks, geese, hogs, sheep, honey, fruits, and vegetables were all widely "harvested" from the surrounding farms. The extent of foraging grew so bold and widespread that orders were issued that all straggling for the purpose of foraging was to cease. Violators were severely punished, yet foraging increased. Haversacks swelled with purloined foodstuffs during this autumn harvest by the Army of the Potomac.

Reaching Snicker's Gap in the Blue Ridge, the 155th was placed on picket duty to guard the passage through the mountain range while the Army of the Potomac bivouacked for the night. The next day the army continued southward through the Loudoun Valley to the town of White Plains, Virginia. At White Plains, the first snow of the season began to fall and, while at this location, the army received word that the command of the Army of the Potomac was changing from George McClellan to Ambrose Burnside.

Little Mac received heartfelt cheers and applause from his troops when he stepped down from his command. Private grumbling about the general gave way to public kudos during McClellan's farewell tour of the troops. Despite his many shortcomings as a commanding officer and his inability to successfully manage his relations with his superiors in Washington, the men saw McClellan as a gallant soldier who resembled Napoleon in more ways than just his stature. He had about him an aura of confidence and personal bravery that his men respected and honored. (Years after the war, when Lee was asked "who was the ablest Federal general he had opposed throughout the war, Robert E. Lee replied without hesitation 'McClellan, by all odds.'"[5])

In his farewell address to the troops, McClellan offered a moving and complimentary goodbye to his men that many would remember for the rest of their lives:

> In parting from you, I cannot express the love and gratitude I bear to you. As an army you have grown up in my care. In you I have never found doubt or coldness. The battles you have fought under my command will probably live in our Nation's history. The glory you have achieved over mutual perils and fatigues; the graves of our comrades fallen in battle and by disease, the broken forms of those whom wounds and sickness have disabled—the strongest associations which can exist among men unite us by an indissoluble tie. We shall ever be comrades in supporting the Constitution of our country and the nationality of its people.[6]

And so George McClellan exited the military stage to reappear on the national political stage in the presidential election of 1864 to face the man who had removed him from command of the Army of the Potomac.

The 155th Regiment drew duty as a rear guard for the Army of the Potomac's Fifth Corps, putting the men behind a long wagon train comprising ammunition, quartermaster, headquarters, commissary, and artillery vehicles. The onerous rearguard duty—no doubt assigned to the 155th because of its lack of military experience—was further complicated because the muddy country roads were quickly churned into a viscid quagmire. Early snow and a rain/snow mix contributed to the mess. Additionally, as anyone with experience employing horses and mules to haul materials knows, equine urinary excretion requires the animals come to a complete halt during the process. The result for a large wagon train is a series of unsynchronized starts and stops as the train rolls along its route.

Burnside lost no time in stepping up the pace of his 110,000-man army to pass through Warrenton and then on to Falmouth, Virginia, a small town that lay upriver across the Rappahannock River from Fredericksburg. By November 22 the 155th was in camp at Falmouth ready to go on the offensive. Several days later, in a steady rain, the 155th left "Camp Misery" (so dubbed because of the mud) and moved down the east side of the Rappahannock to be directly across the river from Fredericksburg. Burnside's plan was to cross the river, take Fredericksburg and then drive straight to Richmond. Once in Richmond, he would seize the Confederate capital city and force an end to the war. At least that was the plan.

The 155th, along with the rest of the Army of the Potomac, was in place, standing by to go on the offensive for the first time since Antietam. Yet one key resource kept the plan from being executed: pontoons. Due to miscommunications about when and where the pontoons would be needed, the Army of the Potomac waited on the banks of the Rappahannock.

The Soldier—George P. McClelland

When the sun rays at last struck full and mellowingly upon the earth, the youth saw that the landscape was streaked with two long, thin, black columns which disappeared on the brow of a hill in front and rearward vanished in a wood. They were like two serpents crawling from the cavern of the night.
—Stephen Crane, *The Red Badge of Courage*

Indian summer temperatures prevailed as George McClelland began the march with his fellow 155th Regiment soldiers in the waning days of October 1862. Traveling over mountainous Maryland roads, at the start in July-like heat, weighed down by gear—knapsack, sixty rounds of cartridges, canteens, haversacks, bayonets, pots, and Springfield muskets—the troops struggled to keep pace as they marched over mile upon mile of roads, up and down hills, through woods, across streams, and around fenced fields.

Later in the march, the temperatures turned briskly cold, signaling autumn's approach. And then came the rains that soaked clothing and turned the roads to barely navigable mire. Despite the weather travails associated with the march, McClelland, like most of his fellow soldiers, was struck by the beauty of the countryside through which they marched, particularly Pleasant Valley near South Mountain in Maryland. Here the land was rich and fertile, dotted with well-kept farmhouses.

As they passed through Harper's Ferry, McClelland noted the debris left behind after the destruction of the U.S. arsenal in 1861. That notion of a "mean dirty looking place" was his lasting impression of historic grounds that still echoed with the memories of John Brown's raid three years before. The town's recent history also included destruction of the arsenal at the start of the war (in an attempt to keep the Confederates from obtaining weapon-making equipment) and the capture of the 12,000-man Federal garrison by Stonewall Jackson just two months earlier.

The nineteen-year-old boy turned twenty as he marched with his unit into Virginia in the fall of 1862. George was becoming proficient in the requirements of being a soldier, and his leadership potential was being recognized as well. During this time he was promoted to third sergeant.

In His Own Words—The Letters of George McClelland

Camp—somewhere between Harper's Ferry and Leesburgh [Leesburg]
November 3, 1862

After waiting for weeks for a letter from home, I have come to the sage conclusion that let-ter writing in Pittsburgh is at a discount—"Blessed are they that expect nothing for they will not be disappointed."

Dear Sister Annie,
    Enjoying a little rest after 3 days severe marching. I feel it to be a "duty" to write you a few lines. You will see by the post mark that we have left the mountains of Maryland. On Thursday, the 30th of October, we broke camp near Sharpsburg and started on the march towards Harper's Ferry. Crossed South Mountain and encamped about 9 PM on a spur of the same mountain Friday.
    Started about daylight after taking our coffee. Took up our line of march through Pleasant Valley. This valley is remarkably fertile [with] rich soil and nice houses along the road. Reached Sandy Hook, about noon, on the Shenandoah [Potomac] River. Pro-ceeded from thence to Harper's Ferry after crossing 2 pontoons. Saw the ruins of govern-ment property here. It is a mean, dirty looking place.
    Once more on the "sacred soil" marched up Loudon Heights and through the valley. The day very warm. Encamped about 5 PM off the Leesburg road.
    Saturday, the first of November. Laid over today. Immense bodies of troops winding their way along the road. The whole army is moving and we can hear the cannon boom-ing away in our front. Our advance is about 8 miles ahead.
    Started again this Sabbath morning. Marched all day up one hill, down two through woods and fields, runs and creeks, and mud. The sun scorching hot. Subsisting on crack-ers all the way until we arrived at our present encampment in a ploughed field. The roads blocked with troops moving on to "Richmond." I lay down on the ground considerably the worse for the wear. Bad cold and lame foot.
    Clark's (Regiment) and our Regiment are encamped in the same field. The boys have scoured the country round. Came in with sheep, calves, turkeys, geese, chickens, etc. etc. Around noon they put guards around us which interfered somewhat with the confisca-tion scheme. I guess we will start tomorrow again either for Winchester or Leesburgh.
    We had quite a number of visitors when we were in Maryland: Dr. Douglass "Sesech" Plumer; a son of James Laughlin's, and others.
    I received in a box some nice underclothing, a can of delicious peaches and a box of sardines, together with a pair of boots. I shall ever remember with fondness those dear ones who have been so kind and thoughtful to me. To Lizzie especially I desire to tender my warmest thanks. The boots were a nice fit for a gentleman, but considerably too small

for marching boots. I turned them over to Tom Dickson and he has sent home for a pair for me. So there is nothing lost, but the delay.

There have been some promotions in Company F, 155th Regiment. I now rank as 3rd Sergeant and John Macken is 6th Corporal. Frank Martyn is 5th Corporal. Corporal Thompson is in good health; makes a good soldier.

It is strange I don't hear from some of my friends. I never heard from Arch, nor didn't get that letter from Tom. I know Father hasn't much time to write and suppose you attend Public School and Normal Class. I received a letter from Henry previous to his departure from Pitt. I should have answered it, but don't know the directions.

Edwin Davis of our mess has been sick for some time in the hospital at Sharpsburg. He was very low when we went through, but the fever has turned and with good care he will recover.

I expect to be in a "scrimmage" in a few days and also expect to be in Richmond in about three weeks. I tell you, Annie, you will hear some grand news before many days.

The weather suddenly changed last night from July to November. Made it in one jump. I suppose it is a peculiarity in this "Ole Virginny".

Well, Annie, I will conclude as I want to write to Father after I make a cup of coffee. Hoping you are all enjoying good heath and all the other needful blessing. I remain,

Your loving Bro
Geo P McClelland
To Miss Annie McClelland, Pittsburgh, Pa

Notes on the November 3, 1862, Letter

After admonishing his sister (indeed, all his family) for not writing to him with greater frequency, McClelland used a break in the march toward Harper's Ferry to write to Annie. Marching dawn to dusk, the unit—now fulfilling rearguard duty—was under pressure to reach the "sacred soil" of Virginia and then head toward Richmond to take the capital. Each day's forced march was made more difficult by the warm autumn sun. McClelland found himself footsore and with a cold because of the physical challenges of the march.

He wrote about the "boys" having "scoured the country round." Foraging was a common problem in the Army of the Potomac and caused General McClellan to take firm steps to prevent straggling and foraging (with little effect.) The army's response to foraging was to use the Regular Army troops to maintain order and discipline among the volunteer ranks. For the 155th, foraging was discouraged by placing guards around the men.

In this letter, Sergeant McClelland also referenced the box sent from home filled with supplies and treats. Boxes from home were a welcome experience for the Union troops throughout the war. John D. Billings, Tenth Massachusetts Battery, author of *Hard Tack and Coffee*, described the "boxes from home":

> If there was a red-letter day to be found anywhere in the army life of a soldier, it occurred when he was the recipient of a box sent to him by the dear ones and friends he left to enter the service . . . The boxes sent were usually of good size, often either a shoe-case or common soap-box, and were rarely if ever less than a peck in capacity. . . . The boxes came, when they came at all, by wagon-loads— mule teams of the company going after them. . . . I think the art of box-packing must have culminated during the war. It was simply wonderful, delightfully so, to see how each little corner and crevice was utilized. Not stuffed with paper thus wasting space, but filled with a potato, an apple, an onion, a pinch of dried apples, a handful of peanuts, or some other edible substance.[7]

Private Edwin Davis, mentioned in the letter, did not recover from his sickness with sufficient strength to remain in the army. He was discharged in late December 1862 on a surgeon's certificate.

McClelland's expectation to be in a "scrimmage" in a few days is off by almost a month and a half. His expectation to be in Richmond in "about three weeks" is off by two and a half years.

Camp in field 3 miles from Warrenton
November 17, 1862

Beloved Sister,

This is not the first time I have opened my writing case to write you since the receipt of your last. For often when I get squatted in our little shelter tent the cry is: fall in. Fall in either for review, inspection, drill or something else. And then, you know, a sergeant ought to be pretty prompt to show an example, and in the absence of the first and second sergeants, I am called on to furnish guards, etc., take the Company out on drill or whatever it may be.

We are encamped on a beautiful field overgrown with briers so thick that you trip and stumble at every step, get your hands scratched, and likely tear one's pantaloons to shreds.

We have been here 3 or 4 days waiting until Burnside gets a firm grip on the reins. And then, on we go. I took advantage of our rest here to do some washing. It took me a whole day to wash those shirts and a handkerchief. You have no idea of the troubles and trials of a soldier.

The modus operandi of washing in this place is first run over [to] the Regiment until you get an axe. Go to the woods close by and fell a tree. Start a fire of green wood. (Fence rails not allowed to be taken.) Then get a camp kettle. Go to the run—a stream as broad as your hand—scoop the water in a tin cup until the kettle is full. Put on the fire. Wash and boil out and then hold each piece to the fire until dried. One dose of this a month is enough for human nature.

Well, Lizzie, the cry is—fall in. I will finish up some other time . . .

Sunday the 23rd

Dear Lizzie,

We have made some severe marches since I wrote the above. We started last Monday about 8 AM and passed through Warrenton, a nice little town with many beautiful buildings. Passed Cattlets Station and reached the junction at 4 PM and bivouacked for the night. It commenced raining which made it very unpleasant. Next morning we started again . . .

(One of my ambrosial locks)

. . . through a drizzling rain with 5 days rations, knapsacks and 60 rounds of ammunition. (Perfect pack horses and mules as we are.) They marched us over horrible roads. Encamped near night and next day at it again. Still raining. Encamped about 6 or 7 miles from Fredericksburg. I was detailed with 90 men to guard 1,100 head of cattle. It poured all night steady. I had to stand and take it all there being no shelter. Was relieved next morning.

The roads being impassable for teams and artillery, we laid over today. Was flooded out of our tents. Got a spade at last and dug a ditch around it. Found ourselves on an island. Called it number 10. It rained all this Thursday night. We sit down on our knapsacks thoroughly soaked while I took out my Bible and read one half of the Book of Genesis. Laid down and slept. I can sleep now any place. The camp is now one vast sea of mud. Yesterday we moved on. No one sorry to leave "Camp Misery" as we called it.

We are now about 2 miles from Fredericksburg. Sumner has demanded its surrender which has not yet been complied with. There is an immense army in this vicinity.

The boys are all well. That is the "Lunies" are. Out of a Company of 98 men, we have not 50 fit for duty. Bob Hill is reported dead. Had his leg amputated again. Macken is well. I don't associate much with him. Could not mess with him. He's too dirty in his habits—slovenly.

Annie gave me the news of your trip to Davenport. I sent a Brother's thanks through her to you for the many gifts and comforts you sent. I hope I may only live to return some of the many favors conferred by you all. I got the finest letter from A. R. the other day. Have already answered it. Will write to H. S. M as soon as I get his address. Glad to hear of T. W. getting along so well. Hope it may always be so with him.

Give my love to Anna, Walter and Georgie. Sorry too you left Pittsburgh as it leaves Annie alone almost. If I ain't shot, I think my next letter will be dated Richmond, Va. I have great faith in Burnside and Hooker. I have seen all the big guns, but Joe Hooker heads them all.

Yours in abiding love,
George P. McClelland

Notes on November 17, 1862, Letter

His busy schedule of marching and drilling left McClelland little time to write letters—or to wash clothes. His complicated, multistep process of washing his uniform might have been essential to rid his clothing of the dreaded "gray backs." Modesty—or pride—may have prevented him from providing these details to his sister.

The 155th regimental history reports that during the march through the "nice little town" of Warrenton, the troops encountered few of its inhabitants other than "one or two indignant females, well up in years, who scolded and denounced the 'Yankee troops' generally as they passed by."[8]

As General Burnside moved his troops into position near Fredericksburg, the rains began. Transportation of wagons and artillery ground to a halt as roads became impassable. The army inched closer to Fredericksburg in anticipation of an attack. General Sumner, on behalf of the Union forces, demanded the surrender of Fredericksburg. The Rebels refused. McClelland was accurate when he wrote an "immense" Rebel army was waiting. At this point, seventy-five thousand of Lee's men were dug in at Fredericksburg and awaiting the next step of the Union army.

Private Robert "Bob" Hill, the unfortunate soldier shot in the foot by a Union camp guard in the Rockville, Maryland, camp in mid-September, was not dead as McClelland presumed, but he had undergone several amputations. Hill was discharged by surgeon's certificate in June 1863 after prolonged stays in various army hospitals.

McClelland acknowledged receiving a letter from his brother Archibald (A.R.) and said that he would write his brother Henry (H. S. M.). He was pleased that his eldest brother, Thomas (T. W.), was doing well and sent his love to Thomas's wife, Anna, and their children, Walter and George, in Davenport, Iowa.

George McClelland's "great faith" in Burnside proved misplaced as events unfolded in the coming weeks, but his faith in General Hooker reflected the feeling of most of the enlisted men in the Army of the Potomac. Major General Joseph "Fighting Joe" Hooker won the respect of his men in the coming months, in part, because of his insistence that his troops be well-fed and sheltered. Many senior officers questioned General Hooker's strategic skills and aggressiveness on the battlefield, but he was held in high esteem by the common soldier because, they felt, he looked out for their most basic needs.

Chapter Four

"Carnage and Destruction"

Fredericksburg, December 1862

The Army of the Potomac

> Those of us who were well acquainted with Burnside knew that he was a brave,
> loyal man, but we did not think that he had the military ability to command
> The Army of the Potomac.
> —Major General Darius Couch, Army of the Potomac

Frustrated with General George McClellan's inability to take the initiative and with his manifest arrogance (to the point of disrespecting his superiors), Lincoln, Stanton, and Halleck sacked the "Young Napoleon" and replaced him with the affable and obedient Ambrose Burnside. Even discounting the usual professional jealousy among senior military men, the generals in the Army of the Potomac found little to recommend Burnside for his new position. Moreover, Burnside himself had reservations about his ability to lead the army. In Washington, Union leadership withheld judgment, preferring to see how the newly appointed leader of the Army of the Potomac performed where it counted—on the field of battle. Burnside's time of testing was fast approaching as November 1862 came to a close.

One of Burnside's first actions was to reorganize the Army of the Potomac into three "Grand Divisions." The "Left Grand Division" was headed by Major General William Franklin; the "Center Grand Division" was led by Major

General Joseph Hooker; and the "Right Grand Division" was under the command of Major General Edwin Sumner. Each Grand Division had two corps of infantry along with artillery and cavalry, giving each general approximately forty thousand men. Burnside's plan, with the endorsement of Washington leadership, was to pass through the city of Fredericksburg, Virginia, and drive on to Richmond where the intention was to capture the Confederate capital and put a swift end to the war. Ostensibly the three "Grand Divisions" would give Burnside the flexibility and muscle to overwhelm Robert E. Lee.

As a doorway to Richmond, Fredericksburg was a key prize on the path to the Rebel capital and had important strategic attributes: the Rappahannock River, which passed by the city, was navigable by shallow-draft vessels; it was the nexus of a significant rail line; and it was located at the intersection of a network of well-maintained roads. One of those attributes was also a major hurdle—the Rappahannock. The river was nearly four hundred feet wide across from the city; the bridges had been burned by the Confederates; and Burnside had to get his army to the other side. Fording the river with an army anywhere close to Fredericksburg was risky, particularly for the newly minted general of the Army of the Potomac, who wanted to make a favorable first impression on his superiors in Washington.

Burnside's method for crossing the Rappahannock was to use a device as old as Caesar's army—the pontoon bridge. Hauled to a crossing site by wagons, the pontoons—each 31 feet long and 5 ½ feet wide—would be linked together, floated across the river and anchored in place to form a proven, albeit unstable, platform on which men and equipment could cross a river. The general's plan was to have Sumner's Right Grand Division cross directly into Fredericksburg and Franklin's Left Grand Division cross on a plain downstream from the city. The two-pronged approach, reasoned Burnside, would stretch Lee's forces across a long front and keep the Confederate general guessing as to where to focus his efforts. Hooker's Center Grand Division would be kept in reserve and deployed where it could have the greatest impact once an attack was begun.

By midmorning on December 11, numerous attempts had been made by Union engineers (primarily the 50th New York Engineers) to span the Rappahannock River; fifty lay dead or wounded near the pontoons. As the fog lifted, the accuracy of the Confederate snipers improved, and the resolve of the Union engineers faded. Burnside, furious with the Confederate resistance that was interfering with the upper pontoon bridge's construction, ordered his artillery to shell the houses along the river in an attempt to drive out the snipers. When the smoke settled, 150 artillery pieces had lobbed over 8,000 rounds into the town destroying or damaging many of the homes and commercial buildings. Yet the Confederates continued firing.

Finally, dismayed by the lack of progress bridging the river, Burnside approved a plan to send troops across in pontoon boats to root out the enemy. Squad after squad of Union infantry established a presence on the Fredericksburg side of the river, causing the Rebel snipers to fall back. Lee had slowed the Union assault across the river by a day.

The next morning, December 12, Burnside's army finished crossing the Rappahannock on multiple pontoon bridges and began occupying the town. Devastation to civilian property had been relatively modest up to this point in the war. Fredericksburg was a turning point. The damage to homes by Union artillery was devastating: buildings were reduced to piles of bricks and wood; standing structures had windows and doors blown out; and grounds were littered with debris discarded by civilians who had hastily packed wagons and carts with a few possessions to escape harm from the clashing armies. Union soldiers took advantage of the chaos to loot and destroy homes and shops. Family libraries were dumped into the streets, portraits slashed with bayonets, silver taken, and mirrors smashed with musket butts.

On December 13, just before first light, Burnside ordered the attack on Lee's lines to begin. A dense fog shrouded the initial movements of Franklin's men, but as the fog lifted, a single division of Union troops under General George Meade—now clearly visible—was raked by Confederate artillery fire. Meade's troops wavered but soon regrouped and advanced into an area the Confederates thought was impassable because it was swampy. Initially successful in gaining ground, Meade's forces were eventually forced to retreat by intense Confederate fire.

Originally planned as a diversion for Union actions to the south of the city, Sumner's troops were now ordered into the city to drive the Confederates from Marye's Heights. Burnside gave Brigadier General William French the assignment of leading his three brigades across a broad plain adjacent to the city, through a drained but soggy millrace and then up to a sunken road where Georgians and North Carolinians lay in wait behind a stone wall. Assessing the situation earlier in the day, Confederate artillery commander Edward Porter Alexander told Longstreet: "General, we cover that ground now so well that we will comb it as with a fine-tooth comb. A chicken could not live on that field when we open on it."[1]

> No troops could have displayed greater courage and resolution than was shown by those brought against Marye's Heights, but they miscalculated the wonderful strength of the line beyond the stonewall. The position held by [Confederate General Thomas] Cobb surpassed strength and resolution.
> —General James Longstreet, CSA

At noon, General French began his assault on Marye's Heights. Three Union brigades braved artillery and musket fire as they advanced toward the stone wall on the Heights. The withering fire from the Rebels quickly turned scores of men into casualties; the wounded and those not struck hugged the earth in the swale before the stone wall using the terrain or the bodies of their fallen comrades as shields from the unending stream of Confederate minié balls. Brigadier General Winfield Hancock led the next Union division toward the wall. The relentless fire cost Hancock 40 percent of his men as they came forward in three waves. Among the casualties were some five hundred members of the famed Irish Brigade.

Behind Hancock's men came Brigadier General Oliver Howard's division followed by Brigadier General Samuel Sturgis's division, which attacked the Heights to the left of the preceding Union units. This change in approach proved disastrous. The men of the First Brigade of Sturgis's division were decimated by Confederate artillery (proving that Edward Porter Alexander's earlier comment to Longstreet that a chicken couldn't survive his artillery was not hyperbole). Sturgis's next brigade went farther to the left, but it too suffered heavy casualties as it was pummeled by Confederate artillery and musket fire.

Rapidly running out of options, Burnside directed General Franklin to resume his assault south of the city and ordered his reserve troops—General Hooker's Center Grand Division—to pick up the attack on Marye's Heights. Hooker, in close proximity to Burnside, went to see the general to express his concern about further attacks on the Heights. Burnside would have none of it. He ordered Hooker to press the attack on Marye's Heights without delay.

The sun was dropping in the mid-December sky when Brigadier General Daniel Butterfield's Fifth Corps was ordered to resume the attacks on Marye's Heights using his three available divisions. Brigadier General Charles Griffin's First Division crossed the middle pontoon bridge at about 2:30 p.m. The men found themselves jumbled up with other troops that had earlier stormed the ground in front of the stone wall at Marye's Heights—some surviving by groveling in the swale, others dying in heaps. In addition to the death and destruction caused by overwhelming Confederate firepower, success was further hampered by the chaos among Union ranks coming on to the field as they mingled with those already there.

By 3:00 p.m. that afternoon, Burnside was anxious to turn his desperate situation around. Despite the grim track record of preceding divisions that had stormed Marye's Heights and the appalling casualties that were stacking up in front of the stone wall, one man welcomed the opportunity to lead his troops over the killing fields: Brigadier General Andrew A. Humphreys burned with the desire to prove that he could succeed where others had failed.

Despite his own paucity of combat experience and the fact that none of his Pennsylvania troops had been in battle before (and six of his eight regiments were nine-month enlistees), Humphreys oozed confidence. He pointed to Marye's Heights in the distance and announced, "We must gain the crest." But if he was exuberant, he was also realistic. Addressing his troops, he characterized their upcoming effort as a "forlorn hope," a term describing "a perilous and hopeless undertaking."

As Humphreys's two brigades made their way to the Rappahannock River and the pontoon crossing to begin the daunting assault on Marye's Heights, General Burnside, on horseback, was caught amid double-quick-timing troops who streamed around him. Brigadier General Erastus Tyler's First Brigade passed over the upper pontoon bridge under sporadic Confederate artillery fire with little problem. Colonel Peter Allabach's brigade, on the other hand, found the bridges unstable. The structures rocked and swayed under the steps of four full regiments of infantry.

General Humphreys ordered Allabach's brigade to advance after 4:00 p.m., and the men were immediately taken under artillery fire. A thick cloud of smoke generated by Confederate and Union cannon fire covered the advancing brigade, among them the 155th Pennsylvania in the front left of Humphreys's Third Division. At this stage in the battle, Confederate soldiers were lined up four to six deep behind the stone wall at Marye's Heights, thereby raining continuous, unrelenting musket fire on advancing Union troops. Deciding that stopping to fire and reload would only cost them momentum on the way to the stone wall, Humphreys ordered all muskets be kept unloaded. He wanted to storm Marye's Heights using bayonets.

In addition to maintaining intense musket fire, the Confederates were able to reposition a 10-pound Parrott gun so that it poured round after round into Humphreys's Pennsylvanians, who had the misfortune of being easy targets directly in front of the repositioned artillery piece. Riding among his men in an attempt to dress ranks and encourage the troops to begin a bayonet charge, Humphreys had two horses shot from under him. Defying the odds, the general himself was not hit. The lead regiments of Humphreys's assault, the 155th and 133rd Pennsylvanians, reached a high-water mark within fifty yards of the stone wall.

In the diminishing light of the December afternoon, it was clear to most of the Union leadership that a further assault on Marye's Heights was futile. General Hooker ordered Humphreys to withdraw his command—what was left of it. Hooker later remarked: "No campaign in the world ever saw a more gallant advance than Humphreys' men made [on the Heights]."

Allabach's brigade retreated to the area near the millrace ravine and Hanover Street, the fading light and distance from Marye's Heights giving them some semblance of safety from Confederate fire. Hundreds of wounded and dead were left where they had fallen near the wall. As darkness settled on the field of battle, freezing temperatures added to the despair of the wounded Union soldiers, who cried out in pain as many of them slowly bled or froze to death in the cold December night. At the conclusion of the fighting, the Union had lost 12,600 men, two-thirds of those in front of the wall at Marye's Heights.

With the cries of the wounded on Marye's Heights audible at Burnside's headquarters across the Rappahannock, the general was planning to resume assaults on the stone wall the next morning. He promised that he would lead the attacks personally with his own Ninth Corps behind him. Most of Burnside's generals in the Army of the Potomac thought that another assault on Marye's Heights—after fifteen brigades had tried and failed to take the summit—was not a wise move. The next morning, when the fog lifted, Burnside saw that the Confederate line had been strengthened at the Heights. Reluctantly, he accepted the recommendation of his generals and cancelled plans for any further attacks. Fredericksburg would remain in Confederate hands. There would be no Union push "On to Richmond" in 1862.

As darkness fell on December 15, the Union troops slipped back across the Rappahannock on the pontoon bridges. By 3:00 the next morning, 60,000 Union soldiers had gained the safety of the east bank. At first light, engineers dismantled the pontoons and packed them up. The battle of Fredericksburg was over, and General Ambrose Burnside's standing as an effective leader was waning in official Washington. Five weeks after Fredericksburg, one feckless maneuver undertaken by Burnside—this one happily without loss of life—would be the final straw that cost him his command of the Army of the Potomac.

The Regiment—155th Pennsylvania Infantry

> The Commander-in-Chief, General Burnside, unmindful of the greatly strengthened position of the enemy so materially added to during the long delay in the arrival of the pontoons, determined to accommodate the willing enemy by making direct attacks upon his strongest positions, and so the battle of Fredericksburg was inaugurated.
> —*Under the Maltese Cross, Campaigns of the 155th Pennsylvania Regiment*

Burnside's organization of three "Grand Divisions" put the 155th Regiment in the center division under General Joseph Hooker, the Fifth Corps under General Daniel Butterfield, and the Third Division under Brigadier

General Andrew A. Humphreys. The 155th was assigned to the Second Brigade under Colonel Peter Allabach along with the 123rd, 131st, and 133rd Pennsylvania Regiments. With the exception of three days on picket duty, the 155th remained in camp near Falmouth, Virginia, about two miles from Fredericksburg, for twenty days, until December 11, before receiving orders to march downriver.

Humphreys's division was held in reserve on the east side of the river. The inexperienced troops were led by a general whose expertise was military engineering: the West Point graduate had only modest combat experience in the Seminole Wars. The general's son, Lieutenant Henry H. Humphreys, accompanied his father.

Another father-son team caused considerable interest as the 155th marched down Stafford Heights on its way to the pontoon crossing. John Mackin, a prominent Pittsburgh city official ("Uncle John"), had jumped through numerous bureaucratic hoops—including personal visits to General Halleck and Secretary of War Stanton in Washington—in order to obtain permission to accompany his son, John Jr., in battle. Halleck and Stanton both rebuffed Mackin as a blustering crackpot. As a last resort, he contacted Assistant Secretary of War Thomas A. Scott, who knew both Mackin and his son from Pittsburgh. Through some creative paperwork, Scott obtained for the father a title of "Chief Inspector of U.S. Military Telegraphs in the Army of the Potomac," with the rank of colonel (without pay). Uncle John rushed to Fredericksburg with his pass in hand to visit his son, who was serving as a color corporal in the 155th Regiment. The commanding officer of the 155th, Colonel E. Jay Allen, welcomed Uncle John with open arms, providing him quarters and food. Somehow this enterprising father was able to borrow a musket. Fully expecting to accompany his son on the field of battle at Fredericksburg, the father marched in the front of the ranks with his borrowed musket on his shoulder as he prepared to cross the pontoon bridge. Colonel Allen, seeing the armed Uncle John in ranks, put an end to his lenient attitude in trying to accommodate "Colonel" Mackin. Uncle John had to be satisfied with a quick farewell embrace of his son as the young man marched down to the river and headed across the pontoon bridge. (Young Mackin returned to his father after the battle without a scratch despite the high casualty rates among the color guard. The son was wounded at Gettysburg, but he recovered. His luck ran out at the battle of the Wilderness, where he was killed on the first day.)

The 155th Regiment, as part of Colonel Allabach's Second Brigade, was the final regiment of Humphreys's division to cross the upper pontoon bridges. While there was sporadic Confederate fire as the troops crossed the bridges, a far greater challenge for Allabach's men was the unstable, swaying movement of the bridge spans. Weighed down by their gear and muskets, the men found that their synchronized marching caused the spans to sway back and forth, creating considerable instability for the final regiment as they crossed the bridges.

Once on the west side of the river (and off the rocking pontoons) the troops saw stacks of crudely made caskets, newly dug graves, and scores of wounded Union soldiers, some with "ghastly wounds," as reported later by a soldier in Tyler's brigade. General Humphreys rode in advance of his columns to shoo away the wounded and their caretakers, sending them down side streets so that his inexperienced men would not be adversely affected by the gory sight of the results of earlier assaults on Marye's Heights. Humphreys pulled no punches in telling his division that they were to be a "forlorn hope" in their assault on the Heights. Now, as the troops approached the active battlefield, the significance of that expression was becoming clearer and clearer. The units halted briefly on Caroline Street, just up from the river, to stow their gear. The division then swung southwest from Caroline Street marching two columns abreast. Allabach's brigade was put in the lead.

Just after 4:00 p.m. Humphreys ordered Allabach's brigade forward. The four regiments, with the 155th and the 133rd Regiments leading the 123rd and 131st, double-quick timed up Hanover Street to the millrace and splashed across the near-dry race as artillery barrages sounded on both sides and thick smoke from the cannonade settled over the approach to Marye's Heights. Once across the millrace, the troops slogged through a swampy area known to the locals as Gordon's Marsh. The Confederates, lined up several rows deep behind the stone wall adjacent to a sunken road on the Heights, were now less than 1,500 feet away. As Humphreys's men charged forward in front of the wall, they were surrounded by the living, the dying, and the dead from the previous assaults. Confederate artillery poured round after round into Humphreys's men while Rebel infantry fired at the advancing Union troops of the Third Division without surcease from behind the stone wall on the Heights. "Forlorn hope" indeed.

One hundred and fifty yards in advance of the position my command was ordered to occupy a heavy stone wall, a mile in length, which was strengthened by a trench. This stone wall was at the foot of the heights in the rear of Fredericksburg, the crest of which, running four hundred yards distant from the wall, was crowned with enemy batteries. The stone wall was heavily lined with the enemy's infantry. The Second Brigade, led by Colonel Allabach and myself, moved rapidly and gallantly up to General Couch's troops under the artillery and musketry fire of the enemy.

As soon as I ascertained the nature of the enemy's position I was satisfied that our fire could have but little effect upon him, and that the only mode of attacking him successfully was with the bayonet.

—Brigadier General Andrew A. Humphreys

An increasingly anxious Burnside reiterated his desire to Hooker that another assault be led against Marye's Heights by Humphreys's division and that the ground should be taken before dark. A less-than-enthusiastic Hooker relayed the command to Humphreys who gleefully passed the order on to Colonel Allabach. The direction coming down through the chain of command was that the bayonet was going to be the weapon of choice for the advancing troops. Firing, stopping, and reloading—so the reasoning went—only slowed the troops' advance.

General Humphreys, a ubiquitous mounted figure moving among his entire division, gave an order that Third Division muskets were to be "rung." That is, each infantryman was to drop his ramrod down the barrel of his musket, and the resulting clanging sound would verify that the piece was empty. With fixed bayonets—and with bayonets alone—the troops were to surge toward the enemy.

Humphreys, brimming with bravado, rode among his troops listening for the telltale ring of empty muskets, waving his hat in the air, and exhorting his division to: "Give them the cold steel. That's what the rascals want."[2] Later Humphreys would embellish the scene: "[The] setting sun shining full on my face gave me the aspect of an inspired being."[3]

As Allabach's forward regiments crossed the field into the swale before the wall, they ran into the prone members of Colonel Joshua Owen's Philadelphia Brigade hugging the ground. Separating the fresh Third Division troops from the infantrymen, who had been in front of Marye's Heights since midafternoon, was the job of Humphreys and Allabach.

Fresh artillery pieces brought in by the Confederates began pummeling the ranks of the advancing Federals. Musket fire tore into Allabach's brigade bringing down both men and horses. At one point, only two mounted riders remained—General Humphreys and his son, Henry. The color guards of Allabach's brigade took exceptionally heavy losses. In the 155th Regiment, Color Sergeant Thomas Wiseman was fatally wounded. Color Corporal Charles Bardeen took Wiseman's place and was felled with a mortal head wound, yet he managed to give the regimental flag to Color Corporal George Bratten. He, too, was struck and passed the flag to Color Corporal Thomas Lawson. When fighting ended, Lawson was one of the few color-guard members still standing in the regiment.

Humphreys then ordered the First Brigade under Brigadier General Erastus Tyler to give relief to Allabach's men so that a bayonet charge could be mounted. But Tyler's men only caused confusion as they poured into the area that Allabach's Second Brigade was holding. The swale before Marye's Heights turned into a tangled mass of men. Attempts by the officers of Tyler's brigade to put some order and cohesion into the ranks were in vain. The loss of officers and color-bearers to the intense Confederate fire, coupled with the growing darkness, made organization among the Union ranks nearly impossible. Tyler's reinforcing surge to the wall soon collapsed.

Under direction from General Hooker, Humphreys began withdrawing his men, using the 123rd and 155th Pennsylvania to cover the retreat of the troops, including Colonel Allabach, who was on foot, having had his horse shot out from under him. Allabach's men withdrew to the area near the millrace and Hanover Street to regroup and make themselves as comfortable as they could on what one contemporary account called "the cold damp ground."

At the end of the day, Humphreys's division lost 1,000 of its 4,500 men in an hour of fighting; Allabach's brigade of 2,300 troops lost 562; and 68 men from the 155th Pennsylvania were killed, wounded, or missing. Most of Humphreys's men retreated to the city of Fredericksburg. Through an oversight in issuing orders, exacerbated by the thick fog that blanketed the battlefield after dark, the two units assigned to cover Humphreys's retreat—the 123rd and 155th Pennsylvania—remained on the battlefield. Several volunteers used that time on the field to gather the wounded under the cover of darkness and fog. When they had completed their task, 120 wounded had been found, loaded into ambulances, and taken to Union hospitals in Fredericksburg. On the morning of December 14, the 155th marched into the city, bivouacked in the street that night and near the Episcopal church the following day.

Burnside thought that there was still time to redeem both the Army of the Potomac and his own reputation. At a council of war he told his generals that he would personally lead his old Ninth Corps against the stone wall on the morning of the 14th. It was a heroic offer, but the generals expressed their strong doubts about the wisdom of another attempt to take the wall—and Fredericksburg. Burnside concluded the only reasonable next step would be to withdraw from the city.

The Soldier—George P. McClelland

There was an ominous, clanging overture to the charge when the shafts of the bayonets rattled upon the rifle barrels. At the yelled words of the command

the soldiers sprang forward in eager leaps. . . . It was a blind and despairing rush by the collection of men in dusty and tattered blue, over a green sward and under a sapphire sky, toward a fence, dimly outlined in smoke, from behind which spluttered the fierce rifles of the enemies.
—Stephen Crane, *The Red Badge of Courage*

When he awoke on the morning of December 13, George McClelland found his camp engulfed by a thick fog. Based on his experience over the past several days, he judged that the fog would burn off by midmorning and the temperature would climb into the sixties. It was a pleasant December day when you were used to cold, raw Pittsburgh Decembers. There was something to be said for this Virginia climate.

George's tent mates—all from Pittsburgh—agreed that the past two weeks had been tolerable. There had been no long forced marches after the exhausting travels from Sharpsburg over the beautiful, but rugged, Maryland and Virginia terrain. Food had been plentiful in camp, thanks to a new supply base at nearby Aquia Creek and a military railroad that transported supplies on a regular basis to the Army of the Potomac. Furthermore, excellent waterproof tents were now available throughout the regiment.

Yet, despite these creature comforts, some aspects of camp life over the past twenty days had been anxiety-producing. Tent mates McClelland, "Doc" Bardeen, John Jamison, and Billy Adams agreed that the long delay in getting the pontoons to the Army of the Potomac had given the Confederates plenty of time to fortify Fredericksburg, making it a formidable armed bastion. From their camp near Stafford Heights they could—with a pair of field glasses—clearly see the enemy and his entrenchments.

The word filtering down among the ranks in the regiment was that, as part of the Fifth Corps, the 155th would be held in reserve, as they had been at Antietam. McClelland and his tent mates speculated that this reserve status was due to their inexperience, the inexperience of their division commander, General Humphreys, and the fact that many of the regiments in the Fifth Corps were nine-month recruits, not those with the three-year enlistment commitment of members of the 155th. Senior Union officers looked on the nine-month recruits with some distain, reasoning that a soldier with such a short service obligation would not be a highly motivated fighting man who could be counted on in the kind of military challenge that Fredericksburg was going to present.

As the day of December 13 unfolded, the fog lifted and artillery fire began booming downriver where McClelland and his fellow 155th soldiers knew the Left Grand Division had been sent under General William B. Franklin. The long-awaited pontoons were now in place at three locations across the Rappahannock allowing Franklin's Left Grand Division and the Right Grand Division, commanded by Edwin Sumner, to cross the river—Franklin's men south of the city and Sumner's troops directly into Fredericksburg.

By noon, the sounds of artillery and musket fire had increased downriver, and the encamped 155th could see the beginning of a Union assault in the city directly across from them. Smoke from the dueling Union and Confederate artilleries began to shroud the city just as the fog had done early in the morning. The fighting in the town in the vicinity of Marye's Heights continued unabated into the afternoon. By midafternoon, the word came down that Humphreys's Third Division was to make a sweeping and final assault to take the Heights.

Colonel Peter Allabach, Second Brigade commander, spoke to his troops, which included the 155th, imploring them to do their duty. As he marched down the bank of the Rappahannock toward the two pontoon bridges that led to Fredericksburg, George McClelland and his fellow soldiers were in a jubilant mood despite the grim designation of "forlorn hope" that defined their mission. In the 155th regimental history, written four decades later, the high spirits of the regiment in the early afternoon of December 13, 1862, were put in historical perspective: "The officers and men of this Division alike—this being their baptism of fire—could be said, for this battle at least, to be 'eager for the fray.' In fact, it can be truly doubted whether they were ever again as 'eager for the fray' as they were upon this occasion."[4]

Years later, James Longstreet, whose troops defended Marye's Heights against the numerous Union onslaughts, paid his former enemies of the "forlorn hope" a sincere soldier's tribute: "When morning broke [on December 14], the spectacle that we saw upon the battlefield was one of the most distressing I have ever witnessed. The charges had been desperate and bloody, but utterly hopeless. I thought, as I saw the Federals come again and again to their death, that they deserved success if courage and daring could entitle soldiers to a victory."[5]

In His Own Words—The Letters of George McClelland

Camp near Fredericksburg
Saturday, December 20, 1862

My Dear Sister Lizzie,
　Your interesting letter of December 4th I undertake to reply at last.
　It seems strange to be sitting in the old tent writing this letter. This day one week ago something different was going on. Carnage and destruction is rife. We went into the

engagement about 3 o'clock. While crossing the pontoon bridge, the Rebs opened on us with shell which fell on either side and in the water doing no damage. We were the eighth regiment of the Division in the crossing. Tyler's Brigade, consisting of four regiments, crossed first; then came Briggs' Brigade; Colonel Allabach commanding 131st, 133rd; 123rd Colonel Clark; and 155th, Colonel Allen bringing up the rear.

The ground ascends with a gentle slope just outside of the town, then descends slightly to the base of the hill which is about 250 yards from the city and rises almost perpendicularly. At the foot of the hill is a stone fence behind which the enemy are posted. The hill itself is bristling with fortifications. To lead men up to such a hill seemed like taking sheep to the slaughter.

It is useless to attempt to describe the engagement. Our Regiment went in first, reached the brow of the knoll, but could go no farther. We lay down behind it, but had to rise at every fire to do any execution. We were totally powerless. The enemy appeared to have it all their own way. Their shells were bursting over our heads, while the lead was flying thick and fast.

Our 1st Lieutenant was wounded on one side of me and several of the boys on the other were crying for their comrades to take them off the field. It was a wonder that I escaped. I stood on my feet and took as deliberate aim as I could. They shot a piece of my gun away, a splinter taking me on the leg doing no damage.

We left the field about 8 o'clock having lost 10 killed and 58 wounded. We got our ammunition replenished and moved out at 3 the next morning (Sabbath) and lay under fire all day. One of our Company was shot in the head while lying on the ground. Were relieved about dark and marched through the town to the Court House. Slept on pavement. The Rebels throw an occasional shell in the streets.

The city is swarming with troops. It is entirely ruined; one half of it burnt and destroyed while the troops have sacked the other half. Splendid libraries lying around the streets together with the most splendid furniture.

Burnside, finding it impossible to take the impregnable hill just back of the town, gave orders to evacuate the town. The wounded were all taken to the other side of the river. This was done all day Monday and Monday night. Before Tuesday daylight, the whole Army was on the other side of the Rappahannock. If the Rebs had known of our retreat in time, what a slaughter there would have been. A Balls Bluff on a ten times larger scale.

Such a time as we had when we did cross. It commenced raining furiously. On we plodded through water and mud 10 inches deep until we reached our old camp thoroughly soaked and benumbed with cold. To make it worse, the weather changed. It blew up cold and commenced snowing.

We only had one piece of tent and were compelled [to] make covering with a blanket, I having lost 2 pieces of tent and gum blanket on the field. As for my tent mates, Doc Bardeen was shot through the head and I could never learn anything about him. He was Color Corporal. John Jamison, cousin of Jack Ralston, lost everything he had. Billy Adams saved *his knapsack. Lieutenant Breed came to our assistance; gave us a piece of tent so now we managed to get along pretty comfortable.*

I am not in Richmond yet and it is extremely doubtful whether we will even get there. I wish you a Merry Christmas and a Happy New Year.

Always, your Brother,
Geo. P. M.

Notes on December 20, 1862, Letter

One week after the battle of Fredericksburg, George McClelland wrote to his sister Lizzie to give her his report on the battle. By this time, over 1,000 Union dead had been interred by fellow members of the Army of the Potomac, Confederate and Union prisoners exchanged, and Congress's Committee on the Conduct of the War rushed to nearby Aquia Landing to conduct a postmortem on the battle and assign blame to those responsible for the catastrophe at Fredericksburg.

As McClelland reported, Company F of the 155th took its share of casualties. First Lieutenant Edward E. Clapp was seriously wounded. Corporal George Bradley and Privates William Clotworthy, Gershon Horner, William McKeever, and Joseph Taylor were also wounded. Color Corporal Charles "Doc" Bardeen was mortally wounded during the assault and later removed from the field and taken to a field hospital, where he died of a gunshot wound to the head. Bardeen was an original "Luny" recruited from Pittsburgh and McClelland's tent mate. When he wrote his letter, McClelland was not aware of Bardeen's death.

McClelland's report on killed and wounded is remarkably accurate coming only one week after the battle. The regimental commander, E. J. Allen, in his official battle report, listed nine killed and fifty-eight wounded from the regiment.

When the regiment withdrew from the field, they headed back toward the Rappahannock and slept on the streets around the court house and St. George's Episcopal Church. In passing through the city, McClelland had a close look at the destruction of the town following the Union shelling and sacking of private homes.

Burnside's withdrawal from the city was one Union maneuver that went right at Fredericksburg. Cloaked in darkness and fog, the sounds of retreat muffled by rain, the Army of the Potomac was able to cross back over the Rappahannock without incident—a remarkable feat considering the men, equipment, ambulances, wagons, and horses that had to pass over the pontoon bridges. In October 1861, a much smaller Union force was routed at Ball's Bluff in Northern Virginia, and in their chaotic attempt to escape over an escarpment and across the Potomac to Maryland, two hundred soldiers were shot, upwards of forty drowned, and seven hundred were captured. One Confederate soldier was reported to have characterized Ball's Bluff as a "turkey shoot." Burnside's troops avoided such a fate. By 3:00 the next morning approximately sixty thousand Union soldiers had slipped out of Fredericksburg, leaving behind a handful of pickets and their unburied dead.

Even though they were only fifty miles from Richmond, no one uttered the old rallying cry of "On to Richmond!" No Union soldier would be celebrating Christmas 1862 in the Confederate capital.

Chapter Five

Mud, Morale, and Monotony

January—April 1863

The Army of the Potomac

After the battle Burnside tried to regain the confidence of the army, and there is no doubt that Sumner did a good deal to help him. Burnside conceived the plan of crossing the Rappahannock a few miles above Fredericksburg, where the enemy were unprepared to receive us. The result was the "mud march" of January 20th—21st. It was Burnside's effort to redeem himself. To start off in the mud as we did with the army in its discouraged state was perfect folly. There did not seem to be anything in the move to recommend itself . . . but it was a hazardous move, with the army out of confidence with its commander and the enemy elated with brilliant success. The general demoralization that had come upon us made two or three months of rest a necessity.
—Major General Darius N. Couch, U. S. Army

Eager for vengeance after the disaster at Fredericksburg, Burnside began exploring ways to recross the Rappahannock and launch a major assault against Lee's army. He was motivated by three factors: he believed that after December 26, 1862, the Army of the Potomac had been sufficiently resupplied and had recovered from the fatigue they had experienced leading up to and at Fredericksburg; the winter weather was unseasonably mild, hence, there was a window of opportunity to move troops and equipment in a favorable climate; and, finally, confidence and morale were sinking by the day in the Army of the Potomac among both officers and men, and in Burnside's mind, a bold initiative would help reverse the downward spiral of the troops' spirits.

Before the offensive could begin, two politically connected brigadier generals (Newton and Cochrane) went to Washington to express their profound lack of confidence in Burnside's ability to lead. Thanks to their ties with Radical Republicans and Cochrane's friendship with Secretary of State William H. Seward, the two disgruntled generals were able to schedule an appointment with the president. Newton and Cochrane laid out a grim and pessimistic picture of a demoralized and vulnerable Army of the Potomac under Burnside's leadership. Just as Burnside was ready to launch his offensive, Lincoln telegraphed him: Burnside was to "not make a general movement without letting me know of it." Already sensitive about the growing discontent and lack of trust among his general officers, Burnside was furious that intriguers were poisoning his relationship with Washington leadership. An angry Burnside went as quickly as he was able to Washington to offer his resignation to the president. Lincoln, seeking to avoid turmoil that would negatively affect the entire Army of the Potomac, rejected Burnside's offer but kept him on a short leash, limiting the general's decision-making authority.

As 1863 began General in Chief Halleck and the president encouraged Burnside to launch a new initiative based on their intelligence that Lee had dispatched a large number of his Virginia-based troops to reinforce the Carolina coast. The Confederate army, in Lincoln and Halleck's view, was in a more vulnerable position than it had been since the battle at Fredericksburg. In response, on January 17, Burnside ordered his division commanders to move out toward two fords on the Rappahannock River, but then he delayed the march for three days in order to gather and assess intelligence on Confederate countermovements. Finally, on January 20, the Army of the Potomac was ordered to move out. It was unseasonably warm, and the army moved under blue skies filled with billowy cumulus clouds.

> You have no idea of how soon the roads turn from good to bad here in Virginia. A clayey soil is hard and the very best for marching on in favorable weather, but let it rain but an hour and troops and wagons march over the road, and the mud is worse than anyone who has not been in Virginia can conceive of. . . . It seems that Mud is really King. He sets down his foot and says, "Ye shall not pass," and lo and behold we cannot. But Mud wields more despotic sway these last two days than ever I saw him wield before. The horses sank into mud up to their bellies. . . .
> —Lieutenant Theodore A. Dodge, 119th New York Infantry, January 22, 23, 1863

The first day's march, over firm, dry roads and under cloudy but fair skies, boosted the spirits of many of the troops. Perhaps they thought that at last the Army of the Potomac had turned the corner and General Burnside would prove to be an effective leader. Still others—including most of the senior officers—remained pessimistic about the future of the Army of the Potomac under Burnside's command. The army went into bivouac on the evening of January 20; the plan was to continue on in the morning, swing west then south and cross the Rappahannock at Bank's Ford. At 7:00 p.m. it began to rain. The Army of the Potomac's weather window of opportunity slammed shut.

The rain—mixing occasionally with snow—continued unabated for the next two days. Clay road surfaces—at first slick with the beginning rain—became saturated quickly then broke down and mixed with the soil beneath. This combination of clay and soil rapidly turned to a viscous sludge when men and wagons and their teams traveled over it. Men struggled in mud up to their knees; wagons submerged to their wheel hubs; mules and horses sank to their bellies in the mud. Efforts to employ "corduroy" support using logs and pulling out stuck vehicles with ropes were all in vain. Horses and mules died of exhaustion, drowned in the mud, or sank so deep in the mire that they had to be shot. Many of the pontoons that were to be used to cross the river were hopelessly bogged down as the wagons used to transport them sank deeply into the mud.

By the evening of January 21, the Army of the Potomac was stretched out from the vanguard of the Sixth Corps, located about a mile from the Rappahannock, all the way back to Falmouth, Virginia, a distance of about ten miles over increasingly impassable roads. And the rain continued. The Union army was virtually immobile. Burnside's delays and weather problems gave Lee an opportunity to respond by ordering two divisions to Bank's and U.S. Fords to check the Army of the Potomac. Once in place, the Confederates saw the Federals' predicament and viewed it with more humor than alarm. Signs began appearing across the river from the Union army: "Burnside stuck in the mud," trumpeted one. "This way to Richmond," offered another sign with an arrow pointing the opposite direction of the Confederate capital city. Having undergone torrential rains, cold, impassible roads, and lack of food, the Army of the Potomac now had to endure the ridicule of its enemies.

The Army of the Potomac's intended advance collapsed. Men grumbled about being sent on a "fool's errand," and Burnside's generals clucked their disapproval of the handling of the "mud march" as it would now be called. (Writing to Halleck months later, General Franklin admitted, ". . . I looked upon the rain which stopped his second attempt to cross the river as almost a providential interference on our behalf."[1])

On January 22 Burnside saw the futility of continuing in the rain and called an end to the campaign. The rain continued into the next day as a misty drizzle fell on the humiliated and discouraged Army of the Potomac. Morale had reached its nadir. Two days later, as the hapless Burnside traveled to Washington to report the calamitous events of the past several days to Halleck and the president, the rain stopped and the sun shone on the encamped Army of the Potomac.

Burnside went to Washington and presented a dramatic proposal that included cashiering nine of the Army of the Potomac's senior officers whom he charged were insubordinate. If the general in chief and president were not willing to accept this plan, Burnside offered his resignation as an alternative. Burnside was especially critical of General Hooker who, in his view, was the cause of much of the discontent and distrust among the Army of the Potomac's senior officers.

Lincoln took the recommendation under consideration, but—bowing to political pressure from the radical wing of the Republican Party—he decided to replace Burnside with the general's nemesis, Joseph Hooker, as the commander of the Army of the Potomac. Not willing to be sandbagged by Burnside's either/or proposal, Lincoln rejected the general's offer to resign, asking that he accept another post to be decided later. Burnside reluctantly withdrew his resignation and awaited reassignment. Later Burnside told Halleck that he acquiesced because, "I do not want to injure the cause."[2]

General Hooker took command of the Army of the Potomac with his own group of outspoken detractors, but the newly appointed commander lost no time in changing the army that had seen three chiefs in four months. General Sumner resigned; Generals Franklin and Smith were relieved of their commands; and the grand-division organization structure was eliminated. The corps commanders now reported directly to Hooker. Lincoln was well aware of Hooker's intemperate remarks and his penchant for second-guessing his superiors. Despite these shortcomings, Lincoln thought that Hooker's self-confidence, wiliness, and aggressive nature more than made up for his flaws and that they could make him a successful leader of the Army of the Potomac.

In addition to command and organization transformations, Hooker set in motion other profound changes that had a significant, daily impact on the lives of the soldiers. He ordered that rations be improved so that fresh vegetables and soft bread were available to all. Under his direction, the sanitary conditions of the camps were greatly improved. As a result, the health of the troops was better, and sick-call lists grew shorter. Hooker also introduced a more liberal furlough system to the delight of the men, both officers and enlisted.

Then, recognizing and tapping into the men's growing pride in their units and corps organizations, Hooker inaugurated the use of distinctive corps badges. Based on a concept conceived by General Philip Kearny earlier in the war, the new badges used shapes and colors to designate corps and divisions within the corps. For example, the Fifth Corps symbol was a Maltese cross; First Division was red; Second Division was white; and Third Division was blue. Originally developed to identify stragglers by unit, the badges quickly became sources of unit pride, further boosting morale in Hooker's Army of the Potomac.

Amid the welcome changes occurring when Hooker took command, paymasters came from Washington bearing sacks with six months' back pay for the troops. Hooker's ascension to the command of the Army of the Potomac brought with it the soldier's perfect formula for improved morale: good and ample food, cleaner living conditions, liberal leave, unit pride, and back pay. These tangible benefits made the now-frequent parade and review demands palatable. The men, marching in grand reviews in regimental ranks, passed the reviewing stand where their benefactor, Fighting Joe, watched them gradually improve their order and discipline as soldiers.

As the winter days passed, the soldiers settled into a monotonous routine of drills and parades. The only change in their lives during this period was the erratic Virginia weather. As one soldier recorded in his diary, "We had plenty and a variety of weather about this time. Here is a record for one week: Monday, nice day; Tuesday, deep snow; Wednesday's rain and Thursday's sun melted the snow and made mud as deep as the snow was previously; Friday and Saturday, wind dried the mud; Sabbath, snow a foot deep and cold."[3]

The Regiment—155th Pennsylvania Infantry

> But fate seemed to be once more against Burnside, as at the end of the first half-day's march a decided change in the magnificent weather took place by a storm of drizzling rain and snow, which in a few hours made the roads over which the heavy wagon and ammunition trains and the troops had to march, impassable by reason of the muddy condition of the same. In many places the roads became almost liquid. It was not unusual to see wagon trains, sutlers' wagons and artillery wagons sunk to the hubs of the wheels, and the poor mules were unable to budge their loads, it being as much as they could do in some cases to keep their bodies or heads above the water and mud.
>
> —*Under the Maltese Cross*

The members of the 155th heard their commanding general, Ambrose Burnside, announce on January 20, as they prepared to resume the offensive against the Confederates that "The auspicious moment had now arrived to strike the enemy a blow." Most of the regiment knew from the grapevine that the planned movement was to be toward the upper fords of the Rappahannock River. Since Burnside's credibility had suffered a major setback among the soldiers of the Army of the Potomac because of his inept leadership at Fredericksburg, the only reason to be at all sanguine about the proposed campaign was the fair weather that the Rappahannock River area was experiencing in late January.

Then the weather did an about-face. By the end of the first day's march, a storm had moved in bringing rain and snow. To add insult to the weather misery, the men saw the Confederates hoisting mocking signs on the opposite side of the Rappahannock where the intended fords were to be crossed. Shivering from the cold, drenched to the skin, and ridiculed by their enemies, the 155th, along with the rest of the Army of the Potomac, marched back to their old camps near Falmouth. It came as no surprise to any of the men of the 155th when, on January 26, Burnside was relieved of command by the president.

> On the 26th day of January, 1863, the official order assigning General Joseph Hooker to the command of the Army of the Potomac was read at dress parade to all the regiments of the army. A few days after this announcement, the One Hundred and Fifty-fifth moved a few miles nearer to Falmouth, to what was probably the finest camp and winter quarters it ever occupied during its term of service.... The memories of the good health and comforts and pleasant days in this camp during February and March, and a large part of April 1863, in the minds of the One Hundred and Fifty-fifth Regiment will never be forgotten.
> —*Under the Maltese Cross*

By February 3, the 155th had established a new camp closer to Falmouth. And under the direction of their new commanding general, Joseph Hooker, the camp was laid out like a small city with streets, comfortable quarters for the men and officers, and excellent sanitary and drainage arrangements. Cedars and other evergreens native to Virginia were planted along the streets of the camp, and a chapel was constructed. The winter quarters (Camp Humphreys) were a pleasant hiatus after the horror of Fredericksburg and the misery of the "mud march."

During this time of regrouping and restoration, leadership in the regiment underwent major changes. The popular Colonel E. J. Allen, regimental commander of the 155th, relinquished his command due to chronic inflammatory rheumatism, turning the responsibility over to Lieutenant Colonel John H. Cain. In addition, five captains and three lieutenants from the regiment resigned their commissions and returned home during the winter months. Regimental history records indicate that some of these resignations were due to health problems; others may have resigned after getting a taste of the lethal nature of their responsibilities as frontline leaders. Union officers had considerably more flexibility in resigning their commissions than enlisted personnel had in getting out of their enlistment commitments. An enlisted man, for the most part, was required to serve the full term of his enlistment obligation unless significant health issues resulted in his being granted a "surgeon's certificate" that led to discharge.

The living quarters for officers and enlisted at Camp Humphrey were log huts built to accommodate three men. Heat was supplied by a wood fire vented through a chimney usually constructed of sticks and mud with a box or barrel placed on top to create sufficient draft to draw the smoke from the hut. The chimneys' drawing power was, more often than not, subject to wind and weather conditions. Chimneys sometimes caught fire, or winds caused the jury-rigged chimneys to draw down rather than up leaving the huts more like smoke houses than living quarters. (Members of the 155th later recounted stories of practical jokers in the unit who covered chimneys of other huts with boards as they went out on guard duty. By the time the unlucky—and smoky—inhabitants discovered their plight, the perpetrator would be away at his post, no doubt laughing at his comrades-in-arms' misfortune.)

Morale steadily improved at Camp Humphreys as the regiment settled into snug quarters and became accustomed to regular meals, vastly improved sanitary conditions, and reliable mail service. The duties required of the soldiers were monotonous but without the danger or discomfort they had undergone in the closing months of 1862. Drills, reviews, picket duty, wagon-guarding, and scouting assignments filled their time with tedious regularity. As a break in the "dull monotony of the soldier's life," the regiment even sponsored a glee club.

The Soldier—George P. McClelland

"Oh, Burnside then he tried his luck,
    Hurrah! Hurrah!
Oh, Burnside he tried his luck,
But in the mud so fast got stuck."
    —Sung to the tune of "When Johnny Comes
    Marching Home," *Hardtack and Coffee*

Despite a time of post-Fredericksburg remorse, random harsh weather conditions, and a command structure in flux, George McClelland retained a positive, upbeat attitude during the period of time when the Army of the Potomac morale was at a nadir. The officers and men of the army then and historians since that time have been in agreement: in the early months of 1863, Union prospects were extraordinarily bleak. McClelland's only serious complaint was the lack of pay. Not until General Hooker took over command were six months' back pay given to the men.

Even young McClelland's response to the poor rations in early January was a lighthearted parody of the army's hardtack cuisine. Rather than communicating a sardonic attitude about his life in the army, McClelland—at least to his sisters—remained droll and self-deprecating about his condition. His thoughts were occupied with observations about his prospects with women and his own lack of letter-writing diligence.

Since McClelland wrote to and received letters from his two sisters on a regular basis, the two women, Lizzie and Annie, were an important link with family and home from which the young soldier took sustenance. Part of McClelland's upbeat attitude was due to his own personality and upbringing, but clearly the ongoing contact with his two older sisters was an important source of strength for him as he faced the cold, dark days of the winter of 1862–1863.

In His Own Words—The Letters of George McClelland

January 10, 1863
Camp near Falmouth, Virginia

Beloved Sister,
I thank you for your kind letter which I received on the 7th.
We are still living in the same old camp, and truly it wears quite a novel appearance. Every tent has its fireplace and chimney built in every conceivable form, there being not two alike. Some few are built scientifically, but the majority are wretched, smoky concerns putting one in mind of the old homily: "A smoky house and a scolding wife" etc. All but the wife. Well, to beautify our camp, we have rows of cedars planted in the different streets which improves its appearance very much.
About a quarter mile from camp there is a church being built for our benefit. It's superintended by our Chaplain, Reverend Thomas, a Methodist preacher from the city of smoke [Pittsburgh] who suddenly made his appearance about a week ago. Query I: Why nearly all our Army chaplains are of the Methodist persuasion? I suppose because there's so many itinerants having no settled charge.
Burnside reviewed our Corps—Mead's [Meade's]—on the 8th. There were 20 Regiments of Infantry and I don't know how many batteries present. It was a grand sight. Among the throng I noticed a number of ladies on horseback. Our Brigade was praised for their splen-

did marching. We are in Hooker's grand Division, Mead's 5th Army Corps, Humphries' [sic] Division, Allabach's Brigade. Now you know our position. In Frank Leslie's paper there is a picture of the "gallant charge of Humphries' [sic] Division." You should get it.

My duties now are most arduous. I have been acting Orderly Sergeant for some time and you may judge I have not much time to myself. It's "Orderly this, that and the other" from morning until night, and the drills have commenced again in earnest. Squad, Company, Battalion & Brigade every day winding up with dress parade.

Lizzie waxeth quite eloquent over the state of the country, and you are about right too. Hardly a week passes without an engagement of the contending forces. The tide of war rolls from east to west, and the minds of the people are no sooner allayed, when they are again startled by another scene of blood. When will this carnage cease? This civil intestine strife is gradually forcing itself into a war of subjugation and even if the Union is again restored whole, generations will have come and gone before the bitter recollections of the war will perish and brotherly concord intervene between the two sections.

The weather here has been very cold for some time back and if this [is] a specimen of the "Sunny South" it's a big thing, but I can't see it.

I was sorry to hear of the loss of the gallant little Monitor. My opinion is Mr. Welles should be pushed overboard for sending her to sea.

I am expecting a letter from Henry every day. I wrote to him at the same time I sent you those lines. Annie is my regular correspondent. Father never writes. Tell Tom I would like to hear from him occasionally. My health is improving and the "hard tack" disappears as fast as ever. It is astonishing the variety of dishes we have. Hard tack plain, crackers "ala mode," "tack Americanais," "cracker scouse," crackers roasted, fried, and boiled. Then we get fat pork and about once a month, molasses, potatoes, and onions. Who says we are not well fed?

It's high time Uncle Sam was coming up with a little dough. There is now 5 months pay due us.

My love to Tom, Anna, and the boys. Goodbye my dear sister. Write soon.

Your affectionate brother,
George

Notes on the January 10, 1863, Letter

Prior to the "mud march," McClelland was in camp near Falmouth unaware that in ten days he would be involved in a major troop movement resulting in physical hardship, the scorn of his enemies, and the dismissal of his commanding general. McClelland's appointment as an acting "orderly sergeant"—responsible for transmitting orders of superior officers—indicated that he had been recognized for his reliability and aptitude in military matters. Never one to shy from expressing his opinion on political matters to his family, McClelland was prescient about the deep divide between North and South that would linger through many generations after the war as the United States struggled to reunite itself.

Bad news traveled fast. McClelland mentioned the ironclad ship, *Monitor,* that had sunk in a gale off Cape Hatteras on the last day of December 1862, taking with her four officers and twelve crew members. McClelland assigned blame for the sinking to Secretary of the Navy Gideon Welles, who initially had many reservations about ironclad vessels. Some in the North thought that once he overcame his earlier concerns about these new types of ships, Welles pushed the *Monitor* into service without the necessary testing and adequate sea trials.

Camp Humphries [Humphreys] near Falmouth, Virginia
February 14, 1863

Dear Sister Lizzie,

Your last epistle was received a day or two ago while we were on picket. I have nothing interesting to communicate in reply. We have moved to a new camp which is dubbed Camp Humphries [sic] in honor of our Division Commander. We have built up quarters and on the whole are fixed pretty comfortably. I received the box Annie sent and emptied it of the contents pretty quick.

I had a letter from Annie brim full of news; also one from Father. He is getting along swimmingly. I received a letter from Arch a good while ago, but did not want to direct a letter to Camden when the battery was under marching, or rather, riding orders. Now I suppose the address of St. Louis will reach him.

Joe Hooker is in command now. Well, my opinion is that he is not "the man." I may be mistaken. I hope so. One thing, however, he is getting very popular among the men by his new orders, such as granting limited furloughs, ordering the issue of soft bread 4 times a week, potatoes, onions, etc., showing great interest in the welfare of the Army. What he intends to do with the Army after he has it remodeled, time alone will tell.

One thing certain, nothing decisive can be done while such weather lasts as we have had for a month back. Rain, freezing, snow, sunshine in constant succession. Roads impassable almost for empty wagons.

I had a visit this morning from Jim McKelvy, a brother of Belle Barbour's. He has been discharged from Colonel Clark's Regiment and is out again in the capacity of Hospital Steward in the Regular Army. He is mustered for five years and reports to Medical Director Letterman. He looks well and reports Pittsburgh the same as ever.

I hardly know what more to write about my little dame. Tell the young ladies you refer to send along their photographs together with a letter of introduction and I will make my choice at once.

My "union" sentiments have not been shaken in the least by a five month's absence in the Army. I have never yet "fell in love," still I have a holy horror of flirts, coquettes and the like. I hereby appoint you, my confidential agent for the State of Iowa, to negotiate a match. I have another operating in Pittsburgh in the person of Sister Annie who has already set up claims of one of the fair sex. But enough of this.

My love to Anna, Thomas and the little ones. I was glad to see a flattering notice of my brother Tom. Go on? Real merit will sooner or later have its reward.

Farewell at this time my dear sister. Always, your brother, George
Miss Lizzie McClelland, Davenport, Iowa

Notes on the February 14, 1863, Letter

McClelland voiced doubts about Joe Hooker as a commander, but was willing to admit he might be mistaken. (Troop sentiment still ran high for their former commander, George McClellan.) Rumors circulated within the Army of the Potomac about Hooker's intriguing and political maneuvering to obtain promotions. His reputation was further sullied when he told a newspaper reporter that the country needed a dictator in order to win the war and subjugate the Confederates. Yet Hooker's commitment to granting liberal furloughs, introducing more sanitary conditions in the camps, and improving food quality and quantity went a long way toward polishing Fighting Joe's image among the troops, including Sergeant George McClelland.

McClelland reported the varying winter weather conditions in Virginia that had had such a dramatic impact on his life over the past month. His mention of the "mud march" was oblique. Perhaps writing a more detailed narrative of the mud march for his sister required recalling things that McClelland wanted to forget.

His reference to the assignment of Jim McKelvy, brother of a woman known by his sister Lizzie, reflected the changes fostered by Hooker in the medical area for the Union army. Jonathan K. Letterman was appointed medical director of the Army of the Potomac by the surgeon general. Under Hooker's leadership, Letterman was a key factor in instituting an effective ambulance corps, implementing a triage method of handling the wounded, and affecting changes in the sanitary requirements for camps. McKelvy was appointed a hospital steward in Dr. Letterman's expanded medical corps.

He acknowledged his sister's earlier reference to his eldest brother Tom's success in Davenport. George clearly admired his brother's entrepreneurial ambition and talents.

March 19, 1863
Camp Humphrey near Falmouth, Virginia

My Dear Sister,

A letter so kind, so interesting and of such length as your last merited no such neglect or delay as I have permitted it to suffer. And I am afraid of being court-martialed for malfeasance of duty. Indeed, I suppose it is already convened. If so, it will probably be as follows: Before a special court-martial held in the City of Davenport, State of Iowa was arraigned and tried George P. McClelland, Company F, 155th Pennsylvania Volunteers, on the following charges and specifications: Charge 1st—"Willful neglect of duty."

Specification: In this, that the said sergeant, George McClelland, having received a loving epistle from his sister, Lizzie, did willfully neglect to acknowledge the same within a reasonable time.

Charge 2nd—"Conduct unbecoming a brother." Specification: In this, that the said G. P. M., Company F, 155th Regiment Pennsylvania Volunteers, when called on to reply to a letter full of tenderness and love, did not only fail to comply, which showed a want of proper regard, but treated it with silence and contempt. Specification 2nd: In this that said G. P. M, etc., when at last he did write, did so in a foolish and nonsensical letter with an [sic] useless jargon of words and a manifest impropriety. All this in camp near Falmouth, Virginia. To which charges and specifications the accused pleaded—not guilty.

The Court after mature deliberation finds as follows—To Specification of 1st Charge—guilty; to the Charge—guilty. To Specification 1st of second Charge—guilty, all but the word "contempt." To Specification 2nd of 2nd Charge—guilty; and to the Charge—guilty. And the Court for this flagrant violation of the ties of blood do sentence him to do penance for the space of two months and—here mercy puts in a plea—in view of the previous good behavior of the accused, the sentence is revoked, provided he seek forgiveness carefully with tears. Such would be your decision my little "dame."

I tell you, Lizzie, military law "takes hold." I am reminded of this fact by the issue of a court-martial in an adjoining regiment. A young man, Fraser by name, 1st Sergeant and acting 2nd Lieutenant, made use of expressions to his Captain not down in "Casey's Tactics" for which he was reduced to the ranks, forfeits six months pay and undergoes hard labor for 2 months with ball and chain. A pretty severe sentence you will say . . .

Our Regiment, which has been cried down and abused by the precious set of "9- month conscripts" in whose Brigade we are unfortunately placed, was cut off from furloughs and other advantages for a time through the influence of the Reverend Colonel J. B. Clark whom I once thought the "Gods had set their seal to give assurance of a man." I may have something more definite to say about him at another time.

We have now been restored to our privileges and the 155th Regiment, Pennsylvania Volunteers will challenge comparison with any other in the field in courage, discipline or intelligence. If I could get a furlough for 25 or 30 days, I would make a flying trip to the west to take in Leavenworth, Davenport and old Pitt. "Wouldn't that be handsome?" But it can't be did [sic] just now for I could get no longer than 10 days under the present regimen.

I have the honor of a slight acquaintance with Mr. Walsh. He is Colonel Allen's orderly and must have gotten an unlimited leave of absence for he went home with Colonel Allen and has not yet returned. The Colonel is not improving and it is doubtful whether he will ever be able to take the field. In the meantime, his position is ably filled by Lieutenant Colonel J. H. Cain.

We are still living comfortably in our old camp feasting on such delicacies as potatoes, onions, peas, molasses and soft bread. Hooker understands human nature. He keeps the men well fed, well clothed and gives them plenty to do. The result is the men have no time to grumble. One cannot fail to note the change in the short space of a month. The whole Army is kept constantly on the alert and discipline and cleanliness is [sic] taught as was never taught before. Tom is right. "Joe Hooker is the best General in the Army of the Rappahannock."

Well, Lizzie, I will not tire your patience. I received letters from Annie and Cousin H. Chess. Also 2 shirts—nice and pretty—which the indefatigable little worker sent on in double-quick time. It is astonishing the resolution and energy she displays. She overcame every obstacle in her path.

I received a letter from Arch some time ago. I have answered it. He is now, I understand, on his way down the Father of Waters. About papers—I have never got any from you. I think a good many papers are "cabbaged" on their way at the different headquarters from Corps to Regimental.

Well, Lizzie, my love, goodbye. I wish you to remember often,

Your brother in arms,
George P.

PS My love to Tom, Anna and the boys.
Miss Lizzie McClelland
Davenport, Iowa

Notes on the March 19, 1863, Letter

With tongue planted firmly in his cheek, McClelland addressed his own neglect in letter-writing with a clever parody of military justice. It's clear that he has been exposed to the technical language used in military law. Perhaps he was a close observer of the court-martial of Fraser—an acting lieutenant—for insubordination. McClelland's role as an acting orderly sergeant may have given him an opportunity to observe the court-martial and become a student of the military justice system.

During the temporary absence of brigade commander Peter Allabach, Colonel John B. Clark, commander of the 123rd Regiment, was given temporary command of the brigade. Due to problems arising from the nine-month conscripts in the brigade, Colonel Clark put a temporary hold on furloughs and other privileges.

Clark's restrictions were short-lived, and the men of the 155th were once again eligible for furlough. But McClelland's ambitious travel plans to visit brother Henry in Kansas, brother Tom and family and sister Lizzie in Iowa, and father and sister Annie in Pittsburgh could not be accommodated within the furlough requirements

The highly regarded Colonel E. J. Allen, commander of the 155th, retired from the regiment on sick leave because of untreatable inflammatory rheumatism. Allen was mustered out in July 1863, four months after McClelland's letter was written. (Allen never returned to his regiment. He lived the rest of his life in Pittsburgh and was an active member in 155th Regimental reunions through the early years of the twentieth century.)

Since writing his February 14 letter, McClelland had changed his opinion about Hooker as a leader. Food, clothing, and activity, coupled with discipline and cleanliness, prove to McClelland that—in his brother Tom's words—"Joe Hooker is the best General in the Army of the Rappahannock." (Tom may have believed that the Army of the Potomac modified its name depending on what body of water it was operating near.)

McClelland's brother Archibald was in the western theater, traveling down the Mississippi. Newspapers sent by Lizzie were stolen ("cabbaged"), which was very frustrating for an insatiable reader such as McClelland.

Chapter Six

"This Coveted Ground"

Chancellorsville, April—June 1863

The Army of the Potomac

Here, on this open ground, I intended to fight my battle. But the trouble was to get my army on it. . . . By making a powerful demonstration in front of and below the town of Fredericksburg with a part of my army, I was able, unobserved, to withdraw the remainder, and, marching nearly thirty miles up the stream, to cross the Rappahannock and the Rapidan unopposed, and in four days' time to arrive at Chancellorsville, within five miles of this coveted ground, and all this without General Lee having discovered that I had left my position in his front. So far, I regarded my movement as a great success.
—General Joseph Hooker, postwar interview, *Battles and Leaders of the Civil War*

In April 1863, General Hooker's elements for a successful offensive campaign began to gel: the weather had improved, making it possible to move troops, artillery, and wagons over the unpredictable Virginia roads; the morale and state of readiness of the Army of the Potomac were high; and Hooker's subordinate command structure—while not stellar—was competent and reasonably loyal. The army now numbered almost 134,000 men and could field over 400 artillery pieces. It was, in Hooker's own words, "The finest army on the planet." The officers and men shared a buoyant optimism that they had not felt in a long time.

Fighting Joe's plan was to use his cavalry corps to cross the Rappahannock upriver from Fredericksburg and swing behind Lee in order to cut the Rebel lines of communications and supply with Richmond. Alas, for Hooker, the rains came in mid-April, quickly turning the Rappahannock into a surging torrent that made it impossible for Major General George Stoneman's troopers to cross the river. Hooker's admonishment to his cavalry general earlier in the month—"On you and your noble command must depend in a great measure the extent and brilliancy of our success"—now turned out to be wishful thinking as the Rappahannock grew in depth and force with the spring rains.

Once news of the aborted cavalry assault reached Washington, a distraught Lincoln, accompanied by Secretary of War Stanton and General in Chief Halleck, met Hooker at Aquia, Virginia, on April 19 to discuss what options Hooker had in mind after the cavalry washout. Hooker's "Plan B" was ambitious and complex. He would send his cavalry corps across the Rappahannock as before, but this time he would simultaneously send three corps of 42,000 men (the Fifth, Eleventh, and Twelfth) upriver to cross at Kelly's Ford, swoop south and east crossing the Rapidan River at Ely's Ford (the Fifth Corps) and Germanna Ford (the Eleventh and Twelfth Corps). The Union force would then come in behind Lee's left flank by marching through a scrubby, overgrown wooded area, referred to as the Wilderness, to converge at the quiet crossroad clearing of Chancellorsville.

In concert with these moves, the Union Second Corps would march to U. S. Ford on the Rappahannock and wait on the east side of the river until the Fifth Corps could move in behind the Confederate troops who were guarding the river crossing on the west side. Once the Rebels were driven from the ford, the Second Corps would cross the river to join the other three corps in the vicinity of the Chancellorsville crossroads.

Adding to the complexity of these maneuvers, Hooker ordered the First and Sixth Corps to cross the Rappahannock downriver from Fredericksburg and attack Lee's right flank. Hooker left the men of the Third Corps at the Union camp in Falmouth to serve as decoys while the other corps were moving into their respective positions up and down the Rappahannock to execute the right- and left-flank pincer movement against Lee's troops.

The brilliant, albeit complicated, battle plan met with official Washington's approval. On April 27, the wheels were put in motion to execute Hooker's grand spring campaign. Years later in his memoirs, Confederate artillery prodigy Porter Alexander called Hooker's plan, "Decidedly the best strategy conceived in any of the campaigns ever set foot against us." Alexander also praised the execution of the plan as, "Excellently managed," adding, "up to the morning of May 1st."

My position at Chancellorsville was a good one for this monotonous country. I felt confident when I reached it that I had eighty chances in a hundred to win.
—General Joseph Hooker

Late in the afternoon of April 30, the Fifth, Eleventh and Twelfth Corps were assembled near the Chancellor family home, a large brick building that— along with some dependency buildings—constituted Chancellorsville. Confederates guarding U. S. Ford had withdrawn to protect Fredericksburg to the south, leaving the Second Corps free to cross the Rappahannock and march to Chancellorsville. Fighting Joe, who traveled with the Fifth Corps, arrived at Chancellorsville where he announced, figuratively rubbing his hands in glee, "The Rebel Army is now the legitimate property of the Army of the Potomac. They may as well pack up their haversacks and make for Richmond."

Robert E. Lee had other ideas, and they did not involve packing up and making for Richmond. He sensed that the Union corps south of Fredericksburg was a ruse and that the main Union thrust would come to his army's left and from behind. In a move that was extraordinarily risky, Lee split his army. He ordered Jackson's infantry and artillery to move on the double west from Fredericksburg along the Orange Turnpike Road to the Chancellorsville area. General Jubal Early was left at Fredericksburg to defend the city with a division of men. By eleven o'clock on the morning of May 1, the Confederates, with Jackson and Lee riding at the head of their troops, moved rapidly west on the Orange Turnpike heading straight toward the waiting Union troops. The two opposing armies were on a collision course. By late morning on May 1, as the armies converged near Zoan Church, the first shots of the battle of Chancellorsville rang out.

The first to make contact was Sykes's division. As the Union division was pushed back on the turnpike by an aggressive Confederate force under Stonewall Jackson, Sykes sent a message to Hooker asking for instructions on how to proceed. Hooker ordered Sykes (and his cohort General Slocum) to pull back and regroup near the Chancellor house. That morning, Hooker went from an offensive to a defensive posture. In this initial confrontation with Lee, Fighting Joe had lost his nerve, and despite his considerable advantage in troop strength, he pulled his troops back to the Chancellor house clearing and dug in. Union troops on the northern River Road route and the southern Orange Plank route faced little opposition and few losses on the morning of May 1; therefore, the corps and division generals were first puzzled by then infuriated over Hooker's orders to withdraw to Chancellorsville. By nightfall, Union units were clustered around the Chancellorsville crossroads with wings stretching left and anchored on the Rappahannock and the right flank positioned along the Orange Turnpike west of Wilderness Church facing south.

While his generals realized that the Army of the Potomac had squandered significant advantage and opportunity on May 1, Hooker seemed almost delusional in his perspective of the situation. Years after the war, General Darius Couch wrote that Hooker told him that evening that Lee was "Just where I want him . . . he must fight me on my own ground." Couch shared the feelings of most of the generals of the Army of the Potomac when he left Hooker's presence that night; he wrote, "It was my belief that my commanding general was a whipped man."

As Hooker fantasized and boasted about a victory, Lee took action. Determining that the Union left and center were well protected and invulnerable, Lee acted on intelligence from cavalryman Jeb Stuart that the Union right was "in the air" and vulnerable to a flanking movement. The Eleventh Corps under Oliver O. Howard—who had lost his right arm in the Peninsula campaign—held the right flank that so interested Robert E. Lee. (The units of the Eleventh Corps were made up largely of officers and men of German descent. After their performance at Chancellorsville, they would be known derisively as the "Flying Dutchmen.")

At an evening council of war to explore how to take advantage of the perceived weakness on the Union right, Stonewall Jackson offered up an audacious plan. It involved taking his entire Second Corps—28,000 men—south on narrow, wood-lined Furnace Road, then west and north on Brock Road until the troops came in behind the Union right flank. They would then sweep down the Orange Turnpike heading east and surprise the Federals. Jackson's plan was indeed bold: it divided the Confederate army, leaving only 14,000 men and 24 artillery pieces with Lee. Despite the high risk associated with Jackson's flanking plan—or perhaps because of it—Lee approved the approach like a confident gambler placing a high-stakes bet. By 7:00 a.m. on May 2, Jackson's men were on the move. To help deflect attention from Jackson's marching columns, Lee made several feints toward the Union lines. Hooker never countered these feigning movements, thereby relieving Lee's worst fear—that his thin line, stretching sparsely for three and a half miles, would be quickly overrun by overwhelming numbers of Union troops.

We had heard that Lee was retreating, and supposed that this unfortunate regiment [23rd Georgia] had been sacrificed to give the main body a chance to escape; but while we were commiserating the poor fellows, one of them defiantly said, 'You may think you have done a big thing just now, but wait 'til Jackson gets round your right.

—John L. Collins, *Battles and Leaders*

Hooker, alerted to the Confederate troop movement, saw glimpses of Jackson's men through his field glasses as they passed by the gaps in the woods along Furnace Road. Major General Howard received several "heads up" messages as to the movement of the Confederate troops and the possibility that they might initiate an attack on his Eleventh Corps units on the right flank. Howard took some halfhearted steps to reposition and strengthen his line, but for the most part he remained indifferent to the warnings.

Jackson, meanwhile, pushed his men hard to cover additional ground so that he would have maximum flanking advantage over the Union right. At a little after 5:00 p.m., following a long day's march, Jackson was satisfied that his "foot cavalry" was finally in the most advantageous position possible. He ordered the men to form up and prepare to attack. Oblivious to the Confederate fury about to be unleashed on them, members of the Eleventh Corps were preparing their evening meals, smoking, and talking with comrades when they noticed numbers of deer, rabbits, and squirrels dart out of the thickets behind them. Their initial laughter at the stampeding woodland creatures turned quickly to gasps of horror as the wildlife was followed by long lines of Confederates breaking out of the woods and thickets.

A few Union soldiers managed to get off a volley, and artillerymen were able to fire a round or two from their pieces, but the charging Confederates soon put the Eleventh Corps to flight. It is said that the corps was "Rolled up from west to east like a wet blanket." General Howard, on horseback with a staff flying the stars and stripes tucked under the stump of what was left of his right arm, tried in vain to rally his men. Remarkably, he was not hit in the hail of rounds that raked the Eleventh Corps. Fighting continued into the darkness as the Union army began to re-form and cover the exposed flank left by the Eleventh Corps.

Not willing to lose momentum because of darkness, Stonewall Jackson, accompanied by several aides, went on a reconnaissance to determine the position of the Union army and its potential weak points. As he returned to his own lines, Jackson was fired upon and wounded by members of a North Carolina unit. The friendly fire resulted in wounds severe enough that they required amputation of the general's left arm. After a brief period of apparent recovery, his condition worsened. On Sunday, May 10—eight days after being wounded at Chancellorsville–Lieutenant General Thomas J. ("Stonewall") Jackson died and passed from being a mortal military genius into the pantheon of exalted Southern heroes.

Union losses by the end of the day on May 2 were primarily in the Eleventh Corps. Late that night and into the early hours of May 3, the First Corps arrived at Chancellorsville, more than making up for the losses in the Eleventh.

By first light on May 3, Fighting Joe was sitting in the catbird seat. He had almost ninety thousand men in position, their fortifications well constructed over the past twenty-four hours. Union troops and artillery were in place on the Hazel Grove plateau giving them a wide-ranging field of fire from an elevated position. The Army of the Potomac outnumbered the Confederate forces by 2 ½ times and—to make matters worse for the Confederates—Lee's two wings were split, separated by the Union army.

Inexplicably, at six o'clock on the morning of May 3, Hooker ordered General Sickles to abandon Hazel Grove, believing that Sickles's corps was vulnerable. Sickles protested, but Hooker insisted, and the plateau was abandoned. Confederates in Stuart's wing quickly started to occupy Hazel Grove and began hauling in artillery. Now holding Hazel Grove, Lee wasted no time in getting thirty artillery pieces—commanded by crack artillerist Colonel E. Porter Alexander—on the summit of Hazel Grove. From this prime position on the plateau the Confederates began shelling the Union ranks located near the Chancellor House and the adjacent area. One of many rounds struck a column on the southwest veranda of the Chancellor house where Hooker had established his headquarters. Leaning against the column watching the battle unfold before him, Hooker was knocked to the ground senseless from the impact of the round that split the column from top to bottom. The bombardment continued. Hooker escaped serious injury, but his dazed, disoriented condition led to the accusations later that he was intoxicated, or worse, had lost his nerve. Hooker remained groggy but was unwilling to relinquish command.

In the meantime, Lee pressed his attack with his infantry to the west and southwest of the Chancellorsville crossroads. The artillery bombardment continued from Hazel Grove eventually resulting in the Chancellor house catching fire and burning to the ground. By midmorning, Union troops had withdrawn from the Chancellorsville crossroads and begun their march back to the ford at the Rappahannock, leaving the ground—and the burning Chancellor house—to the Confederates who quickly moved in and took control of the area.

> "I have always stated that he [Hooker] probably abstained from the use of ardent spirits when it would have been for the better for him to have continued in his usual habit in that respect."
> —General Darius Couch, *Battles and Leaders of the Civil War*

On May 5 the Army of the Potomac began its retreat. Dispirited, marching in a driving rain, the troops crossed the pontoon bridges at U. S. Ford to return to the camps they had left eight days before. Recriminations were sure to follow as Federals, from soldiers to official Washington, felt a sense of shame over the passive image that was left in the minds of their countrymen when they read the newspaper reports of the events of May 1 through May 5. Lincoln was devastated: "My God! My God! What will the country say?"

Despite the victory that the Confederates were quick to claim, the ugly truth was that Lee had lost upward of 13,000 men, 22 percent of his troop strength (versus Union losses of 17,000, 15 percent) and one of his most talented generals—Stonewall Jackson.

The Regiment—155th Pennsylvania Infantry

"President Lincoln, on April 7, 1863, visited General Hooker in the camps at Falmouth, where the winter quarters of the Army of the Potomac . . . had been. General Hooker made ample preparations to extend to the President, on the occasion of his visit, a review of all the corps of the Army of the Potomac. It was conceded that the army had reached the maximum of efficiency and morale at this time, and the display on the occasion of this review by the President had never been surpassed by any similar event since the opening of the Civil War."

—*Under the Maltese Cross, Campaigns of the 155th Pennsylvania Regiment*

On April 7, President Lincoln paid a visit to General Hooker and the Army of the Potomac at their camp near Falmouth, Virginia, across the river from Fredericksburg. Sitting patiently on the reviewing stand under clear skies on a warm spring day, the president watched seven infantry corps, cavalry divisions, artillery batteries, and even a pontoon boat train as they passed in review before him. The men, well trained and frequently drilled during the winter months, were on their best behavior as they passed beneath the gaze of their commander in chief. For the president it must have been a confidence-boosting experience: ninety thousand well-trained, well-fed and well-equipped men led by a general who appeared to be eager to take on the enemy—Fighting Joe Hooker. Perhaps now, at last, the Army of the Potomac would deliver a decisive victory and give the Lincoln administration the political capital it needed as it headed into the elections of 1864.

With the weather improving by the day and Virginia roads now assets rather than the liabilities they had been earlier, it was time for Hooker to put his army to the test. On April 26, Hooker issued orders that each soldier must have in his possession eight days' worth of rations. (The norm in the past had been three days' rations.) Rumors were rampant among the men about their intended destination, but no factual information came from the officers. The men assumed the march would take them where the supply wagons could not venture, hence the need to carry the extra rations.

The 155th Regiment was given the assignment of picket duty at the key fords on the Rappahannock. General Meade and his Fifth Corps staff visited the 155th at the two fords to observe the location, size, and nature of the enemy forces guarding the fords. The 155th was soon relieved of its picket duties so that it could join the rest of Humphreys's division as the spring offensive got under way. As the regiment marched past Hartwood Church northwest of Falmouth, General Hooker and staff rode close by the troops. Seeing the general, members of the 155th cheered and called out: "Eight days' rations! Eight days' rations!" Acknowledging the high spirits of his troops, Fighting Joe smiled and lifted his hat in the air in response.

The next two days were spent marching west and parallel to the Rappahannock. On the evening of April 29, Humphreys's division, including the 155th, crossed the Rappahannock at Kelly's Ford and then marched south to the Rapidan River, where the crossing was to be made at Ely's Ford. A pause of over three hours, caused by a backup of wagon trains, delayed the 155th's crossing. As the wagons cleared, the regiment was given orders to wade the Rapidan, and the men willingly complied. Most stripped off their clothes, bundled them and carried them, along with their muskets, on their shoulders as they waded the cold, swiftly flowing, chest-deep waters of the Rapidan. After spending the night bivouacked in a pine woods where the men warmed themselves before large fires, the march of Humphreys's division resumed on the morning of May 1. By midmorning the men of the 155th had marched through thick woods to reach open ground in the vicinity of the Chancellor house and the crossroads known as Chancellorsville.

The 155th began the morning of May 2 as it had ended the previous day— constructing defensive earthworks. Batteries were also put in place and began shelling the Confederates who gathered in nearby woods in plain sight of the regiment. Toward the end of the day, as Humphreys's division finished erecting defensive fortifications, the men received orders to immediately march to the right of the Union line to check the advance of Stonewall Jackson's attack on the hapless Eleventh Corps. It was clear to members of the 155th as they headed to the area near Wilderness Church, based on the cacophony of musket fire, that Jackson's men had broken through the Union line. As they double-quick timed in the direction of the break, the men of the 155th encountered a mix of noncombatants, cattle, cattle guards, ambulances, and other support personnel blocking the road in a panicked retreat from the scene of Jackson's attack. Working their way around the mass of retreating men, vehicles and animals, the 155th and the rest of the Fifth Corps swapped places with the Eleventh Corps, the latter falling back to the earthworks finished hours before by Meade's men. By 7:00 p.m. the assault by Jackson on the right flank had been checked and a new line was drawn up to meet the Confederate threat. The firing of artillery and rifles continued into the dark under a bright moon, periodically punctuated by the sound of whip-poor-wills calling during the occasional periods when the guns fell silent.

In the morning, soon after daylight, the fighting resumed. Humphreys's men took up position near the Chancellor house. From there, elements from Allabach's brigade, including the 155th, were peeled off from the division to support an artillery battery. After an hour of receiving musket and artillery fire, the units were further split: the 155th and the 131st Regiments were detached from the group and marched close to the Chancellor house. It was in this position during the intense shelling that some members of the 155th were witness to General Hooker being knocked down when an artillery round struck the porch of the house. While other generals awaited the outcome of Hooker's condition, Humphreys ordered the men of his division into line of battle and then, with his customary torrent of profanity, told his regiments that he expected them to perform at the highest standard. These same men, who had fought so valiantly with Humphreys at Marye's Heights, resented his implication that they would not do their best in the coming engagement.

The 155th and 131st Regiments were deployed to the edge of a wooded area near the Chancellor house where fifty-four artillery pieces had been drawn into position. The two regiments were ordered to advance in line in front of the artillery as decoys. The 155th and 131st were sent to draw Confederate fire and then, when attacked, to fall prone on the ground to avoid the enemy's guns and open the field of fire for the Union artillery pieces behind them.[1]

As the Confederates began swarming toward the 155th and 131st, General Humphreys ordered the men to rise up and retreat quickly behind the Union artillery. Once the men of the two regiments were clear, the artillery poured volley after volley into the advancing Rebels. Within minutes, the woods were littered with the bodies of dead and wounded Confederate soldiers. As the men of the 155th and 131st cleared the woods, they could see that the Chancellor house had been set on fire by Confederate shelling.

"We were in this impenetrable thicket. All the roads and openings leading through it the enemy immediately fortified strongly, and planted thickly his artillery commanding all the avenues, so that with reduced numbers he could easily hold his lines, shutting me in, and it became utterly impossible to maneuver my forces. My army was not beaten. . . . But I had been fully convinced of the futility of attacking fortified positions, and I was determined not to sacrifice my men needlessly, though it should be at the expense of my reputation as a fighting officer. We had already had enough grievous experience in that line. I made frequent demonstrations to induce the enemy to attack me, but he would not accept my challenge. Accordingly, when the eight days' rations with which my army started out were exhausted, I retired across the river."

—General Joseph Hooker, comments on Chancellorsville, *Battles and Lead ers of the Civil War*

Tuesday, May 5, Hooker ordered his Army of the Potomac to withdraw from Chancellorsville and go back across the Rappahannock River. To the men of the 155th Regiment the actions were haunting reminders of the battle of Fredericksburg: it was the same river; it was raining; the regiment was assigned rearguard duty to shield the retreating army; and the communications that would give them permission to cross the Rappahannock once the withdrawal of the army was complete were ambiguous. And, as with Fredericksburg, the withdrawal was conducted without enemy interference.

By daylight on May 6, all the troops of the Army of the Potomac—including the 155th—had crossed the Rappahannock safely. The battle of Chancellorsville was over, as were the career prospects for Fighting Joe Hooker.

Hooker's timidity at Chancellorsville was quickly attributed to his propensity for strong drink. For their part, the men of Humphreys's division adamantly refuted the charge that Hooker was intoxicated at Chancellorsville. "The allegation was made at that time that General Hooker's incapacity to command his army at Chancellorsville arose from intoxication. The men of Humphreys' division who saw him on that occasion until disabled by the injuries at the White [Chancellor] House are living witnesses to the injustice of this charge against General Hooker."[2]

The Soldier—George P. McClelland

"Then Hooker was taken to fill the bill,
    Hurrah! Hurrah!
Then Hooker was taken to fill the bill,
But he got a black eye at Chancellorsville."
  —Sung to the Tune of "When Johnny Comes
    Marching Home," *Hard Tack & Coffee*

Spring in Virginia was a welcome time after the harsh winter of 1862/1863 and the harsher experience of Fredericksburg. Gentle spring rains fell. Redbud trees, dogwoods, and rhododendrons began to bloom. Daytime temperatures climbed to the mid-fifties, and the men of the 155th packed their overcoats and heavy outer garments away. Like other soldiers in the Army of the Potomac, George McClelland appreciated the changes made by General Hooker. McClelland had received back pay, the camp's sanitary conditions were vastly better, and the food had improved significantly in both quality and quantity. Even the new corps badges were a boost for morale. McClelland wore his blue Maltese cross with pride (Third Division—blue; Maltese cross—Fifth Corps).

Rumors began circulating during the second half of April that the army would be on the march soon. On April 25 a strong wind blew all day drying up the roads around Falmouth and stirring up rumors about an impending campaign. Surely, the men thought, the conditions were ripe for Fighting Joe to lead a spring offensive against the Rebels.

By April 27 the rumors stopped and the marching began. McClelland and his fellow 155th Regiment troops, the Fifth Corps, and most of the Army of the Potomac were on the move. On April 30, McClelland and the 155th Pennsylvania awoke from their encampment on bluffs overlooking the Rappahannock to watch the Army of the Potomac begin to cross the river over a pontoon bridge: infantry, cavalry, and artillery made their way across the river. By sundown that day the final unit to cross the river—Humphreys's division—had made its way over to the south bank of the Rappahannock. Units of Humphreys's division—including the 155th—were delayed along the route while they waited for the jam of Union wagon trains on the road to clear.

On Friday, May 1, Humphreys's division marched to the open ground near the Chancellor house where, over the next seventy-two hours, they would fight a fierce battle that would take its name from the desolate country crossroads known as Chancellorsville.

In His Own Words—The Letters of George McClelland

Near Falmouth, Virginia
May 17, 1863

Dear Lizzie,

Yours dated May 3rd was received a day or two ago. I am stretched on a rude bunk under a shelter tent literally roasting. The atmosphere is melting hot and has been for a week. It is just two weeks today when I was in the midst of carnage and fierce contending strife. Now a feeling of ennui overpowers me and so it is. This life is ever changing. Most emphatically we know not what a day may bring forth.

What shall I speak of? I need not attempt to describe the battle. Enough has been written on that. I might tell you though how near I came falling into the hands of the enemy. On the night of May 5th the whole Army had retreated with the exception of the 5th

Corps which was left to cover the retreat. Sykes's and Griffin's Divisions were in the entrenchments and our Division was immediately in their rear. In case the troops in front were driven out of the rifle pits, we were to make a grand rush forward and had cleared away the underbrush in the woods to that end.

Towards evening, the firing had almost entirely ceased and a heavy rain commenced falling. The ground in about an hour was flooded 3 or four inches deep. We stood until nearly 12 o'clock in line expecting a night attack. Perfectly exhausted, the men were dropping to the ground and sinking in sleep.

Lieutenant Commanding Edward E. Clapp and myself went on a reconnaissance to hunt a dry spot to lie upon. Directly in rear of our line and about 50 feet from it, we found a brush pile on which we threw ourselves and in a jiffy we were asleep. It was long after daylight when I awoke. I lay still a good while, my head still covered, wondering why the men were so quiet. I could not hear the least noise. I raised my head and looked around me—not a living soul in sight. The Regiment had fell [sic] in very quietly during the night and had gone off.

I looked down in and around the rifle pits, but they were deserted. In the meantime, I awakened the Lieutenant who took it all in at a glance. "Libby Prison!" he ejaculated. I buckled on my knapsack and grub bag and off we bolted for our lines—to reach the river, if possible, before the pontoons would be gone. And what was our satisfaction after going about a mile to see our skirmishers waiting for the Rebs. I tell you, I never felt so good. So on we went and joined the Regiment which was about crossing the river and from thence to camp.

I hope that examination is over and you did not pass. Lizzie, I wish you would banish that word "dependant" from your mind. Your ideas are very good for the masculine gender, but have no application to frail femininity.

Your photograph is very natural—plain black and white, but I turned the envelope inside out and there was nary picture. Don't disappoint me again. Lizzie.

The last 9-month Regiment left this morning for home which leaves us alone. I think we will be put in Sykes's Division among the regulars.

Dear Lizzie, goodbye. Don't let the interval be so long before you again write to,
Your Brother, George
My brotherly love to Anna, Tom and Walter.

Notes on the May 17, 1863, Letter

Back at camp in Falmouth, George McClelland now had sufficient time to write to his sister Lizzie and report on the battle of Chancellorsville and its aftermath. His sister may have read the overall battle coverage in the press, but George is oblique about his unit's role in the battle, the details of which

Lizzie may not have learned from reading the newspaper accounts. While the Fifth Corps was held in reserve for part of the battle, Humphreys's division saw action on May 2 when it relieved the infamous "Flying Dutchmen" of the Eleventh Corps. On May 3 the 155th was engaged in intense fighting as a decoy unit before Union artillery in the woods near Chancellor house and later took heavy artillery fire in the open area around the Chancellorsville crossroads.

Rather than give his sister the details of the battle, McClelland related the story of almost being left behind after the Union withdrawal. Proof of the poor communications to the 155th Regiment—as part of the Fifth Corps rearguard for the Army of the Potomac—Sergeant McClelland and Lieutenant Clapp found themselves abandoned by their regiment. Clapp's first reaction upon discovering that they were in danger of being behind enemy lines is that they would become prisoners and be sent to the notorious Libby Prison in Richmond. (A Union soldier had a better chance of survival on the battlefield than in Libby Prison.) Fortunately for both men, they were able to join their regiment before the pontoons were pulled up from the Rappahannock at U. S. Ford.

McClelland, with a note of sadness, and perhaps envy, mentioned the departure of the 134th Regiment Pennsylvania Volunteers. (The 123rd Regiment had already departed.) Both regiments' nine-month enlistment terms expired on May 9. There were persistent rumors circulating that the 155th was to have had a nine-month enlistment term but through a War Department error had been given a three-year term. Yet wishful thinking did not turn rumors into reality. Instead, a dispirited 155th escorted the nine-month regiments to Stoneman's Switch rail station and bid their comrades goodbye as the nine-month boys boarded trains for the trip back to Pittsburgh and civilian life.

McClelland's intuition about the 155th being assigned to Sykes's division proved correct. Humphreys's division was disbanded after the nine-month regiments were mustered out. The remaining regiments of Humphreys's division: the 91st and 155th Pennsylvania were assigned to the Third Brigade in Sykes's Second Division of the Fifth Corps.

June 3rd, 1863

My Dear Sister,

I received with pleasure your kind letter and accept with joy the undeserved prayers and sentiments of love offered me. I thank you, my dear sister, for the good, big letter. Always write so. I thank you also for that sweet face which you inadvertently left out in your former letter. Your advice I shall endeavor to heed.

We have got settled down in our new camp just opposite the Regulars in Sykes's Division. It's a real nice place, but has got awful dusty. We have streets laid out regularly, sidewalks and all, and covered with gravel. Evergreens planted thickly.

The discipline is very rigid. Drill 5 hours every day except Sunday in the hot sun. And it's very hot. We have had no rain for nearly a month, but very high winds that can only be likened to a "simoom" in the desert of the Sahara. If you close up the tent, you would smother with the heat. And if you leave it open, you are choked with the dust. Still the beautiful moonlight nights, when the wind lulls, atone in great measure for the miseries of the day. When we sit on our camp stools listening to a splendid brass band playing or engaged in conversation—and so it is the world over. Pains and pleasures and joys are the bittersweets that co-mingle in everyone's career.

We are fortifying along the river. Griffin's Division of our Corps has moved up to Kelley's Ford. The Rebels guard every ford along the river with the greatest vigilance. One Regiment of our Division guards the railroad near Stoneman's Switch. It's probable we will relieve them.

Last Sunday Frank and Marion Martyn (Frank is a sergeant and Marion is a corporal) and I went down to our Corps Hospital about 2 miles from camp to see our boys there. I saw for the first time, since the battle, my friend 2nd Sergeant Samuel Walker. Poor fellow with his leg amputated above the knee. He bears up nobly, lively and cheerful. We have seven or eight others convalescing.

G. P. F., our Chronicle correspondent, is George P. Fulton, Quartermaster Clerk—from somewhere up the Monongahela. [He is] by profession a school teacher. A good scholar and well versed in literature and lore. Among his personal acquaintances are judges and legislators, although he is but a young man—not more than 25—a married man too. He and Glass—Willie B.—tent together. He is a good friend of mine and I derive pleasure as well as instruction in his company.

John Ralston is as lively as ever and is a general favorite in the Regiment. Mackin— otherwise known as the "gay little color corporal"—is, well, I may as well speak the truth, the same Janus faced, suspicious youth. The less said about him the better.

So you think General Joseph Hooker a humbug. Truly I am sorry to hear it. I tell you that Joe Hooker is the best General in the army by all odds. I only wish the secret history of the last movement were known! But perhaps it is better as it is.

It is impossible under the present regimen to get a furlough. However much I would like to go home and mingle once more amongst friends, it can't be. Furloughs are granted only on urgent grounds and then but for five days. All the other Corps in this Army are getting 10—15 days. I could get a leave of absence for five days, which would leave me about 24 hours in Pittsburgh. No, I'll wait for a better chance.

I sent a few lines home this morning with Captain Kilgore, a friend of mine and an acquaintance of Father's. He will stop and see the folks.

This is the most civilized camp we have ever yet been in. Mammoth Sutler tents all around us with everything or anything you want. They are driving a good business for the Paymaster has paid the troops off up to the 1st of May.

You have never yet heard from Arch. I would like to know his whereabouts.

There are now 135,000 deserters from the Army of the Union. Short shrift with them in our Division. A lieutenant and two privates are to be shot day after tomorrow for desertion—in the 11th Regular Infantry.

Lizzie, I am going to stop. Be a good girl. Let examinations, school directions and all their paraphernalia go to the dogs. Take warning from Fannie Kyle and Belle Faulkner.

I have two more letters to write today; one to H. S. M., and to Annie. So for this time, au revoir.

Your Brother,
George
To Miss Lizzie McClelland
Davenport, Iowa

Notes on the June 3, 1863, Letter

His sister's photograph, mistakenly omitted previously is in the most recent letter to George. Lizzie was a faithful correspondent and, obviously, a forgiving sister who could overlook her youngest brother's Victorian attitude toward the role of women.

Located at Camp Sykes near U. S. Ford on the Rappahannock, the regiment had settled down to a routine of extensive drill. While the camp time was passed pleasantly, drilling during the day and listening to their regimental band in the evening, there was a palpable tension. Because of their proximity to the Rappahannock, Confederates were posted on all the key fords along the river across from them. The fords, as well as Stoneman's Switch on the Richmond, Fredericksburg and Potomac Railroad, were under constant Union guard in the event of a Rebel attack, which was thought to be imminent.

Yet another reminder of the somber consequences of their duty was evident in George's visit to the Fifth Corps Hospital. He accompanied the Martyn brothers to visit Sam Walker. Wounded during the action at Chancellorsville, Sergeant Walker lost his leg and was transferred to the Veteran Reserve Corps the next year. (Marion Martyn survived the war and was mustered out with the regiment in June 1865. His brother, Frank, was not so fortunate. Frank Martyn, later promoted to sergeant, was killed at Laurel Hill, Virginia, a year after visiting Sam Walker at the corps hospital.)

George Fulton, McClelland's scholarly friend, was a former principal at Brownville Academy, a school located in the Monongahela River town from which it takes its name. Fulton served a dual role as a commissary sergeant and correspondent for the Pittsburgh *Chronicle*.

Two other F Company members in McClelland's "Luny" contingent from Pittsburgh rated comments. John Ralston, a bright, popular soldier who had been promoted to quartermaster sergeant on the regimental staff, got a "thumbs up" from McClelland. John Mackin, on the other hand, got a "thumbs down" for his apparent duplicity. (Mackin was the son of "Uncle John" Mackin, the father who had lobbied extensively in Washington to accompany his son at the battle of Fredericksburg.)

Quick to defend General Hooker, McClelland was not disillusioned as a result of Fighting Joe's performance at Chancellorsville.

Captain Samuel Kilgore of Company D, a McClelland family friend, served with distinction with the 155th. He was wounded at Peebles' Farm near Petersburg, Virginia, in September 1864 and was subsequently discharged in March 1865.

McClelland's guess of 135,000 deserters in the Union army underestimated the seriousness of the problem. By mid-1863, some sources put the number of deserters at 200,000.[3] At this stage in the war, desertion was occurring with increased frequency, and senior officers saw the need to stem the rate by imposing severe consequences on those who were caught deserting. However, McClelland's assertion that a lieutenant—as well as two privates—was to be executed is incorrect. No officer in the 11th Regular Infantry was executed for desertion during the war.

Chapter Seven

Gettysburg and the Pursuit of Lee

June—July 1863

The Army of the Potomac

The battles of Fredericksburg and Chancellorsville raised the confidence of the Confederate Army of Northern Virginia to such a height as to cause its subordinate officers and soldiers to believe that, as opposed to the Army of the Potomac, they were equal to any demand that could be made upon them. Their belief in the superiority of the Southerner to the Northerner as a fighter was no longer, as at the beginning of the war, a more provincial concept, for it was now supported by signal successes in the field. On each of these two occasions the Army of the Potomac had been recently reorganized under a new general, presumably abler than his predecessor and possessing the confidence of the War Department, and the results were crowning victories for the Confederates.

—Brevet Major General Henry J. Hunt, Chief of Artillery, Army of the Potomac

Robert E. Lee gained considerable credibility and stature after Fredericksburg, and this admiration was burnished by his performance at Chancellorsville. Despite Lee's significant loss of men (including the redoubtable Jackson), he was credited with a victory at Chancellorsville by Confederate Secretary of War James Seddon and President Jefferson Davis. Lee tapped this reservoir of credibility when in May 1863 he scotched the idea of sending two divisions under James Longstreet to either Middle Tennessee or Mississippi.

Grant's relentless Vicksburg campaign—not to mention Davis's loyalty to his home state—made a compelling case for sending Longstreet and his divisions to Mississippi to help Generals Johnston and Pemberton whip U. S. Grant, but Lee was not in favor of redeploying key troops needed in Virginia (*his* home state). Reluctantly, Davis and Seddon agreed with Lee. Rather than let a negative opinion linger, Lee came back to Davis with a positive, aggressive proposal: invade Pennsylvania and chalk up another victory in the Confederate column, this time in the Yankees' backyard.

Whatever misgivings Davis and Seddon had about not sending Longstreet's divisions to Middle Tennessee or Mississippi were quickly swept away by Lee's audacious plan. Even Longstreet, who had proposed the redeployment of his divisions to support Johnston and Pemberton, was impressed by the boldness of Lee's plan and how it put the Confederates on the offensive. Lee cited the strategic and tactical benefits of his plan. From a strategic point of view, the invasion could help reignite European interest in recognizing and supporting the Confederacy as well as fuel the ambitions of the northern Peace Party advocates (the "Copperheads") in their attempts to gain political control and end the war. Tactically speaking, an invasion through the Cumberland Valley and Pennsylvania's rich farmlands would provide a necessary and continuing source of supplies for the Army of Northern Virginia, thereby eliminating the logistical problems of transporting large amounts of rations for the men and forage for the animals. An army that lived off the larders of surrounding farmers was an army that was more agile than one bogged down in commissary transportation.

Lee's Union counterpart, Fighting Joe Hooker, enjoyed little confidence from his civilian superiors in Washington. After the battle of Chancellorsville, he met President Lincoln face-to-face, and Lincoln simply handed him a letter in which he expressed tepid confidence in his field general: "If possible, I would be very glad of another movement early enough to give us some benefit from the fact of the enemies communication being broken, but neither for this reason or any other, do I wish anything done in desperation or rashness."

In private conversations with his advisors in Washington, Lincoln fretted that Hooker would again be "out-generaled" by General Lee. Hooker's relationship with general in chief Henry W. Halleck was just short of rancorous. Like his predecessor McClellan, Hooker complained of having too few men to face Lee. In Hooker's defense, this complaint was not entirely without merit.

The Army of the Potomac had been losing large numbers of men as nine-month and two-year enlistments expired. Hooker looked to Halleck to strengthen the Army of the Potomac by reassigning troops from other commands. Specifically, Hooker looked to the garrison at Harper's Ferry under

General William French as a source of additional troop strength. Much like McClellan in 1862, Hooker thought keeping men at Harper's Ferry was a waste of manpower. They should, in his mind, be redeployed to support the Army of the Potomac. Much as he had reacted to McClellan's earlier request to abandon Harper's Ferry and redeploy the troops stationed there, Halleck bristled at Hooker's request. Fighting Joe also proposed that the Army of the Potomac and the Department of Washington (responsible for protecting the Federal capital) be unified under his command; at the same time, he asked for more discretion in planning and executing the actions of the Army of the Potomac. Halleck turned a deaf ear to Hooker's proposals.

When it appeared that Lee was moving his army north, Hooker sought permission to cross the Rappahannock at Fredericksburg and drive on to a vulnerable Richmond, now left unprotected by Lee's army, and seize the Confederate capital. Lincoln, in a curt, sarcastic response, wired back: "I think Lee's Army, and not Richmond, is your true objective point."

While Lee's forces were making their way north, Hooker was still making the case for a drive toward Richmond. Troop-movement intelligence from his cavalry and pressure from civilian leaders in Washington soon convinced the general that Richmond could wait. Washington needed protection. The Army of Northern Virginia was moving north on a relentless path parallel to the Federal capital shielded by the Blue Ridge and South Mountain ranges to the west of the city.

To his credit, Fighting Joe had pushed his 95,000-man army hard to cover ground between the Fredericksburg, Virginia, area and Frederick, Maryland, by June 25. Thanks to intelligence from local civilian spies near Hagerstown, Maryland, and beyond, Union leaders knew that Lee, with approximately 75,000 troops and 275 pieces of artillery, had passed through Maryland.

On the night of June 28, sensing that the movements of his army were becoming apparent to Federal forces, Lee sent urgent messages to his corps commanders ordering them to concentrate on Cashtown Gap in the vicinity of Gettysburg. Furthermore, Lee had intelligence that the Army of the Potomac was in the Frederick, Maryland, area and that his northern campaign needed to focus on a pivotal road hub in the Pennsylvania farmland—Gettysburg. Ewell's Second Corps, poised to capture the state capital at Harrisburg, was redirected to Gettysburg along with Lee's First and Third Corps.

Frustrated by Washington's reluctance to assign him more troops, Hooker asked that he be relieved of command. A quick reply to Hooker, borne by a courier who came by train and then horseback from Washington, arrived on the night of June 27. General Order 194 relieved Joseph Hooker of command and in his place assigned George Meade who, along with his Fifth Corps, was encamped near Frederick.

Forty-seven-year-old George G. Meade, a Pennsylvanian, a career army officer who had been wounded at Glendale, Virginia, during the Peninsula campaign in June 1862, was now commanding general of the Army of the Potomac. Called "Old Snapping Turtle" by the troops for his quick temper or "Old Corduroy" for his obsession with installing and maintaining pristine corduroy roads when moving his troops, Meade was humbled by the offer of command, knowing that he was the fourth change in the army's leadership in the past year.

Once in command, Meade pushed his men hard, ordering the army to march north from the Frederick area with his seven corps in a fan-shaped movement toward Pennsylvania. The pace was to be fast, and there were to be minimal stops to rest along the way. A Confederate spy engaged by Longstreet had reported on the night of the 28th that the Union army's movement north was parallel to that of the advancing Confederate army with the Catoctin/South Mountain range separating them.

Gettysburg—population 2,400 in the 1860s—was a tempting target for the Confederates. Roads fed in on all sides of the small town like spokes in a wheel hub, plus a spur rail line from the east ran into the town. Gettysburg was also rumored to have well-stocked warehouses—including a supply of much-needed shoes[1]—that attracted Confederate interest.

As June 30, 1863, came to a close, two opposing armies had gathered in the vicinity of a bucolic, south-central Pennsylvania town sixty-plus miles from the Federal capital. One army had 95,000 officers and men led by a career army officer who had been in command less than forty-eight hours. The other army was 75,000 strong, commanded by a seasoned career army officer who had developed a reputation as a bold and creative leader. When the sun rose the next morning, the two armies joined battle on a scale never before conducted on American soil. Many men would leave their blood in the Pennsylvania soil. Some of them would not live to see July 2. All who survived would never forget the three days in July 1863. Even as old men these memories could be rekindled by one word: "Gettysburg."

> I shall throw an overwhelming force on their advance, crush it, follow up the success, drive one corps back on another, and by successive repulses and surprises create a panic and virtually destroy the army. . . .[2]
> —General Robert E. Lee, June 27, 1863

July 1

In the early morning hours of July 1, a division of Confederates under General Henry Heth marched on the Chambersburg Pike heading east toward Gettysburg when they unexpectedly encountered John Buford's cavalry division. A sharp delaying action between the Confederate and Union units pulled in additional troops from both sides as each struggled to take possession of McPherson's Ridge northwest of Gettysburg. John Reynolds's First Corps joined in to support the Union cavalry whose breech-loading carbines let them prolong the fight, despite the Confederates' greater numbers, until reinforcements could arrive. Two fresh Confederate divisions from Ewells's corps also joined the fray. On the Union side, the Eleventh Corps under General Howard (whose Eleventh Corps had buckled under Jackson's flanking movement at Chancellorsville) came on the scene to support the First Corps, initially led by Reynolds. During the early action at McPherson's Ridge, Major General John Reynolds was shot in the head and fell from his horse. Firsthand accounts reported that the general was dead before he hit the ground.

By midday, Heth's Confederates had been reinforced by Major General Robert Rodes's division. During the midafternoon, Rodes's division was beaten back, taking heavy losses, but Major General Jubal Early's division struck the weak flank of the hapless Union Eleventh Corps and sent the "Flying Dutchmen" fleeing south toward Gettysburg. At this same time, Heth's troops, reinforced by Major General William Pender's division, stormed forward and sent the Union First Corps retreating toward the borough where they and the Eleventh Corps took positions on the high ground of east Cemetery Hill south of the town.

Lee, seeing an opportunity to press the attack and score a quick and decisive victory, asked Richard Ewell to attack the Union units "if practicable." Ewell's interpretation of Lee's command was that he had discretion in carrying it out. With the daylight diminishing, his troops weary from intense fighting during the day, and the Union troops holding the advantage of high ground, Ewell chose not to attack. The first day of battle at Gettysburg closed with the Confederates, after a vicious nine-hour battle, seemingly on the verge of achieving a major victory.

July 2

George Meade arrived in Gettysburg just before midnight on July 1 from his headquarters in Taneytown, Maryland, thirteen miles to the south. After making a moonlight inspection of the Union lines, he lost no time positioning his infantry corps to make maximum use of the high ground to the south of the town. Subsequently referred to as the "fish hook," Meade's troops were positioned on a three-mile-long front. At the northernmost section, the "barb of the hook," located at Culp's Hill, was the Twelfth Corps. At the "curve of the hook," to the north and west of Cemetery Hill, was the Eleventh Corps. The "shank of the hook," by midmorning, ran approximately two miles south down Cemetery Ridge where the First, Second, and Third Corps were positioned. At the southern end of the shank was the "eye of the hook," a hill (the west slope of which had been clear-cut in the autumn of 1862) known as Little Round Top. Just south of it was a forested hill, higher than its companion, known as Big Round Top. Neither of the Round Tops was, at this point, manned by either army. Meade's remaining corps, the Fifth and Sixth, were rushing to the front.

In the predawn hours of July 2, Lee had to make a crucial decision as to his next step. Aligned along Seminary Ridge and Benner's Hill, Lee's forces were essentially parallel to and a mile from his enemy's forces. It seemed clear to Lee that the Union was digging in with the expectation that the Confederates would take the offensive once they had amassed their troops and decided on a battle plan. Longstreet suggested a plan that was counter to conventional wisdom and might catch the Union off guard. He recommended that the Confederate corps move quickly southeast of Gettysburg and put themselves between the Union army and Washington. By doing this, Longstreet reasoned, they would panic the Federal capital and force General Meade to attack Lee in a position that the Confederates had chosen.

Lee viewed the recommendation as bold and creative but also highly risky, given that without the eyes and ears that J. E. B. Stuart's cavalry provided, the Confederates would have a difficult time determining Union countermovements. They would not have the benefit of advance intelligence as they moved through unfamiliar territory. (Stuart and his troopers were separated from the Army of Northern Virginia, engaged in capturing Union supplies and wagons in Maryland.)

Instead, Lee elected to initiate a pincers move against the Union line. He ordered Longstreet's First Corps troops to launch an echelon attack against Meade's left flank. John Bell Hood's division would spearhead the assault passing over the Round Tops, giving the Confederates the advantage of high ground on the Union left. Lafayette McLaws's division would attack the Union line to the left of Hood through a wheat field and peach orchard. The divisions would then turn north to roll up the Union line with support from A. P. Hill's corps from the west and Richard Ewell's corps from the northeast. The expected outcome: the Union defenses would be crushed in a well-orchestrated pincer movement. The stage was set for the action to begin on day two.

Lee recognized that to take the offensive with the Union line, he had to strike quickly. The longer he waited, the more Union reinforcements arrived and the more difficult his task became. Without specific intelligence from

Stuart's cavalry, he assumed that additional Union Corps were on their way to Gettysburg.

Despite Lee's desire that his offensive be initiated swiftly, it was late afternoon before Longstreet's corps was positioned. Longstreet quickly sized up the situation and recognized the weakness of the Union line where Major General Sickles's Third Corps was situated. After violent and bloody fighting near a grouping of large boulders known as Devil's Den, Longstreet succeeded in pushing Sickles's men back and was prepared to break open the Union line.

Little Round Top, located just to the east of the fighting at the wheat field, peach orchard, and Devil's Den, was the location that Meade had instructed Sickles to occupy and defend—instructions ignored by Sickles. Seeing that the two Round Tops were key to controlling the Confederate assault and that they were not occupied by Union troops, Longstreet ordered John Bell Hood's division to swing to the Confederate right and seize the two hills that appeared ripe for the taking.

Meanwhile, Brigadier General Gouverneur Warren, Meade's chief engineer, had ridden to the Union signal station at the top of Little Round Top to observe the battle taking place below to the west in the wheat field, peach orchard, and Devil's Den. Scanning Big Round Top next to him, he spotted the glint of gun barrels and bayonets carried by Hood's men, who were climbing the wooded hillside. Realizing that the Confederates were about to flank the Union left and gain the high ground of the two Round Tops, Warren moved quickly to order a Fifth Corps brigade under Colonel Strong Vincent—just arriving in the vicinity—to occupy and defend Little Round Top. Seeing that Vincent's brigade of four regiments was insufficient to defend the summit, Warren persuaded Fifth Corps commander Major General George Sykes to release the Third Brigade in his unit—led by Brigadier General Stephen Weed—to rush to the summit of Little Round Top. First came Colonel Patrick O'Rorke's 140th New York Regiment followed closely by the 91st Pennsylvania, 146th New York, and the 155th Pennsylvania Regiments. An artillery battery was dragged up Little Round Top with the help of the infantry regiments so that it could be used to help defend the summit.

The fighting raged until dark with Confederate troops making assault after assault on the eight Union regiments defending the military crest of Little Round Top. Subsequently, the defenders were reinforced by troops of Samuel W. Crawford's Fifth Corps division and men of Sedgwick's Sixth Corps. The Union defense held. From the heroic efforts of the 20th Maine on the Union left keeping Alabama troops of Hood's division in check to the stalwart 155th Pennsylvania on the right who were unwavering in holding their ground, the

Union forces hurled back the Confederate flanking movement. But the triumph came at a steep price. In addition to many soldiers, the Union had lost three of her promising young officers: Colonels Strong Vincent and Patrick O'Rorke and Brigadier General Stephen Weed. (As General Weed was carried from the summit of Little Round Top to the rear, an aide spoke with him. "General, I hope that you are not badly hurt." A barely conscious Weed replied, "I'm as dead a man as Julius Caesar.") Additionally, the officer in charge of the Union artillery battery on Little Round Top, Lieutenant Charles Hazlett, was killed.

Some five hours after Longstreet began his assault on the Union left, General Ewell began an attack on the Union right at Culp's Hill. The Confederates launched another assault against East Cemetery Hill in the evening. Union troops repulsed both attempts.

At the end of July 2, Robert E. Lee again assessed his situation. No Chancellorsville-like victory was in the offing. His men had been battered by Union defenders under the generalship of a capable commander—George Meade. Confederate casualties, in terms of numbers of men and key leadership, were substantial. Thousands fell near the peach orchard, at the Devil's Den, in Rose's wheatfield, and on the slopes of Little Round Top. The only positive news was that the absent cavalryman, J. E. B. Stuart, had returned from his forays into the Maryland countryside and was, once again, available to perform intelligence-gathering tasks for Lee.

After the fighting at Cemetery Ridge had concluded on the evening of July 2, Meade held a council of war with his corps commanders. They discussed the day's battle and the state of their men along with their perceptions regarding logistic needs, strategies, and next steps. When queried by Meade, they unanimously recommended continuing the fight the next day.

July 3

In the early morning hours of July 3, Lee ordered Ewell to launch an attack on the Union right at Culp's Hill. Since the last Confederate attack on Culp's Hill on July 2, the Union Twelfth Corps had strengthened its position by adding batteries of artillery, fortifications, and more troops—reinforcements from the First and Sixth Corps. Under a long and heavy barrage of artillery fire and a fusillade from infantry muskets, the Confederates turned back as they realized the futility of continued assaults.

Seeing that the Union army was strong on both right and left flanks and quite capable of quashing any Chancellorsville-like flanking movement by his troops, Lee concluded that the Union middle, located on Cemetery Ridge, was the weak point, that its strength had been drawn away, shifted to protect the flanks of the line. Lee's plan was to begin bombarding the Union center at the point where he planned to focus his attack. Under the able direction of Colonel E. Porter Alexander, the Confederate cannonade began about 1:00 p.m. The Confederates planned to continue the bombardment pounding the Union center and then storm the weakened area with 12,000 men who would leave the wooded cover of Seminary Ridge, move across open fields and the Emmitsburg Road, and charge up Cemetery Ridge. A small copse of trees on the ridge would be their guide as they proceeded over 1,400 yards of uneven ground toward the waiting Union line. As they marched forward, the mile-long front of Confederates from Major General George Pickett's, Brigadier General J. Johnston Pettigrew's, and Major General Isaac Trimble's units would become compacted because of the terrain and the need to concentrate its attack on the Union center.

The Confederate batteries fired for more than an hour, some rounds finding their marks among Union artillery and the ranks; however, many rounds, even under the direction of the gifted artillerist Porter Alexander, went over the Union line and landed hundreds of yards behind the intended targets. Union artillery commanders wisely held their fire knowing that a heavy artillery bombardment usually preceded a Confederate infantry assault. When the Rebel guns fell silent, the Confederate infantry began to cross the open ground working their way over the uneven terrain and through the thick smoke resulting from the Confederate bombardment. The undulating ground leading to Cemetery Ridge from the west helped conceal the Confederate troops at the beginning of their advance, but as they drew closer to the Union line, the ground rose, leaving them exposed and vulnerable to raking fire from the Union guns that were positioned on Cemetery Ridge and Little Round Top.

Union fire was heavy and lethally accurate. Some of Hancock's Second Corps infantry, firing from behind a stone wall from the elevation atop Cemetery Ridge, remembered another battle and shouted out with revenge in their hearts and vindication in their voices: "Fredericksburg! Fredericksburg!"

By 4:00 p.m. the desperate attempt to break the Union line was over. Some two-thirds of the Confederates who had participated in the assault were casualties. From that day forward, the failed Confederate attack at Cemetery Ridge would be known as "Pickett's Charge." General Longstreet, reflecting on the Confederate action that afternoon of July 3, 1863, later said, "That day at Gettysburg was one of the saddest of my life."[3]

Other than a short-lived cavalry engagement that was fought east of Gettysburg between four brigades of Stuart's cavalry and Union horsemen, the battle of Gettysburg was over. The cavalry actions proved inconsequential in the outcome of the battle. Over the course of three days of fighting, casualties totaled 51,000 for the two armies.[4] The Union casualties represented 25 percent of Meade's army—the army considered to have been victorious at Gettysburg. Historians point out that Napoleon, *defeated* at Waterloo, lost 18 percent of his men.[5]

> "General [Lee], this has been a hard day on you." He looked up, and replied mournfully: "Yes, it has been a sad, sad day to us," and immediately relapsed into his thoughtful mood and attitude. . . . He invited me into his tent and as soon as we were seated he remarked: "We must now return to Virginia. As many of our poor wounded as possible must be taken home."
> —Brigadier General John Imboden, CSA, July 3, 1863, *Battles and Leaders of the Civil War*

Late in the evening of July 3, Lee visited his units to determine their condition for a renewal of the battle on the following day. From this assessment, Lee could see that his command was severely depleted by casualties and that the remaining men were weary and simply not capable of resuming the battle. Instead of laying plans for an attack, Lee dispatched a wagon train of the wounded and braced for an attack by Meade's forces. As the wagon train filled with the wounded assembled to depart for Virginia, a torrential rain began falling. The seventeen-mile-long "Wagon Train of Misery"—as it became known—headed toward the Potomac River crossing at Williamsport, Maryland. The heavy rains continued. Once Lee knew that the "Wagon Train of Misery" was under way, he began the orderly retreat of his army, using the cover of pouring rain and darkness to mask his movements. The main body of Lee's men retreated to Hagerstown, Maryland via Ringgold Pass over South Mountain. Meade's cavalry played cat and mouse with Lee's wagon train and with the main body of Confederate troops as Lee's forces made their way to Williamsport and Falling Waters on the Potomac to cross over into West Virginia. The river crossing was delayed for days because of the surging waters of the Potomac, raised to flood levels by the heavy rains.

Meanwhile, Meade's infantry headed south toward Frederick, Maryland, to resupply with provisions before heading west across South Mountain to intercept Lee at the Potomac River crossings. On July 11 and 12, the Army of the Potomac reached the area of Williamsport and Falling Waters, Maryland, via its circuitous route going south from Gettysburg then west across the mountains to the Potomac. Hard rains continued, preventing Lee's troops from crossing the swollen Potomac and restricting Meade's actions to reconnaissance forays toward the well-entrenched Confederates.

When Meade polled his corps commanders on July 12, as he had done at Gettysburg, the majority "strenuously opposed a fight." Meade deferred to his generals much to the displeasure of President Lincoln, who had General in Chief Halleck telegraph: "Act upon your own judgment and make your generals execute your orders. Call no council of war. It is proverbial that councils of wars never fight." Halleck's telegram was sent the evening of July 13. It was too late to motivate Meade. On the same evening, amid rain and fog, after waiting ten days for the river to subside, Lee began withdrawing his troops across the Potomac to West Virginia, leaving only the rear guard on the Maryland side as Union forces approached the river crossing at Williamsport and Falling Waters on the eve of July 14.

> Fifth day: At daybreak we give the word to advance along our whole line. We "move upon the enemy's works." Works are ours. Enemy, sitting on the other side of the river, performing various gyrations with his fingers, thumb on his nose. . . .
> —Captain Samuel W. Fiske, 14th Connecticut Regiment

As Lee's troops thumbed their noses at their hapless pursuers across the Potomac, President Lincoln was seething in Washington. In a communication to Meade after learning of the Confederate army's successful (and unchallenged) escape across the Potomac, Halleck, at Lincoln's direction, fired off a telegram: "I need hardly say to you that the escape of Lee's army without another battle has created great dissatisfaction in the mind of the President, and it will require an active and energetic pursuit on your part to remove the impression that it has not been sufficiently active heretofore." The president, when discussing the situation with his staff and cabinet, summed up the situation metaphorically: "Our Army held the war in the hollow of their hand and they would not close it."

Following Gettysburg, Lee submitted his resignation to his commander in chief. His offer was refused. After the escape of Lee at Williamsport and Falling Waters, Lincoln wrote a letter to Meade expressing his dissatisfaction, while also acknowledging the success of the Army of the Potomac on the battlefield at Gettysburg. Admonishing Meade, the president wrote: "My dear general, I do not believe you appreciate the magnitude of the misfortune involved in Lee's escape. He was within your easy grasp, and to have closed upon him would, in connection with our other late successes, have ended the war. . . . Your golden opportunity is gone, and I am distressed immeasurably because of it." The president then folded the letter without signing it, inserted it in an envelope, and placed it in his desk drawer. It would remain unopened and unread in Lincoln's and Meade's lifetimes.[6]

The Regiment—155th Pennsylvania Infantry

Wednesday, July 1, 1863, General Sykes's Division of the Fifth Corps, with the One Hundred and Fifty-fifth, was up early and started on the march soon after daylight, and at the end of an hour's travel the state line between Pennsylvania and Maryland was reached. Striking Pennsylvania soil awakened a different spirit, probably more natural than on any previous campaigns, as the troops, and particularly Pennsylvania regiments, deemed the Confederate invasion an aggravation of their offense in fighting the flag of the Union. As a consequence, despite the great fatigue from forced marches, loss of sleep and other privation, speaking for the 155th men, it can be truly said that on reaching the Keystone State their determination to fight to the bitter end was most marked, and no signs of doubt of the results were visible anywhere in the ranks.

—*Under the Maltese Cross: Campaigns of the 155th Pennsylvania Regiment*

The regiment, newly assigned to the Second Division (Brigadier General Romeyn Ayres, commanding) of the Fifth Corps, spent the early days of June encamped along the Rappahannock near U. S. Ford. There members of the regiment communicated with their Confederate counterparts, exchanging newspapers and tobacco and floating paper boats across the waters to each other. Future combat seemed to be far from the minds of troops on both sides of the Rappahannock.

While the regiment was at U. S. Ford, its first commander, Colonel E. Jay Allen, returned from sick leave. Granted leave prior to the battle of Chancellorsville, Colonel Allen spent six weeks confined to bed at his home in Pittsburgh to recover from rheumatism. Disregarding the orders of his physician, Allen returned to his unit with the hope that he could resume his old command, but regimental surgeons quickly determined that the colonel was in no condition to do so, and Lieutenant Colonel John Cain retained command.

Orders came for the Army of the Potomac to break camp and begin marching on the evening of June 13. After a forced march in the rain, the regiment—along with the rest of the army—encamped in a clearing near Hartwood Church. The rain that had inaugurated their march stopped, and the rising temperature, coupled with the punishing pace the regiment maintained, brought on numerous cases of sunstroke and heat exhaustion. Continuing its northeasterly direction toward Washington, the regiment marched by Bristoe Station and the graves of Union soldiers killed there during the Second Manassas campaign. Near Manassas Junction, the 155th joined the rest of the Fifth Corps in camp in the area of First Manassas.

The march resumed at daylight, again at a grueling pace. At this point, the troops turned northwest, away from Washington, through the village of Centerville. That night the regiment camped near Goose Creek several miles from Aldie in Loudoun County, a hotbed of Confederate guerrilla activity. The regiment remained there a week to support the cavalry guarding the Army of the Potomac's wagon trains, which were loaded with supplies and provisions. The cavalry engaged in several clashes in the vicinity of Aldie, Middleburg, and Upperville, but none required involvement of the infantry. The hiatus at Goose Creek gave the 155th time to recover from the rigors of their forced march and to nurse sore feet.

At three o'clock on the morning of June 26, the soldiers of the 155th were ordered to resume marching, ending their pleasant stay at the Goose Creek encampment. After a brief pause in the Virginia town of Leesburg, the regiment crossed the Potomac River at nearby Edwards Ferry on pontoons. Once across the Potomac, they marched to Poolesville, Maryland, where the exhausted troops encamped. The forced march on the 26th was over thirty miles and called by some in the regiment as "the most severe ever experienced up to that date by the Regiment."[7]

The next morning the regiment marched all day, forded the Monocacy River, halted, and bivouacked a few miles from Frederick. The men of the 155th were impressed with the lushness of the Maryland countryside. According to the regimental history, they saw "beautiful fields of golden grain almost ready for the reaper and well-laden cherry trees, ripe and ready for the consumer."

While on the outskirts of Frederick, the 155th came across a macabre scene that was a harbinger of what they would experience before the week was over. Hanging from a tree was the body of a man the troops recognized as a peddler and frequent camp follower suspected by Union cavalry of spying for the Confederacy. They had seized him and in a search of him and his belongings found incriminating papers. Their suspicions confirmed, they delivered swift and brutal justice to "Spy Richardson." The men of the 155th were certain of his identity based on his distinctive facial features and his ever-present linen duster. The men recalled his ready response to their "good morning" or inquiries about his health: "Everything is lovely and the goose hangs high."[8]

In camp near Frederick, the regiment learned that Fighting Joe Hooker had been replaced as the commander of the Army of the Potomac by George Meade, then their Fifth Corps commanding general. Meade's elevation began a domino effect in the Fifth Corps that meant a change for the 155th. Meade was replaced as Fifth Corps commander by George Sykes; Romeyn Ayres took command of the Second Division, Sykes's former command; and Stephen Weed assumed command of the Third Brigade where the 155th served along with the 140th New York, the 91st Pennsylvania, and the 146th New York Regiments.

General Meade lost little time in taking charge of his new command by ordering the army to begin immediately marching north to Pennsylvania. The

155th, along with the rest of the Fifth Corps, on June 29, marched through Frederick and over Maryland roads at an exhausting pace before stopping at the small crossroad of Liberty. Early the next morning, the corps marched north and east toward the Pennsylvania border. The surrounding Maryland countryside offered a pleasant backdrop to an otherwise grim march as the troops passed through large fields of grain and corn and cherry orchards filled with ripe fruit.

Before leaving Maryland, the 155th marched through the village of Frizzellburg, where the "footsore and weary" troops had their spirits lifted by a moving display of pro-Union sentiment. On the steps of the local school building near the roadside, scores of children holding small American flags sang the "Star-Spangled Banner" and other patriotic songs as the troops marched by.[9]

By midnight on Tuesday, June 30, the 155th had halted near the Maryland-Pennsylvania border having marched nearly thirty miles that day. Early the next morning, the Fifth Corps was on the march once again, crossing into Pennsylvania early in the morning. By noon, the Fifth Corps had reached Hanover in York County, Pennsylvania. There the 155th saw grim evidence of a cavalry engagement. Dead horses littered the streets, and buildings bore the scars of artillery and carbine fire. As the troops marched west from Hanover, closer to Gettysburg, they could hear the thunder of artillery fire in the distance. After sunset, the corps stopped to prepare dinner and give the travel-weary troops an opportunity to rest. The men were interrupted when a courier from General Hancock came galloping into camp and dismounted at General Sykes's headquarters. The troops soon learned that the courier was bearing dispatches telling of the day's action, how Union troops had been pushed south through the town, and that the popular commander of the First Corps, Major General John Reynolds, had been killed during the battle.

In less than half an hour, the units of the Fifth Corps had resumed their forced march to Gettysburg to provide support to the imperiled Union forces already in the town. At 1:00 a.m. on July 2, the Fifth Corps halted twelve miles from Gettysburg, the men too exhausted to go farther. To expedite a quick resumption of the march after resting, the troops were given orders to lie down on the road rather than bivouacking in the nearby fields as was the customary procedure. After less than three hours of rest, the Fifth Corps was on the march again. By noon the corps was placed in reserve in the center of the Union line ready to respond when the enemy made his first move.

The enemy is on our soil. The whole country looks anxiously to this army to deliver it from the presence of the foe. Our failure to do so will leave us no such welcome as the swelling of millions of hearts with pride and joy at our success would give to every soldier of the army.

—General George Meade

At the summit of Little Round Top, General Warren had spotted the Confederates making their way up Big Round Top. He feared that they would seize and control both hills, putting the Union forces below in an extremely precarious position. Aided by a member of his staff, Captain W. A. Roebling,[10] Warren acted quickly by pulling two Fifth Corps units out of ranks to defend Little Round Top. First on the scene were the units of Colonel Strong Vincent's brigade (the 16th Michigan, 44th New York, 83rd Pennsylvania, and the 20th Maine), who helped stall Hood's Alabamians and Texans as they stormed up Little Round Top. Close behind Vincent's units were Brigadier General Stephen Weed's brigade (the 140th New York, the 146th New York, 91st Pennsylvania, and the 155th Pennsylvania). An artillery battery under the command of Lieutenant Charles Hazlett was the final Union unit to reach the summit of Little Round Top before dusk. The artillery pieces—four cannons—were hauled up with the help of a squad from the 155th. As the Federals made their way up Little Round Top, they were under constant, heavy fire. With the arrival of Weed's regiments, Little Round Top was now defended in an arc of eight regiments stretching from the 20th Maine on the left of the line to the 155th Pennsylvania on the right.

After a brief lull, Confederate artillery opened up, bombarding Little Round Top. The intense and continuous cannon fire caused the earth to tremble with its power, but for the most part, the rounds passed harmlessly over the top of Little Round Top without causing Union casualties.

The 155th watched as Confederate units formed a line of battle in front of them. They saw the Confederate officers dismount from their horses and, with their swords in hand, lead their men in the assault up the hill. The Union battery on Little Round Top opened fire on the advancing Rebel troops with deadly results. When one Confederate unit was decimated by Union artillery fire, another unit would take it place. After pushing back the Union forces below Little Round Top, the Confederates swarmed across Plum Run—soon to flow red with Union and Confederate blood—and headed toward the eight Union regiments defending Little Round Top.

The 155th was still using the outmoded Harper's Ferry muskets that relied on buck-and-ball ammunition, a firearm and ammunition type effective only at very close range. Because of this limitation, members of the 155th were ordered to hold their fire until the enemy came within twenty yards. Other Union units on Little Round Top were using the longer-range Springfield rifles. Because the 155th was holding fire until the enemy came within effective range, the Confederates assumed that the area of the Union line covered by the 155th was a break in the line and not defended. Confederate units were sent to exploit this area of perceived weakness. When the enemy troops came within firing range, Lieutenant Colonel Cain gave the order: "Aim low. Fire low." The Confederates came within twenty feet of the Union line and were able to pour volley after volley into the 155th, all the while receiving withering musket fire from the old Harper's Ferry muskets. The exchange of fire between the 155th and the Rebels lasted about an hour. After their failure to push back the Union troops on Little Round Top, the Confederates withdrew. Despite the intense fire, casualties among the 155th were surprisingly light. The regimental history offers an explanation:

> ... [I]t was a matter of astonishment to all concerned, in view of the closeness of the range and the number of volleys fired by Confederates, that many more casualties were not reported. Without exaggeration, it can be said with truth that the enemy's bullets flew thick and fast, and it is only owing to their poor marksmanship that their firing was not more destructive. This can be explained only by the fact that the enemy being below the position occupied by Weed's Brigade and firing up hill their bullets fell short of the mark.[11]

Darkness enveloped Little Round Top, and as July 2 came to a close, the defenders at the summit were ordered to use the surrounding rocks to shore up their fortifications in anticipation of another Confederate attack the next day. The warm summer night was absent the boom of artillery and the rattle of muskets that had created such a din hours before. The clamor was replaced by the haunting and heartrending cries and moans of the wounded from both sides who lay in the no-man's-land between the lines of the opposing armies. Even the bone-weary men of the 155th found it difficult to sleep through this chorus of the suffering.

No reveille was sounded the morning of July 3. Instead, officers circulated among the men to rouse them from their sleep. Sounds of artillery fire to the north—near Culp's Hill—and then sporadic artillery fire from both sides at various locations signaled the start of the day. At 1:00 p.m. a Confederate cannonade began pounding the Union line—including rounds fired at Little Round Top—that lasted over an hour. The battery on Little Round Top returned fire during this "artillery duel." Then, as the dense smoke from the artillery fire began to lift, the 155th watched from their vantage point on Little Round Top as a formation of Confederate infantry came out of the woods along Seminary Ridge in the distance. Their position on Little Round Top gave the 155th a unique perspective to watch as Pickett, Pettigrew, and Trimble's men advanced across the open field toward the center of the Union line. At about 4:00 p.m. the 155th heard cheering from the Union line to their right along Cemetery Ridge; and then the word came along the line that the Confederates had been beaten back. Pickett's "great charge" had ended, and Rebel troops could be seen retreating to Seminary Ridge whence they had come earlier in the afternoon.

As July 3 drew to a close, and it was determined that the enemy was not planning any further assaults that day, Colonel Cain sent his men down Little Round Top to recover the Springfield rifles from the Union dead as replacements for the Harper's Ferry buck-and-ball muskets. This battlefield requisition from the dead now gave the 155th arms that were as good as those of their peers in other regiments. The regiment had upgraded its firearms twice—from the clumsy Belgian muskets to Harper's Ferry buck-and-ball muskets and now to the improved Springfield rifles.

Starting the evening of July 3, a heavy, steady rain continued into the morning hours of July 4. Dawn brought with it all the resulting discomforts of a night spent outside in the rain: hardtack was a soggy mess; cooking fires were impossible to start; and clothing was soaked. There were some causes for cheer: the Army of the Potomac could celebrate the Fourth of July knowing that it had acquitted itself honorably—perhaps even victoriously—over the past three days; and with each passing hour, the likelihood of the Confederates resuming hostilities seemed to diminish. Still there remained the grim duty of searching the field for the wounded who survived and transporting them to one of the many field hospitals that had sprung up. And there was the task of burying the dead, many of whom had been lying out for days in the roasting July heat. Identification was an impossible task for even the most compassionate and attentive of the burial detail members.

Sporadic firing continued throughout July 4 between Union and Confederate pickets, but no escalation occurred during the day. At first light on the morning of the 5th, General Warren returned to Little Round Top; there, surrounded by the sleeping members of Weed's brigade, he scanned the Confederate lines with his field glasses. Then to confirm his suspicions, Warren rode to the advanced picket lines of the Union army and made a personal reconnaissance past the Union pickets and out the Emmitsburg Road. As he suspected, Lee's army and wagons had slipped away under the cover of darkness and rain during the night.

The Union cavalry was sent in pursuit of the Rebels; the infantry—including the 155th Pennsylvania—went south from Gettysburg. Meade's plan was to resupply his infantry, which had run low on rations and ammunition, at Frederick and then swing west, cross South Mountain, and intercept Lee's men at their expected Potomac River crossing near Williamsport, Maryland.

But while waiting for the Potomac to subside so a crossing could be made, Lee's men had ample time to entrench and create a formidable defensive position. It was this defensive position that the 155th, along with other regiments of Ayres's division, encountered on July 12. Union skirmishers were sent in to engage the enemy the next day, but no full-scale assault was ordered. That evening Meade conducted his council of war, and the next day, July 14, an assault was ordered. When the Union troops advanced to the Confederate lines they found them deserted. Robert E. Lee and his troops had escaped the "closing hand" of the Army of the Potomac by crossing the river during the night. The Gray Fox, as he had done at Sharpsburg the previous September, had slipped away under a cloak of darkness.

The next day, the Fifth Corps moved down the Potomac to Berlin, Maryland, where they crossed the Potomac on pontoons. Once again, after a twenty-day absence, the Union soldiers were back on "old Virginia soil."

The Soldier—George P. McClelland

The Commanding General, in behalf of the country, thanks the Army of the Potomac for the glorious result of the recent operation. An enemy superior in numbers and flushed with the pride of a successful invasion, attempted to overcome and destroy this Army. Utterly baffled and defeated, he has now withdrawn from the contest. The privations and fatigue the Army has endured, and the heroic courage and gallantry it has displayed will be matters of history to be ever remembered. Our task is not yet accomplished, and the Commanding General looks to the Army for greater efforts to drive from our soil every vestige of the presence of the invader.

—Major General Meade, Headquarters of the Army of the Potomac,
General Order 68, July 4, 1863

George McClelland escaped injury at Gettysburg, but his presence on Little Round Top was not without personal loss. Along with his fellow 155th soldiers, McClelland dropped his knapsack, bedroll, and other nonessential gear near the summit on his way to the regiment's position along the western face of Little Round Top. Musket, bayonet, and ammunition were all he would need to face the Confederates who were swarming up the hill. When McClelland and his comrades went back to retrieve their equipment, they discovered, much to their dismay, that Confederate artillery had obliterated it during a bombardment. Nothing was salvageable.

The intense fighting continued until dark when the firing on both sides began to ebb. When the firing finally stopped and darkness enveloped the summit of Little Round Top, McClelland and others in the 155th used the scattered rocks around them to create breastworks in anticipation of a resumption of attacks by the Confederates. The night passed without a Confederate assault, but McClelland and his brothers-in-arms heard the grim aftermath of the day's battle throughout the night. A soldier in K Company of the 155th described that night in his postwar memoirs: "If the most romantic, or the foremost advocate of war had been there and listened to the moans of the wounded and dying, the whole night long, as we did, were he a human and not a fiend incarnate, he would have longed for the day when the 'sword will be beaten into plowshare.'"[12]

From their vantage point at the summit of Little Round Top, McClelland and the other members of the 155th had a panoramic view of the battlefield between Seminary Ridge and Cemetery Ridge on the afternoon of July 3. They were spectators to one of the most written-about infantry assaults in the annals of nineteenth-century military history—Pickett's Charge.

For George McClelland, the Gettysburg campaign ended as it had begun—with a long, arduous march back through Maryland, over hills and through valleys, across the Potomac and back to Virginia. What he had lost in material possessions during the campaign—articles of clothing, camp gear, and personal accoutrements—he accumulated in remembrances that would last a lifetime: the suffering of exhausting forced marches in stifling heat and drenching rains; being the target of murderous artillery and musket fire; hearing the pitiful cries of the maimed left on the field of battle; and understanding, for the first time, that General Robert E. Lee and his Army of Northern Virginia were not invincible.

In His Own Words—The Letters of George McClelland

"Next came General Meade, a slow old plug
        Hurrah! Hurrah!
Next came General Meade, a slow old plug,
For he let them away at Gettysburg."
    —Sung to the Tune of "When Johnny Comes
        Marching Home," *Hard Tack and Coffee*

Near Snicker's Gap, Virginia
Sunday, July 19th, 1863

Dear Annie,
    I have not heard from you or any of my friends in a long time. Through indirect sources, I have seen that the draft is about completed in Allegheny County.

There is a detail of 3 officers and six men [that will] go on this evening from our Regiment to bring us 400 men to fill us up. Captain Kilgore goes, also Marion Martyn from our Company. I will send this by him. As I informed you, I lost everything at Gettysburg. I borrowed this paper that I am now writing on. Marion will take a small package on his return. There are a great many things I need and would like to have, but for the present I only want articles of the greatest necessity.

This body-distressing infernal marching is done. In the first place, my greatest need is a pocket Bible. Then follows a portfolio to carry paper and envelopes. Something like the one I got before leaving home. A pair of "suspenders" would also come in. My dear girl, I want you to get as much money as you want from Father and make the purchase of the aforesaid articles and (I am) forever obliged, etc. Oh! A needle case or "whatnot"—I almost forgot it.

Well, Annie, here we are in Virginia once more. When we got to Berlin I thought they would leave us lay awhile to recuperate. But no; that wouldn't do. Old Corduroy Meade, after letting them slip through his fingers at Williamsport where we could have demolished the devils easily, now wants to make a show of pursuit. The Army clamors for the reinstatement of the only man who ever knew how to handle the Army of the Potomac. That man is General Joe Hooker.

Our marches from Berlin so far have not been very long or fatiguing. I guess he wants to let "Lee" get a good start and we will follow until we reach the Rappahannock again. A soldier can see a great difference or change since Meade was placed in command. Short rations—one day we marched 28 miles without bread, meat or coffee. Reason? Supply train wasn't up. Another, and a chief cause of dissatisfaction, is in regard to mail matters. We get no mail at all. The last regular mail we got was when near Frederick coming into Pennsylvania. And that, I believe, was under Hooker's reign.

Annie, I understand Ben Ralston is coming on a visit to the Army. I hear that Frank is drafted too. I suppose Pittsburgh has got over its stupendous loaf by this time and business goes on as usual.

That was a terrible state of affairs in New York, was it not? That place wants to be cleaned out.

Now, Annie, write to me often and send me papers. Tell Father to write. I have not heard from Lizzie since about a "century" (counted in marching days.) Goodbye. Don't forget the (things.) My love to all, ever your Brother,

Geo. P. McClelland

Notes on the July 19, 1863, Letter

The punishing pace of marching from U. S. Ford in Virginia in mid-June 1863 gave George McClelland no time to compose letters to his family along the way. Then, at Gettysburg, McClelland was deprived of writing paper and envelopes by the Confederate artillery fire that destroyed his personal effects. For an inveterate letter writer such as McClelland, this loss of his materials for correspondence was a cruel blow. Now, in the third week of July, McClelland had the time and the materials necessary to begin writing letters again.

The Conscription Act, passed by Congress in March 1863, was operational by the summer to begin filling the voids in Union ranks caused by casualties and the departure of nine-month and two-year enlistees. McClelland reported that a detail from the 155th would head to Pittsburgh to bring back draftees from Allegheny County.

Sending his "wish list" of items to replace those lost at Gettysburg, McClelland asked Sergeant Marion Martyn, a friend and fellow "Luny" who has been assigned to the draft detail, to hand-deliver his request to the family. Martyn committed to bringing back a "small package" of items from McClelland's family. Before listing the "articles of greatest necessity" that he wanted, McClelland vented a rare gripe about the marching that has been demanded of the regiment. Generally stoic about army conditions and what was expected of him, McClelland's complaint that the infantry of the Army of the Potomac had undergone extraordinary suffering on the marches during the Gettysburg campaign is an indication of the toll taken on the men. By the time he reached the area near Snicker's Gap, Virginia, where he was writing the letter, McClelland had marched over two hundred miles in about a week's time— from U. S. Ford, Virginia, to Gettysburg, Pennsylvania, and back to Snicker's Gap in the Blue Ridge Mountains.

McClelland's hero, Fighting Joe Hooker, would not be restored to lead the Army of the Potomac, but would be shuttled off to the western front to serve as a corps commander under General George Thomas within Sherman's Federal Army Group. Hooker's strong suit among his men in the Army of the Potomac was his ability to provide good quality and quantity of rations. Meade's failure to provide ample rations and his apparent lack of attention in guaranteeing reliable mail service gave him black marks in Sergeant McClelland's book.

The "stupendous loaf" McClelland attributes to Pittsburgh reflects the lack of replacement troops coming from the city to support regiments such as the 155th. The Conscription Act sought to remedy the depleted numbers of fighting men with a draft. In New York City on July 13, 1863, a mob protesting conscription destroyed the draft office. Political, personal, and racial conflicts sparked the New York riot, which Federal troops eventually quashed. After the New York City incident, conscription activities resumed largely unchallenged in major northern cities.

On the road, about 15 miles from Warrenton, Virginia
July 21st, 1863

My Dear Brother,

I will now endeavor to account for my long silence. We have had an awful time of it since leaving U. S. Ford on the Rappahannock. Our march through Virginia up into Pennsylvania we averaged 25 and 30 miles a day. [We] crossed mountains, waded rivers and creeks, [went] through ravines, swamps and gullies. Fought the Battle of Gettysburg which culminated, as you know, in Lee retreating. We followed and had, near Williamsport, the enemy in our grasp, but "Corduroy Meade" was afraid of a few rifle pits and let him escape without loss. Halleck obtained the removal of the man under whose direction this Army would have accomplished the destruction of the enemy. The fact of the matter is Meade was afraid of Lee.

At Gettysburg we acted solely on the defensive; had a splendid position and held it by superiority of forces, guns, etc. When the enemy found he could make no impression on our lines, he commenced his retreat which he accomplished. And we have got this far in pursuit.

I think we will lie over awhile at Warrenton to recruit for this Army is clean played out. Horses as well as men.

A detail goes to Pittsburgh from our Regiment to bring on the drafted men. We get 400 men. I tried to get on it, but couldn't make the connection.

I have written but 2 letters since the 13th of June: one to Father and one to Annie. In the same time I have got but two. I was gratified a few days ago in receiving your photograph. I will take care not to lose it. I lost all my valuables at Gettysburg.

Things look brighter now for the cause than at any time since the war commenced. Vicksburg, Port Hudson and, I believe, Charleston fallen. Johnston defeated; Bragg discomfited; and the Army of Virginia retreating it for Richmond. Now give us our old commander, Joe Hooker, and we will soon empty Richmond. Oh! If we had had him but for one day at Williamsport.

Well, Henry, I have nothing more at present to write. Drop me a line as often as you can. Weak, sore, weary and worn out, I am still your brother.

George

To Henry S. McClelland, Leavenworth, Kansas

Notes on the July 21, 1863, Letter

McClelland's view that the army was "clean played out" and needed a rest was shared by most of the generals and by official Washington. The addition of four hundred draftees from Pittsburgh was yet another reason to stay in place for a period of time while the new men were being trained.

His optimism about the progress of the war was warranted: Vicksburg had surrendered to General Grant on July 4, and Port Hudson had surrendered five days later. But Charleston harbor, under combined land and sea attack by Union forces, did not fall; the fighting continued and resulted in a stalemate in September of 1863.

Near Warrenton
July 31st, 1863

Dear Sister Lizzie,

Is it possible in the gaieties and joys of this festive season you have lost sight of your "gallus" volunteer brother? Why just think of it, not one letter in a month. Up till yesterday, I have received but one letter from one who used to remember me so often. That letter was dated the 25th of May.

Yesterday I received (it must have been by accident) a letter written on the Fourth of July. Four days were occupied in mailing it and 22 days of rapid marching brought it here. Now, my little dame, if I had had the least chance in the interim, I should have sent you several scolding epistles and rated you soundly. But the "Flying Corps" of the Army was always on the wing until we reached the disloyal, secession border of Pennsylvania where it happened to meet a circumstance in Lee's Army.

What occurred there has been pretty widely disseminated, but all the losses were not reported. You may look in vain the Herald reports for the loss of my knapsack and coffee pot. The former, without joking, was a pretty serious loss to me. All my valuables, including that pretty "trash bag" you gave me, went higher than "Gilroy's Kite." But what's the use of grumbling? I ought to be thankful I did not lose my head on that terrible field of carnage.

I will not picture to you the hardships, the perils and agonies endured during the last 50 days. Let it pass. I don't want to think of it. Suffice it that we have arrived near Warrenton and have had a rest of four days. The heat is intense, perfectly awful.

I have written to Annie, to Henry and to Father. I am especially glad to know that Arch is all right. Much obliged to you for the interesting letter, including your eloquent 4th of July remarks.

We have only stopped here to clothe the men and put everything in ship shape. We move in the morning at 4 AM for Culpepper. I have not great expectations. The Army cries for the reinstatement of General Joe Hooker, to whom—and him only—is due the credit of defeating the designs of "Lee." I only wish that "Meade" had but one-half of his abilities. But the Army has no confidence in "Meade" since that slip at Williamsport.

Well? Let us hope for the best. Our successes in every other part of Rebeldom gives us heart, nerves us on to finish up this intestine strife. And then let "Napoleon" look out for his aggrandizing schemes on American soil.

Lizzie, excuse this rambling scrap. I am, as ever,

Your Brother, George P.
My love to all the household.

Notes on the July 31, 1863, Letter

After chastising his sister Lizzie about her lack of correspondence, McClelland acknowledged that mail had to catch up with the "Flying Corps" that had been constantly on the move. Those in the Union army responsible for making sure supplies reached the Army of the Potomac as it moved quickly to check Lee's northern invasion no doubt put a lower priority on mail than on ammunition and food.

McClelland admitted that losing his personal belongings was an inconvenience but that he was very fortunate he had not been killed or wounded during the struggle on Little Round Top.[13]

He wanted to spare his sister the details of the "perils and agonies" of the battle at Gettysburg, knowing that by this letter he had communicated that he survived unscathed. Any further details would only cause Lizzie to worry needlessly about her youngest brother.

Once again, McClelland praised the military skills of Joseph Hooker and denigrated those of Meade. McClelland's opinion of Meade's lack of aggressiveness and military acumen would be shared by the man who became "Old Corduroy's" commanding officer—Ulysses S. Grant.

McClelland's "Napoleon" was a reference to French Emperor Napoleon III, nephew of Napoleon I, who had designs on Mexico. In June of 1863, Napoleon's forces took Mexico City and a pro-French government was established. Decidedly pro-Confederate, Napoleon had designs on linking up with the Confederacy in Texas to play an active role in supporting the Rebels. Union victories at Vicksburg and Gettysburg effectively dampened Napoleon's zeal to support Richmond in the conflict and further his "aggrandizing schemes on American soil."

Chapter Eight

"Pack Up and March"

August—October 1863

The Army of the Potomac

> I should have no objection to serving out the remainder of my term in camp here, but it is not our habit to stay long in so nice a place, and now we are almost momentarily expecting to receive the order to pack up and march at a double quick pace. . . .
>
> —Private Wilbur Fisk, Second Vermont Volunteers, Army of the Potomac, July 28, 1863

George Meade was steaming over his treatment by Washington leadership after Gettysburg. It was clear to Meade, after less than a month in command, that the Army of the Potomac was being directed from Washington with only minor input from the field generals. Meade doubted privately—in letters to his wife—that he had the necessary temperament to deal with the deskbound second-guessers in the Federal capital. After all, he wrote to his wife, the enemy had been driven "from our soil" (a phrase that he used after the battle of Gettysburg in his July 4 General Order 68 to the troops). There was no urgency in pursuing Lee because his army was back in the Confederacy. When Lincoln read Meade's General Order 68, he was furious with its premise: "Will our generals never get that idea out of their heads? The *whole* country is our soil."

By the end of July, the Army of the Potomac and the Army of Northern Virginia were back where they had been at the end of June. Meade had some legitimate concerns about blindly pursuing Lee. First, he suspected Lee was quite capable of drawing the Army of the Potomac across the Rappahannock and then trapping them—to use Lincoln's metaphor—"like an ox jumped half over a fence." Meade also recognized that his army had been significantly depleted by high numbers of both desertions and casualties and that his remaining men were exhausted from the exertions of the last month. His troops were utterly fatigued, and he had no reserves waiting in the wings.

Meade's lingering self-doubts as an effective leader of the Army of the Potomac and his frustration with the direction he was getting from Washington caused him to submit his resignation. He did not press the matter when his superiors in Washington ignored his request and instead sent him an overdue accolade in the form of a compliment from Halleck for his "superior generalship." Tepid as the accolade may have been, Meade knew that if he resigned his position as commander of the Army of the Potomac that Lincoln had no qualified candidate for the position among Meade's subordinates now that Reynolds was dead and Hancock was recovering from a serious and disabling wound received at Gettysburg. Washington leadership concurred that the slate of generals available to replace "Old Snapping Turtle" was weak. Consistently and unequivocally loyal to the Union cause and to the army, Meade put aside his pride and continued to serve as the commanding general of the Army of the Potomac.

Meade's staying did not result in his becoming more aggressive in pursuing Lee. Over the next two months, Meade had his army repeatedly crossing back and forth over the Rappahannock in a series of tentative thrusts at the Army of Northern Virginia. Some skirmishes resulted, but, for the most part, the Union army spent the late summer and early fall feebly sparring with an elusive Lee and his army.

Meanwhile, Lincoln's star general was distinguishing himself in the western theater of war. After his capture of Vicksburg, Ulysses S. Grant was promoted by Lincoln to major general in the Regular Army for his performance. To Grant's detractors, Lincoln countered: "I can't spare this man. He fights." In retaining Meade, Lincoln knew that Grant could be brought in to shore up Meade if the situation warranted. George Meade would continue in his position in the Army of the Potomac, where he had proven to be marginally effective, until such time as Grant's style of aggressive, bold generalship was needed to achieve a decisive victory over Confederate forces.

[T] he soldiers of the Army of the Potomac had seen many things, but they had never seen anything like the habits and morals of these new comrades in arms.... The men who were coming into the ranks now were for the most part either men who had been made to come or men who had been paid to come. The former—the out-and-out conscripts—sometimes made good soldiers. . . . Unfortunately, however, not many of the new recruits were conscripts. Most of them were men who had joined up only because they got a great deal of money for doing it, and in the great majority of cases, these men were worse than useless.

—Bruce Catton, *A Stillness at Appomattox*

It was becoming increasingly critical that the diminished ranks of the Army of the Potomac be filled. Expired enlistments, low reenlistment rates, and high numbers of casualties had taken a large toll among the regiments. Under the conscription legislation passed by Congress, a man could avoid military service by paying a $300 commutation fee. Those drafted could hire substitutes to take their places. Nearly 90,000 men paid commutation fees. Among the men drafted (170,000), 70 percent hired substitutes.

Conscription enforcement was carried out by members of the military; hence, many Northerners—especially those in large cities—took offense at the house-to-house searches for draftees, the use of troops to break up draft protests, and the armed military presence that inevitably accompanied conscription administration. In New York, political and racial undertones contributed to the volatility of conscription activities, and some New Yorkers even saw parallels between the draft operations of 1863 and the actions of British soldiers in New York just prior to the Revolution. Tempers flared in New York in mid-July 1863, and a full-scale protest riot erupted that resulted in numerous deaths, injuries, and burned buildings.

Official Washington reacted by sending several regiments from Meade's army to New York to maintain order in the streets. Conscription activities were resumed without further incident, but bitterness remained, a sentiment that Copperhead politicians exploited as the elections of 1864 drew closer.

To stem the chronic problem of desertions, the Army of the Potomac instituted harsh and swift penalties on those found guilty of deserting their units. For example, at the end of August 1863, five deserters from the Fifth Corps were executed. The sentences were carried out in front of all the assembled troops and accompanied by appropriate band music. The Fifth Corps executions on August 29 were especially noteworthy because the five deserters represented a broad ecumenical spectrum. Chaplains representing the appropriate faiths were present to provide solace to one Jewish, two Catholic, and two Protestant soldiers. The five blindfolded men were lined up, shot by a firing squad, and buried on the spot. The assembled troops—

excepting only those who could not be spared from picket and other essential duties—marched back to camp to music provided by the corps band.

Despite these widespread draconian measures, desertions continued, the problem being exacerbated by the type of conscripts being brought into the Army of the Potomac. Characterized by one Connecticut infantryman as "bounty jumpers, thieves and cutthroats," these conscripted "burglars and vagabonds" had little compunction about fleeing their units, much to the dismay of their altruistic comrades-in-arms who had enlisted for more noble reasons earlier in the war.

> [W]e were waked up by the bugle sounding, "pack up. pack up." The boys crawled out and commenced packing up; then orders came to draw eight days' rations and to be ready to march at 3 a.m. There was all bustle and confusion. . . . When on such marches we seldom followed any roads and so it was this time. After wading swamps, falling in ditches and other adventures, we re-crossed the Rappahannock back to our Beverly Ford camp. . . . Some of the boys lay down on their old bunks to finish the night's sleep, but before they had time to close their eyes orders came to be ready to march in an hour.
>
> —Brevet Major D. P. Marshall, Company K. 155th Pennsylvania, Army of the Potomac

By mid-September, Washington had intelligence that Jefferson Davis had detached Longstreet's corps from the Army of Northern Virginia and dispatched it to Georgia to shore up Confederate forces there. General in Chief Halleck saw this as an opportunity to move against Lee's reduced army, and he ordered Meade to move more quickly and decisively against Lee. Instead of an aggressive initiative, Meade engaged in a Kabuki dance with Lee that had the Army of the Potomac moving frequently up and down the Orange and Alexandria Railroad, back and forth across the Rappahannock and Rapidan Rivers, and in and out of Culpeper, Virginia, in a bewildering series of movements that confused and exhausted the Union troops. Northern newspapers mocked the army as a "police guard" for Washington and urged that Meade move more aggressively while the weather was still in his favor. Once winter set in, moving the troops effectively along Virginia's road system would become increasingly difficult.

The Regiment—155th Pennsylvania Infantry

> By the bivouac's fitful flame,
> A procession winding around me, solemn and sweet and
>   slow—but first I note,

The tents of the sleeping army, the fields' and
    woods' dim outline,
The darkness lit by spots of kindled fire, the silence,
Like a phantom far or near an occasional figure moving,
The shrubs and trees, (as I lift my eyes they seem to be
    stealthily watching me,)
While wind in procession thoughts, O tender and wondrous
    thoughts,
Of life and death, of home and the past and loved, and of
    those that are far away;
A solemn and slow procession there as I sit on
    the ground,
By the bivouac's fitful flame.
    —Walt Whitman, "By the Bivouac's Fitful Flame"

After Lee and his troops crossed the Potomac at Falling Waters, the 155th spent the rest of July marching back to Beverly Ford on the Rappahannock, where they bivouacked near the site of their camp prior to Gettysburg. Calls to "pack up and march" occurred regularly during August and September as the men crossed and recrossed the Rappahannock River in pursuit of Lee's army, the result of Meade's feeble response to Washington's mandate to crush the Army of Northern Virginia.

When they weren't marching or crossing rivers, the 155th were practicing their drill movements. Colonel Kenner Garrard, who had taken command of the Third Brigade after Stephen Weed's death at Little Round Top, was a strong proponent of frequent close-order drills to sharpen the men's military skills (not to mention minimizing any idle time the men might have when not marching). Garrard was particularly fond of Zouave drill and bayonet exercises. The colonel's zeal for drilling the men in his brigade on the Zouave regimen was not shared by the commander of the 155th, Colonel John Cain, who had led the regiment with distinction at Chancellorsville and Gettysburg. Cain had "a few words" with Garrard, and soon after this outburst he submitted his resignation. Cain said his good-byes to the 155th and returned to Pittsburgh to resume work at his business. (Cain had risen rapidly from private in the 12th Regiment Pennsylvania Volunteers to colonel with the 155th and was well liked by the officers and men who served in the regiment.)

Cain was quickly replaced by Lieutenant Colonel Alfred Pearson who, not surprisingly, was chosen with a strong recommendation from Colonel Garrard. Pearson's love for all aspects of Zouave drill was immediately apparent. He stepped up the frequency of drilling as soon as he took command of the 155th and honed the regiment's skills in skirmish drill and bayonet exercises.

To build the men's enthusiasm for the drills and boost morale, Gerrard sought permission from Washington to outfit the brigade in French Zouave uniforms. Moved by the brigade's gallant performance at Gettysburg and Garrard's assurances of his troops' highly developed skills in Zouave drills, Washington granted permission.

As a young army captain, George B. McClellan had seen the Zouaves in 1855 and declared them the "finest light infantry that Europe can produce . . . the beau-ideal of a soldier." The French Zouaves derived from a tribal group living in Algeria and Morocco who was noted for its bravery and fierceness. While the number of tribal members in French Zouave units dwindled over time, French nationals retained the name and distinctive uniform. The French Zouaves who fought during the 1854–1855 Crimean War were seen as the epitome of courage and military prowess.

The Zouave craze spread to the U.S., and in the opening days of the Civil War, Elmer E. Ellsworth, a dashing twenty-four-year-old law student, dropped his law studies to recruit a regiment of Zouaves drawn from the ranks of Manhattan's volunteer firemen. Called "Ellsworth's Fire Zouaves," the 11th New York quickly attracted attention because of its uniforms and the almost palpable élan that surrounded its members. Further attention came to the Zouaves in May 1861 when Ellsworth was killed in Alexandria, Virginia, as he took down a secessionist flag. After Ellsworth's death as a Union martyr, numerous Union units were raised that would adopt the French Zouave uniform. In addition to the 155th changing to the Zouave uniform, over fifty Zouave units have been identified as serving at some point in the Union army.

The Zouave uniform was described by the men of the 155th Regiment as

being wide—very wide—dark blue knee-breeches with material enough in one pair to make two pairs of ordinary pantaloons, and shaped not unlike the bloomer costume worn by women. . . . Next came the jacket of the same heavy, dark-blue material as the knee-breeches, and trimmed with yellow at the collar and the wrists and down the fronts. A feature of the uniform was the red flannel sash fully ten feet long and about ten inches wide. This sash was trimmed with yellow, and was wound around the waist of the soldier, adding much to the comfort, to the appearance and to the preservation of the health on marches and fatigue duties of the wearer. The footgear consisted of white canvas leggings which came down over the shoes, and were buckled along the sides and around the ankles, reaching halfway to the knees, where the breeches were fitted into them.

Lastly the greatest and most impressive part of the uniform was the turban, after the Turkish plan. It was composed of a sash of white flannel about a foot wide and ten feet long, which would be nicely wound, so as to set or fit on a red fez skull cap to which was attached a blue tassel. The turban was seldom worn except on dress-parade or dress occasions, but the red fez cap with tassel was always worn at fatigue or other duties.[1]

The Zouave uniform had the advantage of distinguishing its wearer as a member of an elite unit, but it also had what some saw as the disadvantage of drawing attention to any straggler who wore the uniform. The ever-alert provost guard could quickly identify members of Zouave units who were straggling and apprehend them for return (and punishment) to their units.

The 155th served with the all-Zouave Third Brigade (Fifth Corps), consisting of the 140th New York, the 146th New York, and the 91st Pennsylvania. It was the only all-Zouave brigade in the Union army.

The Soldier—George P. McClelland

In his great anxiety his heart was continually clamoring at what he considered the intolerable slowness of the generals. They seemed content to perch tranquilly on the river bank, and leave him bowed down by the weight of a great problem. He wanted it settled forthwith. . . . From off in the darkness came the trampling of feet. The youth could occasionally see dark shadows that moved like monsters. The regiment stood at rest for what seemed a long time. The youth grew impatient. It was unendurable the way these affairs were managed. He wondered how long they were to be kept waiting.

—Stephen Crane, *The Red Badge of Courage*

As George McClelland had time to reflect on his past year in the army—when he wasn't focused on combat or on marching great distances in all kinds of weather—he could think of the months of service as a train that had steadily accelerated. From its reserve status at Antietam to its recent action at Gettysburg, the 155th had played an increasingly important role in the battles fought by the Army of the Potomac. Arriving at Antietam after the battle, the 155th had seen the gruesome aftermath as a vivid forecast of what was to come. Green recruits had matured into seasoned soldiers, and untested companies had proven themselves capable of holding their ground under the pressure of intense combat. When he strolled the streets of Pittsburgh as a young man prior to August 22, 1862, George McClelland would never have thought it possible to march twenty to thirty miles a day carrying fifty pounds of equipment over rugged terrain in extreme heat or drenching rains. But he had done just that and survived.

The fierce battles that put them squarely in harm's way took their toll on McClelland's Company F. Of the seventeen original "Lunies" who enlisted on August 22, 1862, four had been seriously wounded and one had died of his wounds in the first year. A 30 percent casualty rate among this small group of friends did not bode well for the future.

The autumn spent in Virginia did not find McClelland and his fellow Army of Potomac soldiers engaging Lee's forces. Instead, during this period, the fighting shifted to Tennessee, where General William S. Rosecrans's Union forces met the Confederates at Chickamauga with disastrous consequences. Camp rumors among McClelland's fellow soldiers were that Rosecrans's reversals in Tennessee would goad Meade (or his superiors in Washington) into taking more aggressive action against Lee to counter the disappointing Union position in the western theater. Instead the cat-and-mouse games continued along the Rappahannock.

In His Own Words—The Letters of George McClelland

Camp in the woods near Beverly Ford
August 22nd, 1863

Hail! Smiling morn. Day ever to be remembered by the members of Company F. The "22nd of August" 1862 when we were taken in the tails by Uncle Samuel and tied fast for the space of three years. And this is the first anniversary.

The question is: How shall we celebrate it? I have proposed to the remnant of the "Lunies" to have a festival and concert. Glass, of course, being Commissary, will furnish the edibles. Bill of Fare: hard tack, pickled pork and bean soup. Ralston will "lead in the singin'." Music: The Gay Volunteer, the "Conscript"—with drafted variations. The whole to conclude with "When This Cruel War is Over." When, of course, we will be completely exhausted and adjourn to the muddy waters of the Rappahannock to cool off.

My dear little dame, your long-expected letter came yesterday while on Battalion drill. Of course I felt good to hear from you, my most backward correspondent.

My dear Sister, you can't expect much of a letter in return for everything is as dry as the parched ground where I am now sitting. We are encamped in the woods about half a mile from the river and occupy our time chiefly in "sweating." (It's a scandalous fact.) It is super-tremendous hot. The long mooted question concerning an expression of David has been decided beyond a doubt: "Rivers of water run down my eyes."

Lizzie, I declare you are becoming quite a politician. Grave matters of state as well as military affairs are discussed with equal ability. Your brilliant 4th of July peroration I have carefully preserved.

Verily, you and the "indefatigable" (I mean your sister) are both becoming prodigies.

Annie is sending me "things" as fast as possible through the Post Office. Letters and papers I receive regularly from Father and her, also Henry.

Lizzie dear, don't be anxious about me and my wants. I am doing very well. Rough and rugged I may be, and do appear, but my heart is still the same, only more fullness of love, of tenderness and silent yearning than ever. The time is fast approaching, I hope and believe, when with "wings as swift as meditation on the thoughts of love" I can greet you "propria persona." In conclusion, I have only to say farewell for this time.

Your Brother in arms, George P

PS My tender regards to the "sweet and interesting young lady" Miss Mattie D—and sincere thanks for her generous offer. I don't quite understand the sentiment. "Preferences" and "forget me not." How can I remember one whom I have never seen? Please have it elucidated.

Yours as ever,
George
Miss Lizzie McClelland, Davenport, Iowa

Notes on the August 22, 1863, Letter

An entire year had passed since McClelland and the "Luny" city boys enlisted in Pittsburgh, and they did not intend to let this anniversary pass without a celebration. Drawing on their various resources, the "Lunies" planned their event. William Glass was assigned to the regimental commissary in early September 1862; therefore, he was tapped to provide the appropriate food. John Ralston, assigned to the regimental staff in the quartermaster area, was asked to serve up the appropriate music. The three songs mentioned (*Gay Volunteer*, *The Conscript* and *When This Cruel War Is Over*) were popular among the troops throughout the Union army.

George paid Sister Lizzie a compliment for her Fourth of July letter to him. According to George, it reflected her skill as a writer as well as a growing understanding of things political. He was beginning to resupply himself with personal items after losing much of his gear to Confederate artillery fire at Gettysburg. George's belief that he would be able to greet his sister *"propria persona"* (in person) would have to wait. The current troop level within the Army of the Potomac meant that not a man could be spared.

The identity of young "Miss Mattie D" from Davenport whose "generous offer" and "forget me not," passed along by his sister, will have to remain a mystery. Miss Mattie D never reappears in McClelland's surviving letters.

Near Rapidan
September 22nd, 1863

My Dear Sister,

Your long-expected letter came at last. It's just one month since I wrote you. In that time I have received 4 letters from Henry, the same number from Father and 5 from Annie, while I can but coax one from you. If it can possibly be done, I make it a point to answer immediately and you know a soldier's facilities for writing are not always of the best. A letter from you has borne me up when almost ready to fall on many a former weary march.

The Army of the Potomac is again on the move for Richmond. A battle is impending. I think Meade will have to fight a battle to counteract the reverse of Rosecrans in Tennessee—give King and take Pawn. If he fights here there will be another Fredericksburg slaughter.

We are now encamped near the property of General A. P. Hill CSA. He has a very pretty house around which soldiers of our Brigade stand guard. That did not deter me, however, from making a midnight raid on his sweet potato patch.

Eight days rations were issued last evening to us which betokens a move away from our lines.

I am delighted to know you have been enjoying yourself so well. Throw study like physics to the dogs, but don't neglect to pore into the words of Sterling Anthony.

"When this cruel war is over" as well as its "answer" are sang out. Perhaps you were not aware we have a glee club. Still I prize the "Gold and White" song for your sake.

I received Arch's letter from Leavenworth and hope to see him soon. He says Henry treats him like a "Christian and Scholar." He forgot to add "Brother."

You need not be surprised if you do not hear from me for sometime. Everything looks like a forced march. Other Corps and Divisions are sending their surplus clothing to Washington. The wagons and pack mules are ordered to the rear. The impression is that we are to make a bold dash and take Richmond by coup de main.

I have just received a letter from Annie. A box containing 2 pairs of boots, some shirts, etc. has been shipped to me. It's doubtful whether I will ever get it.

Some 2 weeks ago, I sent up an application for a furlough for 20 days in order to go to Davenport. Ralston sent up one at the same time. His came down "disapproved" while I have never heard from mine—very probably mislaid. Under any other circumstances, I would send up a note in reference to it, but there's going to be a lively mill and I'm bound to be in.

Excuse this lame scribble. Remember me to all the household. I am as ever,

Your loving Brother,
George
Write me soon . . .

Notes on the September 22, 1863, Letter

George McClelland admitted to his sister Lizzie that the letters he received from his family members—brothers, sisters, and father—were an important support for him. His frequent complaints about a lack of letters from his siblings were more than peevish rants from the youngest brother. The letters had become an important psychotherapeutic means to motivate and sustain him during periods of high physical and emotional stress. The daily routines of the family—especially his sisters—expressed in the letters brought a sense of calm and peace to his tumultuous life as a soldier.

A. P. Hill's boyhood home near Culpeper, Virginia, was the site of the 155th's encampment. Despite an armed Union guard (assigned by Meade to protect the house from desecration—he wanted no repeat of the Union vandalism at Fredericksburg), McClelland managed to forage sweet potatoes from the garden.

McClelland had written to his sister before to counsel her on the need to abandon her scientific studies. This time he encouraged her to study a more fruitful subject for a woman—the singing of popular songs of the day. (Sterling Anthony was a composer of such songs.)

McClelland anticipated a forced march to Richmond based on some key signals: surplus clothing was being transported to Washington, and wagons and pack mules were being sent to the rear to get them out of the way. He envisioned a sudden attack on Richmond and expected that his requested twenty-day furlough would be denied because of the imminent move. McClelland's expectation of participating in a "lively mill" was premature. For that he would have to wait until the spring.

Culpepper [Culpeper] Court House, Virginia
October 5, 1863

Dear Sister,

Sitting in my tent in quietness, thoughts came up of ones far away: of a dear parent, of the best of sisters and brothers, and then I thought of all dear ones to me. Your communications were less frequent, so without any favor of yours to reply to, I would write it (this letter) for no other reason than to thank you for your beautiful gifts sent in a box from Pittsburgh.

I was thinking over the past year. That is, of the war. I read of Father's prosperity with pride. I see Annie climbing the rugged paths of learning; "onward and upward" being her motto. I look on the features of Henry and can see the brilliant future in store for him. Of Thomas—what need I say for him? Energy and steadiness of purpose are bearing him along, blessed as he is with the best of wives and his two lovely boys. A well directed ambition will carry him to his proper sphere.

And what cause for thankfulness have we in the restoration of Arch to us. Who, it was thought more than once, was irrevocably lost. And for my dear, good little sister who I am now addressing. A kind and noble husband is in store for her and she deserves one high-minded intellectual with all good grace to grace a gentleman. So hurry up, mister— what's your name?

Well Lizzie, what shall I write about this cool, clear October day? Movements in this vicinity remain in the "status quo." We are lying very quietly in camp, eating, drilling and sleeping away the time. No excitement. Executions, one or more of which occur daily, are not even remarked. Our community is as silent and orderly as any village on a Sabbath morning. You know this state of affairs ain't going to last long.

Our 1st of April comes a little oftener than it does in old Pittsburgh. A couple of weeks ago we were going to Richmond right strait. After that died out, the knowing ones held that Texas was our destination and lastly we were ordered to Tennessee to reinforce "Rosey" (Rosecrans.) Well, we haven't gone to any of those places and, what's more, ain't likely to.

Our good old fighting cock, Joseph Hooker, is in that vicinity now. He took the 11th and 12th Corps with him. His right arm is worth a thousand men.

My hopes in regard to seeing Arch are dashed. Military business is conducted a little loosely out west, it strikes me. I only wish Arch could shake off that "viper." He'll never do any good until he does.

I am in good trim, living in good style on soft bread and butter and sweet potatoes. Tried to get home to vote for Curtin forgetting that October comes before November. Given, secondly, ain't quite of age.

Well, Lizzie, goodbye. My love to all the folks and hurry up a word or two for your brother in Virginia.

George P. McClelland
1st Sergeant, Company F, 155th Pennsylvania Volunteers

Notes on the October 5, 1863, Letter

George McClelland's strong family bonds once again came through in this letter to his sister Lizzie. He was strengthened by his relationships with his geographically dispersed siblings and his father, and he took great pride in their accomplishments. Thomas and Henry found success in the West; sisters Annie and Lizzie continued their education beyond secondary school with the prospect of entering the teaching profession.

Even Arch, the second-oldest brother after Thomas, was in his thoughts. George was hoping that his errant brother abandoned his dissolute ways, including his use of alcohol ("the viper"), and found himself after having lost his way.

Rumors that the 155th would be sent into action took on an April fool quality. At first the unit heard that it would be sent to take Richmond; then the prospect was raised of being reassigned to the western front in support of General Rosecrans in Tennessee. Neither rumor proved true as September faded into October. Of course, George McClelland, ever the Hooker man, was pleased with the prospect of following his favorite general to the western front.

Hoping that he could return to Pittsburg to vote for the popular Republican governor of Pennsylvania, Andrew Curtin, who was running for reelection, McClelland realized that he would not turn the voting age of twenty-one until November—a month after the elections.

(Opposite) 1, 2, 3, and 4 George P. McClelland (clockwise, beginning top left) Pittsburgh, 1862; Davenport, 1867; Davenport, c. 1870; Davenport, c. 1880 (courtesy of the author)

(Above) "General McClellan and staff passed just now. The boys gave him a hearty cheer. A great many think he is no man for Jackson." September 20, 1862 letter (Major General George McClellan – Commanding General, Army of the Potomac 1861-1862, courtesy of the Library of Congress)

"Burnside, finding it impossible to take the impregnable hill just back of the town, gave orders to evacuate the town." December 20, 1862 letter (Major General Ambrose Burnside – Commanding General, Army of the Potomac 1862-1863, courtesy of the Library of Congress)

"So you think General Hooker a humbug. Truly I am sorry to hear it. I tell you that Joe Hooker is the best General in the army by all odds." June 3, 1863 letter (Major General Joseph Hooker – Commanding General, Army of the Potomac 1863, courtesy of the Library of Congress)

"A soldier can see a great difference or change since Meade was placed in command. Short rations – one day we marched 28 miles without bread, meat or coffee." July 19, 1863 letter (Major General George Meade – Commanding General, Army of the Potomac 1863-1865, courtesy of the Library of Congress)

"I can't get it into my thick noddle that Grant is *the* man. I want to believe and hope he is, but there it is." April 23. 1864 letter (Lt. General Ulysses S. Grant – General in Chief of the Union Army, courtesy of the Library of Congress)

"They say that the 5th Corps was on a high old spree and the 6th and 9th Corps looked on us with envy when they saw almost every man with a turkey, chicken or leg of mutton marching on that raw 12th of December." December 15, 1864 letter describing the "Apple Jack Raid" led by General Warren. (Major General Gouverneur K. Warren – Commanding General, Fifth Army Corps, Army of the Potomac, courtesy of the Library of Congress)

"The fact of the matter is Meade was afraid of Lee." July 21. 1863 letter
(General Robert E. Lee – Commanding General of the Army of Northern Virginia,
courtesy of the Library of Congress)

"McClellan's strategy is played out. Pope doesn't appear to do much better. Stonewall Jackson is a match for the whole of them." August, 1862 letter. (Lt. General Thomas ("Stonewall") Jackson – Commanding General, 2nd Corps, Army of Northern Virginia, courtesy of the National Archives)

Crossing at Jericho Mills where McClelland was wounded May 23, 1864, at the battle of North Anna River. (courtesy of the Library of Congress)

Fairgrounds Hospital in Petersburg, Virginia, where Annie McClelland found her brother George on April 18, 1865. (courtesy Chris Calkins, Sailor's Creek Park, Virginia)

Annie McClelland's letter, April 1865 (courtesy of the author).

One of George McClelland's letters, which he signs, "your brother in arms." (courtesy of the author)

Chapter Nine

"Shooing Geese across a Creek" and Decision at Mine Run

October—December 1863

The Army of the Potomac

To avoid misunderstanding, let me say that to attempt to fight the enemy slowly back into his intrenchments at Richmond, and there to capture him, is an idea I have been trying to repudiate for quite a year. My judgment is so clear against it that I would scarcely allow the attempt to be made if the general in command should desire to make it. My last attempt upon Richmond was to get McClellan, when he was nearer there than the enemy was, to run in ahead of him. Since then I have constantly desired the Army of the Potomac to make Lee's army, and not Richmond, its objective point. If our army cannot fall upon the enemy and hurt him where he is, it is plain to me it can gain nothing by attempting to follow him over a succession of intrenched lines into a fortified city.

—Abraham Lincoln, instructions to General Meade, Autumn 1863

Much like a large dog confronting a wily, agile fox, George Meade's Army of the Potomac was superior in size (90,000 troops versus the Army of Northern Virginia's 60,000), but Meade knew the "fox" was capable of quick attacks and could use its acknowledged boldness to circumvent his army and trap it between the Rappahannock and Rapidan Rivers. Daily admonitions from

Washington for Meade to seize the initiative and crush Lee's army with his numerically superior forces only frustrated the general since the communications came in the form of "suggestions," never direct orders, from Halleck or the president.

In addition to having an abiding respect for Lee's ability to direct his men in daring flanking movements, which they could accomplish with speed and ferocity, Meade also knew his own command limitations. Despite his army's numerical superiority, the five corps remaining with Meade had three new commanders: the highly respected Reynolds (killed at Gettysburg) had been replaced by John Newton, Sickles (wounded at Gettysburg), by William French, both unproven corps commanders. Former engineering staff officer Gouverneur Warren had replaced the redoubtable Hancock (wounded at Gettysburg) as Second Corps commander. Consequently, Meade's confidence in three of his five corps commanders was not high as he moved his army along the Orange and Alexandria Railroad through Rebel territory in the late fall of 1863.

To protect his army, Meade kept the five corps close together so that they could support one another in the event of a sudden move by Lee's army. With official Washington urging him on (though still not offering specifics) Meade looked for an opportunity to turn the tables on the elusive fox. That opportunity came midday on October 14 near a rail station on the Orange and Alexandria Railroad.

Confederates under General Henry Heth, with urging from his corps commander, A. P. Hill, saw an opening to strike a Union force, all of whom were ostensibly in the midst of crossing a stream—Broad Run. Anticipating the vulnerability of the fording Federal troops, Heth ordered two of his brigades forward to attack the Yankees in midstream. What Heth did not know was that Warren's entire Second Corps was in close proximity, concealed by an embankment. Warren's men poured enfilading fire into the surprised Rebels. Instead of taking advantage of a small Union force that was vulnerable during a crossing, the Confederates were themselves the victims of, "as fine a trap as could have been devised by a month's engineering. . . ."[1] At the conclusion of the thirty-minute battle, 1,400 Confederates had been killed or wounded and 450 taken prisoner. Union forces sustained 300 casualties, 50 of which were deaths.

The engagement at Bristoe Station was an embarrassing bloody nose for General A. P. Hill, who had authorized the action, and a significant boost in the reputation of General Warren as an effective field commander. Meade's subsequently increased confidence in the former staff officer would serve Warren well at a critical decision point in the final days of November 1863.

Meade again kept the Army of the Potomac on the move after the action at Bristoe Station. (The army had crossed the Rappahannock three times in four days prior to that battle.) Thinking that Meade would be energized by his success at Bristoe Station, Lee expected his enemy would opt for an expansive engagement at Manassas, where the Union army seemed to be headed. Meade demurred. He had no desire to add his name to an 1863 entry at Manassas and join those Union generals who had lost engagements there in 1861 and 1862. Instead, Meade's cavalry—a division under Judson Kilpatrick—was drawn into a five-mile chase of Jeb Stuart's horsemen in the vicinity of a place called Buckland Mills. Within a few hoofbeats, Stuart's men reversed direction and turned from the pursued to the pursuers, running Kilpatrick's cavalry ragged and capturing 200 troopers along with Union wagons and equipment. The "Buckland Races," as the engagement came to be known, resulted in 1,250 Union casualties compared to 200 Confederate losses.

If you cannot ascertain his [Lee's] movements, I certainly cannot. If you pursue and fight him, I think you will find out where he is. I know of no other way.
—General in Chief Henry Halleck, telegram to General George Meade, October 18, 1863

If you have any orders to give me, I am prepared to receive and obey them, but I must insist on being spared the infliction of such truisms in the guise of opinions as you have recently honored me with, particularly as they were not asked for.
—General George Meade, telegram to General in Chief Henry Halleck, October 18, 1863

The sniping between Meade and his superiors in Washington continued through October as the Army of the Potomac marked time after its victory at Bristoe Station. On October 23, Meade headed to the capital to confer with the president and brief him on the battle at Bristoe Station among other topics. During their exchange at the White House, Lincoln offered Meade one of his rural analogies: "Do you know, General, what your attitude toward Lee for a week after the battle reminded me of?" Lincoln asked. When Meade replied, "No, Mr. President, what is it?" Lincoln responded, "I'll be hanged if I could think of anything else than an old woman trying to shoo her geese across a creek."[2] Meade held his temper in check, but he was clearly glad to escape the political atmosphere of Washington and return to his troops in the field.

Meanwhile, Lee was looking for a way to divide the Army of the Potomac or employ a flanking movement to catch the Union army off guard using the Rapidan and Rappahannock Rivers to his advantage. He waited for the peripatetic Yankees to straddle the rivers as they maneuvered daily over the Virginia roads while the weather was still good. But this time it was Meade who seized the initiative. On November 7 he attacked Lee's forces at Kelly's Ford on the Rappahannock. Two regiments of Confederates were overcome by Union troops who took control of the ford and built a pontoon bridge to facilitate the movement of troops and supplies. Later in the day, just prior to the rise of the moon in the clear autumn sky, Meade's forces overran the Confederate entrenchments near Rappahannock Station. Deeply disappointed that his offensive move against Meade was now in shambles, Lee withdrew his forces. At Kelly's Ford and Rappahannock Station, the Confederates suffered the loss of just over 2,000 men while the Union lost about 500 casualties.

Two days later, the Confederates consolidated their retreating forces into a defensive position between the Rappahannock and Rapidan Rivers expecting that Meade would be eager to capitalize on his momentum. Meade did not press his advantage, and the two armies faced each other across the Rapidan and waited while a cold rain soaked the combatants, turned the Virginia roads to a quagmire, and engorged nearby rivers until they were difficult, if not impossible, to cross.

> The men and guns stood ready. He [Meade] had only to snap his fingers, and that night would probably have seen ten thousand wretched, mangled creatures, lying on those long slopes, exposed to the bitter cold, and out of reach of all help.
> —Lieutenant Colonel Theodore Lyman, aide to General Meade, November 30, 1863

Motivated by improved weather, intelligence about the diminished number of Lee's effectives (40,000 to 50,000 Confederates versus 84,000 Union), and goading from his superiors in Washington, General Meade resumed his pursuit of the Army of Northern Virginia. Crossing the Rapidan on Thanksgiving morning, the Union troops marched south to advance to the Orange Turnpike and Orange Plank Road not far from the infamous Wilderness area of Virginia near Chancellorsville where Meade's predecessor, Joe Hooker, had floundered only seven months earlier. Meade's strategy was to move quickly to overwhelm Lee's smaller force with greater numbers, speed, and the element of surprise. The still-muddy roads and tricky river crossings slowed the Union troops and helped eliminate the element of surprise. There was intermittent fighting between the two armies during November 27, but Meade's grand strategy to overwhelm Lee's army fell victim to road and stream conditions and Union tactical missteps. Despite the faltering Union advance, Lee saw his vulnerability once the Federals got their forces coordinated. That night

Lee ordered his troops to move back to the west and occupy the high ground adjacent to the western bank of Mine Run. Confederates used the darkness to build formidable entrenchments to repel the anticipated Union attack.

On November 28, the Army of the Potomac organized a line along the east of Mine Run in anticipation of an attack on the Confederate line established the day before. The following day heavy rains drenched the armies facing each other across Mine Run. The Union attack was delayed.

That evening the rain stopped and was replaced by numbingly cold temperatures. Some Union soldiers later reported that the water in their canteens froze during the night spent waiting at Mine Run. Meade's plan was to attack early the next morning. At 7:00 a.m. on November 30, an artillery barrage would initiate the attack with General Warren leading the assault. Huddled in a forested area near the run and shivering in the early morning hours (fires were prohibited), the Union soldiers grimly awaited their orders for the assault—an assault that the Union troops referred to as a "death warrant" because of the well-entrenched Confederate forces on the western slope facing Mine Run.

Pessimism—or a grim practicality—ran through the ranks as the Federals awaited the attack at dawn. Many of the men pinned pieces of paper on their uniforms that gave their names and ranks; more fatalistic soldiers also wrote on their tags: "Killed in action, November 30, 1863."[3]

Prior to the scheduled attack time, General Gouverneur Warren rode out from the Union lines to explore the state of the Confederate line. What he saw in the early morning light surprised him: the Rebels had created formidable fortification improvements during the night that dramatically changed the attack dynamics. A military man who saw a field of battle through an engineering prism, Warren assessed the fortified works before them and calculated that it would take his troops about eight minutes to run up to the fortifications during the attack—eight minutes during which his men would be under unrelenting musket and artillery fire from a well-protected enemy. An assault would be suicidal.

Warren made the decision not to attack and sent Captain Washington Roebling, one of his staff who had accompanied him on Little Round Top when both men served on the engineering staff, to convey his decision to General Meade.

Outraged by this eleventh-hour refusal, Meade and several of his staff officers rode to Warren's position to assess the situation for themselves. Upon seeing the enemy's position firsthand, and respecting Warren's judgment based on his performance at both Little Round Top and Bristoe Station, Meade called off the attack. Several days later, in a letter to his wife, Meade reflected on his decision at Mine Run: ". . . I would rather be ignominiously dismissed, and suffer anything, than knowingly and willfully have thousands of brave men slaughtered for nothing. It was my deliberate judgment that I ought not to attack; I acted on that judgment, and I am willing to stand or fall by it at all hazards."[4]

In the days immediately following the Mine Run campaign, Meade weighed his options for an offensive against the Army of Northern Virginia and found that none warranted serious consideration. With reluctance and a deep sense of lost opportunities, Meade withdrew his forces and headed north of the Rapidan, crossing the river in the early morning hours of December 2. The following day, the Fifth Corps crossed the Rappahannock to guard the railroad supply lines. Meade's main body of the Army of the Potomac spent several weeks at various temporary encampments before settling into winter camp in Culpeper County, Virginia, north of the Rapidan River. There the army could rest, recuperate, and reflect on a year of humiliating losses, stunning victories, lost opportunities, and a war closing out its third year with no end in sight.

The Regiment—155th Pennsylvania Infantry

"All quiet on the Potomac. Nothing to disturb autumnal slumbers," Stanton had wired the Chattanooga quartermaster on October 4, proud of his management of the transfer west of two corps from the army down in Virginia, which apparently had been accomplished under Lee's very nose without his knowledge, or at any rate without provoking a reaction on his part. Three days later, however, Meade's signalmen intercepted wigwag messages indicating that the rebels were preparing for some sort of movement in their camps beyond the Rapidan, and two days after that, on October 9, word came from the cavalry outposts that Lee was on the march, heading west and north around Meade's flank ... Presently things were anything but quiet on the Potomac. ...

—Shelby Foote, *The Civil War, A Narrative: Volume 2, Fredericksburg to Meridian*

Responding to intelligence regarding the movements of the Army of Northern Virginia, the men of the 155th found themselves constantly crossing the Rappahannock River as they shifted almost daily between offensive and defensive postures. Like wary fencers, the two armies thrust and parried, the Rappahannock and Rapidan Rivers and the Orange and Alexandria Railroad circumscribing their strip. Between October 11 and October 13, the 155th crossed the Rappahannock three times in a bewildering series of marches and countermarches, often avoiding roads, traveling at night, plunging through thickets and wading through swamps.

On October 14, when the Army of the Potomac made contact with the Confederates at Bristoe Station, General Warren's Second Corps executed a brilliant trapping movement. The 155th, as part of the Fifth Corps, was sent in to support the Second Corps. Despite fears of being flanked by the Confederates, the Second Corps handled the situation skillfully and did not require backup reserves. The only enemy soldiers seen by the 155th were some of the 450 prisoners taken during the engagement at Bristoe Station.

Intermittent rain in late October made any offensive actions by the Army of the Potomac unfeasible. Rather than send his troops slogging over muddy roads, Meade ordered them to establish camp near Warrenton Station and hoped that November would bring clearer, drier weather, if only for a brief time, so that an offensive could be conducted before winter set in. On November 7, the general judged the time was right to make his move. The weather was favorable, and Meade had developed a plan that he thought would succeed. His superiors in Washington agreed. Meade split his army into two wings. The plan was to catch Lee's army between the wings and crush it.

As the sun began to set on November 7, the right wing was in place. Brigadier General Kenner Garrard had skirmishers in position to the east of the Orange and Alexandria Railroad and north of the Rappahannock. Stretching from Garrard's skirmishers on the north and east to Colonel Emory Upton's brigade on the south and west, the Confederates guarding the pontoon bridge were surrounded by Yankees. The Rebels' only ways escape were to cross the exposed pontoon bridge or swim the freezing Rappahannock River.

The Union assault began and quickly turned to hand-to-hand combat as the line stormed into the Confederates. By nightfall the bridgehead at Rappahannock Station was in Union hands. Once the Confederate leadership on the south side of the river realized that no more of their soldiers could cross to safety, they ordered the bridge burned to keep the Yankees from using it.

Confederate forces at nearby Kelly's Ford suffered a similar fate. General William H. French's Third Corps overran the Confederates, resulting in 360 casualties for the Rebels (and only 42 Union casualties). Casualties at Rappahannock Station were similarly unbalanced: 1,700 Confederate; 400 Union. Although both engagements were "vest pocket" battles, the unambiguous Union victories improved morale among Meade's men, and increased official Washington's confidence in the Army of the Potomac's commanding general.

The 155th Regiment remained in camp until November 24 when plans were formulated for the entire Army of the Potomac to cross the Rapidan

River in pursuit of the Confederates. The weather intervened when a severe storm made such a large-scale troop movement impractical. The following day the movement from camp was resumed, and the Fifth Corps crossed the Rapidan at Germanna Ford and marched south stopping in the vicinity of New Hope Church. By 4:00 p.m. on November 29, the 155th had taken up a position in a thickly wooded area in front of Mine Run across from the Confederate entrenchments. The west side of Mine Run, where the Confederates were dug in, was elevated one hundred feet above the run with a cleared slope of a thousand yards rising from the bank of the run to the Confederate fortifications. Meade called for the assault to begin at 8:00 on the morning of November 30 starting with Warren's troops. Then, at 9:00 a.m., Sedgwick—leading his own Sixth Corps and the Fifth Corps commanded by Sykes—would join in the Union assault.

From their position in the Fifth Corps, the men of the 155th had a clear view of the Confederate positions. The sight was daunting. The Rebels had dammed Mine Run so that Union units attacking would have to wade a broad, deep, cold stream, surmount a cordon of felled trees, cross an open area, and, finally, climb steeply rising ground to reach the Confederate entrenchments. It reminded many of the Union soldiers of the situation they had faced at Marye's Heights at Fredericksburg. Their apprehension about the significant disadvantages presented by the field of attack was compounded by their physical discomfort. The word came down from the generals that there were to be no fires to give the Union troops' location away to the enemy. Instead, the men shivered in the cold, dark woods awaiting the dawn and their fate.

Earlier in the day the men had left their knapsacks in the rear, but they were encouraged to take their blankets in the event they were wounded during the assault. That way they might be able to survive the frigid hours waiting to be removed from the field. Selected to be among the first to wade Mine Run and storm the Confederate works, the 155th gave their valuables to the regimental chaplain for safekeeping and possible return to their next of kin. Some of the men wrote their names on slips of paper and pinned them to their uniforms in the event they were killed on the field of battle. Then they settled down to wait.

First light came and went. At 8:00 a.m. the Union signal gun fired on schedule and was followed by a smattering of artillery fire. Curiously, the men of the 155th thought, there was no sound of musket fire coming from the left, where General Warren's men were to launch the assault. Nine o'clock passed with no order to proceed with the planned attack. At midmorning, the word came down that General Meade had called off the assault after a strongly worded recommendation from General Warren, who had determined that the reinforced Confederate works represented an insurmountable obstacle for the Army of the Potomac.

The men of the 155th pulled the paper name tags from their uniforms and reclaimed their knapsacks. They waited until darkness fell then withdrew and headed back north. After crossing the Rapidan River on December 2, the 155th continued on to the Rappahannock, where the regiment made its fourteenth crossing of the river in a year's time. Cold, tired, and running short of rations, the men of the 155th stopped to bivouac at Bealeton Station on the Orange and Alexandria Railroad line where they rested and were resupplied. The day after Christmas 1863, the 155th remained north of the Rappahannock to guard the railroad.

The Soldier—George P. McClelland

> The weather was extremely cold, so much so that the men were in danger of freezing. At early dawn the enemy's position could be seen. During the night they had greatly strengthened it by formidable earth works and by damming the Run so that it had filled & spread into quite a river. . . . Every man in the command felt that death would surely be met with on these terrible slopes. But I did not hear any one decline to go forward. No one thought of backing out.
>
> —Captain Francis Adams Donaldson, Fifth Corps, Army of the Potomac, at Mine Run, November 30, 1863

As October's days unfolded, George McClelland and his unit found that a bewildering and exhausting series of predawn reveilles and early morning marches were becoming the norm: up at 1:00 a.m., ready to march at 3:00 or 4:00 a.m., crisscrossing the Rappahannock, and plodding—more often than not—through swamps, across ditches, and over such obstacles as wind-fallen trees rather than marching over the conventional Virginia roads. No sooner would McClelland and his fellow soldiers make camp and begin a quick rest than a bugle would sound and the entire process would begin all over again. The Army of the Potomac was no closer to crushing the Army of Northern Virginia than it had been in the months following Gettysburg.

On November 7, McClelland was on the march again, this time toward the Rappahannock River, where his unit halted in the vicinity of the Orange and Alexandria rail station near the river. An advance unit of skirmishers, selected from throughout the Fifth Corps, joined units from the Sixth Corps to attack Confederates protecting a bridgehead. Maine, Wisconsin, and two Pennsylvania units led the engagement and met with quick success. McClelland's regiment—in sight of the Confederate fortifications—never had to come to the support of their fellow soldiers in the Sixth Corps. Instead they watched as the Confederates were dealt a sound thrashing.

McClelland and his fellow soldiers had a respite from the fighting, but increasingly cold weather, lack of sleep, and diminishing rations were beginning to take their toll on the men. Complicating the logistics of resupplying the troops, it began to rain as the Army of the Potomac moved to cross the Rapidan River in pursuit of Lee's army. On November 26 weather conditions improved significantly, thereby permitting McClelland and his fellow soldiers to cross the Rapidan and take a position near the Confederate lines at Mine Run. Over the next three days McClelland and his comrades endured numbing cold and uncertainty about whether they would at last launch a comprehensive army-wide assault on a well-fortified enemy.

As 1863 came to a close, McClelland was spared the requirement to "dash forward into the face of death," as one Union soldier described the prospect of attacking the enemy at Mine Run.[5] The decision to abort the attack was made initially by the very man responsible for sending McClelland and the 155th into battle at Gettysburg—General Gouverneur Warren. Their benefactor at Mine Run would soon become their corps commander, holding that position through the conclusion of McClelland's active service in the Union army.

In His Own Words—The Letters of George McClelland

Camp near Kelly's Ford, Virginia
November 15, 1863

My Dear Sister,

I have written you in answer to every favor of yours. It's strange you do not receive them. I direct all letters the same as usual, viz: care of T. M.

I have written a great deal today and feel kind of exhausted. Not fit to reply to your splendid letters. I must say, Lizzie, you are very happy in your choice of language; beautiful ideas clothed in beautiful language.

Well, Lizzie, we have been used pretty roughly on the race course nearly all the time. I last wrote you from camp near "Auburn." We moved from thence to near Warrenton Junction and from that place to Rappahannock Station.

Our Brigade was the second line of battle. The noise of artillery all around us and the sharp rattle of musketry directly in our front made us feel a little anxious. Waiting every moment to hear: "Forward—double quick." We got tired. Paid no attention to the thunder. At last, and towards evening, little fires began to twinkle all along the line and hundreds of dirty little tins were fizzing away in the process of coffee making. And we just got it made in time to pour in our canteens when we started out in front to relieve a Brigade of the 6th Corps.

We had just got out of the woods and in sight of the Rebel fortifications when we heard a terrific yell followed by the roar of 10,000 rifles and we had no need to go farther for the Maine and Wisconsin boys finished up the work thoroughly.

The only part of the 2nd Division (our Division) engaged was a skirmish line of 600 Regulars commanded by our Brigade General Garrard. And I am sorry to say they wouldn't stand, but run [sic] like hounds. Even Sykes could not rally them. We rested on our arms that night and, before daylight next morning, we were well on our way to Kelly's Ford.

We are now encamped amongst a lot of deserted Rebel quarters about 2 miles south of the river. A. P. Hill's Corps, 10,000 strong, had erected bully huts here, intending to winter in this vicinity. They now [are] transformed into Yankee huts. There are no Rebels north of the Rapidan.

I think we will remain here until the railroad is repaired. We have to wagon our supplies 20 miles all the way from Warrenton Junction. The "eight-day ration" is still in force. No commander will ever be popular who does not feed the men right. A full half of the Army is in a starving condition, the hard bread not being fit for swill. I am well and want for nothing but a little good "grub."

"They say" there is no winter quarters for this Army this year. "Meade is going straight to Richmond." It can't be done. My opinion is we'll winter north of the Rappahannock. I don't care how soon we lay up. Reorganize the Army, bring out the 300,000 men by doing away with the substitute swindle, commutation humbug, etc. Enforce quarter deck discipline with them and by the 1st of June, 1864, we'll form a junction with Grant and Gillmore and sweep the Rebels into the Gulf. Hurrah!

I want to see the men to fill up our Regiment anyhow. Then, and not till then, will my condition be ameliorated—or [I] can't assume the duties of 1st Lieutenant. In the meantime, with my musket on my shoulder and knapsack of worms and other rubbish, I am ready to go anywhere.

My love to all,
Your loving Brother, George

To Miss Lizzie McClelland
Sergeant G. P. McC

Notes on the November 15, 1863, Letter

McClelland acknowledged the proximity of the battle at Rappahannock Station and the fulfillment of Meade's strategy featuring the close cooperation of the army corps to quickly respond with support where required—as the 155th was called on to support the Third Brigade of the Sixth Corps. That brigade—consisting of the 6th Maine, the 49th Pennsylvania, the 119th Pennsylvania, and the 5th Wisconsin—acquitted itself well and didn't require the active involvement of the 155th Pennsylvania. However, the skirmishers from the Second Division (under Brigadier General Kenner Garrard) faired poorly. These "Regulars" fled under fire and could not be turned back to fight even by their Fifth Corps commander, Major General George Sykes. George McClelland took some measure of satisfaction in knowing that U.S. Army Regulars, who often looked down their noses at the reserve forces of "nonprofessional" soldiers, had buckled under pressure. Never had the 155th fled under fire on the field of battle.

McClelland's complaints about the quality and quantity of the food were not without merit. The men had expended tremendous amounts of energy as they pursued the Confederates, and the provided rations were not sufficient to fuel hungry men. In addition, the hardtack issued to the regiment was found to be filled with worms and "not being fit for swill." After numerous complaints, the wormy crackers were replaced and the old supply burned. When McClelland and his fellow 155th cohorts broke open this new supply of hardtack, it too was found to be wormy. Resigned to eating the infested crackers or going hungry, the regiment "Soon learned that the best time to eat them was after night and before daylight."[6]

McClelland's prediction that the army would "winter north of the Rappahannock" and not go "straight to Richmond" was correct. Meade, in fact, received unambiguous direction from Washington not to view the conquest of the Confederate capital as his goal. McClelland also put his finger on a key issue facing the entire Union army: the lack of fresh manpower. Both substitution and commutation had an adverse effect on successful recruitment. His desire to see the Army of the Potomac "form a junction" with the armies under Ulysses S. Grant and Quincy Adams Gillmore did occur organizationally when Grant was appointed commander of all Federal armies on March 12, 1864. This unification of armies under one strong general effectively accomplished McClelland's hoped-for result; and he would not have to wait until June for action to be taken by Grant. The Army of the Potomac would be back on the battlefield a month sooner than that.

McClelland's desire to see the ranks of the 155th bolstered also stemmed from his wish for a personal benefit. Sergeant McClelland had been considered for a commission as a lieutenant, but this promotion was dependant on increasing the numbers of men assigned to the regiment and his company.

Camp near Kellysville, Virginia
November 21, 1863

Dear Lizzie,

Thinking a word or two from your brother in the Army of the Potomac would be acceptable, I will write you briefly and trust you are in enjoyment of all the blessings vouchsafed to mortals in this mundane sphere.

I have written, you, Lizzie, before from this place. We are expecting to move every day and now that General Meade has returned from Gettysburg and his orders from Halleck in his pocket, I suppose he will try another move on Richmond by this route (by way of Gordonsville), for this is the way. Halleck has staked his "military reputation" on it and it must be so.

Notwithstanding what Meade has achieved since he took command, or the success that have been imputed to him, he hasn't obtained the confidence of the Army. The men are afraid at every move of being drawn into a trap. They know that everything we have gained has been owing to the brilliancy of subordinate commanders. The feeling was far different with Hooker—even after the Battle of Chancellorsville, where our high hopes were checked (and by no fault of his either.) He was obliged to retreat.

When almost drowned by 72 hours [of] rain, roads almost impassable by reason of mud, we at last got across the swelling river and struck out for our old camps near Falmouth, a march that never could have been made by human bone and muscle if it had not been "home" we were striving to reach. Not a murmur or grumble escaped the lips of a single soldier, except when a "crescent" was seen (the mark of the 11th Corps) plodding along. "There goes one of Sigel's Flying Dutchman," and other remarks not so polite.

Well, the whole Army that had started on the night of the 6th of May reached "home" before the close of the ensuing day. The next morning, every soldier had his loaf of soft bread, potatoes, onions and so forth. (What we seldom see now.) Then came orders to move again; and would you believe it created joy, enthusiasm? Every man felt that he was going to certain victory. But the powers at Washington decreed otherwise and his hands were tied.

Chancellorsville was the greatest defeat the Rebels had received, and if Hooker had only been allowed to pursue his advantage, there would be no "Army of Northern Virginia" in existence. As it was, they lost the greatest general they ever had, "Stonewall Jackson" . . . .

This day is wet, cold and very disagreeable—calculated to give me the blues. We were paid day before yesterday and the men are sending nearly all their money home, a thing they wouldn't do if there was any chance of spending it . . . .

I was thinking where I would like to be today, but I am not there, so I won't think. Very sensible ejaculation, isn't it?

Well, Lizzie, I am very dull and stupid. I'm afraid it's becoming part of my nature—I have been musing again. I was thinking, should I ever get through this war safe and in after years looking back over my past life [I] should ask myself where three years have gone. How was that period of maturing youth (19—23) been spent? I could not answer. A perfect blank. Three years lost, gone, forever gone for which I have nothing to show.

I have received a letter from Henry since I last wrote.

The Chaplain has just been in and given me a book with a paper cover: "What is Calvinism?" I will close this scrawl and proceed to find out what it is.

Goodbye. Write me soon. I send you a trifle. My love to Tom, Anna, Walter and George.

Ever your Brother,
George
Miss Lizzie McClelland
Davenport, Iowa

Notes of the November 21, 1863, Letter

In his letter to Lizzie, McClelland told of General Meade returning from Gettysburg, where, two days earlier, the general had attended the dedication ceremony at Gettysburg National Cemetery and heard President Lincoln's immortal address. McClelland's expectation that the Union army would move was accurate, but Lee's army, not Richmond, was the objective. General in Chief Halleck's "military reputation" rested entirely on meeting Lincoln's wishes, and the president wanted the Army of Northern Virginia, not the city of Richmond, in Meade's sights.

Confidence in Meade remained low among his troops. The general had very little residual goodwill left after his performance at Gettysburg; he was viewed by the soldiers as wholly dependent on the competence of the corps and division commanders who reported to him. Fighting Joe Hooker—at least for McClelland—remained the favored general despite his less-than-superb leadership at Chancellorsville a little more than six months earlier.

McClelland and his fellow soldiers endured the three days of cold rain and the exhausting marches without "a murmur or grumble," but seeing some of the hapless members of the Eleventh Corps—who had fled the field under fire at both Chancellorsville and Gettysburg—they mocked them as the "Flying Dutchmen." (Their crescent insignia gave away their corps affiliation just as the Maltese cross identified members of the Fifth Corps. Many of the members of the Eleventh Corps were of German stock, hence the term *Dutchmen*.)

Reflecting briefly on Chancellorsville, McClelland recalled that they had been well fed and under the command of a general (Hooker) who could have subdued the Army of Northern Virginia had he not been restrained by "the powers in Washington." To consider Chancellorsville a great Rebel defeat was an exercise in wishful thinking on McClelland's part, but his assessment of the impact of the loss of Stonewall Jackson on the Confederate army was an accurate and commonly held belief among Union soldiers.

McClelland engaged in a rare acknowledgement of melancholy as he reflected on his time in the army. Perhaps it was the dreary weather, the lack of clear military progress in quashing the enemy, the loneliness of a young man separated from his very close family just ten days past his twenty-first birthday, or a combination of all those factors that caused him to feel the emptiness he experienced as a soldier. The "What is Calvinism?" tract given to him by the regimental chaplain may have helped him view his experience as a predestined trial which he had to endure with perseverance and grace.

Bealeton Station, Virginia
December 19, 1863

My Dear Sister Lizzie,

I avail myself of some spare time to write you my good little sister.

In the first place, briefly, the situation: we are now encamped near Bealeton, a station about 4 miles from the Rappahannock. The boys went to work with a will erecting quarters and I tell you we are pretty well defended against "Old Bones."

My present residence is composed of logs built up about four feet from the ground, 2 shelter tents on top. It is 11 feet long in the inside and 6 feet wide. Then in one end there is a three-cornered fireplace, while a bunk, consisting of tolerably straight saplings cut into 6 foot poles and raised 2 feet from the ground, is in the other end. The other boarder and lodger is Tom Dickson, my mess mate, my wife. "Let's play house. You be the Mother and I'll be the Pop."

Our fire place is a "contrary thing" like a good many people. Sometimes it will smoke and persist in it in spite of everything or everybody. But I'll fix it. I have run the chimney about 11 feet high. I'll get a pork barrel and then a flour barrel and on top of that I'll put a vinegar keg. I'm bound to make it draw.

The winter is upon us. It is cold, bitter cold (that is outside.) It's pretty comfortable where I'm sitting now.

Lizzie, I got that "box" which was sent me from Pittsburgh. The eatables were pretty badly spoiled being almost a month on the way. I also received a letter from Annie enclosing a notice of a new Davenport firm (success to it, I say) and of the promotion of A. R.; and he was doing better and better. If that ain't encouraging, I don't know what is.

As for this "chile," he hangs on to the "gun and cartridge box" with tenacity—or maybe they have a grip on him that he can't shake off. The latter must be the case. However, I ain't going to cry because I haven't got a pair of shoulder straps or a sword dangling at my side.

Tell Walter and his "aide" George I will consider on his offer of a Colonelcy. I want Anna's, Tom's, Walter's and George's pictures sent me as soon as convenient.

Lizzie, I think you had better close communications with Miss family "K" and if I hear any more such suggestions coming from that source, I'll open my battery and pour in a raking fire.

The Army of the Potomac, yes, the Armies of the Union everywhere are settling down to inaction and repose. Questions of great and momentous importance to the Country now take the precedence. The wise and beneficent suggestions of our noble President are to be codified in the laws and statutes. Then, in the first opening of spring, with largely increased armies, we advance and put the quietus on armed rebellion.

But just now it's too cold to think of fighting. The near approach of the Holidays suggest turkeys, mince pies and such like. A good many of the boys are going home on short furloughs. Will Glass is at home now. Ralston goes after his return. Adjutant Montooth left for Pittsburgh yesterday. I'll get as far as Pittsburgh (but I think no farther) about the 1st of February. Can't get any more than 10 days and I couldn't get to Davenport on that time.

I wish you all a Merry Christmas and a Happy New Year.

Affectionately,
Your Brother,
George

Notes on the December 19, 1863, Letter

The forced marches in rainy, cold weather came to an end for the season. The Mine Run campaign, started with high expectations, had reached an uneventful conclusion for the Army of the Potomac. A year that had begun in the mud of Virginia finished in a snug encampment thirty miles to the northwest.

McClelland acknowledged a letter from his sister Annie telling of his eldest brother's new sash, door, and blind business in Davenport, Iowa, and the army promotion of his brother Archibald in the west. George McClelland's promotion to commissioned officer ("shoulder straps or sword dangling from my side") was in limbo for the time being, but he was willing to bide his time and not complain about the delays in his advancement. For his two young nephews, Walter and George, he considered a "commission" for the rank of colonel and asked in return that Lizzie send him photographs of the two boys and their father and mother.

Now, during the lull in military action, McClelland saw the need for legislative action to strengthen the Union—included in which might be stronger conscription measures. President Lincoln was now "our noble President"— a sea change in McClelland's perceptions since August 1862, when he wrote to his brother about "Granny Lincoln" having "again forgot the dignity of the President. . . ."

Chapter Ten

Winter Encampment

January—April 1864

The Army of the Potomac

In the east the opposing forces stood in substantially the same relations toward each other as three years before, or when the war began; they were both between the Federal and Confederate capitals . . . Battles had been fought of as great severity as had ever been known in war, over ground from the James River and the Chickahominy, near Richmond, to Gettysburg and Chambersburg, in Pennsylvania, with indecisive results, sometimes favorable to the National army, sometimes to the Confederate army, but in every instance, I believe, claimed as victories for the South by the Southern press if not by the Southern generals. The Northern press, as a whole, did not discourage their claims; a portion of it always magnified rebel success and belittled ours, while another portion, most sincerely earnest in their desire for the preservation of the Union and the overwhelming success of the Federal arms, would nevertheless generally express dissatisfaction with whatever victories were gained because they were not more complete.

—Lt. General Ulysses S. Grant, *Personal Memoirs*

The fires of the Army of the Potomac had essentially been banked by January 1864 as most of the troops focused on constructing snug log huts that would afford some refuge from the Virginia winter. Culpeper County north of the Rapidan River, where winter quarters were established, became a military city with officers' residences at the head of streets followed by enlisted quarters arranged according to rank. Chapels, infirmaries, cookhouses, and commissaries sprang up in orderly rows to provide for the needs of the army in cantonment.

While most of the officers and enlisted men were enjoying the respite from marching and fighting, one man had no desire to sit by the fireside until spring. Judson Kilpatrick, West Point graduate and cavalry division commander, had a plan to strike at the heart of the Confederacy, a plan that he believed would surpass in audacity and daring those of his Confederate counterpart, J. E. B. Stuart.

Kilpatrick envisioned a "hit-and-run" cavalry raid on Richmond that would unnerve the civilian population and Confederate government, sever Lee's communication and supply lines with the capital, and leave the Army of Northern Virginia encampment isolated and vulnerable. Known derisively by his men as "Kill Cavalry," Kilpatrick had contacts in Washington who were able to get his bold plan to Secretary of War Stanton and even to the president. This end run around both his cavalry commander, Alfred Pleasonton, and the commander of the Army of the Potomac, George Meade, gained a swift response. Lincoln asked Meade to send Kilpatrick to Washington. Once at the capital, Kilpatrick presented his plan to Stanton, who liked the boldness of the proposal. Saying that he was speaking for the president, Stanton told Kilpatrick that he was to add to his mission the distribution of Lincoln's amnesty proclamation[1] to the civilian population as his troopers rode through the streets of Richmond. As it was envisioned by official Washington, each cavalryman in Kilpatrick's division would be given one hundred copies of the proclamation to pass out to Richmond's residents. Further signaling his agreement with Kilpatrick's plan, Stanton made a provision to reinforce his division; Kilpatrick would command 4,000 troopers for his raid on Richmond.

Both Pleasonton and Meade grumbled about the infeasibility of the operation and its recklessness as a military initiative. The accompanying political mission—distribution of amnesty proclamations—would be best accomplished by undercover agents, not cavalry troopers, the generals argued. Kilpatrick's operation was fully approved by Washington, and the impetuous cavalry general was given full discretionary power to execute the raid by his Army of the Potomac superior officers.

Just prior to the launch of the raid at the end of February, Kilpatrick was sent a twenty-one-year-old cavalry colonel with significant Washington connections and a level of bravado to rival that of his new commander. Ulric Dahlgren, son of Rear Admiral John A. Dahlgren, had served previously in staff positions in the Union army after receiving his commission as captain early in the war from Secretary Stanton. Young Dahlgren was returning to duty in early 1864 after recovering from a serious leg wound sustained while pursuing Lee's army following Gettysburg. Recovering in Washington after having his leg amputated, Dahlgren was promoted from captain to colonel, fitted out with a prosthetic leg, and then sent back to the Army of the Potomac. Kilpatrick saw an opportunity to use the well-connected colonel to lead a 500-trooper detachment as part of his pincer approach in raiding Richmond.

An hour before midnight on February 28, the Kilpatrick-Dahlgren operation began with the riders crossing the Rapidan River at Ely Ford and then heading on to Spotsylvania Court House. Just beyond that Dahlgren and his troopers split off from the main body to head south of Richmond and cross the James River into the city. Kilpatrick's main body of men—some 3,500 troopers—were to approach Richmond from the north.

Kilpatrick lost contact with Dahlgren and, upon running into the northern defenses of Richmond, found the resistance considerably more potent than he had expected. The "government clerks, old men and boys" proved to be spirited defenders of the capital. Kilpatrick stalled, awaiting evidence of Dahlgren's success to the south. After waiting over six hours for Dahlgren's breakthrough—all the while watching as Confederates beefed up their lines with additional artillery and more infantry—Kilpatrick's ardor for battle cooled, and he decided to withdraw.

At dark, Kilpatrick ordered a relaunch of his attack, but Rebel cavalry had come to the city's defense by this time, and the prospect of facing Confederate Regulars convinced Kilpatrick to withdraw. Soon Kilpatrick's main body of troopers was joined by about half of Dahlgren's men. The men told of being unable to ford the James River, which was flooding from heavy rains. In the dark, Dahlgren's unit had split in two; one group suffered some casualties after contact with Confederates before they found Kilpatrick's camp. The other group, led by Dahlgren, ran into a Confederate ambush. The brash colonel rode headlong into the Rebel lines. The Confederates responded by killing Dahlgren with a barrage of musket fire. Most of the troopers accompanying him were either killed or captured during the engagement.

Later, when Union troopers went back to recover the Union dead, they found that Dahlgren's personal effects—watch, boots, coat, and a ring, along with the ring finger—had been taken. The unfortunate cavalry colonel had even been stripped of his artificial leg. Also removed from Dahlgren's person were documents that he had been carrying that proved to be highly inflammatory. The papers called for the Union cavalry to destroy bridges, burn Richmond, and kill President Davis and his cabinet. Confederate leadership was outraged. In an unprecedented action, Lee sent copies of the offending papers with a note to General Meade inquiring if the actions spelled out in

Dahlgren's papers were authorized by the U.S. government or Dahlgren's superior officers in the Army of the Potomac. Meade responded promptly to Lee: "Neither the United States Government, myself, nor General Kilpatrick authorized, sanctioned, or approved the burning of Richmond and the killing of Mr. Davis and his cabinet. . . ."

When the raid was concluded, 300 Union troopers had been taken prisoner, 40 Union troopers killed, and over 1,000 horses either lost or too broken down to be of any further use. Admiral Dahlgren's young son was dead, and it was reported that several thousands of the president's amnesty proclamations were scattered about the Virginia countryside. The Confederates had suffered no losses.

> I was a stranger to most of the Army of the Potomac; I might say to all except the officers of the regular army who had served in the Mexican war. There had been some changes ordered in the organization of that army before my promotion. One was the consolidation of five corps into three, thus throwing some officers of rank out of important commands. Meade evidently thought that I might want to make still one more change . . . that I might want an officer who had served with me in the West, mentioning Sherman especially, to take his place. . . . He urged that the work before us was of such vast importance to the whole nation that the feeling or wishes of no one person should stand in the way of selecting the right men for all positions. For himself, he would serve to the best of his ability wherever placed. I assured him that I had no thought of substituting any one for him.
>
> —Lt. General Ulysses S. Grant, "Preparing for the Campaigns of '64," *Personal Memoirs*

The hiatus in significant fighting early in 1864 made it possible to adjust the command structure of the Army of the Potomac. To begin, official Washington reaffirmed its commitment to retain George Meade as commander. It was not a ringing endorsement. Few saw Meade as an outstanding leader; he was just marginally better than the generals who had come before him in that command.

Then, by general order in March, the First and Third Corps were eliminated and the men distributed among the Second, Fifth, and Sixth Corps. Generals French and Newton were relieved of command. Winfield Hancock, regaining strength after his severe wound at Gettysburg, commanded the Second Corps. Gouverneur Warren was assigned to lead the Fifth Corps, replacing George Sykes.

John Sedgwick was to be relieved of his command of the Sixth Corps, but Meade had a high degree of confidence in "Uncle John" so Sedgwick remained.

Congress revived the rank of lieutenant general, a general officer grade last held by George Washington, and Lincoln promoted Grant to the rank also making him the "general in chief." Henry Halleck, who had been serving in that role, stepped aside to become "chief of staff." To round out Grant's team, Lincoln gave William Sherman command of the western armies and Philip Sheridan command of the cavalry. To familiarize himself with the eastern theater and to watch over Meade, Grant decided to make his headquarters with the Army of the Potomac.

During one trip by rail to confer with the secretary of war and the president in Washington, Grant narrowly missed encountering John Mosby at Brandy Station on his return trip. The rebel guerrilla leader and his men frequently harassed Union cavalry, trains, and supply wagons along the Orange and Alexandria Railroad.

Now that he had his command structure in place, a good working relationship with official Washington, and an understanding of the strengths and weaknesses of the Confederate armies in the field, Grant was poised to begin the campaigns of 1864.

The Regiment—155th Pennsylvania Infantry

We marched about three miles through the rain and mud, each company stopping by itself . . . We passed Catlett's [Station] and arrived at Warrenton Junction at night, wet, weary wicked and muddy, very tired if not wiser men. We have never been able to discover why we were marched day and night through rain and mud, first one direction and then turn and go the other way. This is likely to remain one of the unsolved problems of the war. We were now back in the same place we had left three weeks previous."
—D. P. Marshall, *Company K 155th PA Volunteers,* December 1863

The troops of the Fifth Corps, while in winter camp at Rappahannock Station, were responsible for guarding the railroad lines against raids by John Mosby's rebel guerrillas, who seemed, at times, to be omnipresent. The mounted Confederate partisans swooped in, raided unsuspecting Union units, and then disappeared into the surrounding countryside. As a precaution, Union trains that collected at various rail junctions in the area would keep their steam up all night in the event they had to move quickly to avoid Mosby's men. Guerrilla activity put an abrupt end to the Union practice of allowing wives of senior officers to accompany their husbands in winter camp. Several of Mosby's men, dressed in Union uniforms, replaced Union pickets and raided camps near the railroad. After this incident, visitation by wives was no longer allowed because of the "attending risk and danger."

As personnel were being shifted at the top of the Army of the Potomac command structure, changes closer to the 155th were also occurring. Colonel Garrard, brigade commander, was promoted to brigadier general and reassigned to lead a division of cavalry in the western theater. Garrard, a strong proponent of the Zouave drill, had been instrumental in outfitting the 155th in Zouave uniforms. By the end of January 1864, the transformation of the 155th to a Zouave unit was complete. During this period, John Cain, 155th regimental commander, resigned to return to his business in Pittsburgh. Colonel Alfred L. Pearson was put in command of the unit. He took great pride in seeing his men outfitted in Zouave uniforms and invited his wife to attend some of the early dress parades and reviews until permission for wives to enter winter camp was withdrawn.

The threat of rebel guerrilla raids persisted, but the prospects for a major campaign by the Army of the Potomac decreased as 1863 came to a close. Soldiers who had not seen family for nearly a year and a half thought that the reduced military activity, coupled with the onset of Christmas and New Year holidays, made for an optimum time to request furloughs in order to travel home to see relatives and friends. The demand for ten-day furloughs was high, yet the barriers to obtaining such leave were even higher.

While the Confederate army, encamped south of the Rapidan River, suffered a miserable winter with meager rations and a depleted number of fighting men, the Army of the Potomac enjoyed an abundance of food and fresh recruits arriving by train. Their encampment surrounding the Orange and Alexandria Railroad proved propitious for helping supply the Union army with provisions and additional manpower.

Unlike their Southern counterparts, Union men enlisted for a specified period of time. The Confederate soldiers were in for the duration of the war unless released by disablement or death. By the end of 1863, the Confederacy was forced to make military service compulsory for all able-bodied men aged fifteen to seventy. The bottom of the Southern manpower barrel was being scraped.

Some Union soldiers elected to reenlist when their terms of service expired. Nearly 136,000 made the choice to extend their service, but 100,000 decided to return home in 1864 rather than remain in the army. Inducements of a four hundred dollar federal bounty plus state and local bounties did not have a significant impact on retention and recruiting. In February and March 1864, only 16 new recruits showed up to fill the places left by casualties in the 155th. As 1863 came to a close, the regiment had lost 103 men to enemy fire or illness. Death took a brief holiday for the 155th as 1864 began. An absence of military engagements, along with the improved camp sanitary conditions, had a positive impact on lowering mortality rates in the regiment. Burial details enjoyed a welcome hiatus in their duties, broken by one tragic exception.

On January 24, Captain Joseph B. Sackett, company commander of E Company, rode to visit friends in a group of Regular army soldiers bivouacked at a camp about five miles away from the 155th. Accompanying Captain Sackett was Quartermaster Sergeant John H. Ralston, a Pittsburgh native, a "Luny," and good friend of George McClelland's. (Ralston had returned from a ten-day furlough along with McClelland just two weeks earlier.) Sackett was scheduled to go on leave the next day, traveling to Pittsburgh to see relatives and friends. During their visit to the Regular encampment, torrential rains passed through the area turning local streams into sluices of surging water.

By 9:00 p.m. Sackett and Ralston were returning to the 155th's camp and attempted to cross at the ford they had used earlier in the day. But the heavy rains had flooded the ford, and the depth and speed of the water caused Sackett's horse to lose its footing and throw the captain into the frigid waters of Kettle Run. His body was later recovered by the Regulars who dragged the stream to find the corpse.

Captain Sackett was accorded full military honors as his embalmed body was transported from regimental camp to the railroad a mile away. The entire Zouave Brigade, outfitted in their new uniforms, turned out for the occasion. Under most circumstances, battlefield deaths left no time for the pomp and circumstance of full military honors, but the funeral procession consisted of Sackett's coffin borne on an artillery caisson, thirty-two musicians with instruments, the brigade commander and staff, the men of 155th Regiment, and a regiment of Regulars. Captain Joseph B. Sackett—the well-liked officer who had led his company at Fredericksburg, Chancellorsville, and Gettysburg—was buried in his family plot in Allegheny cemetery near Pittsburgh.

The Soldier—George P. McClelland

Uncle Sam voluntarily distributed gratuitously old rye whiskey, styled "commissary," to the men, in honor of the day, in the proportion of one quart to twelve men. No excesses or abuse of this infinitesimal distribution of whiskey was apparent in the camp, and the best of feeling prevailed. The usual thoughts and reminiscences of the year just ended impressed the soldier, and thoughts of home and friends as well as anticipation of what the future might have in store for the Nation and for the individual in the army, also occasioned more than passing thought.

—*Under the Maltese Cross,* New Year's in camp, 1864

George McClelland was one of the fortunate few who were able to do more than have "thoughts of home and friends." He received a ten-day furlough just before the end of December. The proximity of the rail line made it possible to be in Pittsburgh in a relatively short period of time. Whether McClelland's furlough was the "luck of the draw," as most applications were handled, or the result of a senior officer wanting to reward a promising young soldier who was a viable candidate to receive a commission is not known. Commissions for officers in volunteer units were granted by the state, and the bureaucratic process that approved commissions was slow and often politically motivated. Additionally, there had to be a sufficient number of enlisted men in a company to justify additional officers beyond the company commander. Those who had the power to grant furloughs may have seen that McClelland's situation required a reward in the form of a furlough to make the waiting period for a commission more palatable. (By accepting a commission, McClelland would also be extending his time in service.)

In addition to his interests in writing letters to his family and reading serious literature, George enjoyed singing, and he performed in what must have been some of the most unusual venues for a Union army choral group. A small contingent of Company F men—led by their company commander, Captain Edward E. Clapp—knocked on the doors of some prominent Virginia families and "took possession of the parlors" that had pianos. There the small group of Union soldiers serenaded the residents of the homes with songs such as the poignant "Rock Me to Sleep, Mother," a Civil War-era favorite, with words by Florence Perry and music by John Hill Hewitt.

At the conclusion of the singing, the courtly Captain Clapp would thank the women and children of the house for their hospitality and bid them farewell. He and his men would gather up their firearms and equipment and depart into the winter day leaving behind an astonished (and relieved) Confederate family with a story to tell for generations to come. For a brief time, music and lyrics transcended the differences between North and South.

> Backward, backward turn backwards, O Time, in your flight,
> Make me a child again for just tonight;
> Mother, come back from the echoless shore,
> Take me again to your heart as of yore.
> Kiss from my forehead the furrows of care,
> Smooth the few silver threads out of my hair;

Over my slumbers your loving watch keep,
Rock me to sleep, Mother, rock me to sleep.
  Rock me, rock me, rock me to sleep;
  Rock me, rock me, rock me to sleep. ·

In His Own Words—The Letters of George McClelland

Warrenton Junction, Virginia
January 13, 1864

Dear Sister Lizzie,

Since last writing you, I have been to Pittsburgh on a 10 day furlough. I had delayed sending up my application until after Christmas and shortly after we received orders stating no more furloughs would be granted; so I thought no more about it. But I was agreeably surprised on the night of the 30th of December when an orderly came in and handed it over.

John Ralston and I started together next morning, and on New Year's afternoon I bounced in on the folks—Father and Annie and all the rest. Wasn't it a Happy New Year? But still I missed your familiar face where I left you 17 months ago.

I had not much rest while there. Went to Birmingham; saw Aunt Chess's dear old face that I always loved to look on, reminding me of a mother whose features I can scarcely remember. Went to Allegheny. Called and received cordially by Belle Kane. Well, I saw everyone there that I cared about. I was very much pleased to see Father looking so well—strong and active and working as vigorously as ever. The "Little Indefatigable" hasn't changed. I only wish she had a good husband instead of teaching 50 young ideas how to shoot.

Well, here I am back in my little kingdom pursuing my duties as heretofore, my trip appearing like a dream or a journey to another world . . .

I have not exactly been cheated out of my commission, although if I had not made a stir, but submitted quietly, it would have been done. I have assurance of a Member at Harrisburg that it is alright. If the other appointment had been made, I could have got every officer in the Regiment to protest against it. It would not do me any special good just now as I could not be mustered in there not being enough men in the Company. Still it would be a satisfaction to have it.

The weather has been very cold and the duty of the men is severe. They hardly have time enough to obtain sufficient wood to keep themselves warm.

We have a very strong guard; one half of the Regiment on duty every day for the reason we have an important post to guard and guerillas are as plenty as blackberries in summer. No one durst stray half a mile from camp or he will be "gobbled" up. It is really dangerous as we are liable to be picked off by murderous assassins at any time. I would sooner be in "front"—that is, with the main Army.

Well, Lizzie, to conclude, I need scarcely tell you I am well—not quite either, for I have a very bad cold with a cough and I want some of Mrs. Winslow's soothing syrup. "Commissary" was prescribed, but I don't indulge.

I had a letter from Henry; both Arch and he are well.

Pardon this scribble. I never take time to punctuate. I require a lecture from you or somebody else, then I'll be better.

Ever Your Brother,
George
Miss Lizzie McClelland
Davenport, Iowa

Notes on the January 13, 1864, Letter

McClelland was granted one of the prized ten-day furloughs. Fellow "Luny" John Ralston and George took advantage of the nearby rail line to travel to Pittsburgh, a trip taking a day and a half thanks to steam-powered rail transportation. His family saw a George McClelland very different from the boy who had left Pittsburgh seventeen months earlier. He had left a teenager and was now twenty-one years old. He left a student and apprentice carpenter and returned a veteran of three of the most significant and bloody battles of the war thus far. He left a boy imagining that he could be brave enough to fight the Rebels to preserve the Union and returned knowing that he had been tested under the most demanding circumstances and proved that he was capable of leading men into battle.

George continued to fret about his sister Annie, the "Little Indefatigable." Continuing his often-stated desire to see his sisters married and not pursuing professions, he thought that Annie teaching her fifty students—"young ideas how to shoot"[2]—was not as worthy a calling as being a wife for a "good husband." (Before the end of the war, George would come to value Annie's indefatigable character and find that her determination and independence were qualities that helped save his life.)

The prospect of receiving a commission to serve as an officer was held up in bureaucratic red tape and politics, but McClelland was optimistic that once the additional number of men required to justify another officer in the company was realized, he would receive his commission. Assurances from a member of the Pennsylvania legislature in Harrisburg, the state capital, gave McClelland an additional source of hope.

The threat of guerrilla activity (Mosby and his men) occupied McClelland's thoughts. His concern was justified. The following month, a Union mail carrier was killed by the guerrillas near the camp.

McClelland was suffering from a bad cold, but he refused to drink whiskey ("commissary") in the absence of Mrs. Winslow's patent medicine. Avoiding the use of alcohol out of preference for the patent medicine, McClelland was not aware that Mrs. Winslow's Soothing Syrup contained laudanum—an opium derivative—and possibly codeine.

Warrenton Junction, Virginia
January 30, 1864

My Dear Sister Lizzie,
 I do not owe you a letter, nor, in fact, any one of the family. But a feeling to be doing something impels me to write, and not having any fair Dulcinea to discourse to, I shall direct a few remarks to you and begin——Tis a morning bright and clear. All nature has been disenthralled of the icy bands of stern winter, and the warm, genial sunshine and the balmy spring-like atmosphere insinuates itself and is felt all around.
 It's too warm to remain under canvas roofs, and the boys are gathered outside on rude benches or lounging about camp lazily and listlessly. It is truly glorious weather for the lover of beauteous spring or full bloom of summer. But I don't admire it, never did. And more especially, don't like it when out of season, as it is now. Jolly Old Winter, with its irresistible storms, its cutting winds singing through the trees putting life and motion into men, is the season for me. It has with it associations, pleasures, enjoyments without number.
 Well, Lizzie, I intended writing you a letter—something concerning your soldier Brother and his associates, but have half a notion to turn it into an article to the "Continental" on the seasons. But now I think of it, Young has done full justice to the same subject.
 To be business-like, the weather has been and is now unusually mild. Here I am seated in my sanctum sanctorum, Headquarters Company F. I am in command of the Company for the next ten days on account of the absence of our worthy Captain Edward E. Clapp.
 A most unfortunate and sad occurrence took place of the evening of the 26th. Captain J. B. Sackett and John Ralston left camp in the morning on horseback to visit some friends in the "Regular Brigade" which is encamped about five miles from us. Upon returning, they had to cross Licking Creek [Kettle Run] and, not thinking it worthwhile to go round where was a bridge, plunged in the stream. Ralston was carried safely across although the water was ten feet deep. Not so with the Captain. He followed. The horse was swamped and the rider was drowned. His body was dragged and brought to camp, embalmed, and—with high honors—escorted to the cars and sent home.
 I was well acquainted with the Captain. His was a noble spirit, kind and gentlemanly. His fine qualities had endeared him to all who knew him. His remains were followed to the railroad by all the officers in the Brigade. He has a brother serving in the same Com-

pany who does not realize his loss. He is but 17 years of age. Captain Clapp accompanied the remains to Pittsburgh.

We have recruiting officers at work now to fill up the Regiment. It remains to be seen whether they will be successful.

The people have to be aroused and be dreadfully in earnest if they desire the war brought to a successful termination. It they have not their whole hearts in the work (and they have not), they will regret it when it is too late. Jeff Davis and his Myrmidons, reduced to the most desperate straits, are conscripting the whole male population; and it's high time the people of the loyal states were fully alive to the fact. They will enter the field in a few short months with tremendous armies, both east and west. Armies which in their shattered strength the veterans of two years bloody campaigning cannot successfully cope.

Do the people of the North, lolling in ease and opulence and a false sense of security, realize the position? Do they weigh the disastrous consequences of defeat attending our arms at this time when a vigorous support to our depleted ranks crushes the rebellion and ends the strife before the winter of 1864 fully sets in? Or will they hug the delusive phantom of hope until the war is carried to their very hearths? I hope not. I trust they will become sensible of the situation, fill up our Army to an overwhelming strength, give their whole support—moral and pecuniary—to the government, smite every appearance of treason in their midst, bend their whole energies to the prosecution of the war. And the spring of 1865 will open and smile on a regenerated, a purified country.

There are symptoms of a "move." I think retrograde; I have for a long time thought that this long line of operations will be abandoned. It has been tried often enough to prove its futility. The Army of the Potomac will be distributed to other points: Tennessee, Georgia and perhaps some sent to Butler on the Peninsula, leaving a Corps of Observation around the Capital—this is only an opinion of mine.

There is quite a town building up around here in the shape of government buildings— which could easily be turned into comfortable dwelling houses. There are plenty of families who would be glad to get them.

About three miles from camp is a little village called Weaverville. The inhabitants are not so reserved and sullen as when we first came. Grim want has made them communicative. Whole families pass though the Regiment daily on their way to the Commissary after provisions. I have noticed several pretty lasses who are not at all bashful. But they are Rebs and if one should go to "see them to hum," he would very likely never return to relate his experiences.

I have as good a crowd of boys under my command as ever shouldered a musket. I am proud of them and hate to let them go, as they do, one by one. If any men are wanted for clerks, assistants in any of the departments, or any duty requiring reliable men, Company F has to furnish them. These and other causes have reduced the Company to the present strength of 37 men.

I was delighted on receiving your letter yesterday evening with a photograph of Thomas. He looks well with matured expression on his face indicating manhood. I am very thankful—the more so as I am so unfortunate to not have any sweetheart—to have (a) dear sister whose letters breathe sentiments of tenderness and affection. I don't know what I would do without them.

I might take to inserting advertisements in the "Waverly" in some such style as this:

A gallant young soldier, etc., etc. wishes to open a correspondence with a handsome, accomplished, witty—and 99 other qualifications—young lady between the ages of 17 and 70, etc., etc.

And Captain Hoskins, our Brigade Quarter Master, got his wife in just such a way. He had never seen her and through the medium of the "Waverly' opened a correspondence which culminated in matrimony. He received a leave of absence, went to Washington, was married and has his wife now here. I saw her last Sabbath in our log chapel at divine service, the only female present. The sight was strange.

But, Lizzie, it's time to draw this incoherent medley of a letter to a close. So without more ado, I remain, as ever, your loving Brother,

George
(My love and regards to all who inquire.)

Notes on the January 30, 1864, Letter

With the approach of Valentine's Day, McClelland acknowledged that his lack of a sweetheart required that he share his thoughts with his sister Lizzie. (Dulcinea is Don Quixote's ladylove in Cervantes's novel.)

His passing reference to "Continental" referred to a magazine *Continental Monthly* published from January 1862 to December 1864. It contained a variety of travel stories, essays, and reviews of literature.

McClelland raised the issue of low manpower levels in the Union army. He accurately described the situation among the Confederates, where every healthy male from fifteen to seventy was subject to conscription. Jefferson Davis and his "Myrmidons" knew the desperate manpower shortage could only be solved by an aggressive and comprehensive recruitment effort. (Myrmidons were members of a Thessalian tribe who accompanied their king, Achilles, to the Trojan War. The term was used pejoratively to mean a subordinate who obeys orders without question or comment.)

He predicted the break up of the Army of the Potomac into smaller units that would be disbursed out to the forces in the western theater. A small contingent, McClelland theorized, would be kept to guard Washington. General

Ulysses S. Grant had other ideas for the deployment of the Army of the Potomac, and they did not include leaving Virginia soil.

Visits by local families to the Union commissaries were commonplace—including the presence of attractive Southern girls who caught McClelland's eye. The local guerrilla activities precluded any soldier leaving the safety of the camp alone to visit a Virginia belle.

Camp of the 155th Pennsylvania Volunteers
Warrenton Junction, Virginia
March 7, 1864

Dear Sister Lizzie,

Your highly interesting and romantic letter was received. I am truly glad to know the right one has come at last, and he must be the right one if the description you give is correct. Still I must know something more particular about him ere I can say: "Take her!"

He must be a man in the highest and best sense of the word. None other is worthy of my dear, good sister, Lizzie. But I have no right to doubt him. I am a believer in the doctrine of the electric sympathy of hearts, of kindred spirits uniting souls who have never been present to each other, of a sympathetic cord that draws souls together though they may be a thousand miles apart, etc., etc.

He's a brave fellow no doubt and I want to hear from him. You say, Lizzie, that you "was urged on all sides to accept him." Surely that did not influence you. You consulted your own heart, of course. You love the "gallant little Major" and show it in a variety of ways.

Love is very exacting—you will want a letter every 24 hours in his absence. And when the [left blank] Iowa goes on an extensive march, you will be in dire suspense. Something must have happened him and then you will have a terrible dream. He will be wounded on the dropping of a fork from the table. Or omit to place a knife and something awful has befallen him. Then you will be seen gazing abstractedly in the depths of a tea cup and, lo, he will be seen in the dregs. And at the first intelligence of a battle—Oh! He's killed, and forthwith cry yourself to death.

But, Lizzie, don't do any of these foolish things. Treasure the bright pictures of the future when the gallant little Major comes home covered with glory and claims his prize and then paint the joys of your future life. "Cor unum via una, durante vita."

Ye poor sergeant of ye Army of the Potomac is doing well. He talks glibly with ye whole family.

The spring campaign is about opening. Kilpatrick is only a preliminary. We expect to be relieved here pretty soon and go to the front. And in the next affair, look out for the "1st United States Zouave Brigade."

There is a little musical talent in the Regiment. Colonel Pearson is a good singer and several others, but our Captain beats them all. The Regiment went on a new fangled scout the other day. Stopped at every good looking house, took possession of the parlors, sat down at the piano and sang. Called on the family of ex-Congressman Bouldin and other FFVs [First Families of Virginia]. Captain Clapp sings a very pretty piece: "Rock Me to Sleep, Mother" and the answer.

With this jargon, Lizzie, you will get an ambrotype of the undersigned and if worthwhile, you can get it photographed.

Lizzie, I won't take any more excuses. It seems hard to hear so seldom from you—not once a month. Henry keeps me well posted. I always hear from Arch through him.

And now, I have hardly room to sign myself,
George

Notes on the March 7, 1864, Letter

While his sister was most likely amused by her youngest brother's pretentious counseling on matters of love, the chilling possibility that George raised about her betrothed being a casualty of war was a thought that he should have kept to himself. George may be tactless in this letter, but he was prescient about Lizzie's fiancé, Major Noel Howard of the 2nd Iowa Infantry Regiment. McClelland's reassurance that the major will come home after the war and be "one heart on one path, while life continues" (*Cor unum via una, durante vita*) was faint consolation after he raised the possibility—in such a graphic way—that the young man might be wounded or killed.

McClelland mentioned the Kilpatrick-Dahlgren raid that had occurred a week before he wrote to Lizzie. The raid was not, as he suggested, a precursor to a spring offensive, but a stand-alone assault—an ill-fated flash in the pan. Going to the front under Grant's command did not occur for nearly a month.

McClelland's reference to the "new fangled scout"—where Captain Clapp, accompanied by McClelland and others, sang in the parlors of the First Families of Virginia (FFV)—was as audacious as it was whimsical, considering the Confederate guerrilla activity in the area. John Mosby and his men would not have been as receptive to Union gentlemen choristers as were the women and children in the FFV homes. McClelland did not report (nor do other sources) whether senior Union officers were aware of these songfests in the homes of Confederate sympathizers.

McClelland included an ambrotype with the letter. In this early form of photography the image was made on glass. The ambrotype replaced the costlier daguerreotype. Since an ambrotype was glass and fragile, the images were kept in protective metal frames. McClelland would have sent his framed ambrotype to Lizzie in a protective box. Copies of the ambrotype were made from the original glass plate.

Warrenton Junction, Virginia
April 2, 1864

Dear Sister Lizzie,

The above heading is becoming stereotyped, but it is not my fault that we have remained so long at this place.

I received your letter containing the pictures. Sister Annie and Brother Tom are lifelike. My little nephew very much resembles his Pa, all but his eyes, which are his Mother's. My collection is now complete with the exception of Arch.

The "artists" have been ordered to Washington and it will be impossible to procure a picture for Arch as I promised, so I'm obliged to call on you the second time to get that ambrotype photographed. Do this please, Lizzie, and send me a few copies.

It does not flatter me a bit to be talked about by 1 or a dozen young ladies. Still if they are in earnest, mean business, tell them to hold on a while. I'll marry the whole of them and immigrate to Utah. But, to avoid trouble and dropping prevarication, I think I had better tell all; make a clean breast of it. While at home on furlough, I married a widow with nine small children and one at the breast. If John Rodgers [Rogers] was a martyr, so am I. It is terrible—the never-ceasing clattering of her tongue and the demoniac yells of the young whelps, like Bedlam let loose. My responsibilities are woeful indeed. But enough; let the veil be drawn over the scene.

By the way, Lizzie, I wonder what "Thomas McFadden" it is who Stanton has commissioned Chaplain of the 2nd Colored Regiment rendezvousing at Leavenworth?

Dearest Sister, what shall I say? I am sitting in my high-backed arm chair—you smile! It is true. I procured a clothing box from the Quarter Master, took it apart, and have made me a royal chair. You may loll in your velvet cushioned mahogany, on your spring bottomed sofas, lounges and high fashioned whatnots, but I would not give my easy chair for any of them. Tis a luxury to sit on it.

Well, as I was saying, I am sitting in my high-backed arm chair, the wind is howling piteously and the crows are keeping up a ceaseless clamor in the leafless oak trees. The view is wild, bleak, desolate. The elements, which have been warring for the last fortnight, have called a truce and left a sea of mud.

I must say, we have beautiful spring weather. On the 22nd of last month, snow fell to the depth of 12 inches and it has been alternating rain and snow ever since. Outdoor amusements and exercises have been suspended and I have remained pretty much indoors, putting in my time reading and this has been more varied than I could have hoped for.

I have had the Bible, Military Tactics, Soundings from the Atlantic by Oliver W. Holmes, Hawthorne's Marble Fawn, besides the Atlantic Monthly (sent by Annie) and a variety of newspapers. So on the whole, I have enjoyed the inclement weather.

Well, I can enjoy anything. I care not what it is. Lizzie, if you can get any satisfaction out of this letter, I must say you are easily pleased. Remember me in love and friendship to all.

Fraternally Yours,
George P. McClelland

Miss Lizzie McClelland
Davenport. Iowa

Notes on the April 2, 1864, Letter

The feminine gender was once again on George's mind and in his letter to his sister Lizzie. She had been talking up her youngest brother to the young ladies of Davenport who, having seen Sergeant McClelland's latest ambrotype sent with his last letter, commented about her young, handsome, dashing, and available soldier brother. George offered a polygamist's solution to the numerous inquiring ladies by offering to marry them all and head to the Mormon enclave in Utah Territory where having a plurality of wives was still practiced. Then, shifting his tongue to his other cheek, George confessed that while on his ten-day furlough he had married a widow with ten children. He equated being a husband and father of such a brood with being a martyr in the same league as John Rogers. (Rogers was a Protestant clergyman who became England's first Protestant martyr under Queen Mary I. He was burned at the stake in 1555 for his heretical views.)

McClelland's reference to Thomas McFadden is a false rumor. No person of that name was commissioned chaplain in the 2nd Kansas Colored Regiment or at any other black unit.

He noted—with a trace of sarcasm—the "beautiful spring weather" of snow and rain that kept the Virginia roads unfit for large troop movements. Another member of the Union army was also closely watching the weather conditions. The troops reported seeing General Grant pass the encampment by rail on March 10 and again on March 24, no doubt examining the conditions to evaluate the appropriate time to launch a spring offensive. The Army of the Potomac would not have to wait long. Soon the long winter encampment would end. The recently appointed general in chief, Ulysses S. Grant, was eager to deploy the 100,000 soldiers of his new command amassed on Virginia soil. The campaigns of 1864 were about to begin.

Chapter Eleven

The Wilderness, Spotsylvania
Court House, and North Anna River

The Overland Campaign and
Hospital Recovery, April—July 1864

The Army of the Potomac

"General Grant, about how long will it take you to get to Richmond?"
"I will agree to be there in about four days—that is, if General Lee becomes
a party to the agreement, but if he objects, the trip will undoubtedly be pro-
longed."
—Exchange between a newspaper correspondent and General Ulysses S.
Grant, *Campaigning with Grant*

Ulysses Grant chose to establish his headquarters at Culpeper, Virginia, for
a variety of strategic and practical reasons. Culpeper's proximity to Washington made a quick trip by train to the Federal capital convenient. Grant
also could increase his understanding of the Army of the Potomac while
he kept an eye on its commander, George Meade. Grant concluded that his
knowledge of the western theater—based on his recent experience there and
the high level of confidence he had in his western commander, William T.
Sherman—made remote command of that army feasible. And, on a more
personal note, Grant was eager to take on the mythical Robert E. Lee and the

Army of Northern Virginia. While Grant respected Lee as an innovative and tenacious commander, he thought that the Army of the Potomac leadership put too much stock in Lee's reputation and needed to be more aggressive in their conduct of the war. Grant knew he had overwhelming superiority in numbers of troops and—thanks to the genius of his chief quartermaster, General Rufus Ingalls—the Army of the Potomac had a supply system second to none.

The end of March brought snow, hail, and rain that turned roads into quagmires and made troop movement inadvisable. Not wanting a repeat of Burnside's 1863 Mud March debacle, Grant kept the Army of the Potomac in winter camp through the end of April. Early April saw a snowstorm at the start of the month that changed to rain as temperatures climbed slowly into the fifties by midday. Roads throughout April remained a problem for troop movements. Once the intermittent rain and hail were over on May 2, the days warmed under bright spring sunshine and roads began drying out. At last the time had come to begin the spring offensive.

Grant's spring campaign strategy was a three-directional choreography of Federal units focusing on Lee: Meade's Army of the Potomac—supplemented by Burnside's Ninth Corps—would cross the Rapidan east of the Army of Northern Virginia, flank the Rebels, then turn west and confront them head on. Butler's Army of the James would head toward Richmond, proceeding up the James River, and separate Lee from the Confederate capital. And Sigel would move his army south through the Shenandoah Valley ("up the Valley"), cut Lee off from his supplies, and imperil his left flank.

To keep movements of the army under wraps as long as possible, the infantry of the Army of the Potomac was not told of its routes of march until just before midnight on May 3. By first light the next day, the Army of the Potomac was on the move, with the Fifth Corps, under Warren, heading down the Germanna Plank Road to cross the Rapidan at Germanna Ford followed by Sedgwick's Sixth Corps and with Hancock's Second Corps crossing at nearby Ely's Ford to avoid the congestion of three army corps crossing the river at the same point at the same time. Burnside's Ninth Corps crossed at Germanna Ford later in the day. The plan called for the Army of the Potomac to pass through the Wilderness—a sixty-square-mile area of tangled thickets, pine, scrub oak, and cedars.

Andrew Humphreys, Meade's chief of staff, wanted the Federal troops to move quickly through the Wilderness so that they would not be trapped in this inhospitable maze where they could not easily maneuver, fire with accuracy, or use artillery. Meade's numerical advantage, in Humphreys's view, would be lost in this impenetrable thicket. Meade rejected his chief of staff's recommendation and halted the army in the Wilderness so that the wagon trains could catch up with the troops. (The supply train of 4,300 wagons with food, forage, ammunition, 835 ambulances, and a herd of cattle, if lined up end to end, would stretch from the Rapidan to Richmond.)

From their lookout on Clark Mountain, the Army of Northern Virginia leadership could see the mass movement of Union troops over the Rapidan by midday on May 4. Reacting quickly—with much more alacrity than the Union generals expected—Lee ordered Lieutenant General Richard Ewell's Second Corps to abandon the fortifications near the Rapidan, march down the Orange Turnpike, and confront the Federals in the Wilderness, where the Confederate general knew familiarity with the terrain would give the Confederates an advantage. Simultaneously, Lee sent Lieutenant General Ambrose P. Hill's Third Corps on a parallel route—the Orange Plank Road—toward the Union troops at Wilderness Tavern.

To bolster his two corps moving east, Lee ordered Lieutenant James Longstreet to move elements of his First Corps northeast from the area near Gordonsville, Virginia. When Stuart's cavalry scouts reported that the Army of the Potomac was camped in the Wilderness, Lee decided to take the offensive and attack immediately. Ewell was directed to continue to move out along the Orange Turnpike; Hill's men were to proceed down the Plank Road where they would hold the Union forces in check until Longstreet's forces arrived; then the three Confederate units would close their grip on the trapped Army of the Potomac and crush them despite the smaller number of Confederate troops.

By five o'clock on the morning of May 5, the sun was beginning to rise in the eastern sky and the Union Fifth Corps was starting to march toward the Orange Turnpike when pickets, stationed along the eastern end of the turnpike to guard the troops under way, spotted a dust cloud rising in the warm morning air on the turnpike to the west. Out of the dust cloud emerged Ewell's corps marching with determination, sun in their faces, toward the Federals. Warren immediately alerted Meade of the approaching Confederates. Union Fifth Corps men were ordered to attack what Meade presumed was a small Confederate force. Warren spread his three divisions along a north—south axis.

Warren could see that his right flank was vulnerable and that an assault on Ewell's men—dug in along a wooded area at a rise across an open field (Saunders' Field)—would result in his men receiving enfilade fire from Confederate forces. Warren appealed to Meade to wait until Major General John Sedgwick's Sixth Corps could be brought in to protect the Union right. Meade objected, repeating his order to attack the Confederate line.

Forming on the right at Saunders' Field, one of the few open spaces in the Wilderness, Brigadier General Romeyn Ayres's Zouave Brigade took withering

Confederate fire as they moved across the field in what one soldier later called a "killing bowl." To Ayres's left, Brigadier General Joseph Bartlett's brigade was able to move west along the turnpike, his lead units breaking through the Confederate lines, if only for a brief period before they were repulsed. Other Union units of the Fifth Corps were similarly beaten back. Warren ordered artillery pieces into the struggle on Saunders' Field which began lobbing shells indiscriminately into both the defending Confederate lines and the advancing Union troops. A blistering fusillade of artillery and musket fire set the tinder-dry field and woods on fire trapping scores of wounded men. Some were carried to safety; others were incinerated in the flames at Saunders' Field.

By 3:00 p.m. Sedgwick's corps had arrived at Saunders' Field, two hours after the attack began. By then, fighting had wound to a close. Once in position, Sedgwick's men restarted the assault against Ewell's line, and fighting continued into the late afternoon and evening, with neither side gaining the advantage.

The Union attack resumed early the next morning, May 6, and the Army of Northern Virginia was in danger of folding under intense pressure from the Union Second Corps and Wadsworth's division of the Fifth Corps. Then, as the Confederate situation seemed to be going from bad to worse, advance forces of Longstreet's troops, refreshed after a night's rest, arrived on the scene and counterattacked the Federals. Later in the morning, taking advantage of an unfinished railroad grade to flank the Union line undetected, Longstreet's men attacked Hancock's troops, rolling up his line—as Hancock later described it—"like a wet blanket." The Union forces withdrew east to the Brock Road to re-form.

In the evening of May 6, Brigadier General John B. Gordon, with Ewell's approval, attempted a flank attack on the Union line north of Saunders' Field. Darkness and Union reinforcements put a stop to Gordon's pursuit of his advantage. Several hundred Union prisoners were taken during the fighting (including two general officers), but no important Confederate breakthrough was achieved. The two-day battle of the Wilderness had ended leaving in its wake 18,000 Union and 12,000 Confederate casualties.

> More desperate fighting has not been witnessed on this continent than that of the 5th and 6th of May . . . Our victory consisted in having successfully crossed a formidable stream, almost in the face of an enemy, and in getting the army together as a unit. . . . With my staff and a small escort of cavalry I preceded the troops. [May 7]. . . . The greatest enthusiasm was manifested by Hancock's men as we passed by . . . No doubt it was inspired by the fact that the

movement was south. It indicated to them that they had passed through the "beginning of the end" in the battle just fought.
—Lieutenant General Ulysses S. Grant, *Personal Memoirs*

From private to general, the men of the Army of the Potomac recognized that their new general in chief was not cut from the same cloth as previous generals who had commanded their ranks. There was to be no holding back, regrouping, or biding their time in camp. This was a general who would press his enemy at every opportunity and not be satisfied with a tactical draw as an outcome. Grant's plan was to move the army south to the county seat of Spotsylvania Court House, placing his troops between the Army of Northern Virginia and Richmond, thereby forcing Lee out of the Wilderness to fight on terrain more favorable to the Union army.

Warren's Fifth Corps moved out first at dusk on May 7 and proceeded south on its way to Spotsylvania Court House. When the men realized that they were heading south to continue the campaign against Lee rather than heading north to withdraw over the Germanna Plank Road, the men let out a roaring cheer of approval. Hearing the cheering from their entrenchments, some Confederates assumed that a night attack was under way.

Lee reacted quickly to the Union troop movement and ordered Major General Richard Anderson to head toward Spotsylvania Court House to intercept the Army of the Potomac. Anderson, without urging from Lee, recognized the necessity of reaching the hamlet at Spotsylvania as rapidly as possible. The race between the Army of the Potomac and the Army of Northern Virginia to the pivotal crossroads at the court house was on. Warren's Union Fifth Corps and Anderson's Confederate First Corps marched inexorably toward a confluence on the Brock Road, where they collided on the morning of May 8 at the Spindle Farm, less than two miles north and west of Spotsylvania Court House.

Confederate cavalryman Fitzhugh Lee and his troopers had harassed Warren's corps delaying Union forward progress and giving Anderson's men an opportunity to move into position along the heights of the Spindle Farm near Laurel Hill. Warren assumed the hill was being defended by Confederate cavalry so he ordered his corps into action giving Brigadier General John Robinson's Second Division and the First Division, under the irascible Brigadier General Charles Griffin, the lead.

Within minutes after the assault began, Warren's men relayed that the hill was defended by more than a small cavalry unit. Confederate musket fire poured into the Union ranks as they ascended Laurel Hill in the vicinity of the Spindle farmhouse. Reminiscent of their experience at Saunders' Field three days earlier, Griffin's division found itself taking heavy casualties as the men attempted to storm up the hill toward the entrenched Confederate position, Ayres's undaunted Zouave Brigade once again in the forefront of the action.

Despite the addition of two more Fifth Corps divisions and Warren's personal attempt to rally his stunned troops by riding among them and urging them on, the Confederate firepower was too great. The Fifth Corps men pulled back to the foot of Laurel Hill to begin re-forming at the edge of the clearing there. The Union Sixth Corps that joined in the attack at midday met similar results. Ewell's Confederate Second Corps troops arrived at sunset after the fighting had concluded at Laurel Hill and occupied an area of high ground northwest of Spotsylvania Court House. That night they constructed stout earthen fortifications, including a salient known as the "Mule Shoe" because of its bulging inverted "U" shape.

By midmorning on May 10, Grant realized that he needed to jump-start his offensive after a disappointing show at Laurel Hill. He ordered Major General Winfield Hancock to withdraw all his Second Corps with the exception of Brigadier General Francis Barlow's division to be left behind as a distraction to the Confederates. Rebel artillery hammered Barlow's position, and Major General Henry Heth's division stormed into the Union lines, the Confederates screaming Rebel yells as they came. Barlow's men folded under the merciless pounding of artillery and musket fire and the sheer fury of the advancing Confederates. Those Union men of Barlow's division who survived fled across the Po River to safety.

> I am heartily tired of hearing what Lee is going to do. Some of you always seem to think he is suddenly going to turn a double somersault, and land on our rear and on both our flanks at the same time. Go back to your command, and try to think what we are going to do ourselves, instead of what Lee is going to do.
>
> —Lieutenant General Ulysses S. Grant, *Campaigning with Grant*

On May 10 Grant, breaking tradition with the way the Army of the Potomac had been led in the past, sought to keep the pressure on Lee by ordering a 5:00 p.m. assault across Lee's entire line. However, Warren was itching to restore his reputation after the debacle at Laurel Hill two days before. Upon convincing Meade that his Fifth Corps could take Laurel Hill on the second try, Warren began his assault at 4:00, an hour prior to the scheduled grand assault on Lee's line. Warren's second attempt at Laurel Hill was no more successful than the first.

After 6:00 p.m. elements of the Union Sixth Corps, under the command of twenty-four-year-old Colonel Emory Upton, attacked the Confederate works at the "Mule Shoe" where they burst through the Rebel lines. Upton expected support to hold his position, but the young general was forced to pull his men back into the surrounding woods. Following the Upton assault, Grant remained confident. Always seeing the glass as half full, Grant concluded that if Upton could breach the line, then Lee's defenses were vulnerable. With the advantage of numerical superiority, the Army of the Potomac could overwhelm Lee and squash the Army of Northern Virginia in one comprehensive, bold move.

On the morning of May 11, Grant solidified his plans for the grand assault. Hancock would lead his Second Corps in an assault on the "Mule Shoe" salient. Simultaneously, Burnside's Ninth Corps would attack the eastern leg of the salient while Warren and Wright with their corps would hold the Confederates in place at Laurel Hill. The plan had all the earmarks of a Grant initiative: bold, brave, and decisive.

A rainstorm during the late afternoon and evening made Union maneuvers disorienting as well as miserable for the men as they trudged through mud on their way into position for the assault the next day. On May 12, thirty minutes before sunrise, Hancock's men plunged through the mist and fog to storm the Confederate entrenchments. Fighting at the salient and surrounding area was fierce between the infantries of the two enemy forces, and Union artillery fire on the Confederates continued unabated, leading one soldier to later remark that they fought "Onward thro' hissing shot and screaming shell . . ."

While intense fighting was occurring at the Bloody Angle, Meade—with Grant's urging to press the Rebel flanks—ordered Warren to send his men back to Laurel Hill once more. Wearied from their prior attempts to rout the Confederates there, Warren's men balked at being sent yet again into a certain catastrophe. Warren's attempts to convince Meade that further attacks would be fruitless only enraged Meade, who finally directed the Fifth Corps commander to attack at once, "at all hazards with your whole force, if necessary." Having run out of appeals, Warren did what Meade ordered: he directed his division commanders to attack Laurel Hill. Warren's assessment of the plan's foolhardiness was as accurate as had been his assessment of the risks of an assault at Mine Run the previous December. This time, however, Warren did not receive the benefit of a considered decision by Meade, who was, himself, under intense pressure from Grant to press the attack on all fronts. Warren proved to be prescient about the outcome at Laurel Hill. Griffin's First Division and Brigadier General Lysander Cutler's Fourth Division of the Fifth Corps were raked by fire from the well-entrenched Confederate units. Laurel Hill turned out to be a "slaughter pen," as one of Griffin's men described it later. Warren's reluctance to put his men in harm's way was interpreted by Grant—and to some extent by Meade—as a sign of weakness. It was a black eye for Warren at Laurel Hill from which he would not fully recover.

As the curtain came down on the battle of Spotsylvania Court House, the best information available showed that 18,400 Union casualties occurred during fighting and 10,200 Confederates were casualties at Spotsylvania. Senior officer losses on both sides were especially severe as a result of the fighting at the Wilderness and Spotsylvania Court House. Moreover, during the same period, Lee lost his esteemed cavalry commander J. E. B. Stuart, who was killed in a separate action at Yellow Tavern, Virginia.

Eager to maintain the offensive momentum of the Army of the Potomac, Grant disengaged from positions near Lee's line and began a march to swing around the right flank of the Army of Northern Virginia in hopes that Lee would rise to the bait by leaving his fortifications near Spotsylvania and attack the Union on open ground. Lee did not accommodate him. On May 21, Lee learned from his cavalry that the Army of the Potomac was on the move and might possibly threaten the intersection of two Confederate supply lines to Richmond at Hanover Junction. The Army of Northern Virginia left its fortifications at Spotsylvania and marched quickly south to protect the railroad junction stopping near the North Anna River on the morning of May 22.

On the same day, Meade sent Warren's corps down Telegraph Road toward the north side of the North Anna River along with Wright's corps. Meade had deep misgivings about confronting Lee at the North Anna River, but Grant had no reservations and ordered the move south to the river over Meade's objections. Grant's relentless pursuit of Lee had political motivations. The general in chief did not need any reminders from the civilian leadership in Washington that the November presidential election was growing near and that a demonstrable victory over Lee was required to improve Lincoln's standing going into the election.

Grant's own reputation also needed bolstering. The spring campaign thus far had yielded no military breakthroughs for the Union army but had resulted in huge numbers of Federal casualties with many of the wounded sent to Washington turning that city into a growing, highly visible hospital ward that was a grim reminder of Grant's campaign in Virginia.

As Warren's Fifth Corps moved south toward the North Anna River, he and his staff were bedeviled by inaccurate maps of the area. Nonexistent roads and bridges were depicted, distances were not to scale, and other essential details bore little relation to the reality of the terrain. To speed their progress on the march south, Warren split his corps in two: Griffin's and Crawford's divisions proceeded on a western route; Cutler's division took a more eastern route.

Despite poor maps and periodic shelling by errant Confederate artillery units, the Union army proceeded down Telegraph Road reaching the North

Anna River by the morning of May 23. Hancock's Second Corps troops took control of the Telegraph Road Bridge over the river while Warren's troops headed upstream of the Second Corps to cross at Jericho Mills. (Their maps showed a bridge at Jericho Mills, but no bridge existed.) Warren's corps, with Griffin's division in the lead, rambled to the river looking for a likely spot to ford with the help of a civilian guide.

Warren's men forded the river and set up camp on the south side of the North Anna. As part of Grant's objective to have his army positioned in a line five miles long and stretching along the river facing Hanover Station, Warren was ordered to hold the south bank of the river at Jericho Mills ford. Once all the troops in Warren's corps had crossed and formed up, they busied themselves building entrenchments and preparing for their evening meal. After the last Fifth Corps unit crossed the river, the 50th New York engineers came behind them and put in place a 160-foot-long pontoon bridge to facilitate subsequent crossings.

The Union troops' crossing had not gone unnoticed by the Confederates. A. P. Hill ordered an attack to commence before dark using Major General Cadmus Wilcox's division, made up of Carolinians and Georgians. The Union troops were taken by surprise by the advancing Confederates. Warren quickly provided reinforcements to plug the gap opened by Colonel William Robinson's Iron Brigade. The Confederates did not press their advantage of surprise. This hesitation gave the Union reinforcements an opportunity to strengthen the line, and the Confederate assault soon collapsed. (Later Lee would chastise A. P. Hill for his lack of aggressiveness at Jericho Mills: "Why did you not do what Jackson would have done—thrown your whole force upon these people and driven them back?")

The next day Lee and his generals devised a brilliant scheme to array Confederate forces in the shape of an inverted V with the point on the North Anna River at Ox Ford—still held by the Army of Northern Virginia—midway between Jericho Mills and the Telegraph Road Bridge. This formation effectively cut Grant's line into three sections, which would allow Lee to concentrate his forces against the elements of a divided Union line. Further strengthening the Confederate position, Lee's men had constructed formidable fortifications that made a Union assault very risky.

On the evening of May 24, Union troops—Burnside's Ninth Corps—were thrashed during an engagement at Ox Ford in the driving rain. The Union Second Corps received a similar drubbing that included hand-to-hand combat. Scattered skirmishes occurred over the next two days before Grant decided to withdraw and head toward the Confederate capital. As Grant marched "on to Richmond" Lee was incapacitated by illness and made no attempt to spring the trap he had set at North Anna for Grant. The general in chief and his Army of the Potomac moved on to the next way station on their drive to bring a rapid conclusion to the war. The next stop in Grant's drive toward his goal of crushing Lee: Cold Harbor.

> In the opinion of a majority of its survivors, the battle of Cold Harbor never should have been fought. There was no military reason to justify it. It was the dreary, dismal, bloody, ineffective close of the Lieutenant-General's first campaign with the Army of the Potomac, and corresponded in all its essential features with what had preceded it. . . . No great or substantial success had been achieved at any point.
> —Brevet Major General Martin T. McMahon, Army of the Potomac

> I have always regretted that the last assault at Cold Harbor was ever made . . . At Cold Harbor no advantage whatever was gained to compensate for the heavy loss we sustained.
> —Lieutenant General Ulysses S. Grant, *Personal Memoirs*

Starting on June 1, Union and Confederate forces fought a series of inconclusive battles to control the crossroads at Cold Harbor. On June 3, at first light, after an evening of drenching rain, the Union Second, Sixth, and recently arrived Eighteenth Corps, under the command of Major General William Smith, began an attack on the Confederate lines. Union troops got within fifty yards of the Confederate breastworks before the Confederates opened fire with artillery and muskets. The men of Hancock's highly regarded Second Corps were mowed down in a hailstorm of Confederate lead. One participant from a New York regiment reported: "It could not be called a battle. It was simply a butchery, lasting only 10 minutes."

At the conclusion of Cold Harbor hostilities, there were 13,000 Union casualties, resulting in a total for the entire campaign—May 5 to June 3—of 50,000 men. The Confederates 5,000 casualties at Cold Harbor, bringing their May/June total to about 30,000 men. Despite an outcome judged to be a stalemate by most, Grant took heart that he had driven Lee and his army out of their strong defensive line, nudged the Confederate troops closer, to Richmond, and, at the same time, significantly reduced the Confederate general's options to maneuver.

The Regiment—155th Pennsylvania Infantry

> The sun, in blood-red splendor, as if ominous of the dreadful carnage which was soon to follow in the dense entanglement of the jungle in which Grant's

entire army was soon to become enmeshed, was pouring his slanting beams through the openings in the woods so richly clad in the green robes of early summer.

—*Under the Maltese Cross*

On Sunday, May 3, Brigadier General Romeyn Ayres's brigade, including the 155th Pennsylvania, the 91st Pennsylvania, and the 140th and 146th New York Regiments along with seven regiments of U.S. Regulars, halted their march from winter encampment near Culpeper. Expecting to stay the night, the troops had begun making preparations to bed down for the evening when, at eleven o'clock, the regimental bugle sounded, signaling that they would soon be required to be on the march again. By daylight the next morning, Ayres's brigade—the 155th Regiment in the lead—had begun crossing the pontoon bridges at Germanna Ford on its way down the Germanna Plank Road.

Sheridan's cavalry swept the area for Confederate pickets—dislodging a handful—and made the river crossing and road on the other side of the ford free from rebel activity. The regiment was halted at the intersection of the Germanna Plank Road and the Orange Turnpike to let the supply wagons catch up. There, in the temperate afternoon air, the men began building cooking fires and preparing their meals while several brass bands assigned to the Regular units began to play familiar, inspiring music. It was an idyllic setting that held no hint of the horror that would swoop down on Ayres's brigade within the next twenty-four hours. As darkness closed in around them, there was no evidence of the enemy; the only sounds were "the song of the whippoor-will and the occasional screeching owl," according to the regimental history. The troops quickly came to appreciate that the "impenetrable jungles and undergrowth of saplings" that defined the Wilderness were no place to maneuver infantry, artillery, or cavalry.

At dawn, orders came down that a move was to begin. Ayres's brigade was put in the advance and headed west on the Orange Turnpike. The 140th New York was positioned on the front line of battle on the left along with elements of the Regulars on the right. The second line, directly behind them, was made up of the 146th New York on the left and the 91st and 155th Pennsylvania Regiments behind the Regulars on the right. Combat being regarded as imminent, the men in the two battle lines left their knapsacks to be guarded while they made an assault. At noon the order to march was given, and the two lines moved forward without talking; the only accompanying sound was the rattle of tin cups, bayonets, and canteens as the troops pushed their way through the tangle of brush and woods.

Soon the advancing battle lines reached the Union pickets, then encountered Confederate skirmishers, who fell back as the men of Ayres's brigade moved slowly and deliberately through the brush and woods of the Wilderness. Within minutes the brigade came to a clearing in the woods. Saunders' Field—an uncultivated old cornfield about four hundred yards deep and eight hundred yards wide—lay before them. The undulating ground of the field rose to a crest where Confederate infantrymen were positioned, waiting for the Yankee assault.

As the first Union troops entered the field, the men at the crest opened fire with devastating effect. The commanding officer of the 140th New York, Colonel George Ryan, ordered his men down so that they could fix bayonets for the assault across the field to the crest. The call to advance was given, and the first battle line of Ayres's brigade swarmed across Saunders' Field toward the Rebel position on the hill, a position split by the Orange Turnpike running west.

From their fortifications on the crest of Saunders' Field, Ewell's Confederate riflemen poured volley after volley of musket fire into the ranks of Ayres's two battle lines. The 140th New York swung slightly to the left toward the turnpike; the U.S. Regulars, on the right, moved straight ahead into the Rebel fire.

Griffin, seeing his battle lines withering under heavy fire as they struggled to cross Saunders' Field, ordered a battery of the First New York Light Artillery up to take some of the pressure off his infantry. The artillery men, coping as best they could with Confederate sharpshooters perched in the trees, eventually were able to unlimber their field pieces and began firing across the field. Rounds of grape shot and canister shells fell upon Rebel defenders and attacking Yankees indiscriminately.

The second battle line, including the 155th, was ordered into the fray, and Warren, knowing that Griffin's men were taking a beating, shifted Colonel Jacob Sweitzer's brigade to reinforce Ayres's men. Saunders' Field was now filled with Zouaves, some moving forward under heavy fire, others scattered in an attempt to find cover from the Confederate fusillade. The wounded, dead, and dying covered the field, their bright red-and-blue Zouave uniforms contrasting sharply with the tawny colored ground beneath them. The 140th New York, first on the field, was "melting away like snow," one survivor said later. The air was filled with the din of musket and artillery fire; a thick, white smoke settled over the battleground and shrouded the participants. Sweitzer's troops moved up the south side of the Orange Turnpike. Like Ayres's brigade on the north side of the turnpike, Sweitzer's brigade came under heavy fire, yet it maintained forward momentum and pushed back the Confederate line.

On the north side of the turnpike, the men of Ayres's brigade began to pull back. Disorganization and confusion among the Confederate ranks allowed the 155th to withdraw successfully to their lines and to bring many of the wounded back. The survivors of the 155th regrouped behind Union lines and assessed the damage to their unit. Both officers and men of the 155th agreed, "[We had] not been whipped, but simply overwhelmed by the enemy."

During the evening of May 5, members of the 155th began digging entrenchments in their newly formed lines as the glow of fires continued in the wooded areas where they had been ignited during the day's battle by musket sparks and artillery fire. Many men from Griffin's division were unaccounted for—including some from the 155th—presumably incinerated in the fires that has sprung up on the battlefield.

Men from the 155th were deployed as skirmishers that evening. While on the skirmish line, they could hear the sound of the Confederates felling trees and digging to strengthen their fortifications. At dawn the skirmishers from the 155th watched as the Rebels opposite them formed a battle line and began advancing. The 155th men opened fire as they began to fall back into the breastworks completed by Ayres's brigade during the night. The Union barrage soon had the Rebels withdrawing, leaving behind a few of their fellow infantrymen, who quickly became prisoners.

By the evening of May 7, it was understood by the men of the 155th that Grant wanted to evacuate the Wilderness area, but unlike his predecessors at Fredericksburg and Chancellorsville, Grant had no desire to retreat and regroup. At 8:30—well after sunset—the men of the Fifth Corps were on the march south to Spotsylvania Court House. It was a race to see whether Grant's forces or Lee's would arrive there first.

The 155th struggled over narrow roads, across small streams, and around obstacles thrown up by the Confederates as they made their all-night forced march toward Spotsylvania Court House. At six o'clock on May 8, after a quick breakfast, the 155th, as part of Griffin's division, formed up to replace Brigadier General John Robinson's division, which had been repulsed by Confederates entrenched at Laurel Hill, an area less than two miles from Spotsylvania Court House.

After two attempts, the 155th, as part of Ayres's brigade, succeeded in pushing back the Confederates into the tree line at the crest of Laurel Hill. An enthusiastic Ayres even called out his brass band to provide stirring music to motivate his men. Some remembered "Hail Columbia" being played over the roar of gunfire at Laurel Hill.

During the 155th Regiment's assault on Laurel Hill, Company F commander Captain Edward Clapp was killed; after the fighting stopped, Clapp was buried on the battlefield. (After the war, Clapp's parents visited the grave and had his remains removed to the family cemetery in Massachusetts.)

On Tuesday, May 10, as temperatures climbed to nearly ninety degrees by midafternoon, the 155th spent most of the day in the brigade's breastworks trading occasional fire with the enemy. Later in the afternoon, the 155th was ordered—as part of Ayres's brigade—to drive the Confederates back to their works. The following day was occupied preparing for a major Union assault. The entire Fifth Corps, supported by the Sixth Corps, was to attack the Rebel's works.

On the morning of May 12, Hancock's corps stormed the angle of the salient in the Confederate lines—the "Bloody Angle"—and broke through capturing prisoners and severing the Confederate line. The 155th was brought in to hold the captured works in support of Hancock's men. The regiment, as well as other units in Warren's corps, was required to change positions often in order to counter the enemy's efforts to regain their captured works. On May 21 the Union army abandoned the Spotsylvania Court House area and proceeded southeast toward the North Anna River.

> We marched early in the morning, came to the North Anna River at Jericho Ford and crossed by fording. We came in on a private road, where they did not expect us and where they had only a few pickets. We advanced three-fourths of a mile from the river. Although the skirmishers in front kept pipping away we did not apprehend any trouble. We lay about carelessly and at 6 p.m. many of us had coffee made, meat fried and were just ready to eat supper when we were ordered to fall in . . . Before that was done, we heard the Rebel yell and knew what that meant.
>
> —First Sergeant D. P. Marshall, Company K155th Pennsylvania Volunteers, May 23, 1864

The 155th Pennsylvania Regiment forded the North Anna from the north bank rather than wait for the engineers to build bridges with pontoons being carried on the Union wagon train that followed them. Once across, the troops quickly established a skirmish line on the south side of the river and began driving out the Confederate outposts to positions farther south of the river. The opposition they faced in crossing and moving forward (although light), coupled with their exhaustion after a grueling march, made them welcome the chance to set up camp, prepare supper, and relax.

Muskets were stacked, cook gear was in use, and the men were savoring a warm meal and a respite for their sore feet when there was an urgent call to "fall in" immediately followed by the now-familiar Rebel yell as Confederates swarmed across the field in front of them. Local farm animals—hogs, sheep, cattle, and ducks—flushed out by the advancing Confederates, preceded the attackers in a barnyard stampede. Reacting quickly, the men of the 155th collected their muskets and prepared for the onslaught by taking up firing positions along a quickly formed line. The regiment advanced up to their pickets and pushed back the Confederates' frequent attempts to storm the Union position. General Ayres personally led the advance of his brigade and rallied the troops around the Fifth Corps flag.

Generals Grant and Meade commended the members of the Fifth Corps, Griffin's division, and Ayres's brigade for their performance in standing firm against the surprise attacks. Praise even came from an unlikely source, according to D. P. Marshall in his memoirs: "Our Brigade was sometimes called Ayres's Regulars. Rebel prisoners said they called it the 'Stonewall Brigade' which, of course, we received as flattering to us."[1]

At the end of May, the 155th Pennsylvania, as part of the Army of the Potomac, headed for the crossroads of Cold Harbor, the next stop in Grant's continuing strategy to pursue Lee and crush his army. One member of the regiment would sit out this next phase of the "Overland Campaign" as he recuperated from a wound received at North Anna River: Sergeant George McClelland.

The Soldier—George P. McClelland

> "We fought the fight in detachments,
> Sallying forth we fought at several points, but in each the
> luck was against us,
> Our foe advancing, steadily getting the best of it, push'd us
> back to the works on this hill,
> Till we turn'd menacing here, and then he left us."
>   —Walt Whitman, "The Centenarian's Story"

After an April that brought snow and intermittent rain along with cool temperatures, May arrived "fair and lovely," as one of the men in the 155th praised the beginning of the month. As the midday temperature climbed to sixty degrees and above, George McClelland also observed that the roads surrounding camp were drying out and would soon reach a state where the Army of the Potomac could move its men, horses, supply wagons, and gun carriages without fear of getting bogged down in the red Virginia clay.

On the afternoon of May 4, McClelland, his company, his regiment, his division, and his corps were marching across pontoon bridges over the Rapidan River and down Germanna Plank Road. After countless prior pontoon crossings, the men were becoming proficient at maintaining stability while moving quickly across the bobbing structures.

Continuing down the road, McClelland and his fellow Fifth Corps men could not help but savor the beauty of the spring day and be awed by the massive blue-clad army—some said the largest army ever assembled—that moved confidently and inexorably, regimental flags waving, gun barrels gleaming, toward its inevitable rendezvous with the Army of Northern Virginia.

Just before noon on May 5, McClelland with his regiment lined up behind the Regular units of Ayres's brigade. To his left were all the other members of the Zouave Brigade. The units were ordered forward at noon. McClelland and his company struggled through dense thicket that tore at their uniforms and made an orderly formation impossible. Soon the sound of metal against metal—tin cups, bayonets, canteens—was punctuated by the sound of musket fire coming from the area directly in front of them. As they broke out of the woods and into a field, the men automatically dressed ranks, stopping to fire and reload as they proceeded forward. The pace picked up to double-quick as they plunged across Saunders' Field, their shoes crunching the stalks that were scattered across the old corn patch. Puffs of smoke appeared at the crest of the rise to the west of the field ahead of them where the Confederates were entrenched. The puffs grew more numerous as the Rebel infantry and sharpshooters began to focus their fire on the two lines of Ayres's men entering Saunders' Field.

As the 155th moved forward, the Confederates on their right moved around them. Within minutes, the 155th was receiving the infantryman's worst nightmare—sustained enfilade fire into their ranks. Whether in fear or anger or a combination of both emotions, men shouted and screamed as the opposing armies came together. McClelland and his company stepped over the fallen bodies of the men they had been following across the field—the 140th and 146th New Yorkers. Artillery fire sent a shower of twigs and broken branches down on them. Almost immediately the 155th realized that the fire was from their own artillery behind them.

The tumultuous engagement caused both sides to become disorganized in the "pandemonium of horrid sounds and panorama of awful scenes."[2] The men of the 155th were able to take advantage of the Confederate confusion to withdraw to their lines. When he had an opportunity to assess the losses, McClelland found that five of his company had received serious wounds. (One subsequently died of his wound; three were discharged due to the seriousness of their wounds; and one was transferred to the Veteran Reserves to serve in a limited duty role.)

Along with the remainder of Ayres's brigade, the 155th pulled back into breastworks that it then occupied for several days awaiting its next assignment. While there were plans and preparations for additional assaults, nothing materialized. The battle of the Wilderness had ended for Sergeant McClelland.

On the afternoon of Saturday, May 7, the Army of the Potomac was on the move again. As much as Sergeant George McClelland appreciated General Grant's aggressiveness in pursuing the enemy, it required all Sergeant McClelland's leadership skills to motivate the men of Company F on a forced march to Spotsylvania Court House, fifteen miles to the south, in what was sure to be a race between the Confederates and the Federals. All the men of the 155th were exhausted by two days of fighting, and now it was clear that they were heading into the teeth of another firestorm as they lured Lee's men out of their defensive positions.

In the vicinity of Spotsylvania Court House, Warren ordered Brigadier John Robinson's division toward what was thought to be Confederate cavalry units. The division proceeded past a farmhouse owned by Sarah Spindle, toward an open field, and up a rise known as Laurel Hill. From his position behind Robinson's men, George McClelland watched as two brigades of Robinson's division worked their way up Laurel Hill. At the brow of the hill—where a woods joined the open field—McClelland could see a breastwork that appeared to be fashioned of logs and rail fence sections.

A volley of fire erupted from the crest of the hill, yet it appeared that Robinson's men would succeed in overrunning the breastworks due to their numerical superiority over a modest Confederate contingent. Then, suddenly, as Robinson's men drew closer to the summit of the hill, an enormous fusillade of fire poured into their ranks. General Robinson dropped from his horse amid his men. To the cacophony of musket fire was added the boom of Confederate artillery. Through the din came orders for Ayres's unit—the 155th in the lead along with U.S. Regulars—to join the fray. Behind them the brigade's brass band started to play "Hail Columbia."

As they advanced toward the front, the most devastating fire was coming not from the front of their line, but from the left flank. Like a murderous hailstorm, minié balls raked their ranks. Ahead of McClelland's company, Colonel George Ryan of the 140th New York—who had so valiantly led his men at Saunders' Field three days earlier and escaped without a scratch—was hit several times with such force that he was propelled from his horse and lay sprawled on the field. Also killed during the engagement was Captain Edward Clapp, company commander of McClelland's unit, Company F.

Slowly the Union advance was losing steam, and men started to break ranks and fall back toward the Union lines. Soon the flood tide of Union troops moving forward became an ebb tide as the word came from regimental and brigade leadership to begin a withdrawal from the hill.

The youth was not conscious that he was erect upon his feet. He did not know the direction of the ground. Indeed, once he even lost the habit of balance and fell heavily. He was up again immediately. One thought went through the chaos of his brain at the time. He wondered if he had fallen because he had been shot.

—Stephen Crane, *The Red Badge of Courage*

With the death of Captain Clapp at Laurel Hill, George McClelland was given interim day-to-day command of Company F of the 155th Regiment until other arrangements could be made. McClelland's ambition for advancement was tempered by the grief he was suffering over Edward Clapp's death. The captain had been highly respected, a model leader, and McClelland thought of him as a friend as well as his superior officer. When he fell at Laurel Hill, the captain was carrying papers for a leave of absence so he could be married.

By midmorning on May 23, the Fifth Corps had reached Mt. Carmel Church, just east of the North Anna River where the Confederates were presumed to be encamped. Meade's plan was to have Hancock's Second Corps cross the North Anna at Chesterfield Bridge and the Fifth Corps cross upriver from Hancock's men at Jericho Mills.

As part of Ayres's brigade of the First Division, the 155th Regiment was one of the first units to cross the North Anna. McClelland and the troops waded the 150-foot-wide river at Jericho Mills. The current there was swift, but the bottom was firm and the depth never over four feet. While confusing maps and lack of current experience of their guide caused some concern, the crossing was completed without incident other than an irate local landowner complaining about Union troops stealing vegetables on their march though his lands to the river.

Once the entire Fifth Corps was across the river and formed up in a defensive line facing south, thoughts turned to preparing dinner as late afternoon slipped into early evening. Several pigs wandering in the nearby woods did not escape the attention of McClelland or his men. If not immediately taken for a pork roast, they raised the prospect of a future banquet.

Thoughts of roasted pork and hot coffee soon vanished when McClelland and his men saw farm animals being flushed by advancing Rebels out of the woods directly in front of them. McClelland's men grabbed their stacked arms and took cover behind the just-erected entrenchments. As the enemy advanced toward them, screaming the Rebel yell, McClelland and his company poured round after round into the charging Confederates, thankful that this time they were in the defensive position behind breastworks.

Over his shoulder, McClelland and his unit heard the distinctive, gruff voice of General Griffin bellowing: "Sock it into them boys! Give them regular hell . . . Pay them up for the 5th and 12th!"[3] (referring to Saunders' Field and Laurel Hill).

Ayres' and Sweitzer's brigades held firm and beat back the Confederate assault. During the fighting, Private Theodore Baldwin of Company F—a fellow "Luny" from Pittsburgh—was struck by a round coming from the increased Confederate fire on the right. Then, as he was performing his new duties as company commander, George McClelland was hit in the foot by a minié ball.

The gunshot wound to McClelland's right foot near the heel caused substantial blood loss, but the flow of blood had an important benefit—it kept the wound free from infection in its early stages. McClelland was removed from the North Anna battlefield to be treated at the Fifth Corps field hospital. Diagnosis: *Vulnera sclopetarius*—wound cause by a single minié ball.

After five days in the field hospital, McClelland was sent to Second Division (Fifth Corps) hospital in Alexandria, Virginia, and then, on June 2, moved to the Union General Hospital in New York City. During the time he was in New York, McClelland began walking with the aid of crutches and, later, a cane. Following nearly a month in the New York hospital at Fort Columbus, including fifteen days' furlough in the city, McClelland was sent to the general hospital in his hometown of Pittsburgh, where he was treated on an outpatient basis. By July 29, just over two months following his wound at North Anna, McClelland was judged fit for duty and was transferred back to F Company of the 155th Pennsylvania, now located outside Petersburg, Virginia. During his two- month absence, Sergeant McClelland missed the battle at Cold Harbor.

Private Theodore Baldwin of Company F was less fortunate than McClelland. He died of the wound he received at North Anna River on May 23, 1864. His burial site is unknown.

In His Own Words—The Letters of George McClelland

Warrenton Junction, Virginia
April 23, 1864

Dear Lizzie,

Your welcome letter of April 13th is at hand and in reply would say "move." I believe this Army has got "move" on the brain. Talk about the inalienable rights of man, or discuss the lost planet, I don't care what the subject is, it's all the same, swallowed up in the simple verb "move." I "move"; thou or you "moveth"; he "moves"; we "move"; you "move"; they "move." After it's conjugated, it's not so terrible a thing after all. The world moves—why shouldn't the Army of the Potomac move? Well, I'll hurry on—I was going to say "move."

The Army is stripped of all useless appendages and I am sure every good soldier wants to go in and win and send the hell-born Confederacy where it was conceived. The campaign has opened inauspiciously for us. The news of Banks' defeat comes like lightning on the fiendish massacre at Fort Pillow. And I am not very sanguine of the victory here in Virginia.

I can't get it into my thick noddle that Grant is the man. I want to believe and hope he is, but there it is. I cannot explain it.

It's a fearful crises has come upon the Nation. The best blood of the Country has been shed. God grant the sacrifice is sufficient, for the patriots are needed at home. The ravings of the traitorous Copperheads must be silenced. Public opinion must be molded and kept in the right channel. The people must be taught, next to God, to reverence their Country. This is the work devolving on the flower of the Nation now in the field.

My congratulations on the birth of another man child. Why is my third nephew called "Wilson"? Is it after the Massachusetts Senator? I took it for grant-ed it would be "Ulysses" after the fashion of the world. George Washington McFinegan, William Pitt O'Flaherty. Any number of these great men can be found on the line of a projected railroad or an incipient canal. If their names don't go down to posterity, still they are no less the benefactors of the race.

You say, Lizzie, that a certain night in the autumn of 1862 was "the saddest night you ever passed." Say rather, "the proudest night of your life," for on that night your Brother went forth to battle for the honor, the integrity, yes, the very existence of this great Union.

I hope, Lizzie, you don't show my scribbling out of the family. I don't indulge in endearing epithets, never consulted the "polite letter writer" as my correspondents are all of the male gender, excepting two dear sisters. (This is to palliate my bluntness.)

When I next write, it will be from a different locality and if I was not like a heavily-burdened mule on the march, I might give you some "wayside jottings", "life in the open air" experiences. But a fellow gets so confounded tired that nothing interests him, oblivious of everything but self and that self's comfort. "There's where Washington's mother was buried." Sotto voce—"Let her RIP." "There's the house in which President Monroe lived." "Who cares?"

Well, Lizzie, my candle is bout flickering out, so I'll flicker likewise. My love to Anna, Tom and the "b-hoys."

With undiminished affection,
Your Brother,
George P.

Notes on the April 23, 1864, Letter

By late April, when McClelland wrote this letter, the worst of the rains had occurred, and Virginia's roads were drying out, fit, once again, for an army on the move. The expectation of starting the spring offensive was palpable (and conjugated!) in McClelland's letter to his sister in Davenport.

Major General Nathaniel P. ("Nothing Positive") Banks had floundered in the western theater of war at the beginning of the Red River Campaign in Louisiana, and there was shocking news about Fort Pillow: At this Union garrison on the Mississippi River, Confederate General Nathan Bedford Forrest's men killed black soldiers after they surrendered. The infamous "Fort Pillow Massacre" occurred on April 12, just eleven days before McClelland wrote his letter.

Perhaps it is understandable that McClelland had reservations about Grant. The odds, at that date, were not in the general's favor: Neither McClellan, Burnside, Hooker, nor Meade had been able to whip Robert E. Lee and his outnumbered Army of Northern Virginia.

Peace Democrats or "Copperheads" were becoming more active and outspoken as the national elections drew closer. Molding public opinion in wartime was a tall order for any president, but Lincoln knew well that some unambiguous Union victories would go a long way to fueling positive public opinion for support of the war. The "work devolving on the flower of the Nation now in the field" acknowledged that the pressure was on the Union army to renew its efforts to beat the Confederate forces at every opportunity.

Department of the Monongahela
Friday, June 17, 1864

Dear Sister Lizzie,

Here I am at home once more. In consequence of the severe service rendered and the great losses suffered (being cut up dreadfully), I have been placed in reserve. Old Grant told me to go home and rest myself awhile.

"I could a tale unfold, would harrow up thy very soul, freeze thy young blood, etc." but I won't unfold it. All I would say is that after 19 consecutive days of fighting, the enemy succeeded in inflicting a slight wound. For about two weeks I could not walk. Now I get around without the aid of either crutch or stick.

Well, Lizzie, I must tell you that after being confined in New York Harbor some days, I managed to procure a leave of 15 days. (If it had been 60 you may be sure I would not have halted until I reached Davenport.) Left New York on the night of the 15th. I had been sight-seeing all day—Central Park, "Barnum," etc., etc.

Arrived at noon yesterday. Surprised the folks somewhat. Was shocked myself to find another brave boy had gone—poor John Mackin. I attend his funeral today. I have been received very kindly here by everyone, but my thoughts and desires are with the gallant remnant left before Richmond.

Let brotherly love continue. I have not time to write more just now.

Ever your devoted Brother,
George

(Love to all.)

Notes on the June 17, 1864, Letter

Three weeks after he was wounded and had been treated in four hospitals, George wrote to his sister once again. He was vague about his battlefield experience and how he came to be wounded, relying on a quote from Shakespeare's *Hamlet*, act I, scene 5, to communicate the horror of the Overland Campaign: "I could a tale unfold whose lightest word / would harrow up thy soul, freeze thy young blood, / make thy two eyes, like stars, start from their spheres."

He spent some of his time in New York City as a tourist, visiting Central Park and the P.T. Barnum exhibit.

Upon his return to Pittsburgh, he learned of Corporal John Mackin's death. Mackin enlisted with McClelland, was one of the original "Lunies" from Pittsburgh, and was the son of "Uncle John" who was able to accompany his boy up to the crossing of the Rappahannock prior to the battle of Fredericksburg. Macklin had been wounded at Gettysburg but returned to his unit where he served until the battle of the Wilderness. He was wounded during the assault at Saunders' Field on May 5 and died of his wound at the General Hospital in Washington, D.C., on June 12, 1864.

Department of the Susquehanna
USA General Hospital
Pittsburgh, Pennsylvania
July 3, 1864

Dear Sister Lizzie,

Your kindly sympathizing letter was received some days ago and I am constrained to ask your forgiveness for this dilatory reply.

I was very glad you had reconsidered your intention to fly all the way to Pittsburgh to see me, for although it would be my greatest joy to behold my dear Sister Lizzie, yet under the circumstances, it would not be right for you to make the journey. My only regret is that I did not procure a leave for a longer time (which I might have done), but it was not to be so. And I am confident that the time is not far distant when there will be a meeting of joy and gladness of loving brothers and sisters.

I told you, Lizzie, about being furloughed from New York. When my time expired, I reported at the hospital at this place—for I thought that not being well, I might as well be near home as lying in hospital in New York.

There are over 700 patients—nearly all wounded—here and it is very much crowded. Buildings, sheds and tents all full. The accommodations being very poor, I asked the privilege of remaining at home, merely reporting at stated intervals, but the Surgeon in Charge would not grant it. So, as the next best thing, I was admitted to the office assisting in the business and since I have been treated first rate.

I eat my meals in a nicely furnished room with the Hospital Steward and Chief Clerk—regular hotel fare—and go home every evening and go out in the morning. So you see, Lizzie, I have a pretty good time. My foot is healing slowly and I am in good health. Expect to go back to the Regiment about the 10th of this month.

I will be "in at the death" yet. I think that is the reason of the delay in taking Richmond. Grant is waiting for me. It is curious—the sympathy existing of a soldier for his comrades. I can't feel contented, nor won't be, until I am back with my boys. I left them without a commander and that is the reason I am so anxious concerning them. Our dear Captain, the noblest soul I ever met, Edward E. Clapp, we lost in the 3rd day's engagement and I am the senior officer although without as yet a commission.

Well, Lizzie, excuse this note. My thanks are due Brother Tom for his kind and prompt intentions in my behalf. So goodbye. Love and greetings to Anna and the boys.

Devotedly, Your Brother,
George

Notes on the July 3, 1864, Letter

McClelland had negotiated a situation where he could sleep at home then report for duty at the general hospital in Pittsburgh as he performed clerical tasks during his recovery. Since the hospital was at or near capacity, McClelland's offer to lodge at home provided some relief to hospital administrators trying to accommodate the growing number of wounded.

McClelland once again mentioned his desire to be back among his fellow 155th Pennsylvanians. The power of serving with comrades with whom you "have shared the incommunicable experience of war"—as veteran Oliver Wendell Holmes Jr. expressed it—was a powerful draw for McClelland to return to his unit and finish the task he had begun in August 1862.

The death of Captain Edward Clapp at Laurel Hill on May 8 resulted in McClelland being selected to lead Company F until he became a casualty at North Anna. Now McClelland would return as a commissioned officer (after the requisite authorization from officials in the state capital in Harrisburg, Pennsylvania).

McClelland had served with Edward Clapp since his enlistment in 1862. Wounded at Fredericksburg as a first lieutenant, Clapp returned to his regiment and company after his recovery and was promoted to captain in November 1863. McClelland respected Captain Clapp's leadership style, his bravery, and his character (Clapp being "the noblest soul" he ever met). Clapp, McClelland, and others from the company enjoyed singing together during the winter encampment of 1863/1864. In the 155th regimental history, Clapp is referred to as "a model officer . . . who cared for the men of his Company."

Chapter Twelve

"Hold on with a Bull Dog Grip"

Petersburg, July—September 1864

The Army of the Potomac

> The Army of the Potomac was given the investment of Petersburg, while the Army of the James held Bermuda Hundred and all the ground we possessed north of the James River. The 9th Corps, Burnside's, was placed upon the right at Petersburg; the 5th, Warren's, next; the 2nd, Birney's, next; then the 6th, Wright's, broken off to the left and south. Thus began the siege of Petersburg.
> —Lieutenant General Ulysses S. Grant, *Personal Memoirs*

The Overland campaign, fought from early May to early June at four contiguous locations—the Wilderness, Spotsylvania Court House, the North Anna River, and Cold Harbor—had cost the Army of the Potomac 54,000 casualties (compared to the Army of Northern Virginia's 32,000) and resulted in little tangible success. Union ranks were depleted, the men's fighting spirit—from top to bottom of the corps—was drained, and the pervasive feeling in the North was that the war could drag on inconclusively for years to come. The dog days of summer for the Army of the Potomac in the field at Petersburg were matched by the dog days in the political climate in the north as the presidential election of 1864 drew closer.

To the west, Sherman was gearing up for a campaign to Atlanta while, in the east, Grant was making plans to disengage from Cold Harbor and focus his

Army of the Potomac on Petersburg, a vital hub for rail lines serving Richmond. Sever the rail lines that supplied the Confederates in their capital, Grant reasoned, and he could choke off the city and bring about an early end to the war, perhaps giving Lincoln a battlefield victory and a fighting chance in the autumn election.

On June 14, the army began to transport troops using the James River. Grant, wanting to keep steady pressure on Lee's forces, ordered the Eighteenth Corps under Major General William ("Baldy") Smith and Hancock's Second Corps to attack the Confederate lines surrounding Petersburg. The Eighteenth Corps moved very slowly toward its objective while the Second Corps did not receive clear communication regarding its role in the attack. Consequently, the Eighteenth Corps went into the attack on the eastern side of the Confederate line at Petersburg on its own.

When they finally did attack the Rebel entrenchments at Petersburg, Baldy Smith's men succeeded in capturing over a mile of the Confederate line. Despite the unit's significant advantage in troop strength and its penetration of the line, Smith believed that the Confederates were quickly feeding in reinforcements and would soon surpass his numbers of troops. The sporadic Union attacks that followed on June 16 were all repulsed by the Confederates who were growing in strength by the hour.

Additional troops from the Ninth Corps were sent in to strengthen the Federal lines, but it was to no avail. On June 18, General Pierre G. T. Beauregard's Confederates, though outnumbered, were able to throw the Union troops into disorder. Disorder led to confusion; confusion led to disaster; and disaster led to defeat. After four days of fighting, Union losses totaled 10,000 men. While the Confederates had an impressive defensive position in place to fend off Union assaults on Petersburg and Richmond, the Federals had taken control of two of the five railroad lines that supplied Petersburg—the Petersburg and Norfolk Railroad and City Point Railroad.

Meanwhile, Grant was using his artillery to shell Petersburg. Beginning on June 16, artillery units took the city under fire, causing thousands of civilians to abandon their homes and flee to the surrounding countryside. Among the guns eventually used was one called the "Dictator," a 13-inch mortar capable of firing 200-pound shells up to two and one-half miles.

July was spent digging trenches at the Union lines. Midday temperatures remained in the nineties for most of the month—soldiers called the heat "oppressive" in diaries and letters. The heat and an absence of rain turned the entrenching activities into dusty, baking exercises involving prolonged physical exertion. Men collapsed from the heat, and a few even died from acute heatstroke. The troops on both sides were plagued by flies, chiggers, ticks, and lice that thrived in the Virginia summer heat.

As the surface digging came to a close, another form of digging was getting under way under the direction of Lieutenant Colonel Henry Pleasants. Manned by a contingent of coal miners from Schuykill County, Pennsylvania, Pleasants's 48th Pennsylvania Regiment recommended that a tunnel be dug up to and under the Confederate lines and that it then be mined with gun powder. Pleasants took the idea to Burnside who, in turn, sent the idea up the chain of command with his concurrence. Meade had reservations, and he decided to pass the idea up to Grant with a lukewarm endorsement. After Meade and Grant gave their approval to proceed, Burnside developed a battle plan that involved sending in his black troops after the mine exploded, allowing them to demonstrate their prowess in battle and the military skills they had developed through extensive training and drilling.

Dawn on July 30 was set as the detonation time. Four tons of gunpowder, packed into a gallery, lay at the end of a tunnel that stretched 511 feet and ended beneath the Confederate line. The fuse was lit. It fizzled, requiring two miner volunteers to reenter the tunnel to investigate. Finding that the fuse had failed at a splice, they relit the fuse and quickly exited.

Far more consequential than the failed fuse, was Meade's decision, before the detonation, to change the order of battle. He wanted the white divisions under Burnside to go in first, not the black division. General Grant later testified before the Committee on the Conduct of the War that he agreed to a change in the order of the divisions sent in because he was concerned that the military and northern civilians alike would think that the black unit was sent in first because it was considered expendable. Others argued that Meade lacked confidence in the black troops and had orchestrated the change. Regardless of the motivation, the result was disastrous for black and white Union troops alike.

Further compounding the ill-advised decision to change the lead unit prior to the explosion and subsequent attack was the choice of which white division was to go first. The division—untrained in how to conduct the attack once the explosion had taken place—was under Brigadier General James Ledlie, an officer with an acute fondness for strong drink.

The explosion created a crater 170 feet long, 60 feet wide, and 30 feet deep—over 11,300 cubic yards of earth—that stunned Confederates and Union troops alike. Ledlie's men stumbled into the smoke-filled crater and failed to mount a coordinated flank attack. Rather than being at the front with his troops, Ledlie was reported to be in the rear with a bottle.

A second white division followed closely on the heels of the first division and was, itself, followed by a third. All failed to break through the Confederate line. Finally, the black division was sent in, but by this time the advantage had been lost. From the Federals' standpoint, the assault collapsed quickly, disorder ruled, and desperate hand-to-hand combat for survival was the result. Infuriated Confederates were reported to have bayoneted or shot black soldiers who attempted to surrender in a scene reminiscent of the Fort Pillow Massacre. When the battle of the Crater came to a close, there were 4,000 Union and 2,000 Confederate casualties. Particularly distressing for the Federal troops was the refusal of the Confederate leadership to allow the wounded and dead to be removed from the crater area immediately after the engagement.

> July 31st, PM. Seeing a flag of truce going out from our line toward the Rebel recaptured line, some of us went down that way supposing it was to bring off the dead and wounded, who were still lying between the two lines where they fell in battle . . . but the Rebels inhumanely refused to let us remove them, but permitted the giving of water and stimulants to them. They would not allow any shelter or protection to be put over them to keep off the burning sun. We supposed these requests were refused because they were mostly colored soldiers. The flag of truce returned and we returned to our posts, from which we could see these poor fellows lying there in all their misery.[1]

The afternoon temperature on July 31, 1864, in the Petersburg area was recorded at ninety-eight. On August 1, the Confederates acceded to the Union request for a truce so that the Union might bury their dead and remove any survivors.

In a message sent to Washington after the conclusion of the battle, Grant admitted to Halleck: "It was the saddest affair I have witnessed in the war. Such an opportunity for carrying fortifications I have never seen and do not expect again to have."

Burnside was angered by the decision to replace his black division as the lead unit. The disastrous consequences at the Crater fueled his anger. After the battle he argued with Meade, their mutual recriminations reaching a level just short of physical violence. Following their confrontation, Meade wanted Burnside court-martialed for insubordination, but Grant intervened and offered Burnside home leave to cool down the volatile situation. The distraught Burnside subsequently resigned from the army and returned to his home in Rhode Island, where he prospered in business. (Only forty years old when he left the army, Burnside eventually went into politics and served three terms as governor and two terms as a U.S. Senator from Rhode Island. Never a bitter former general who dwelt on past military decisions or slights, Burnside moved successfully into the civilian world where the Crater became a distant, albeit haunting, memory.)

I have seen your dispatch expressing your unwillingness to break your hold where you are. Neither am I willing. Hold on with a bulldog grip, and chew and choke as much as possible.
—Abraham Lincoln, telegram to Ulysses S. Grant, August 17, 1864

On Thursday, August 18, after a rain-soaked Wednesday, Grant ordered Warren and his Fifth Corps to do some "chewing and choking" at the Weldon railroad line (also known as the Petersburg Railroad). Warren's corps—some 20,000 strong—reached the railroad at Globe Tavern, about four miles south of Petersburg, at 11:00 a.m. Warren then sent two divisions up the Halifax Road toward the city and ordered his remaining troops to begin tearing up the track and disfiguring the rails.

Some of the men Warren had dispatched were seen by Confederate scouts who reported back—incorrectly—that a small Union force was heading north along the Halifax Road. Initially, the Confederates were able to turn back the Federals, but the Union forces rallied and pushed ahead.

Warren operated in the mode of defending his position at the rail line. Grant, on the other hand, had a more aggressive posture in mind. Communicating through Meade, Grant made it clear what Warren's role was to be: Warren was to halt destruction of the Weldon Railroad and to entrench his position, which was now an extension of the Union siege lines.

On August 19, Confederate forces under Beauregard moved some units down the Halifax Road while others were ordered to hit Warren's right flank—an area that they saw as a weak point in the Union line. The flanking units, under the command of Major General William ("Little Billy") Mahone, attacked in the late afternoon and soon overran the Federals. As the sun set, the Confederate units began to lose steam, and they pulled back to Petersburg, leaving the Union force still in position. The fighting resumed the next day, by which time Warren's forces had been strengthened by the addition of two Ninth Corps divisions.

On August 21, Beauregard resumed his assault on the Union position, this time heading toward the Federals' left flank. Despite a fierce attack by the Confederates and the presence of Robert E. Lee on the scene later in the day, the Rebel assault failed. While Union casualties again exceeded Confederate casualties, by 2,000 men, the Army of Northern Virginia had lost strategic ground. A key supply line had been cut; they now had only one remaining rail route to supply Petersburg.

Now that the Union siege line had been extended, Grant sought to resume the task Warren had started of destroying the Weldon rail line. Keeping the Fifth Corps and the units of the Ninth Corps assigned to Warren in place to maintain the siege line, Grant sent Hancock's Second Corps to handle the rail line destruction.

On the afternoon of August 24, Lee sent eight infantry brigades out of Petersburg toward the Union lines. This group linked up with two cavalry divisions south of Globe Tavern and attacked Hancock's men near Reams Station. Hancock's troops, depleted and wearied by earlier fighting in the Overland campaign, quickly folded when pressed by the Rebels. The Confederates were jubilant while Hancock sulked, claiming that his men had received inadequate support from the rest of the Army of the Potomac.

While Grant was making some slow headway in tightening the noose around Petersburg, Sherman was making considerable strides in Georgia. By September 1, Hood and his Rebel forces had evacuated Atlanta, and the next day Union troops marched triumphantly into the city. Sherman telegraphed Washington: "Atlanta is ours, and fairly won."

Only two days prior to the fall of Atlanta, the Democratic convention had ended, and the peace plank of the Democratic election platform, crafted with much zeal in Chicago, started to lose its appeal when Sherman's unequivocal win in Atlanta became known. Even George McClellan, Democratic presidential candidate, backed off his own party's "Peace Platform," not wanting to have to tell Union veterans that the "labor and sacrifice of our slain and wounded brothers had been in vain." On the Republican ticket, Lincoln was no longer a pariah: "The president was now a victorious leader instead of a discredited loser."[2]

Eager to further isolate the Army of Northern Virginia and to cut off the remaining Rebel supply lines, Grant ordered Warren (through Meade) to move two divisions of his Fifth Corps, along with two divisions from the Ninth Corps, west to reach Boydton Plank Road and take control of the South Side Railroad. Proceeding over a narrow corduroy road to reach the plank road, Warren's men ran into a small Confederate cavalry detachment located behind earthworks dug at Peebles' Farm on September 30. Warren's troops easily overran the small enemy unit and halted to regroup and assess their new position. The delay allowed A. P. Hill time to send a division-sized unit from Petersburg to intercept Warren's men. Fighting continued in a series of separate actions in the vicinity of the Jones Farm during the day, but the Union had lost its momentum, and Warren directed his men to turn their attention to digging fortifications.

As September 30 came to a close, Warren had once again shifted from an aggressive offensive against the Confederates to a cautious defensive posture. The Union attempt to secure Boydton Plank Road and take control of South Side Railroad was dead in the water.

The Regiment—The 155th Pennsylvania Infantry

We waited until nearly sun-up, when there was a rumble, and the earth shook as though in an earthquake. On casting our eyes toward the fort we saw a sight long to be remembered . . . it looked to us though there was about an acre of ground heaved up in the air from 50 to 75 feet . . . Some compared it to a weeping willow. The column of black earth in the center was the highest, while beneath and around the black column great clouds of white smoke rolled out. Oh! It was grand!

—D. P. Marshall, *Company K, 155th Pennsylvania Volunteers*

On the evening of July 29, members of the 155th learned that a mine, placed in a tunnel under the Confederate line, would be exploded. Fellow Pennsylvanians from the 48th Regiment had performed the work. While the 155th was digging trenches above ground, members of the 48th were burrowing beneath. The mine lay in front of the Ninth Corps, a piece of terrain well known to the 155th since the regiment had made an assault at that point in the Confederate line on June 18.

According to historians of the 155th, the Confederates were aware that some activity was going on beneath the earth in the vicinity of their lines. Confederate artillery men, lying with their ears to the ground, could hear the work going on below. Yankee pickets fueled their suspicions by calling out: "Johnny, you're going to heaven soon," or "We're going to blow you up next week."[3] Confederate engineers, based on rumors and reports coming from the rank and file, made several unsuccessful attempts to locate the mine and counter it with their own explosives, but these efforts were soon abandoned.

Minutes before five o'clock on July 30, as the sun was rising, there was "a deep rumble and the earth in the neighborhood trembled as with an earthquake, and then with a tremendous explosion a conical mountain, seemingly half an acre in extent, rose in the air, carrying with it stones, timber, caissons, bodies and limbs of men, and some of the heavy guns of the fort."[4]

Once the dust settled, the 155th , waiting in reserve, watched for the Ninth Corps divisions to go streaming through the gap in the Confederate line. Instead, Brigadier General James H. Ledlie's division slowly moved into position, hesitating and then halting at the crater left by the explosion. Their position blocked other Ninth Corps divisions from moving forward. The men of the 155th questioned why Burnside was not present to direct his corps when both Meade and Grant were at the scene to observe the action.

The Confederates reacted slowly to defend their line—too slowly according to a perturbed Robert E. Lee—but they were still faster to react than the muddled Union Ninth Corps. Seeing the opportunity to break through the Confederate line and head to Petersburg evaporating with each passing minute, General Warren requested that his corps be sent into the action. Both Meade and Grant refused Warren's request. Other than firing into the Confederate line during the anticipated attack, the men of the 155th could only be appalled observers of the calamity unfolding at the Crater.

For the next eighteen days, the members of the 155th lived the life of trench warfare soldiers, digging entrenchments by night and remaining undercover during the day to protect themselves from artillery rounds lobbed periodically from the Confederate lines. Baking ninety-degree days and warm evenings added to the misery of those living as animals in burrows. By August 17 several consecutive days of thunderstorms had provided some relief from the heat and dust that permeated entrenchments.

On August 18, the 155th and the rest of the Fifth Corps were ordered to leave the trenches and proceed to the Weldon Railroad. The regiment, part of Griffin's division that was the advance infantry unit of the corps, was preceded by a brigade of cavalry on their march. Once Griffin's division reached Six Mile Station on the railroad, they were detailed to start tearing up track as part of Grant's plan to sever the Confederate supply lines into Petersburg. Two other divisions—Ayres's and Crawford's—marched north up the tracks toward Petersburg. Soon two brigades of A. P. Hill's corps were sent double-quick time down the rail line to thwart the Union attempt to disable Weldon Railroad. The two groups clashed in the vicinity of Globe Tavern and, thanks to Warren's Fourth Division under Brigadier General Lysander Cutler, who rushed to the scene to reinforce Ayres's and Crawford's men, the Confederates were turned back. The Union troops held their position and began immediately constructing earthworks, a task that lasted into the next day.

On the 19th, the 155th began an advance north with Griffin's division toward Petersburg, constructing entrenchments as it moved forward. After an initial contact at midmorning, the Confederate forces, under Major General Henry Heth, conducted a full-scale attack at 4:00 p.m. in a heavy rain. The Confederates, "yelling like demons," overran the advanced picket line and entrenched skirmishers before being pushed back by Griffin's division. The Rebel assault resulted in heavy Union losses, especially among the First Brigade of U. S. Regulars, whose commander, Brigadier General Joseph Hayes, was wounded and captured during the action.

The Fifth Corps maintained its line through the next day under heavy Confederate artillery fire, but there was no advancement of infantry on either side. The following day, August 21, the Rebels renewed their attack on Warren's men, driving back Union skirmishers, but ultimately they were repulsed by the main Federal line.

The 155th spent the remaining days of August entrenching and solidifying its position near Weldon Railroad, a position won after three days of hard fighting and significant casualties. Once again, the regiment had demonstrated that it could be counted on to perform with effectiveness and bravery when its soldiers were placed in key positions on the front line of battle.

As the 155th and the Fifth Corps held their position adjacent to Weldon Railroad near Globe Tavern (where Warren established his headquarters), a daring raid behind Union lines by Confederate cavalry under General Wade Hampton took place. Hampton's troopers—dressed in Union uniforms taken from Army of the Potomac pickets—rounded up several thousand beef cattle at the rear of the Army of the Potomac. As a diversion, the Confederates attacked the picket lines at the Union front near the Fifth Corps on the morning of September 16. The 155th was called to arms in anticipation of an assault on their entrenchments. The attack on the line never materialized, but twenty miles to the east, the Confederates were successfully raiding the Yankee storehouse.

On September 29, Union troopers from David Gregg's cavalry division were scouting the area in the direction of Southside Railroad when they came in contact with a large body of Confederate infantry and artillery. The 155th was ordered to "pack up" and move quickly to a position to the north and west of their line to support the cavalry. Gregg's troopers fell back from the advancing Confederates to take refuge behind the lines just formed by the 155th. Once the Rebels realized that they were coming upon a Yankee infantry brigade, they halted their skirmish and withdrew to the west leaving the Union troops formed up and at the ready until dark. Only when they were sure that the threat had passed did the Union troops march back to camp.

The next day, Griffin's division was ordered back to the position it had left the evening before. Forming a line of battle, the division pushed on in a northwestern direction when it came under fire from Confederate artillery. The division marched down a steep, wooded ravine, stopping several times to align its advancing column. Meanwhile, Confederate artillery fire lopped off trees that grew in the densely forested ravine.

The 155th proceeded across the ravine and into a cleared field. An abandoned farmhouse, barn, and outbuildings were located in the center of the open ground. On the opposite side of the field was the Confederate's Fort Archer, which offered an unrestricted view across the field that the Union troops would have to cover in their assault.

The 155th, along with other units of Griffin's division, advanced double-quick across the field, cheering loudly, yet without the benefit of an order from their superiors to proceed. The commander of the 155th Regiment, Colonel A. L. Pearson, attempted to gain order over his men, but finally, seeing the futility, called out, "Well, if you will go, then go!"[5] The division troops swept through Fort Archer taking control of the redoubt and planting regimental flags, the 155th Regiment's being one of the first flags put in place.

Following the taking of Fort Archer, Brigadier General Robert Potter's Second Division of the Ninth Corps marched through the captured fort to pursue the fleeing enemy. Within an hour, Potter's division had been pushed back and its line flanked by advancing Confederates. Over a thousand Union soldiers of the Ninth Corp's division were taken prisoners and the rest scattered by the Rebels. The 155th together with other infantry and artillery from Griffin's division were able to rally and stop the Confederates approaching to retake the fort. Artillery and musket fire from the 155th and other First Division units lasted until dark and was able to check the Confederate attempt to retake Fort Archer. Griffin's division ended the long day of fighting by digging modest entrenchments using their bayonets and tin plates as tools

The Soldier—George P. McClelland

> He thought that he was about to start for the front. Indeed, he saw a picture of himself, dust-stained, haggard, panting, flying to the front at the proper moment to seize and throttle the dark, leering witch of calamity.
> —Stephen Crane, *The Red Badge of Courage*

George McClelland returned to his regiment after an absence of two months. During his recovery period away from his unit, the men had fought in the ill-fated battle of Cold Harbor and, just three days before his arrival, witnessed the mine explosion at the Petersburg siege line. The twenty-one-year-old soldier had come back with a new level of responsibility. He was mustered in as a commissioned officer. The granting of a commission was contingent on his signing up for three more years of service, and McClelland willingly did so.

During McClelland's absence, Sergeant William H. King had taken charge of Company F. (Past officers of the company had resigned, or—in the case of Captain Clapp—been killed.) King, described in the regimental history as both an "MD" and a "practicing dentist,"[6] had been granted a commission as a second lieutenant in early July 1864, a month prior to McClelland's return. When McClelland arrived and was given a commission as first lieutenant, he was put in charge of Company F with the expectation that he would be promoted to captain once the necessary bureaucratic hurdles were cleared in Harrisburg. King became a subordinate to McClelland, a position he held until he took temporary command of Company F when McClelland was called to serve as aide-de-camp at brigade headquarters.

George McClelland's strong motivation to return to the front and his willingness to extend his service time by accepting a commission can be attributed to several factors that were not uncommon during the Civil War. Like most of his volunteer peers, McClelland enlisted with neighbors and friends, all the while maintaining close community ties to Pittsburgh throughout his service. As a result, McClelland felt a strong sense of responsibility to the men with whom he served. He had grown up with many of them and knew their families. He demonstrated strong leadership qualities, and the trust he engendered among his senior officers put him in the position of holding the fate of his men in his hands, a position he took very seriously as he led this "band of brothers."

The second factor that motivated McClelland to accept a commission and return to the battlefront was pride in his unit. Historian James McPherson cites the power of regimental pride in the Civil War: "The pride and honor of an individual soldier were bound up with the pride and honor of his regiment, his state, and the nation for which he fought, symbolized by the regimental and national flags."[7] The 155th Pennsylvania Infantry was justifiably proud of its performance since the early days of its service: taking on the role of "forlorn hope" during the assault on Marye's Heights at Fredericksburg; turning back the enemy at Little Round Top; and fighting courageously at Saunders' Field, Laurel Hill, the North Anna River, and Cold Harbor during the Overland campaign. Being granted the status of a Zouave unit further lifted the unit's esprit de corps. McClelland took pride in his unit, and attaining a leadership position in the regiment carried with it the prestige of past accomplishments and the high regard in which the unit was held by the general officers of the Army of the Potomac.

In His Own Words—The Letters of George McClelland

Before Petersburg, Virginia
August 5, 1864

Dear Lizzie,

On returning to the Regiment, which I did on Tuesday the 2nd August, I found a letter from my little sensitive Sister who got angry once upon a time because I thought it was not her duty to come to Pittsburg, although I would have been overjoyed to have seen her. However, I judge the spell wore off ere she wrote me last so kindly, so affectionately. I, of course, also received the gorgeous pictures.

Well, Lizzie, to inform you of the situation both individually and generally, I went to work and made out my discharge papers and they have gone to Corps Headquarters for approval. When they come down, I will be mustered into the US Service for three more years as a First Lieutenant, Company F.

This mustering business is creating a great deal of dissatisfaction. No muster is made, under a recent order, for less than 3 years and at every promotion you are mustered for three years from that date. A number of men and officers have refused commissions solely on that account. It has not scared me a bit, for I think I will go home with the Regiment.

My commission as Captain will be here ere many days. I think I realize the responsible position I will soon occupy and will labor to make myself worthy of the trust. To secure the love and affection of my men and to do my duty faithfully and unflinchingly is my chief desire. I may make mistakes, but they will be from want of experience and from the head, not the heart.

This is a curious region of country to one who has never seen it—all cut up with works of every description. We are on the front line and the spires of Petersburg are distinctly visible. We are protected by bomb proofs—great holes dug in the earth, rendered necessary for protection from the enormous bombshells thrown from mortars—which they can throw anywhere almost.

Our pickets in front of us are also buried in the earth about 10 paces from the Rebels who are protected in the same manner. Both sides are peaceably inclined and walk about with impunity—but just on our immediate right the firing is kept up incessantly by "Burnside's Niggers"; the Rebs seem to have a spite at them.

The fort that was mined and blown up is in plain view from our position. It has been discovered that the Rebels are mining two of our forts and we say: "Go in John Williams! Blow away!" We are prepared to give them a warm reception. If they can take works, such as we have, I say they ought to have them.

The weather is awfully hot, almost unbearable and there is no shade here, but the sun beats down with remorseless heat on the burning sand.

You tell me that Thomas is going East. I wish that he could have arranged it when I was at Pittsburgh. I received a letter from Henry when I got here. He was contemplating a visit to the old town and would have come if he had known I would have made so long a stay.

Well, Lizzie, you must pardon this lead pencil scribble. Keep up to your good resolutions and probably you may provoke something like a letter from your little Brother, George. I send affection to Tom, Anna, Walter, George and Wilson. Also, to all friends who inquire, I would be remembered.

There is going to be some very hard fighting before long and notwithstanding blunders and miserable failures, there is not a doubt of the issue. Continue your prayers in my behalf and may God's grace be abundantly manifested to us all. Lovingly, I bid you a fond farewell.

Ever Your Brother,
George

PS Don't forget my brother in arms, the Colonel.

Notes on the August 5, 1864, Letter

George McClelland was back with his regiment and had taken the necessary steps to receive his commission as an officer. Under the terms of the commission, he had to agree to serve three more years. His original enlistment term—with a year of service left—was abrogated.

Generally sanguine about an end to the war occurring soon, McClelland was still taking a leap of faith in extending his service time. The war's end was on the horizon, but his new responsibilities increased his exposure to harm exponentially. His commitment to his men and his willingness to shoulder those responsibilities, however, were unequivocal.

The new first lieutenant had returned to an army that was in the midst of trench warfare, facing an enemy that was in a superb defensive position. The skyline of Petersburg—less than two miles away—was clearly visible and a daily reminder that the Confederates remained a tenacious and formidable enemy. On the right side of Warren's Fifth Corps was the Ninth Corps, embittered after its devastating losses at the Crater less than a week earlier.

At the location of the 155th, McClelland had a clear view of the Crater just north and slightly west of the regiment's lines. Rumors abounded about the Confederates trying a similar mining attempt. His reference to "Go in John Williams . . ." may refer to one of two Union Medal of Honor recipients, both navy men. Boatswain's Mate John Williams had manned an eleven-inch gun on the USS *Mohican* against the Confederate fleet in November 1861. His courage under intense enemy fire earned him the Medal of Honor. Seaman John Williams—from Pennsylvania—held his position on the deck of the USS *Commodore Perry* as his ship took Confederate batteries under fire at Franklin, Virginia, in October 1862. Seaman Williams was also awarded the Medal of Honor for gallantry.

At the close of the letter, McClelland shared his confidence about the defeat of the Confederates but recognized that there might be some Union stumbles along the way. His postscript acknowledged Lizzie's fiancé, Colonel Noel Howard (2nd Iowa Infantry Regiment), who had been promoted from major during McClelland's hospital leave.

Weldon Railroad
August 22, 1864

Dear Sister Lizzie,

Yesterday I received your interesting letter, but the condition we are now in precludes the possibility of anything but a lead pencil scribble in return.

I was very much pained to hear of the Colonel being so severely wounded. The first information was from Annie, but your hopeful letter allayed my fears. Send him my sympathetic and consoling regards. The Army of the Potomac sends greeting to the noble Army of Tennessee. My greatest wish, as from a soldier to another brave defender, is that he may soon be enabled to rejoin his brothers—never to sheathe his sword until the last vestige of armed rebellion disappears from the land.

Well, Lizzie, I must tell you how I am fixed and why I send you such a scrawl. To begin, you must know, despite insinuations of the Richmond Whig, Sentinel and Enquirer, that Grant's army still remains intact; that the siege has not been raised; that the mortality is not more than the ordinary rate, swamps, malaria, etc. to the contrary notwithstanding.

About one week ago, the 9th Corps relieved the 5th and we marched out of the works, rested in camp a couple of days and then started on the Jerusalem Road—away to the left. This was on the 18th. Soon reached the advanced pickets of the enemy and drove them in. Advanced in line of battle through an almost impenetrable woods [that was] very swampy and, without hardly a shot having been fired, struck the Petersburg and Weldon Railroad and of course took possession. Cut the wire and destroyed the road, then took a good position.

The Rebels coming down to see what was the matter, pitched into Ayres' Division (our old Commander) and thrashed him. We suffered severely, but finally regained what we had lost. The enemy, seeing that we were in some force, ran down troops from Petersburg and assaulted all parts of the line, but without effect.

Yesterday, the 21st, they undertook it on the left. I guess they did not know that Griffin's Division was here. A charge was made, General W. [H.] F. Lee's cavalry division in advance, followed by infantry. We were so well fixed for them that it cost no effort at all to send them back in confusion, capturing 1,200 prisoners. (Old Company F bagged a Lieutenant and 7 men.)

Our loss was very slight—none in my Company. The prisoners all agree in saying that Lee (Robert E.) swore that he must have that railroad if it cost the annihilation of his army. We are just as determined that he shan't have it. The Army is all up and well in hand—the Sixteenth [sic], 10th, 9th, 2nd and 5th—strong along about 12 miles.

So here I am sitting behind a breastwork we worked on all night (expecting another attack) writing on an ammunition box. I don't know whether I can send this away or not. I expect orders to advance and feel the position of the enemy. I have several letters to write—but have no way of writing them. I received two envelopes from HSM. Tell him I will acknowledge the receipt the first chance I get.

There will be some severe fighting, but don't be anxious concerning me. I will try and be prepared for any contingency. So until you hear from me again, good bye.

Love to all—Your loving Brother,
George
Direct
Lt. George P. McClelland

155 Pa Zouaves
Washington, DC

Notes on the August 22, 1864, Letter

Unfortunately, McClelland's earlier letter to his sister Lizzie (March 7, 1864) regarding the possible wounding of her fiancé had proven prescient. The brother's "greatest wish" regarding Lizzie's wounded fiancé—that he "soon be enabled to rejoin his brothers"—was no doubt far from his sister's mind as she contemplated her fiancé's condition. Colonel Noel Howard was severely wounded while leading his unit on July 22, 1864, at the battle of Atlanta.

He assured his sister that, contrary to Confederate newspapers (which Lizzie was unlikely to be reading in Davenport, Iowa), the Union army was in a good state and had taken control of the northern portion of the Weldon Railroad, tearing up the track and cutting telegraph lines to further constrict supplies and communications that went to the Confederates.

McClelland's listing of the Union army resources, five army corps spread along the Union line twelve miles long, was testimony to Grant's numerical superiority against a withering Confederate force. (McClelland incorrectly identified the Eighteenth Corps—Major General E. O. C. Ord commanding—erroneously calling it the Sixteenth Corps.)

He had recently received two letters from his brother Henry ("HSM") but had been unable to reply in anticipation of engagements to follow. Grant was pressing his troops to break the stalemate at Petersburg, and McClelland was keenly aware that under these conditions there was little free time to write letters.

Headquarters 2nd Brigade, 1st Division, 5th Corps
Weldon Railroad
September 4, 1864

Dear Sister Lizzie,
Your expected bimonthly epistle reached me this morning, as usual full of instruction and entertainment. I am glad to know the Colonel is improving and trust he will be soon restored to health.
The announcement on the envelope was a little premature. It hurt me a little—as yours was not the only letter endorsed in that way. And I can't imagine why Annie should have so written you. It is something I always disliked myself and generally excites remark in others. So that it shall not occur again, I now tell you that my position is 1st Lieutenant.

There is a hitch in Harrisburg regarding affairs in the Regiment and until matters are arranged, no more commissions will be issued. The fuss is in reference to Major. The senior Captain is entitled to the position providing he is competent—which the majority of the officers think he is not. So a strong effort is being made to run in Ed Montooth, Adjutant of the Regiment. Therefore, Lizzie, please call me Lieutenant.

I had got thus far in this when the Colonel, Colonel Gregory of the 91st Pennsylvania Volunteers I mean, commanding the Brigade, came into my tent and told me to come with him to see and hear Reverend H. Stewart [Stuart], President of the Christian Commission who had arrived in company with a number of delegates and was to speak before the two Brigades of our Division. (Of that I will speak anon.)

I need not speak of the movements of this Corps on the Weldon RR as it is old and we have settled down here as though we were permanently fixed.

You talk of the war and the length of the campaign. It has been a hard one—a campaign of such severity, such hardships, such exposures that I would surely sink under had it not been for the cheering, the consoling and inspiring words which came flying to me from those I love. Now don't forget your resolutions in regard to writing me. . . .

After repelling all different assaults of the enemy, we set about strengthening our hold and have now quite a formidable network of forts, redoubts, breastworks, etc.

I have been very busy attending to the business of the Company. There is always a great amount of work at the close of the month—and it has all devolved on me. In fine, I have been acting Company Clerk. We have received reinforcements. Until now, my Company numbers 95.

While in the midst of a complicated muster roll, an order came from Brigade Headquarters detailing me on the staff as ADC. I hesitated some time before accepting as the interests of the Company required my presence with them, but a man has to look after his own interests in the Army and I concluded it was only a duty to myself to accept. And I did, and here I am now.

The advantages are obvious: I mix and come in contact with a better class of men; make acquaintances that I would never do in the lines and am brought to the notice of General officers; have a horse to ride; always a good bed to sleep upon; and no disagreeable duties to perform. This will not last long, however, for when my commission comes as Captain, I will return to my Company.

I have made the acquaintance of Captain Ed Bennett, Inspector General on the staff— a Massachusetts boy and a man of refinement and great intellectual powers. One who has read a great deal and [is] perfectly conversant with all the standard authors. I have derived both instruction and pleasure in his society.

Colonel Gregory, the senior Colonel, commands the Brigade—a good, religious man, but not much of a military one, and is not liked amongst the officers and men.

Today we had for dinner two delegates of the CC (Christian Commission.) They informed us that Mr. Stewart would be along sometime during the day. Towards evening, went up to the Corn Exchange Regiment [118th Pennsylvania]. Found where a congregation is waiting for the distinguished visitor.

Short addresses were made by Reverend Stowe of Massachusetts, Mr. Ames, one of the secretaries of the Commission after which a powerful address was delivered by Mr. Stewart. At the conclusion of the services, I was introduced to the "Merchant Prince" of Philadelphia who has done so much for the cause of Christ—especially among the soldiers of the Union. And then I returned to complete the few lines commenced to my little dame.

Now I have about come to an end. While the political horizon is agitated by cries of "Peace" and the doings of that mongrel convention in Chicago, the military aspect is cheering. Old Salamander is making history fast. That finished soldier, Sherman, has taken Atlanta and Grant has fingers of steel closing around the throat of Rebellion in Virginia.

In a very short time you may expect to hear stirring news from this Region. The reinforcements are only now beginning to come. You perhaps have known that the Army has been greatly depleted by expirations of service, deaths on the battlefield and by disease. This is the reason why we have not moved faster, but now the men are arriving 1,000 per day and before a month, we assume again the offensive; 100,000 men now would terminate the war in 60 days—Grant has said it. I am full of confidence that my prophecy will prove correct. . . .

I replied to your last letter—hear regularly from Henry and Arch and Father and Annie. Have no reason to complain at all.

The weather is hot by day and cold by night. We are surrounded by swamps on every side. The men are kept busy. Whiskey mixed with quinine issued morning and evening. A man must keep moving or he will certainly die.

In kindness and love remember me to Tom, Anna and the boys. And to brother soldier, send greeting.

With loving affection, I remain,
Your Brother,
George
Direct Lt. G. P. M.
2nd Brigade, 1st Division, 5th Corps, Washington, DC and give HS the same directions

Notes on the September 4, 1864, Letter

Good news arrived from Lizzie that her fiancé, "the Colonel," was recovering well from his wound. This time, fortunately, the youngest brother spared his sister the hope that the colonel would be quickly reunited with his unit.

Lieutenant McClelland was embarrassed that both his sisters had jumped the gun and addressed their letters to him as "Captain McClelland." Other positions—including a major rank—were holding up his promotion in Harrisburg. In the meantime, he admonished his sister to address him as "Lieutenant."

The new Second Brigade commander, Colonel Edgar Gregory, formerly commander of the 91st Pennsylvania Regiment, personally requested that McClelland accompany him to a talk by George H. Stuart, the founder and chairman of the United States Christian Commission. In November 1861, at the direction of the board of the New York City YMCA, the commission was created to serve the religious needs of Union soldiers and sailors. The commission promoted Sabbath observance, temperance, creation of libraries and symposiums, and the securing of qualified chaplains to serve the armed forces. The commission's mandate was expanded to help distribute emergency medical supplies, food, and clothing.

Things quieted down for the 155th and McClelland on the Weldon Railroad line, but he was reminded, after reading a letter from Lizzie, of the duration and severity of the war. In one of his rare acknowledgments of the personal toll the war has taken, he cited the value of the letters he received from loved ones. His frequent complaints about the lack of correspondence and the long gaps between letters are evidence of his psychological dependence on the letters he received from brothers, sisters, and father. Letters from home comforted and sustained McClelland during periods of uncertainty and stress.

In seeking to understand the motivation of Civil War soldiers, James McPherson has written: "Convictions of duty, honor, patriotism, and ideology functioned as the principal sustaining motivations of Civil War soldiers . . . But without a firm base of support in the homes and communities from which these citizen-soldiers came, their morale would have crumbled."[8] As for so many soldiers, letters from home were McClelland's lifeline during the most trying times.

While coping with administrative duties in conjunction with the growing number of recruits arriving, McClelland was tapped to become an aide de camp on the Second Brigade staff. He was pleased by the recognition of his aptitude by his superior officers and glad he was considered qualified to serve in a staff position—assignments usually reserved for well-educated and well-connected junior officers—but McClelland was torn by the decision. In the staff position he would gain visibility among senior officers, but remaining with his company would fulfill his desire to be loyal to his band of brothers. The young former carpenter from Pittsburgh was not immune to the lure of a staff position: being in frequent contact with general officers; being assigned a horse for transportation; staying in better quarters; and having a variety of high-visibility assignments. Any remorse he had over leaving his company was mitigated by the knowledge that he would return to Company F when his captain's rank was granted.

In the staff position, McClelland rubbed shoulders with men he admired; for example, Captain Bennet, who was a well-read New England gentleman. But his opinion of the brigade commander, Colonel Gregory, was equivocal. Another soldier in the 155th—not on brigade staff—did not share McClelland's reservations about Gregory: "Colonel Gregory, of the 91st PV commanding our Brigade, was one of the best men of the Brigade. He had worship regularly in his tent, of which he required all his staff to attend, nor would he allow any whiskey in his command."[9] George McClelland may have been handpicked by Colonel Gregory because of the young lieutenant's strong Presbyterian roots and his abstention from alcohol.

McClelland's attendance at the Christian Commission assembly with Colonel Gregory gave him an opportunity to hear commission notables, including George H. Stuart, the "Merchant Prince of Philadelphia." Stuart's clothing store later evolved into a highly successful department store. A native of Philadelphia, Stuart had strong ties to the local and national YMCA.

His reference to the "political horizon" reflected McClelland's contempt over the "Peace Democrats" and their election platform. The Democratic convention was held in Chicago starting August 29, and delegates nominated George B. McClellan, former commander of the Army of the Potomac, as their candidate for president. While the Democrats were crafting an election platform that favored ending the war with a negotiated peace with Richmond, the Union military position strengthened considerably. "Old Salamander," Admiral David Farragut, won the battle of Mobile Bay. ("Damn the torpedoes! Full speed ahead!") And the "finished soldier" (i.e., consummate, highest degree of excellence), Sherman, had taken Atlanta. McClelland was part of Grant's "fingers of steel" that were "closing around the throat of Rebellion."

In mid-July 1864, Lincoln issued a new call for 500,000 men. A draft was planned to fill any shortfall in the recruiting effort generated by the call. The results of that call were beginning to show up at the Army of the Potomac encampments near Petersburg. McClelland's prophecy that the war would be over in two months was very optimistic, as events would bear out. The tenacity of Lee and his threadbare legion was greatly underestimated at all levels of the Union army.

The dog days of August continued into September, and the heat, in conjunction with the mosquito-breeding swamps all around, made McClelland and his fellow soldiers subject to illnesses that were to be warded off by twice-daily rations of whiskey and quinine. While this mixture had questionable medical efficacy, the social and morale-boosting benefits to the men—with the exception of abstainers such as McClelland—were well documented.

Headquarters 2nd Brigade, 1st Division, 5th Corps
Weldon Railroad
September 20, 1864

Dear Lizzie,

Your welcome letter reached me this AM. Many thanks for the same. I have held a convention and of course have a platform and one of the planks says: That you will bend your whole energies and with unswerving fidelity to the Union and the Constitution and—and—write a little oftener. Twice a month won't do for me. It may do very well for How[ard]. If he objects, just turn him over to me. I'll send him one or two Henry A. Wise letters.

Well the convention decided briefly, but unanimously, that my constituents in Iowa must write at least one letter per week during the existing rebellion from now henceforth until it is squelched. Which period, thank the Lord, is near at hand. With this proviso: that in case of sickness or other cause of disability, you will procure a suitable substitute. If you have any McClelland friends about the bluffs of Davenport (real nice you know) who desire to know more of me and my platform, just give them my address.

All remains very quiet in this Army. Our thinned ranks are receiving large accessions daily, but they are not the same stuff as the old levies. The major portion are substitutes—from every country in the world except America. And of course, fighting for the almighty dollar, they cannot be greatly relied on.

There is no disguising the fact that our Army is deteriorating slowly but surely. The best men gone home or going and their places filled by those whose hearts are not in the cause. Still, by rigid discipline, we can make them effective enough to whip the forces of the Confederacy for their veterans are scarce enough.

We (I mean everybody from General on down) were expecting a last and more desperate effort of Lee's to regain possession of this road. But if there ever has been a time when he could have broken our hold here, that time is now past. And in a short time we will strike the blow. Some think that both armies will remain quiet until the results of the election are known and that if Lincoln is re-elected, Davis will abandon the struggle.

My opinion is that Grant will hazard nothing by an offensive movement unless he has a sure thing, because he can afford to wait. Every day we become stronger and the enemy weaker and I think there will be one desperate battle and not more . . .

I am still at my summer residence (Brigade Headquarters) for so it appears to me coming from the line.

I am glad to know my oldest brother is prospering. Tell him to vote for Lincoln and not for the tool of unprincipled anti-Republican-liberty men. Three-fourths of the Army will vote for Uncle Abe.

I heard from Annie a few days ago. All goes well in the Smoky City. Henry and Arch have been silent for a long time. My love to all. I would like to know more of that fair one you have in reserve for me.

Truly and devotedly, your Brother,
 George
Direct According to Heading

Notes on the September 20, 1864, Letter

Henry A. (Augustus) Wise was a well-connected naval officer who wrote several popular books about his travels in the 1850s. While a native Virginian, Wise chose to serve with the Union navy. Lincoln appointed him chief of the Bureau of Ordnance and Hydrography in 1864.

Drawing on the terminology of the recent political party conventions to nominate the presidential candidates, McClelland wrote about "constituents" and "platforms" as they pertained to family correspondence to him (i.e., more letters!).

Recruits from the July call continued to arrive at the regiment, but they were not of the caliber that McClelland and his fellow veteran soldiers were used to having in their units. Substitutes, particularly those of foreign birth who were motivated only by cash bonuses, filled the ranks of the new recruits, according to McClelland. Despite the lackluster talent coming into the Army of the Potomac, he recognized that even those substandard additions could help beat a greatly diminished Confederate army.

With national elections less than two months away, McClelland was correct that the Union army leadership would not undertake any offensive movements that had any possibility of failure. Yet McClelland underestimated the longevity of the Confederacy—Jefferson Davis would *not* "abandon the struggle" when Lincoln was elected in November, and there would be several more "desperate battles" before the war concluded seven months hence.

McClelland's request for Lizzie to lobby their eldest brother, Thomas, to vote for Lincoln was a dramatic turnaround from his position as a young recruit regarding the president: "Granny Lincoln. . . . forgot the dignity of the President of a great republic . . ." He was accurate in his estimation of the vote within the Union army. Of the twelve states permitting absentee voting for soldiers and providing separate tabulation of results, Lincoln received a 78 percent majority of the votes versus McClellan. The civilian majority in those same states was 53 percent for Lincoln.[10]

Chapter Thirteen

"Strong Men Strengthened and the Weak Made Strong"

Petersburg and the Weldon Railroad Raid, October—December 1864

The Army of the Potomac

> And then amid it all, General Griffin came along, resolute, heroic, impressive, with assuring words and comforting promises of help. The wavery lines stiffened; strong men were strengthened and the weak made strong. From now on it was his fight, and his presence in inspiring the men was almost equal to the promised support of his batteries.
> —118th Pennsylvania Regimental History

Like beads on a necklace, Union forts hung around the neck of Petersburg linked by breastworks to form a siege line that was a feat of engineering skill and a testimony to the excavating endurance of the Federal soldiers. Using a variety of tools, from picks and shovels to mess plates and cups, the Army of the Potomac had constructed an integrated string of over thirty forts and redoubts with connecting entrenchments by autumn 1864. Each Union fort—named for an officer killed in battle—was an original, no two the same in design. Accompanying the siege lines—one line facing toward Petersburg, the other a reverse line to ward off attacks from the rear—were a variety of age-proven defensive accoutrements: abatis, chevaux-de-frise, and gabions, all devices used in military defensive operations for hundreds of years.

After the engagement at Peebles's Farm on September 30/October 1, Warren's Fifth Corps dug entrenchments extending Union siege lines further west, thereby forcing the Confederates to stretch their lines along a 35-mile-long front. Robert E. Lee's men were spread thin in order to protect their remaining ground surrounding Petersburg. While their line held despite Union attacks, the Confederates had lost access to a number of key roads leading into the city and, consequently, their supply lines were significantly reduced. The civilian residents of Petersburg anticipated a difficult winter, knowing that fewer supply routes would mean shortages of food and fuel.

October began with gloomy, drizzly days that remained cool through the late mornings and then, after sunset, settled into cold dampness that reinforced the concerns about a fuel shortage among the residents of Petersburg. The first frost on October 10 offered civilians and soldiers from both armies a harbinger of the approach of winter weather.

Grant could almost taste a Union victory and knew that it would be only a matter of months before he overwhelmed Lee's ragged, diminished army. Motivated by both the window of opportunity before winter set in and the bad press he was getting in the North, Meade approached a receptive Grant with a plan to cut one of the few remaining Confederate rail lines that supplied Petersburg. Meade's plan involved using Hancock's Second Corps to flank the Confederate's right, cross Hatcher's Run, move along Boydton Plank Road and then head for the South Side Railroad, two key transportation routes that, once taken, would further choke off Confederate supplies to Petersburg and Richmond. A Union cavalry division would screen the Second Corps's advance and protect its left flank. Meanwhile, the Ninth Corps would put pressure on the Confederate lines at Peebles's Farm, and the Fifth Corps would be available to support either the Second Corps or Ninth Corps as battle conditions warranted. General Butler's men were to provide a diversion north of the James River commencing at the same time as the main assault on October 27.

The attack plan, as conceived by Meade, was daring, sweeping, and promising —in theory. In fact the ferocity of the Confederate response and the idiosyncrasies of the local terrain caused the Union plan to collapse. On October 27, the Ninth Corps began its attack against the Confederate lines opposite Peebles's Farm, but the Federals were not able to break through the resilient Rebel forces. The Second Corps marched down a country road ill-suited to such use, many places in the road being impassable for the large body of troops. Further complicating the progress of Hancock's men, pockets of Confederate resistance harassed the Union troops as they attempted to cross streams along the route.

Hancock's corps reached Boydton Plank Road at midmorning in the vicinity of Burgess's Mill. Rather than Confederate cavalry and scattered Rebel resistance, the Second Corps now confronted a major force of enemy infantry and artillery gathered across Hatcher's Run and the Boydton Plank Road bridge. Reinforcements to the Confederate line had been pouring in from Petersburg all morning.

The Fifth Corps, called into action to support the Second Corps, became entangled and hopelessly lost in the thick underbrush east of Hancock's men. The Second Corps was on its own. By early afternoon, Hancock was assessing his next steps when Grant and Meade, along with their staffs, arrived at the front. Grant reconnoitered the Confederate line at Hancock's position and decided that a direct assault was unwarranted. Instead he told Hancock to hold his position for twenty-four hours hoping to lure Lee's men out of their defensive position. Soon after Grant and Meade departed, Confederate cavalry and infantry attacked the Second Corps from multiple directions. A fierce battle followed with both sides inflicting heavy losses.

After dark, Hancock ordered his men to withdraw over the same route they had traveled to reach their position earlier in the day. The inadequate road and lack of ambulances meant leaving most of the wounded behind on the battlefield. When the day was over, Union casualties were 1,800 men; Confederate casualties, 1,300. No additional ground was taken or entrenchments extended by the Union; the Confederate position remained unchanged, but fewer troops were available to man the 35-mile-long Rebel siege line.

Tuesday, November 8 was the long-awaited election day in the North, with the presidential race pitting the incumbent, Abraham Lincoln, against the former commander of the Army of the Potomac, George B. McClellan. Both sides of the siege line closely followed the election results. If McClellan won, the Confederates viewed their prospects for a favorable cessation of hostilities more likely than if the incumbent prevailed in winning the vote. Union troops had a mixed reaction to their former commander, Little Mac. When all the popular votes were counted, Lincoln won just over 55 percent of the total votes cast, with the Union army voting four to one for "Old Abe." Union army votes were responsible for Lincoln's carrying Connecticut, New York, Illinois, Pennsylvania, Maryland, and Indiana. In the end, Lincoln would receive 212 electoral votes to McClellan's 21, his victory due, in large part, to members of the Federal army.

From this time forward the operations in front of Petersburg and Richmond, until the spring campaign of 1865, were confined to the defense and extension of our lines, and to offensive movements for crippling the enemy's lines of communications, and to prevent his detaching any considerable force to send south.

—Lieutenant General Ulysses S. Grant, siege of Petersburg, *Battles ands Leaders of the Civil War*

As late-autumn temperatures dropped into the forties during the day and daylight hours slowly diminished, the men of the Army of the Potomac began to think of a winter cessation of hostilities as they had been accustomed to under previous commanders. However, Ulysses S. Grant was not willing to send the Army of the Potomac into winter hibernation just yet. The general in chief wanted to maintain pressure on the Confederate supply and communications lines.

Grant's target was the Weldon Railroad, which, despite Federals' efforts, was still being used by the Confederates to transport supplies. The rail line's lower southern section was usable through North Carolina to Stony Creek (Virginia) Depot located sixteen miles below Petersburg. Rebels transferred the supplies from rail cars to wagons and brought them north via Boydton Plank Road through Dinwiddie Court House and into Confederate lines. The only other rail line available to the Confederates was the South Side Railroad, which had been the object of unsuccessful Union assaults at Peebles's Farm and Burgess's Mill.

Grant's choice to take the rail line and render it unusable was the Fifth Corps commander, Major General Gouverneur K. Warren. The general, who had so distinguished himself at Little Round Top, had been under a black cloud since his perceived lack of aggressiveness and courage at Laurel Hill during the battle of Spotsylvania Court House. Warren was eager to redeem himself and willingly took the assignment from Grant and Meade to head the expeditionary force consisting of 26,000 men. The force got under way on December 7 in brisk December weather, heading down the Jerusalem Plank Road toward Sussex Court House, Virginia. To assist them in crossing the numerous streams and rivers that they would encounter along the way, the expedition transported with them a 250-foot pontoon bridge made of canvas.

Operating as the lead unit, the Union cavalry reached the rail line on the morning of December 8. By noon, the infantry had reached the tracks at Jarratt's Station and begun the task of ripping up the rails and burning the rail station. Once pulled from their beds, the rails were heated in fires stoked by the rail ties and then twisted so they could not be reused in any attempt to rebuild the rail line. (The sixteen-mile section of track remained out of service until March, when the Confederates completed repairs.)

Despite the cold weather and arduous marching required to get to the rail line in southern Virginia, the Union soldiers were in high spirits and happy to be away from their muddy burrows along the Petersburg siege line. Contemporary reports tell of the Fifth Corps infantry twisting the rails into the shape of Maltese Crosses, the symbol worn by members of Warren's corps on their uniforms.

High spirits among the troops were further fueled by the availability of potent apple brandy—"applejack"—from the well-stocked farms along the expedition's route. In addition to foraging for chickens, ducks, geese, and turkeys as they passed through the Sussex County countryside, the troops commandeered large quantities of the powerful intoxicant to help celebrate the coming holidays. Officially known as the "Hicksford Expedition" or "Weldon Raid," the foray was dubbed "The Apple Jack Raid" by the troops.

Drunken Union soldiers became stragglers in their befuddled state, many falling victims to Rebel guerrillas—or "bushwhackers"—who shadowed the expedition. One Union soldier was found dead, pinned to the ground with a stake driven through his mouth. At Sussex Court House, the bodies of six Union soldiers, stripped bare, were discovered aligned side by side in front of the court house building.

Several documented instances of rape by drunken Union soldiers were reported, with both white and black women the victims as the troops returned from the Weldon Raid. While not widespread, these attacks on females contributed to the animosity among some of the local population on the expedition route and may have caused the brutal treatment of intoxicated Union stragglers.

Along the route of the expedition, Union units were harassed by Wade Hampton's Confederate cavalry. Lee also sent A. P. Hill to support Hampton to challenge this Union action against the key Confederate supply line. A severe sleet and rain storm curtailed the Confederate attacks and prevented Hill's men from intercepting Warren's force as it moved north on its return toward Petersburg.

By December 12, Warren's expeditionary force had arrived at the encampment near Petersburg after marching through nasty weather that coated everything with a thin veneer of ice. Warren considered the expedition an unmitigated success. He had pulled up tracks, rendered the rails ineffective, and returned to his original position all in six day's time suffering only 300 casualties in his 26,000-man force. Others—primarily Confederates, but even some Union troops—saw the expedition tainted by drunkenness, theft of civilian property, and the criminal assault of females.

The Regiment—155th Pennsylvania Infantry

When he [Corporal George Clever] got on the works a Rebel officer saw him and called out, 'Look at the Yankee s_____ of a b_____! Shoot him!' When George saw their guns raised he jumped and ran. There were a good many shots fired at him, but all missed.

—D. P. Marshall, Company "K" 155th PA Volunteer Zouaves

Early October brought falling temperatures and drizzling rain that made the digging of entrenchments dank duty. Originally modifying the captured Confederate works to fit Union needs, the regiment was moved back to an earlier position after threats of a Rebel counterattack. Despite Confederate shelling and brief skirmishes, the days were uneventful. During this lull, the regiment dug new defensive positions and cleared timber in front of its line to open the view and used the fallen timber to construct defensive fortifications.

On October 26, the 155th was ordered to pack up and be ready to move out early the next morning. Under the command of Colonel Alfred Pearson, the 155th joined with the other regiments of the Second Brigade in Griffin's First Division to march from the area near Peebles's Farm to begin a flanking movement to take the South Side Railroad. Moving ahead of the main column, the skirmishers from the 155th soon ran into the Confederate's first line of works but were not given an order to attack.

Several impetuous men from the regiment—including Corporal George Clever of Company K—mounted the enemy's defenses in a display of bravado that surprised the Rebel defenders. Before the Confederates could draw a bead on the brazen Yankee infiltrators, the Union soldiers realized the danger and quickly retreated.

Located along Hatcher's Run, the 155th was in the second line of battle in Griffin's division. During the ensuing engagement, members of a New York regiment in the first line panicked under intense Rebel fire and began retreating through the ranks of the 155th, leaving behind their coats, knapsacks, and other equipment, which the members of the 155th took as deserved "spoils of war" from their New York comrades in arms who chose to run rather than stay and fight.

When it was discovered that the Second Corps and Fifth Corps would not be able to connect to form a unified line of battle and that the Confederates had sent in numerous fresh reinforcements, the assault was abandoned and the regiment ordered to withdraw to their entrenchments near Peebles's

Farm. Most of the men in the 155th thought that this late October engagement would be the last before they went into winter encampment mode for the remainder of 1864. General Grant had other ideas before any winter hiatus would begin.

> [W]hile the sleet was giving the ground and bushes a coating of ice, a soldier belonging to some other regiment of the Third Brigade passed through the column of the One Hundred and Fifty-fifth resting on each side of the road. The mud was ankle deep. The comrade was hatless. His canteen was full of apple-brandy and his head with the effects of it. He had a brace of chickens fastened to his belt, his gun strapped over his shoulder, and a willow basket filled with honey on his head. As the joyous soldier waded through the mud, perfectly indifferent to the trickling down of the honey over his head and shoulders, his voice rang out in the strains of a patriotic song. The One Hundred and Fifty-fifth, with hearty cheers, sped the joyful soldier on his way.
> —*Under the Maltese Cross,* describing the "Apple Jack Raid," December 1864

On December 6, the 155th joined the rest of the Fifth Corps along with a division from the Second Corps and Gregg's cavalry division to form an expeditionary force. The troops were not told their destination, but the soldiers surmised that with the four days' rations given to them to carry and the news that the supply trains accompanying them carried an additional eight days' rations for each man, the expedition would be lengthy. As they began to march south, some speculated that their destination was Wilmington, North Carolina, where the troops would attack the Confederate rear by land while the Union navy attacked the front by sea.

The 155th—in company with the rest of the Warren expedition—marched down Jerusalem Plank Road, crossing the Nottoway River by pontoon bridge. In the early hours of December 8, the expedition marched through Sussex Court House, Virginia, and later that afternoon the 155th began tearing up the Weldon rail lines. Their work continued until midnight when all the rails had been pulled up, ties burned, and rails twisted into various shapes. Fires of burning ties dotted the landscape along the path of the destroyed Weldon Railroad, glowing links in a chain of destruction that stretched as far as the eye could see in the December night.

The next day, as temperatures dropped below twenty degrees, the expedition continued its march to Belfield, forty miles south of Petersburg, where it faced some minor Confederate resistance at Three Creek, a small stream where a railroad bridge had been previously destroyed. The Rebels were soon driven back by Warren's artillery fire and the men of Tenth New York Cavalry Regiment.

The next day Warren ordered the expedition to turn back for the Union lines. Grant considered its mission accomplished, and he wanted the troops back in position on the Union siege line. With the rail line rendered useless, the troops were needed in place to help "chew and choke" the enemy at Petersburg.

Initially, Warren had issued orders prohibiting foraging along the route of march, but during the return trip, this restriction was revoked, perhaps in retaliation for the hostile activities of guerrillas that grew in frequency and intensity. The lifting of the ban gave Union soldiers license to raid the autumn cornucopia of foodstuffs found on farms along the Federals' path. Turkeys, chickens, sweet potatoes, honey, jams, and jellies were pilfered from local larders. There too, the men found supplies of applejack, which was consumed by many of the troops, most unaware of the potency of the drink. Some applejack-saturated soldiers became disoriented and straggled from their units only to be captured—and some killed—by local "bushwhackers" who hovered at the periphery of the Union expeditionary force. Members of the 155th reported a number of stragglers were brutally murdered during the return march.

Warren retaliated for the random acts of guerrilla cruelty by ordering the burning of public buildings at Sussex Court House and the vicinity. Ironically, members of the 155th commented favorably on the positive response and "kindly feeling" they experienced among the local population along the route. The white residents were reported to have gathered on their porches and balconies to watch the Union infantry, cavalry, and artillery of the expedition "pass in review" by the farms and homesteads, while slaves stood at the sides of the road to offer the passing soldiers springwater ladled from buckets.

The Soldier—George P. McClelland

> Suddenly there was a hollow rumble of drums. A distant bugle sang faintly. Similar sounds, varying in strength, came from near and far over the forest. The bugles called to each other like brazen gamecocks. The near thunder of the regimental drums rolled.
> —Stephen Crane, *The Red Badge of Courage*

Plucked from Company F as a newly commissioned officer, George McClelland served in a staff position in Colonel Gregory's Second Brigade. As a member of the brigade staff, McClelland was issued a horse. While being issued a mount carried with it an aura of prestige, it also had a very practical purpose: Aides-de-camp were expected to be highly mobile, carrying messages and orders from the commander and staff to officers in the field. This role was especially important during engagements where communications between staff and field forces were critical and other means of communications—such as signal flags—were not feasible because of terrain or weather. The aide-de-camp was expected not only to relay messages to the field forces, but also to carry back messages and observations to the brigade commander and staff. McClelland's considerable battlefield experience as an infantry noncommissioned officer was invaluable as he carried out his brigade staff duties.

During the battle of Peebles's Farm, the role of communications for the Union Fifth Corps was crucial. Coordinating the various units (two divisions, totaling seven brigades) located in a thickly wooded area with ravines cutting through it required military choreography executed with the utmost precision. As the action accelerated, General Griffin held his advance on the Confederate lines until he could complete the deployment of his troops in the area of a ravine. Individual regiments needed to be repositioned in order for his division to spread out in a single line of battle facing the Confederate entrenchments north of Popular Spring Road. Historian Richard Sommers explains the complex maneuvers conducted by Griffin: "The experienced Griffin was not about to expose his troops to danger. . . . He, accordingly, directed that as soon as the soldiers advanced from the shelter of the ravine, each brigade would execute a half-right wheel that would shift its axis northwestward toward Fort Archer. [General James] Gwyn would then follow the skirmishers; Gregory would move up behind him; and Sickel would take position behind the Second Brigade."[1]

The elegantly orchestrated movement began falling apart when the Union regiments started charging toward the enemy fortifications without receiving orders. Understanding his veteran troops, and knowing their courage, Griffin was reported to have said: "Never mind about keeping the men in line. Tell them to go and they will go if only you will let them."[2]

McClelland and his fellow aides-de-camp in Griffin's division had their hands full helping convey the orders from division and brigade leadership during the day as their units assaulted Fort Archer. McClelland's skills as a mobile aide-de-camp came into play the remainder of the day as Gregory's brigade was called on to push the Confederates past Fort Archer to an area known as Pegram's Farm. Fighting continued past sunset, which kept McClelland in the saddle performing his duties until late that night. The young lieutenant—a month and a half shy of twenty-two—now saw the larger picture of tactics and strategies as they played out on the field of battle.

In His Own Words—The Letters of George McClelland

Headquarters 2nd Brigade
1st Division, 5th Corps

Near Petersburg, Virginia
October 8, 1864

Dear Sister Lizzie,

Your kind letter was received and now, after being all day in the saddle, I want to write you a word in reply.

Since I last wrote you, I have been under fire and a hot one too. You read a shabby account of it in the papers. Honor to whom honor is due. Our little Division, General Griffin's, did all the fighting. Yes, we charged a most formidable fort and line of works and captured them cheaply, that is with little loss. The Johnnys don't fight with the vim or same vigor they did in the Wilderness.

After we had secured the position so handsomely, up came 2 Divisions of the Ninth Corps and took the front. We marched back some distance, stacked arms and prepared to rest the night, which was approaching.

About 5 PM the enemy charged the Ninth Corps and they broke. In five minutes we were double-quicking to the rescue, rushed into the gap and hurled the confident Rebs back. They came on again in 3 lines of battle, but our little Division of 3,000 muskets stood like a wall of iron. By this time, it was quite dark and I had been riding backwards and forwards along the line, bullets flying like hail and shells bursting on all sides. Yet both I and my good horse escaped.

It was a grand terrific sight. The streak of fire along the whole line, the red flame of thousands of muskets, the huge volume of fire belching from the cannon's mouth, the illumination of shells bursting overhead—all was distinctly visible in the surrounding darkness.

Well, I can't describe a fight just now. I want to tell you that we whipped them handsomely and I came out alright.

I won't say anything about the disagreeable duty I had posting a picquet line that night in an almost impenetrable woods—swampy at that. I slept nearly all the next day, however, and then we set about building works, forts, etc. Next day they attacked General Ayres on our immediate right, but were repulsed beautifully and we have lain in quietness ever since until today.

This morning at 7 AM we advanced our skirmish line along the whole front and our Brigade supported the movement. I was just this whole day riding through dense woods filled with undergrowth and thickets; and now we have our line butting right against the Rebel's rifle pits. Did it too without losing a man.

Another word and I have done. My connection with these headquarters is about dissolved. I have asked to be relieved. Rank, military etiquette, etc. I have mustered as Captain and will assume command shortly of the department of Company F, 155th Zouaves.

I desire you, Lizzie, not to decry our President. Any man who could cope successfully with the lamented Douglas is not "common" or "coarse." Look at his opponent, a man *whose statesmanship consisted in superintending a third-rate railroad. Who, in his long connection with the Army, could not submit a plan of campaign. But he hasn't the ghost of a chance. Let him go to obscurity.*

When you write, Lizzie, direct to the Regiment. Love to all.

Ever Your Brother,
George

Notes on the October 8, 1864, Letter

George McClelland wrote from Second Brigade headquarters in his position as an aide-de-camp to Brigadier General Gregory. He spent his days on horseback covering the terrain on brigade business. His reference to "under fire" was the battle of Peebles's Farm that began in late September and spilled over into October. McClelland's role in the brigade came at a critical time. The maneuvers conducted by Griffin's division during the assault and subsequent actions at Pegram's Farm drew heavily on the mobility and communications skills of the division and brigade staffs. Far from his having a sedentary staff role, McClelland's responsibilities found him playing a vital role in helping Generals Warren, Griffin, and Gregory execute the actions of the day on the battlefield. After the collapse of the Ninth Corps, McClelland played a key role helping orchestrate a response to Confederate assaults that sought to break through the Union line. With his perspective as a mounted staff officer, McClelland was able to see the canvas of the battlefield in broader terms than he had ever seen before when he was serving as a foot soldier with his company.

McClelland's commission as a captain had broken through the bureaucratic logjam in Harrisburg, and he had asked to be relieved of his staff duties so that he could return to his company as its commander. That request had been granted, and McClelland soon returned to his beloved Company F.

In a stark turnaround from his judgment of Lincoln at the start of the war, McClelland challenged his sister's low opinion of the president. Compared to Stephen Douglas—a skilled orator, but a man of questionable substance—Lincoln demonstrated the leadership qualities that McClelland so prized. And the former commander of the Army of the Potomac—Lincoln's opponent in the upcoming election, George McClellan—was summarily dismissed as a second-rate railroad man and an ineffective general.

Camp of the 155th Pennsylvania Volunteers
Pegram House, Virginia
November 4th, 1864

Dear Sister Lizzie,

Your last interesting letter I received while just on the point of starting on the reconnaissance towards the south side road. I need not tell you anything in reference to it as it has been fully published. The impression had prevailed among us all that something grand was about to be accomplished from the fact that the preparations were on such a grand scale and the heavy force that was sent, comprising about all the Army of the Potomac.

We started at 3 AM and I read your letter by the glimmer of a campfire. Of course we had not far to go until we butted against the enemies' works protecting the railroad. I had the good fortune to be sent on the skirmish line with 200 men of our Regiment; and we advanced our line to within 50 yards of the Rebel breastworks, driving their skirmishers into them.

Their sharpshooters then got at work firing through loopholes and killed and wounded quite a number of our Regiment. Anybody showing himself in one spot was almost sure to be hit. Every man had his tree and if, in an unguarded moment, he disclosed any part of his person, he was almost sure to be shot.

It's an exciting place—a skirmish line—fascinating to me. It's dreaded by a great many, but I would sooner fight so than in line of battle. I had provided myself with a number of bandages and staunched the poor fellows' wounds as well as I could and sent them to the rear.

I remained all that day and night on the line—most a miserable night it was—rain pouring in torrents and no protection, no fire. I had coiled myself up around the trunk of a tree and finally forgot all my troubles in sleep. I was aroused about midnight by a lantern glaring in my eyes and a voice calling: "Captain, Captain!" The owner of the voice was a Colonel on Warren's staff and he wanted to know the position of the line and the connection on our left. I told him, but he was not satisfied; wanted to see it himself, so I had to go down the line with him along the edge of Hatcher's Run about a quarter mile. When I got there, I left him and started back alone.

The darkness could almost be felt. It was as black as misery. It took me just two hours to reach my post. I had to feel my way and only fell into the Run once which did me no harm as I was soaked anyhow.

Next day we fell back and reached camp about 3 PM. Since that time, I have been very busy attending to Company business, etc. and these are the reasons I have been so long replying to your letter.

My impression about the move is that it was a decided failure, caused chiefly by the disgraceful conduct of the new Regiments which acted shamefully.

The weather has become very cold and disagreeable and the men are busy erecting quarters, building chimneys, etc. Every board and brick in the country being pressed into the service for this purpose.

I am glad to know How[ard] has recovered. Give him the compliments of his brother and fellow soldier.

Well, Lizzie, I have come to the end of my string. I regret that I have been unable to send you a remittance. It requires a little self denial as it is to live within my income. The tariff on officers is very great. An enlisted man can make about as much as a Subaltern. Officers are resigning by the scores on the plea of inadequate compensation. Coffee 15 cents per pound; sugar 45; ham 30; and everything else in proportion. Then I pay $30 per month for a servant and it takes about all.

But I will close this dry, stale, flat unprofitable letter by tendering love and affection to all the household. I have just received a word from Arch. No, about three words. He said: "We have cleared Price out of Kansas and I have a slight scratch." I judge he is wounded.

Ever Your Brother,
George

Notes on the November 4, 1864, Letter

In this letter, McClelland reflected on the battle of Burgess's Mill that had occurred a week earlier during the army's attempt to seize and disable the Southside Railroad. Despite extensive preparation and the perceived weakness of the Confederate army, the battle's outcome was inconclusive.

In his new role as captain and company commander, McClelland led a group of 200 skirmishers (unlike some of his contemporaries, McClelland liked skirmish duty) to within 50 yards of the Confederate fortifications. A number of his men were killed or wounded by Rebel sharpshooters who manned the breastworks.

The assault on October 27 did not achieve its objectives, as McClelland pointed out, and the Union army suffered the loss of some 1,800 men (to the Confederates' 1,300) due to a host of factors, the least of which was the performance of new regiments in the Army of the Potomac. Difficult terrain, poor communications, and inadequate coordination among Union units played more crucial roles in the outcome.

McClelland reported to Lizzie that he had received a letter from their brother serving with the cavalry in Kansas. Arch had apparently suffered a slight wound and reported to his brother that Confederate Major General Sterling ("Pap") Price had been defeated and his forces run out of Kansas.

Camp in the Woods, Virginia
Near Park [Parke] Station
December 15, 1864

Dear Lizzie,
I am just recruiting my exhausted energies consequent on the great raid down the Weldon Railroad. We were about six days; marched 80 miles; devastated the whole country

on our line of march. Pushed through mud, slush, rain, snow and hail. The 3rd day, while we were near Bellefield [Belfield], the next station past Jarratt's, the whole country was covered with a sheet of ice, fully an inch thick. The javelin leaves of the pines looked like clusters of silver spears, while the fields looked like myriads of Lilliputian silver palaces. This soon melted away making the country a sea of mud.

The 5th day the weather was chilling cold and on that night (the 11th) everything inanimate was frozen solid. Animation was about suspended in me. Still 15 miles from our lines and the rough frozen roads rendered pedestrianism difficult and painful so that when we did at last reach home, I was most emphatically "played out."

We suffered but little damage from the enemy. A few men who had straggled from the column were found with their throats cut and bodies stripped of clothing. One man of my Company is missing.³

The country on our line of march was remarkably rich. Large palatial residences, splendid farms well stocked. Wheat, corn, rye, oats and sweet potatoes in abundance. Poultry and Apple Jack in amp[le] quantity.

The men had their Thanksgiving on the 2 last mentioned. They say that the 5th Corps was on a high old spree and the 6th and 9th Corps looked on us with envy when they saw almost every man with a turkey, chicken or leg of mutton marching in on that raw 12th of December.

But to see the quick work made of the railroad: the whole Division deployed along the line and at a given signal, the whole track was upset for 5 miles. Then we set to work separating the ties and railroad iron. Built up the ties in piles and the rails on top. Then started the fires. Very soon the iron was warped and bent. For 18 or 20 miles it was a complete wreck. The boys will never forget the raid to North Carolina [southern Virginia].

Here we are now in the woods on the frozen ground watching for something to turn up. I trust that "something" will be winter quarters. Now that the daring Sherman has got through all right, there will be no necessity for us to make any feints.

I had been expecting at least half a dozen letters when we returned from our great tramp and although it took over two hours to distribute the mail to the Regiment, I had not a single letter. That made me feel worse, but I was consoled last night by your sprightly letter. Your former letter enclosing one from George the Younger was also received. I will have him court martialed for disrespect to his superior officer if he writes any more such hieroglyphics.

Well, Lizzie, you are having quite a brilliant time. I have been thinking and studying how to procure a 20 day leave in order to go to Davenport. I think I will try it about the last of January.

Excuse this sprawling sheet. I have a tent without fire in it and am compelled to run out every minute to warm my fingers.

Love to all,
George
GPM postwar note on the letter—Apple Jack raid December 1864/

Notes on the December 15, 1864, Letter

McClelland's final letter to Lizzie in 1864 was written after the infamous "Apple Jack Raid" to southern Virginia near the border of North Carolina. His vivid description of the ice storm that swept through the area, the thaw and then refreezing of the ground indicates the challenges that the 26,000-man expedition faced on their trek. Horses, wagons and artillery also had to be transported through this changing weather pattern that turned roads from ice to mud back to frozen, rut-ribbed byways.

The official Union casualty rate for the expedition was just a little over 1 percent of those participating, but the brutal death inflicted on stragglers by local guerrillas left lasting impressions on Warren's troops. McClelland's man, Private Frederick Rutert, a draftee, was captured on December 11. Presumably taken while straggling, Rutert was held prisoner by the Confederates at an unknown location until February 14, 1865, when he was released. Private Rutert never returned to the 155th Pennsylvania but was transferred to the 191st Pennsylvania Volunteer Regiment where he served until his discharge in June 1865.

His nephew, "George the Younger," age three, had "written" his uncle a letter that was enclosed by Lizzie with one of her letters. Uncle George, tongue in cheek, threatened Nephew George with a court-martial for disrespect because of the toddler's indecipherable writing.

McClelland's hopes for a twenty-day leave to visit Davenport would not be fulfilled. Grant and Meade wanted all of their army in place at Petersburg and the traditional granting of leave during the holidays was curtailed.

Chapter Fourteen

"He Knows Not What a Day or Hour May Bring Forth"

Dabney's Mills and Second Hatcher's Run,
January—March 1865

The Army of the Potomac

> Taking new resolution from the fate which our enemies intend for us let every man devote all his energies to the common defense. . . . The advantages of the enemy will have but little value if we do not permit them to impair our resolution. Let us then oppose constancy to adversity, fortitude to suffering, and courage to danger, with the firm assurance that He who gave freedom to our fathers, will bless the efforts of their children to preserve it.
> —General Robert E. Lee, February 11, 1865

As both sides settled into winter encampment at the close of 1864 and the beginning of 1865, the Confederates were at a decided disadvantage: their food and supplies had been severely reduced by Union successes in seizing and controlling Rebel rail lines and roads; Union forces outnumbered their own in the Petersburg fortifications by a 2:1 margin; and the November presidential election in the North had resulted in a resounding victory for Abraham Lincoln that seemed to close any doors to a negotiated peace between the two armies. Lincoln did, in fact, pursue several peace overtures, but his insistence on unconditional surrender and his rejection of Southern independence scotched the possibility of negotiations between the two sides.

Union regiments in the Army of the Potomac were beginning to receive cold-weather clothing that had been packed up and placed in storage during the summer. And the Union supply train and wagon network brought ample provisions to the Federals on a regular schedule. On the other side, cold and hungry Confederates began trickling into the Union lines to surrender. The 155th Pennsylvania reported receiving squads of five or six deserters at a time into their line. As historian James McPherson has described it, Lee's army of 55,000 was "melting away by desertions"[1] during the winter of 1865.

Under pressure from Lincoln to pursue Lee while the Confederate army was so vulnerable, Grant made plans for an operation to attack the Confederates where the Army of the Potomac had left off at the end of 1864. The primary objective of this renewed effort was to inflict casualties and force Lee to extend his already thin siege lines a bit more. This was not war on an epic scale but a continuation of the "bull dog grip" approach, advocated earlier by Lincoln, where the enemy is strangled into submission. Meade objected to the foray, insisting that there was little to be gained from such a move and that maneuvers in winter could be subject to disastrous weather conditions. (The memory of Burnside's "Mud March" lingered on.) Meade was overruled by Grant.

Grant's orders, issued on February 4, were for the Second and Fifth Corps, accompanied by General David Gregg's cavalry division, to intercept and capture Confederate wagon trains carrying supplies from Belfield. Warren's Fifth Corps–starting out from Globe Tavern—would provide security for Gregg's troopers, who would ride south on Boydton Plank Road to locate and seize Confederate supply wagons. The Second Corps—now under General Andrew Humphreys—departed the vicinity of Globe Tavern to hold positions north of Hatcher's Run to protect the Union operation from a northern attack by the Confederates coming out of Petersburg.

Once he saw the Union's intention, Lee ordered reinforcements into the area: the Second Corps of General John B. Gordon joined General Henry Heth's division. Held in reserve along Boydton Plank Road was General Mahone's division, now under General Joseph Finegen, who temporarily commanded while Mahone recovered from an illness. Because of severe forage limitations for mounts, the only Confederate cavalry unit nearby was that of William Henry Fitzhugh ("Rooney") Lee, Robert E. Lee's son.

Beginning on the afternoon of February 5, the Confederates began taking the Federals under fire that lasted over an hour. They then followed artillery fire with an assault on the Union line that was turned back at dusk. After sizing up the situation in the early evening, Grant sent reinforcements to support the Second and Fifth Corps. Joining Humphreys's and Warren's men were divisions from the Ninth and Sixth Corps.

On February 6, Warren's men crossed to the south of Hatcher's Run and marched up the Dabney's Steam-Sawmill Road toward the site of a former steam-operated sawmill. Flooding into this mixing bowl of troops were General John B. Gordon's Confederate corps along with "Rooney" Lee's cavalry division. Fierce fighting occurred at Gravelly Run and at the site of Dabney's Sawmill. Then rain, hail, sleet, and freezing temperatures turned the battlefield into an ice-encrusted *tableau vivant*. Those severely wounded, left behind as sunset and weather made further fighting impossible, likely froze to death during the night.

The freezing rain and snow continued into the next day making an assault by either side less and less likely with each passing hour. The temperature never rose above freezing. Late in the afternoon, there was a feeble Union artillery bombardment, but it was without consequence, and, thus, the battle of Hatcher's Run (or Dabney's Mill) ended. By nightfall, the Union had withdrawn to the defensive position they had held at the start of the day.

Lee, on February 8, wrote to Secretary of War James Seddon in Richmond: "[S]ome of the men had been without meat for three days and all were suffering from reduced rations and scant clothing, exposed to battle, cold, hail and sleet. . . ." Both sides were eager to return to the relative warmth, comfort, and safety of their winter encampments.

While the Hatcher's Run/Dabney's Mill engagement ended in a stalemate, Lee lost 1,000 men, over 7 percent of his troops, further depleting his diminished force. Now his line needed to be stretched even thinner to maintain the integrity of his siege line around Petersburg.

Grant, on the other hand, lost some 1,500 men killed, wounded, and missing out of the 34,000 Federals from the Army of the Potomac that were involved in the battle, a loss of just over 4 percent. In a war of slow attrition, Lee was at a decided disadvantage. Each loss for him cut away at the muscle and sinew of his army.

> The cool, frosty morning made every sound distinct and clear, and the only sound heard was the tramp! Tramp! Of the men as they kept step as regularly as if on drill.
> Brigadier General James Walker, division commander in John B. Gordon's corps, on the opening phase of the attack on Fort Stedman, March 25, 1865

As temperatures rose slowly, signaling the approach of spring in Petersburg, Robert E. Lee began exploring ways to break the stranglehold the Union had on the city and his army. It was clear after discussions with Jefferson Davis in Richmond that there would be no negotiated end to the war. There were no political cards to play; only military options were left to the Confederate general. Lee asked Major General John B. Gordon to put together a plan to break the siege.

Gordon reconnoitered the lines and chose Fort Stedman, a Federal fortification due east of Petersburg located midway between the Appomattox River and the Crater. His plan of attack was to employ all three of his divisions in a predawn assault on the fort. A small contingent of Confederates, equipped with axes, would precede the infantry in order to clear a path through the abatis barriers that blocked the approach to the fort. Once openings were made, a small force would storm the fort, take control of the batteries, and seize positions in the Union rear to prevent reinforcements from filling the break in the line. Once this Confederate advance group had done the initial work in securing the area, the major part of Gordon's force would stream into the fortress. In total, Gordon would have at his disposal 11,500 men, a full cavalry division and a reserve of an additional 8,200 men to support the attack after it was under way.

A breakthrough at Fort Stedman also had the advantage of putting the Confederates close to a major Union supply depot on the City Point Railroad at Meade Station. The Gordon plan was bold, but it was also an action born of desperation. Lee knew that Phil Sheridan's cavalry had disposed of Jubal Early's force in the Shenandoah Valley and was moving rapidly toward Petersburg to join the Army of the Potomac. The addition of Sheridan's troopers would give the Federals increased flexibility and agility to strike at the Confederate right and likely the ability to shut down the remaining Rebel supply lines. The situation required quick action, and Lee chose to begin the attack on Fort Stedman in the early morning hours of March 25.

Gordon's advance contingent was successful in clearing a path through the Union obstacles, surprising the enemy picket line and seizing control of Fort Stedman's batteries exactly as planned. The Rebel infantry began to double-quick time across the no-man's-land into the fort (with General Gordon among his troops to evaluate the assault). The temporarily dazed Union troops began to react, and when they did they were able to prevent Gordon's men from widening the breach in the line. By 8:00 a.m. a Union counterattack was in full force and began to smother the Confederates with sheer numbers of men. Union forces quickly overwhelmed Gordon's men, trapping many behind the Federal line. Scores of Confederates who were boxed in surrendered rather than face continuing Union musket and artillery fire as they attempted to extricate themselves from the fort. The daring Confederate effort to take Fort Stedman collapsed like a punctured balloon, and Lee called off the attack while the morning was still young.

Figuring that Lee must have depleted his right flank to support the effort at Fort Stedman, Grant smelled blood and ordered an attack on the Rebel lines near Hatcher's Run. Union forces succeeded in overrunning the Confederate lines, inflicting heavy casualties and taking nearly a thousand prisoners. When casualties were counted at the end of the day, the Confederates had lost 4,800 men; the Union, just over 2,000. For the Confederates it was a bad day at Fort Stedman made worse by the losses at Hatcher's Run.

In late March, Sheridan joined his force with Meade's at Petersburg after successful operations in the Shenandoah Valley. Now, with the considerable combined resources of the Army of the Potomac and the Army of the Shenandoah, Grant was in the catbird seat. His focus now was to prevent the wily fox from slipping out of Petersburg and to crush the enfeebled Confederate forces with an aggressive spring campaign.

The Regiment—155th Pennsylvania Infantry

> Every fresh advance into the enemy's strongholds by General Warren's Corps involved the greatest dangers and necessitated not only courageous fighting qualities on the part of his troops, but the ability to perform very hard manual labor. Every new position gained had to be fortified; every intrenchment captured from the enemy had to be remodeled so as to make it a defensive position for the Union troops.... [D]uring the greater part of the winter of the Petersburg campaign, the One Hundred and Fifty-fifth Regiment was constantly engaged either in fighting, or through details of men, digging and shoveling in the trenches.
> —*Under the Maltese Cross*

On the evening of February 4, much to the surprise of all the regiment, the 155th received orders to be ready to march at a "moment's notice." Officers and men alike thought that the inclement winter weather precluded any attacks on the Confederate lines. At the direction of their senior officers, the men would take only the most essential items; anything not deemed critical to an attack were to be left behind.

Early the next morning, Bartlett's brigade (of which the 155th was one of eight regiments) marched down the Weldon Railroad track several miles before heading southwest to Rowanty Creek near the Confederate breastworks. The large Union force soon routed the small Confederate contingent in the vicinity and took some Rebel prisoners. Griffin's division crossed the stream and advanced in a column to Vaughan Road. Pausing to rest for several uncomfortable hours in the cold evening air on frozen ground, the troops were then ordered to resume their march at midnight toward the rear of the Confederate lines at Hatcher's Run where they bivouacked. Early the next morning they set about reworking the abandoned Confederate works to strengthen them, wielding their shovels and pickaxes in the bitterly cold weather.

At midafternoon, the Second and Third Divisions of the Fifth Corps were ordered to advance on the Rebel lines. They encountered little resistance and drove the enemy back following light, sporadic musket fire. Griffin's First Division—including the 155th—was then ordered to cross the Confederate works and advance over a broad field to a woods where the Rebels were positioned, raking the open area before them with artillery and musket fire.

As the regiment began crossing the open space, they encountered an elderly black man and woman who were taking turns carrying a white child about two or three years old. Members of the 155th directed the frightened couple and child to seek cover behind a fallen tree as the unit continued their advance across the field. The Confederates fell back and were then joined by Mahone's division. The newly reinforced Rebels now outnumbered the Federals, and brigade commander Joseph J. Bartlett, seeing the futility of his unit attacking a force of such superior numbers that held an exceptionally strong defensive position, ordered his men to fall back. Firing into the Confederates as it withdrew, the 155th was able to slow the pursuit by Mahone's men.

Nearing its own lines at the edge of the open space where it had started the advance earlier in the day, the 155th was met by members of the Second Brigade of Griffin's division—a unit comprising New York regiments manned by raw recruits. Stationed at the edge of the woods, the New York units were to have provided covering fire while Bartlett's brigade withdrew, but instead they panicked at the rush of men and enemy fire and began firing into the ranks of the 155th. Caught between "the devil and the deep sea"—as regimental historians later characterized it—the 155th chose to charge the New York Units in an effort to disrupt the friendly fire. The New Yorkers broke and fled in chaos behind the Union lines. Once the mob of New York regiments had dispersed and Bartlett's brigade, including the 155th, had cleared the field of fire, Union artillery opened up with a barrage that halted the advancing enemy. Order was restored among the Union troops after the initial confusion, and, after regrouping, they were ready to repel a Confederate assault that started after sunset. The Rebels were pushed back easily, and the 155th settled down for a cold, wet night.

Memories of that night and the following days were recalled in the regimental history: "On the night of the 6th of February, 1865, to the 13th, the One Hundred and Fifty-fifth and Griffin's division suffered extremely from the cold and exposure. Having left all camp paraphernalia in their former quarters, some soldiers even leaving their blankets, and the weather continuing very inclement, the ground being frozen hard, it was impossible to attain a restful sleep. In fifteen minutes after lying down the part of the body in contact with the frozen earth would become numb with cold, compelling the weary soldier to turn continually from side to side. . . . A more miserable week than that spent by the One Hundred and Fifty-fifth during the lull following the Dabney's Mills campaign could hardly be imagined."[2]

> Soon the brazen-throated engines of war with ear-splitting detonations began to fill the air with missiles of destruction. The musketry firing increased to a continuous roar; again subsiding to sounds resembling the ripping of canvas or the rattling of a stick over a paling fence. The firing increased and subsided continually, and as the battle extended the contending hosts became enveloped in the smoke and lost to view.
> —The Second battle of Hatcher's Run, *Under the Maltese Cross*

On March 25, the regiment woke to the sound of artillery fire coming from the direction of Petersburg. The men of the 155th, along with the rest of Bartlett's brigade, were roused out of their warm, comfortable quarters into a fog-shrouded landscape. They marched several miles and then halted to await further orders while they watched a division of the Second Corps maneuver in front of them. During this halt, they learned that the artillery fire they had heard earlier in the morning was from the Confederate attack on Fort Stedman.

An hour before sunset, the 155th marched in the direction of heavy firing and formed a line of battle behind the Irish Brigade and then advanced to relieve them. The fire between the 155th and the enemy was intense, resulting in extraordinarily high casualties in the regiment, including the wounding of Lieutenant Colonel John Ewing and Major John Cline, both of whom served on regimental staff. Among the regiment four men were killed and sixteen wounded during the Second Hatcher's Run engagement.

The enemy pulled back at 9:00 p.m. affording members of the 155th the opportunity to collect the dead and wounded and to exchange their muskets with those of the dead men if they judged that the deceased's weapon was in better condition than their own. For two days following the "Second Battle of Hatcher's Run," the regiment "slept on their arms." That is, the men's weapons were stacked in Company "streets," their knapsacks were packed and ready to go, and their haversacks held four days' worth of rations. If required, the regiment could be on the march in five minutes after receiving orders to move. The winter hiatus in activity—such as it was during the first three months of 1865—was over. A spring offensive was in the wind.

The Soldier—George P. McClelland

> It occurred to me how soon the quietness of this pleasant morning may be broken by the shrieking of shells, the murderous rattle of musketry, the rush of steeds and men in deadly conflict and the heart-piercing groans of the wounded and dying. Yes, this is the lot of the soldier—above all others he feels that he knows not what a day or an hour may bring forth.
> —Captain George P. McClelland, March 15, 1865

Bone-chilling cold accompanied by frequent freezing precipitation, including snow in the Petersburg area, made for a gloomy start of 1865. Yet, for the Union forces, there were signs of hope that the conflict might end by spring. The regiment was buoyed by word that Fort Fisher in North Carolina had been taken by Federal forces. (There was also a rumor that Wilmington, North Carolina—the final sanctuary of Confederate blockade-runners—was now in Union hands. That rumor proved to be false.) A salute of one hundred guns honored the capture of the fort among the ranks of the 155th. Added to news of Union victory in the West and Sherman's expedition through Georgia and South Carolina were McClelland's firsthand observations on the Petersburg front. Desperately hungry Rebels raided Union lines ("Haversack Raids") to take food. Confederate deserters, who made their way to McClelland's area on the Union line, related the desperate situation of the remaining soldiers spread thin over the siege line, ill-fed and -clothed, devoid of their earlier zeal and optimism. McClelland heard the prisoners speak of a "hopeless cause." Yet, despite the growing optimism of McClelland and his fellow soldiers, hard fighting still lay ahead. The Confederate army might have been haggard, but it was not about to roll over.

At Dabney's Mill, McClelland's company was sent in to block the breach in the First Division's line in the vicinity of the sawdust pile left behind from the mill. McClelland soon found his unit holding the center of the Union line as the right and left flanks were pushed back by the enemy. Nearly surrounded by Confederates and initially regarded as lost by Union officers, McClelland's men fought their way back from the sawdust pile to sanctuary behind Union lines.

On March 25, while the right side of the Union line was fighting the Confederate assault on Fort Stedman, McClelland, as part of Bartlett's brigade, was sent back to Hatcher's Run to take advantage of what was thought to be a weakened Confederate line. McClelland and his company were sent in at about 6:00 p.m. and advanced to a position close to the Rebel works, where they fought vigorously until nine o'clock, when they were relieved.

McClelland's Company F, along with Company A, situated on the right of the assaulting Union line, received heavy enemy fire because of its exposed position. Units on the left were protected by the sloping terrain, which shielded them from the worst fire. During the firing, a voice from the 155th ranks called out: "Fire right oblique!" By directing their fire to the right at an angle, the members of the 155th were able to break the Rebels' advance.[3] The enemy fire diminished and then stopped; soon the Confederates withdrew behind their entrenchments. At the end of the day, Company F had lost two men to mortal wounds; one man was wounded but survived. The Confederates might have lost some of their zeal in the beginning months of 1865, but they could still deliver a powerful sting to their adversaries.

In His Own Words—The Letters of George McClelland

Camp of the 155th Pennsylvania Volunteers
January 20, 1865

Dear Sister Lizzie,

I received a day or so ago a letter soaked in tobacco juice. The only part of the superscription legible being—"lland". It had fell between flooring of the Adjutant's office and was only by accident discovered. The letter was from you and I was glad to get it for I had not heard from you in a long time. I have heard from Pittsburgh in the shape of letters and "box of luxuries" which were gladly received and duly appreciated.

Arch and Henry I have not heard from for two months. I received a letter—very interesting—from my young friend and schoolmate Captain Thad G. Sloan of Knapp's Battery now at Savannah. He is connect[ed] with that heroic band of Sherman's. It is reported that we will join Sherman, but I think not—so long as General Meade commands the A of P. The 5th is Meade's old Corps and is the standard or criterion of the Army. The end is drawing nigh and there is but two months left me and for the War, or I am a false prophet.

The weather has been uniformly cold for the past few weeks with the exception of one severe rainstorm which covered our camp like an inundation of the Nile and left a sea of mud. This territory being naturally marshy made it very disagreeable.

All is quiet around the beleaguered cities of Petersburg and Richmond, even the inevitable picket firing has almost entirely ceased. We have to vary the general monotony [with] an occasional dash on our lines. The boys call them "Haversack Raids" food being their principle object. This evinces the desperation of the enemy. We have intelligence tonight of the capture of Fort Fisher with its entire garrison and also Wilmington—this last not confirmed, but very probable.

I am getting along admirably—a little busy at times—yet I would rather be employed than idle. I am now detailed on a Board of Examination to pass upon officers of the 1st Brigade of our Division. As I am the junior member, I am, of course, the recorder of the proceedings.

You must not be too sanguine, my dear Sister, of seeing me on a visit to Davenport. Furloughs and leaves are only granted in extreme or urgent cases. Said urgency consists of important business, expressly stated, or a sick wife or child or parent, sister or brother. Now none of my kith are fortunate enough to be attacked with illness, so unless I take hold of the temptation held out and concoct a falsehood, I will be necessitated to stay it out. I sometimes think the best policy would be to remain my seven months and then I will not be hampered by want of time.

It's the usual, yet unnatural way of mankind. One generation rises after another and scatters over the world. Look at us, for example. And in a few short months there will be another of the family to commence the elbowing and jostling of this life. Sometimes I shrink from the thoughts of it. The world is cold, unfeeling, heartless and I must work my way through it all. But if I can only get a start, I'll fight it. Then sometimes the feeling creeps over me that this is the only fight I am called to engage earthly—and it behooves me to fight that good fight heavenly.

Here I leave you with the fervent hope that at last, in the unveiled presence of that infinite, all perfect and eternal One, we may again meet. That Eternal One in whose presence there is fullness of joy and whose right hand there are pleasures for ever more.

George

Notes on the January 20, 1865, Letter

McClelland could have spared his sister the story of his retrieval of her tobacco juice-soaked letter from the adjutant's office. If she had harbored any doubts prior to this revelation, Lizzie surely now knew that the soldier's life was one surrounded by indelicate masculine habits.

The letter he received from a school friend, Thad Sloan, caused McClelland to think about Sherman's role in the Army of the Potomac. There was considerable speculation among officers and enlisted men alike about Sherman replacing Meade. It was Grant, however, who decided that Sherman was not a good fit in the mix of resources at Petersburg. The general in chief favored keeping Meade in the position he had held since the summer of 1863. Meade was deemed adequate for the job, and moving Sherman into the position would only complicate the command structure when simplicity and constancy of command were necessary. On the other hand, Grant welcomed Sheridan because of the additional cavalry resources he brought with his Army of the Shenandoah. The joining of Meade's and Sheridan's armies was not viewed as replacing leadership but as supplementing the Union forces with a key resource.

McClelland's prediction about the end of the war was off by half a month. Yet, for McClelland and the others in the Army of the Potomac, some of the most vicious fighting of the war would take place in the coming two months.

The "Haversack Raids" mentioned by McClelland were evidence of the desperation of the Confederate troops. With their supply lines effectively cut off and foraging constrained by wintry weather, the Confederates had to resort to forays into Union lines to steal food.

Fort Fisher, North Carolina, was taken in mid-January 1865 by Union General Alfred H. Terry after heavy bombardment by Admiral David Porter's warships. The city of Wilmington, North Carolina, however, would not be in Federal hands until February 22, 1865.

McClelland realistically had low expectations for a potential visit to Davenport. Only the most urgent family matters warranted the granting of leave during this crucial period of siege. He resigned himself to spending his remaining time in the army without a furlough.

McClelland's thoughts turned uncharacteristically melancholy at the end of his letter to Lizzie. He thought about the end of the war and his eventual need to make a living upon his release from the army. Then he contemplated his own mortality and closed with the thought that brother and sister might only meet again, not on earth, but in the presence of God. Reading this letter, Lizzie must have felt a chill when she came to these lines. Never in past letters to his sister had George discussed the possibility that he might not survive the war.

Camp of the 155th Pennsylvania Volunteers
February 15, 1865

Dear Lizzie,

I have the pleasure to acknowledge the receipt of your welcome letters; one from Iowa City and the other from home in Davenport. I am almost afraid to write an answer to your letter for the simple reason that I can't do justice to them. You are undoubtedly an accomplished letter writer, choice in language and apt in expression. But you must consider, my dear Sister, that for the past two and one-half years, I have had no opportunity for the cultivation of the mental powers excepting in a military sense. All my energies were turned in that direction because it was my duty. I think I can say now, without egotism, that I can support the dignity of the position I now hold.

But to the matter at hand. You no doubt have read of the fight we had at Hatcher's Run. They had me killed for the space of an hour, but I finally turned up all right. I had been on the skirmish line all day (it was the 6th) and our Brigade advanced through the

line on a double-quick. My skirmishers were collected as rapidly as possible and we dou-
bled-quicked to join the Regiment.

The firing was now heavy and when I reached the front, General Pearson threw me
with my detachment into a breach the enemy had made in the Division line. We accordingly went in and planted ourselves on a sawdust pile near a deserted mill. Before long,
Mahone's Rebel Division came up and pushed back the right and left of our lines. My
small handful of men clung to their position in the center until we were almost enclosed
by the enemy's lines, when it required some nice maneuvering to get out. But I finally did
all right.

I found the Regiment when I had got back and, being the senior officer, took command—formed the line hurriedly as the enemy were still gaining ground, made a charge
and—night put a stop to any further operations. This is very interesting, I know. The
losses in the Regiment were 55 killed, wounded and missing. I lost five men wounded in
my Company.[4]

We are now turned out of house and home in the dead of winter (and real winter it
is), compelled to build huts again in our new position near Hatcher's Run. My fingers
are stiff with cold—I sigh in vain for my cozy little hut with the alcove that I shall see no
more forever.

Freezing outwardly, my heart beats warm for my Brothers and Sisters and our dear
Father.

Your Brother,
George P

Notes on the February 15, 1865, Letter

McClelland's reference to the battle on February 6 was to Dabney's Mill
where McClelland and his unit were nearly overrun by Confederates. The
famous "sawdust pile" near the abandoned mill site was the subject of numerous recollections by soldiers of the Fifth Corps who fought that day at
Dabney's Mill near Hatcher's Run.

As senior officer among the withdrawing 155th Regiment, McClelland took
charge, forming up a line to stop the enemy from advancing. He was successful in bringing order out of the chaos on the battlefield and stopping the enemy from continuing its advance.

Dabney's Mill proved a costly battle for the 155th Pennsylvania. While not
the levels that McClelland reported in his letter, the official casualty count was
twenty. Some of the men McClelland counted as "missing" from the regiment
may have turned up before the official count was taken. Official regimental
records show no men missing at Dabney's Mill.

On the day McClelland wrote his letter to Lizzie, it was sleeting in the Petersburg area and temperatures remained in the midthirties during the day, dropping into the twenties at night. Her brother had every reason to be "freezing outwardly" as he concluded the letter.

Headquarters, Company F, 155th Pennsylvania Volunteers
Hatcher's Run, Virginia
March 15, 1865

Dear Sister,

Yours, ever welcome, came to me on the picket line on Sunday, March 12th. I will tell you what I jotted down in my memorandum book on my tour of duty:

I am on picket; the line runs along a tortuous stream with gnarled trees with unsightly branches shooting from [them]. The banks on either side are hid by impenetrable thickets of bushes and vines. I am sitting in my lodge of pines—not sighing for a "lodge in some vast wilderness" as someone says, but looking across at the picket posts and still further to the forest of evenly grown pines and wondering what is going on beyond where the blue smoke curling upwards and settling like a veil among the tops of the trees denotes that a hostile party watches and waits for they know not what.

I visit the entire line and return to my post. The warm sun has sunk behind the horizon and in a short time night throws her sable garment over the world; but not long—for the moon in its fullness sheds a rich mellow light on nature and I drink in the hallowed influences that impress me.

The last bugle has sounded, the last shrill pipe of the fife and the last stirring drum beat and the Army of the Potomac sleeps—all but the watchers on the outposts. As the last tune of martial music expires, the duties and trials of a soldier seem to vanish and I am transformed into another nature.

Memory carries me back to infancy and the retrospection is sad. I think of our once bright, cheerful home when all was joy and gladness. I think of the gradual disruption of that home, broken up piecemeal. I think of the cares of an aged father, of sisters and brothers struggling through the world. I think of it all—of those saddest of all words "what might have been" down to the living present. Then the bitter pang of self accusation thrills through me when I consider what little I have done; the many things left undone; the hitherto profitless life spent.

Standing in the pale moon light, looking on the bright firmament above me, I thank God for his infinite mercies and goodness. Thank Him for the watchful and tender love of parent, sisters and brothers. I thank him for the blessed hope of immortality where our love and praise will be blended together around the great white throne.

Hark! A musket shot breaks the stillness and my reverie at the same time. My responsibility of guarding a sleeping army admonishes me to be vigilant. A careless sentinel has discharged his piece. I throw myself on the ground and am soon asleep.

Monday morning—this morning I was awakened by the slanting rays of the gentle sun streaming in my face and the merry singing of the birds as they caroled their songs, flitting from tree to tree. And it took some time to dispel the gleam of peace and happiness it all suggested. I finally awoke to the stern realities of my position.

It occurred to me how soon the quietness of this pleasant morning may be broken by the shrieking of shells, the murderous rattle of musketry, the rush of steeds and men in deadly conflict and the heart-piercing groans of the wounded and dying. Yes, this is the lot of the soldier—above all others he feels that he knows not what a day or an hour may bring forth. But a truce to this.

I sit down to tell you that we had a review of the Corps today. That when we returned to camp, the news was published of a victory of Schofield over Bragg and that he was near Fayetteville; and that shortly afterwards (just two hours ago) the order came to be ready to move at a moment's notice—with four days rations and sixty rounds of ammunition.

We have had a week of warm, dry weather and the roads are pretty good. This move is particularly unfortunate for me as I expected a north-west trip of twenty days, but if we move it kills it. The clouds are lowering tonight and a rain may delay the movement.

Four deserters came in on my line and they confirmed the status told by others that Lee's army is in a desperate condition, almost open mutiny, mutterings—not loud, but deep and wide spread—of a hopeless cause. Of a return to their homes and let the consequences be what they may. All this the utmost efforts of the officers have failed to stop. The final crush of the reeling Confederacy is at hand—God Save the Republic.

With the reiteration of my changeless love to you all, I am your Brother,
George

Notes on the March 15, 1865, Letter

McClelland vividly described the scrubby surroundings at Hatcher's Run while on picket duty with his men. He wondered what was going through the minds of the enemy located across from him, an area marked by clouds of smoke rising from their campfires. His reference to a "lodge in the wilderness" was borrowed from William Cowper, eighteenth-century English poet.[5]

During this lull in the action, surrounded by the quiet beauty of nature, the soldier reflected on the past and his thoughts stirred sad memories: of a widowed father; brothers gone off to war; an eldest brother on the frontier struggling to establish his own life with wife and children; and sisters who pursued their own careers outside the family. Rather than see siblings who were independent, mature adults successfully making their own way in the world, George saw the disruption of a nuclear family. And, curiously, he saw his own life as without accomplishments. That he had served as a skilled and respected soldier, most recently as a commissioned officer, seemed to be overshadowed by the uncertainty of what he would do after his military service.

At age twenty-two, George had a life of bright possibilities before him. Perhaps a more fundamental uncertainty filled his thoughts—not concern for the dissolution of his childhood family or frustration over the lack of achievements thus far in his young life but the prospect of his own death. For over two years, he had been surrounded by death on the battlefield. Friends, senior officers, and his enemies had fallen around him. He had been in the maelstrom of combat countless times and had been struck only once by enemy fire. On a quiet, moonlit March evening in Virginia, George McClelland may have sensed that the odds of death were increasing with each new battle. How many more battles would be fought before the Confederacy finally collapsed? In how many more battles would he fight before his luck ran out?

Union General John Schofield's encounter with General Braxton Bragg in North Carolina in mid-March was much less conclusive than McClelland's letter implied. Bragg did withdraw but only after inflicting heavy losses on the Union army. Sherman moved through Fayetteville, North Carolina, destroying the Confederate arsenal there.

McClelland's hopes for a "northwest trip" to Davenport for twenty days would not be realized. The tension in the Petersburg siege line was building, and there was little thought of granting furloughs as both armies geared up for additional fighting.

The despair evidenced by the Confederate deserters was palpable. A "final crush" was indeed imminent, but there were several major engagements for McClelland to participate in before the war could be concluded. One of these occurred weeks after McClelland wrote this letter, when he and his company faced the enemy at the crossroads of Five Forks, Virginia.

George McClelland would not write another letter to his family from the front lines of the war. Two and a half weeks later, after periods of intermittent fighting, destiny met Captain McClelland at Five Forks.

Chapter Fifteen

"The Beautiful Captain"

Five Forks, March—April 1865

The Army of the Potomac

> It is natural to suppose that Lee would understand my design to be to get up to the South Side [Railroad] and ultimately to the Danville Railroad, as soon as he had heard of the movement commenced on the 29th [of March]. These roads were so important to his very existence while he remained in Richmond and Petersburg, and of such vital importance to him even in case of retreat, that naturally he would make most strenuous efforts to defend them. He did on the 30th send Pickett with five brigades to reinforce Five Forks.
> —Lieutenant General Ulysses S. Grant, *Memoirs*

As March drew to a close and weather appeared conducive to a major offensive using the combined forces of Sheridan's Army of the Shenandoah and Meade's Army of the Potomac, Grant was guided by three interrelated objectives: (1) to force Lee to stretch his siege line even further by threatening the Confederate right flank; (2) to seize the South Side Railroad, cutting off Rebel supplies to Petersburg and Richmond; and (3) to crush the Army of Northern Virginia with the Union's overwhelming number of troops. These objectives were not mutually exclusive endeavors; they were compatible approaches combined to deliver a knockout blow to Lee's army and the Confederacy.

On March 29, Warren's Fifth Corps—17,000 men strong—set out in a light rain to march up Quaker Road toward Boydton Plank Road. Warren's mission was to provide infantry support to Sheridan who was on the road to Dinwiddie Court House with 9,000 troopers as part of a coordinated effort to take the South Side Railroad. Serving as the vanguard of the Fifth Corps, the First Brigade of the First Division, commanded by Brigadier General Joshua L. Chamberlain, ran into resistance from Confederate units located just off Boydton Plank Road near a farm owned by the Lewis family. Reinforced by the Second Brigade of the division, Chamberlain moved his unit forward and began driving the Confederates back toward their entrenchments aligned to the north along White Oak Road.

The Confederate general who watched the Union drive his men back, Lieutenant General Richard Anderson, responded by quickly dispatching a brigade of South Carolinians under Brigadier General William H. Wallace. Wallace's reinforcements helped stop Chamberlain's advance after thirty minutes of intense fighting. The action see-sawed back and forth as Union artillery came on the scene provoking a third Confederate brigade to join the fray. Concerned about the probability of his advance collapsing beneath the hammering by three Rebel units, Griffin sent in four fresh regiments, including the 155th Pennsylvania, that had been held in reserve. The newly introduced regiments swarmed past the Lewis farmhouse and used sawdust piles at an abandoned sawmill near the farm as makeshift breastworks.

The pressure on the Confederates was overwhelming, and the Rebels began to fall back. When the action was over, the Confederates had lost 371 men to the Union's 381. Yet, despite the ostensible equity in casualties, the Union had scored a major gain: it now had a foothold on Boydton Plank Road, an important supply route for Lee's army.

Grant was pleased with the turn of events and saw an opportunity to send his most aggressive general officer, Phil Sheridan, around the right of the Rebels in order to get behind them. This meant giving up the effort to take the South Side Railroad—at least for the time being. Grant was responding to a dynamic battlefield situation, and he knew that Sheridan and his cavalry troopers had the mobility to quickly take advantage of the situation while the plodding Fifth Corps would—in Grant's mind—not be able to move quickly, particularly under the direction of General Gouverneur Warren whose reputation had plummeted with Grant.

On the morning of March 31, General Ayres—with the approval of corps commander General Warren—began an assault on the Confederate lines along White Oak Road. Meanwhile, the Confederates, under direction from Lee, began their own assault on the Union lines facing White Oak Road. The two opposing armies were like billy goats battering each other, but the Confederates had the advantages of an earlier start and forward momentum. They could not be stopped. The Rebels pushed both Ayres's and Crawford's divisions back and took the entrenchments occupied by Union troops earlier in the day.

The retreating troops of Ayres's and Crawford's divisions re-formed, and Warren then ordered a second advance, this time with General Griffin directing the efforts. The combined force of Ayres's and Crawford's divisions and some of Griffin's men, along with two brigades of Humphreys's corps, advanced and held their ground.

The Union units entrenched on this newly taken field and faced the enemy in front of White Oak Road. After a close observation of the enemy's facing entrenchments, Warren advised Meade that a full-scale attack would be a useless sacrifice of men. Instead, the corps commander had to be satisfied that he had cut off a Confederate division from the rest of its army. Warren saw this as a Union foot in the door that could lead to a breakthrough in the Confederate line. At 5 P.M, Meade sent a message to Warren ordering him to hold his position and send a unit to establish a link with Sheridan at Dinwiddie Court House. Bartlett's brigade—including the 155th Pennsylvania—was selected and sent out to make contact with the Union cavalry.

While Warren's men had been fighting Lieutenant General Richard H. Anderson's corps on March 31, Sheridan's troopers had run into Major General George Pickett's division of infantry and cavalry led by Major General Fitzhugh Lee at Dinwiddie Court House. Sparring with the Confederates the entire afternoon, Sheridan had to halt his northern progress to Five Forks. While he was stopped in his tracks by Pickett's men, Sheridan saw the glass half-full: "We at last have drawn the enemy's infantry out of its fortifications, and this is our chance to attack it."

Sheridan wanted infantry support to supplement his attack and specifically requested the help of General Horatio G. Wright's Sixth Corps. He did not want Warren's Fifth Corps; he made that clear in communications to Grant. The general in chief responded by telling Sheridan that Wright's corps was holding an important position and could not be released. Furthermore, Warren's corps was closer and could be quickly moved into position to support Sheridan.

By the evening of March 31, Bartlett's brigade had reached a point in the rear of Pickett's left flank, at the plantation of Dr. James P. Boisseau, as they carried out their orders to make contact with Sheridan at Dinwiddie Court House three and a half miles to the south.

Spooked by the presence of Bartlett's brigade at his rear and surmising that more Union forces would soon arrive, Pickett began a withdrawal of his men to Five Forks.[1] The complex chess game being deftly played over the past three days by Union and Confederate generals was inexorably leading to a confrontation at a country crossroads thirteen miles southwest of Petersburg.

Hold Five Forks at all hazards . . . Protect the road to Ford's Depot and prevent Union forces from striking the Southside Railroad.
    —General Robert E. Lee, instructions to George Pickett, March 31, 1865

What I want is that Southside Road . . . I want you men to understand we have a record to make, before that sun goes down, that will make hell tremble—I want you there!
    —Major General Philip H. Sheridan, instructions to his officers, April 1, 1865

The convoluted reporting structure of the Union army gathered around Five Forks suited Grant's preference for issuing orders to those in whom he had a high degree of confidence rather than using the chain of command. This arrangement confounded effective communications. Sheridan (in whom Grant had unqualified confidence) reported directly to the general in chief. Warren (in whom Grant had little or no confidence) reported to Meade but was now taking orders from Sheridan. Delays and miscommunications were rampant in the lead-up to the action at Five Forks. Anticipating that Warren would lack the necessary aggressiveness, Grant gave Sheridan the option of relieving the Fifth Corps commander if conditions called for a change in leadership.

On Saturday, April 1, the sun rose at 6:45 over the bucolic landscape surrounding the five-road intersection. The area around the crossroad has been described as: "A rural setting . . . a mosaic of a few large plantations and small farmsteads, mainly the property of Widow Mary Elizabeth Gilliam . . . and the farms of James and Benjamin Boisseau. To the east of the junction were the Bass and Robert Sydnor houses, the ruins of an old place referred to as The Chimneys, along with a little white frame meeting house called Gravelly Run Methodist Episcopal Church. The surrounding terrain was largely covered with tangled thickets and pine woods, which were cut by ravines and interspersed with bogs and an occasional clearing."[2]

While the Confederates completed their entrenchments along White Oak Road just east of Five Forks, Sheridan sent men to reconnoiter the Rebel lines facing him and began to formulate the details of his attack. His plan was to use his cavalry to assault the enemy front, fighting both mounted and dismounted, while Warren's infantry corps went streaming in around the enemy's left flank. Simultaneously, Major General George Armstrong Custer would lead his Union cavalry division on a feinting move on the Confederate right. It was a simple, straightforward plan; however, Sheridan's scouts got one vital piece of intelligence wrong: they had the Confederate left flank stretching further east than it was actually positioned.

Called in to support Sheridan's cavalry, Warren's corps did not reach its required position until 4:00 p.m. due to difficult terrain and the exhaustion of the infantry. Sheridan was furious, attributing Warren's delay to a lack of aggressiveness on the part of the Fifth Corps commander.

Initially organized at a clearing adjacent to Gravelly Run Church, the corps was sent quickly into combat: Ayres's division was to attack the Confederates at the angle on the eastern flank of Pickett's line; Crawford's division was to sweep past the Confederates' left flank and come in behind them; and Griffin's division was to be held in reserve, prepared to provide support where needed as the assault unfolded.

Despite Sheridan's straightforward plan, the Union advance had a fumbling and misdirected start. The cavalry was unable to mount a sustained assault against the White Oak Road line. Warren's infantry fell victim to the poor intelligence provided by Sheridan's scouts earlier in the day. Ayres's division, aiming for the left center of the Rebel line, took heavy fire on its left from the angle. Crawford's division, which was to flank the Confederates and come in behind the Rebel line, went well north and west of its intended target. Quickly adjusting to compensate for the faulty troop-position intelligence, Ayres redirected his men to begin attacking the Confederate flank. Griffin seized the initiative and directed his men to begin attacking around and behind the Confederate left flank to the north of Ayres's division. Bartlett's men of Griffin's division closed in on the Rebels, and several regiments—including the 155th Pennsylvania—engaged in hand-to-hand combat with the collapsing Confederate line.

Warren rode off to bring Crawford's errant division back into the fold, while Sheridan, in a display of martial theatrics, spurred his horse, "Rienzi," to leap over the Confederate earthworks while leading Ayres's men as they broke through the Rebel line. Warren located Crawford's division, turned it south where it could put additional pressure on the Confederates who were starting to buckle under the formidable Union assault.

The Confederates had difficulty organizing resistance due, in part, to the absence of their leaders, Pickett and Fitzhugh Lee. Both generals had left Five Forks earlier in the day—without telling their subordinates where they were going—to attend a shad bake hosted by General Thomas L. Rosser north of Hatcher's Run. The freshly caught and cooked fish were no doubt accompanied by strong beverages that contributed to a relaxed feast atmosphere. Some have insisted that an "acoustic shadow" prevented the Confederate generals from hearing the battle raging one mile away. Whether caused by acoustical phenomena, strong drink, or a combination of both, two key Confederate leaders were "missing in action" during the critical phases of the battle of Five Forks.

When the fighting stopped after dark, the Confederates had lost 3,000 men, many of those captured by the Union. The Union lost 800 men. Now the way was cleared for the Union to take the South Side Railroad; Lee's escape route south and his final supply line were closed.

General Warren cleared the field at the cessation of the fighting, believing that he had helped bring victory during the critical hour of the battle by getting Griffin's division quickly into the fray when Ayres's division ran into trouble and by pulling back Crawford's division after it had strayed out of the location where it was needed. Instead of being hailed as a conquering hero by Sheridan, Warren was shocked to learn that he had been relieved of duty as corps commander. Despite impassioned pleas to both Grant and Sheridan, Warren was rebuffed by both generals. (Gouverneur Warren spent the rest of his life trying to clear his name. On November 21, 1882—seventeen years after the battle of Five Forks—Warren was vindicated by a federal court of inquiry. Unfortunately the dispirited general died three months prior to the release of the court's findings.)

> I have just heard from Sheridan. He has carried everything before him. He has captured three brigades of infantry and a team of wagons, and is now pushing up his success.
> —Lieutenant General Ulysses S. Grant, telegram to President Lincoln, April 1, 1865

Wishing to move quickly while his enemy was on the ropes, Grant ordered an all-out assault on Petersburg to take place early on the morning of April 2. The Ninth and Sixth Corps were the focal points of these attacks. Of the two, the Sixth Corps was most successful in breaking through the Confederate line. In an attempt to rally his beleaguered troops during the Union assault, General A. P. Hill was riding among his men when he was shot, mortally wounded by a soldier from a Pennsylvania unit.

During the day, the Federals piled on the attacks. Just after one o'clock the next morning, Union pickets reported that the Rebels were abandoning Petersburg, the troop movement illuminated by burning tobacco warehouses. By 3:00 a.m. Federal troops had entered the city and raised the Stars and Stripes over Petersburg's courthouse, ending a nine and a half-month siege that had cost the Federals about 42,000 men and the Confederates 28,000. (Incredibly, civilian casualties in the city due to military action were less than half a dozen.)

With Union troops in dogged pursuit, Lee's army moved west to Amelia Court House on April 4, on to Jeterville on April 5, and then toward Farmville and the Appomattox River on April 6. In the retreat, Lee lost one-quarter of his men when they were captured as his force split near Sailor's Creek. On April 7, Lee held off Union forces at Farmville and resumed his retreat north of the Appomattox River, proceeding toward Appomattox Court House. On the morning of April 8, Lee saw the campfires of Sheridan's men blocking his retreat path to the west. He knew that Grant and Meade were behind him and closing in fast

By April 9, after a few halfhearted attempts to engage the Union army encircling his troops, Lee agreed to meet Grant to discuss surrender terms. Meeting at the home of Wilmer McLean, the two generals reached a surrender agreement that permitted Lee's men to take their horses home with them. Lee and Grant signed the surrender document, shook hands, and departed, leaving their subordinates to work out the details of the agreement.

Three days later the formal surrender ceremonies were held with Brigadier General Joshua Lawrence Chamberlain given the honor of receiving the surrender of the Rebels' arms and colors. Chamberlain was deeply moved by the "sad great pageant" as the Confederate ranks passed in front of the Union troops, stacking arms, dropping cartridge boxes, and laying down their battle flags—some "rushing from the ranks, kneeling over them, clinging to them, pressing them to their lips with burning tears," according to the general from Maine.

The Regiment—155th Pennsylvania Infantry

> The victory at Five Forks had swept away a flying buttress of the enemy's stronghold. We had broken down the guard of a tactical movement to hold their threatened communications and cover their entrenched lines. We may be said to have virtually turned the right of the defenses of Petersburg and broken the Confederate hold upon Virginia. It was, indeed, a brilliant overture, giving courage to our hearts and stimulus to our energies.
>
> —Joshua Lawrence Chamberlain, *The Passing of the Armies*

During the engagement at Lewis Farm, the 155th's commander, Brigadier General Alfred Pearson, grabbed the regimental colors from a surprised color sergeant and rode toward the Confederate lines bellowing, "Follow me, men, or lose your colors!" The regiment rallied behind their commander, the troops taking cover behind scattered sawdust piles as they advanced toward the Confederate lines. Chamberlain later expressed his appreciation for the aggressive assault of the 155th at Lewis Farm that rescued his brigade: "Up came that handsome Zouave regiment, the 155th Pennsylvania, the gallant Pearson at their head, regimental colors in hand, expecting some forward work, sweeping so finely into line that I was proud to give them the center, joining on the heroic [Brevet Lieutenant Colonel] Glenn, holding there alone."[3]

By 4:00 p.m. on April 1, Warren's entire Fifth Corps, including the 155th Pennsylvania, was assembled on the grounds surrounding a small country church—the Gravelly Run Methodist Episcopal Church—after an arduous night march across a swampy landscape and over surging streams. Orders were issued for the Fifth Corps to advance north over Gravelly Run Road toward White Oak Road and then wheel left when it was past the enemy's flank and come in on the Confederate rear. While Warren's infantry was executing this flanking move, Sheridan's cavalry would dismount and attack the front of the enemy line.

The 155th, along with the 1st Michigan and the 20th Maine, swooped into the Confederate line where they fought hand-to-hand with the entrenched Rebel infantry. Chamberlain saw the pressure that Bartlett's three regiments were experiencing and sent in reinforcements. The Confederates buckled when faced with the reinforced Union line and began falling back to Ford Road, the northernmost road into Five Forks. By nightfall, Ayres's and Griffin's divisions had succeeded in rolling up the Confederate line from the enemy's left flank all the way to Five Forks.

By the time the fighting had subsided and the Confederates had cleared the field of battle, the 155th had taken a Rebel prisoner for every man in the regiment as well as three artillery pieces and numerous wagons and ambulances. But these prizes of war came at a price: eight of the regiment's men were killed and sixteen more were wounded in the engagement.

After the battle at Five Forks, the regiment marched to the South Side Railroad on April 2 with plans to proceed east and take Petersburg. Before the 155th could start an invasion, the Confederates abandoned the city and soon after that left Richmond. For the next several days, the 155th chased Lee's dwindling forces, sometimes marching in large circles in pursuit.

On the afternoon of April 9 the regiment was pausing after a series of exhausting marches when it was called to the front and quickly formed into a line of battle. As the Union forces pressed in on the Confederate position, a mounted courier bearing a white flag rode up to the Union line near them. The Confederate courier was met and taken to General Chamberlain, now commanding the First Division of the Fifth Corps. The messenger was then escorted to General Griffin's Fifth Corps headquarters from which orders were soon delivered back to the 155th to stand down. A cease-fire was called.

While Grant and Lee signed the terms of surrender on April 9 at the McLean house, the men of the 155th, from their vantage point on a nearby ridge, could see the surrounding landscape, including the Confederate army in position, the village of Appomattox Court House, and the McLean residence. The regiment watched as General Lee stepped from the porch of the house to mount his horse and ride back to the Confederate lines. Within minutes a Union staff officer passed among the regiment to announce that the Army of Northern Virginia had surrendered.

General Meade ordered the Fifth Corps to receive the final surrender of the Confederate forces. General Chamberlain was to receive the arms and colors of the surrendering army. As part of the First Division, the 155th was assigned the role of lining the road along which the Confederates would pass to relinquish their arms. From 9:30 a.m. until 5:00 p.m. on April 12, the Confederate brigades passed through the Union troops to stack their arms and deposit their flags as part of the terms of the surrender.

When the final arm had been stacked and the last color surrendered, those present could honestly report: "The Army of Northern Virginia, the pride of the Confederacy, the invincible, upon which their hopes and faith had been reposed, had disappeared forever, existing thenceforth in memory only."[4]

The Soldier—George P. McClelland

The two bodies of troops exchanged blows in the manner of a pair of boxers. The fast angry firings went back and forth. The men in blue were intent with the despair of their circumstances and they seized upon the revenge to be had at close range. Their thunder swelled loud and valiant. Their curving front bristled with flashes and the place resounded with the clangor of their ramrods.
—Stephen Crane, *The Red Badge of Courage*

By late afternoon of April 1, McClelland, his company, the 155th, and the rest of the Fifth Corps reached their marshaling area in a clearing near a small, wood-frame country church at the intersection of White Oak and Gravelly Run Roads. The Gravelly Run Methodist Episcopal Church would become a focal point for George McClelland prior to the attack as the units of the Fifth Corps formed in lines of battle and after the engagement when the church served as a way station for the wounded, the dying, and the dead.

McClelland's Company F formed up as part of Griffin's division just behind Ayres's and Crawford's divisions. By 4:00 p.m. the Fifth Corps had received its instructions and begun marching north on Gravelly Run Road toward the Confederate lines aligned along White Oak Road. Ayres's division wheeled left and passed through thick woods and then across an open field toward the left flank of the Confederate line. It was headed dead on to "the Angle," where the left flank of the Rebel line was crooked like a shepherd's staff.

Crawford's division moved in a northwesterly direction to get in behind the Confederate lines. As Griffin's men made their way behind the other two divisions of the corps, McClelland saw a clearing through the woods ahead, and as he and his unit moved through the pine, cedar, locust, and scrub oak woods into the open field, they saw the Confederate left flank firing at Ayres's troops. Crawford's men were nowhere in sight. General Bartlett spotted the opening around the back of the Confederate line and sent his regiments in behind the Rebels' left flank. As they wheeled left and headed west, the sun began dropping below the tree line in the distance.

The members of the Confederate line pivoted around to fire at the approaching members of McClelland's Company F that had come in behind Brigadier General Matthew Ransom's North Carolinians. As the distance closed between the advancing Union ranks and the Confederate line, Captain McClelland was hit in the upper left thigh by a minié ball fired by one of the North Carolina soldiers defending "the Angle." The impact of the round knocked McClelland to the ground. Unable to move and bleeding profusely, he was, for a brief time, behind enemy lines as the fighting surged back and forth in the late afternoon.

After the fighting subsided and the Confederates began withdrawing from the field, McClelland was surrounded by soldiers from his unit. Sergeant James McDowell of his company directed efforts to lift the captain and lay him on a blanket as a makeshift stretcher. The soldiers discussed transporting him to a nearby field hospital. As gently as they were able, the Zouaves of Company F carried McClelland to the small country church that had been near their marshaling area several hours earlier. The captain slipped in and out of consciousness as the stretcher-bearers transported him from the battlefield to the church.

The little Gravelly Run Church was aglow with lamps when the stretcher-bearers reached their destination. Pews had been pulled from the church and were scattered around the perimeter of the building. The Zouaves stepped gingerly around the men lying on the pews and the grounds of the church as they carried Captain McClelland into the interior. With Sergeant McDowell as their spokesman, the men made certain that a surgeon examined the captain. Sergeant McDowell spoke to the surgeon after he finished examining McClelland, suggesting that the men could carry Captain McClelland to the railroad at Humphreys's Station so he could be sent to a hospital. The surgeon responded: "What is the use, the Captain's wound is fatal!"[5]

The men made Captain McClelland as comfortable as possible in the small structure that was now more like an abattoir than a place of worship. Sergeant McDowell volunteered to stay with the captain through the night, and the other Zouaves from Company F departed leaving behind their captain and the haunting scene of human suffering they had just witnessed at Gravelly Run Church.[6]

Surgeons continued to treat McClelland's wound over the next several days. They determined that a .58 caliber minié ball has passed through his upper left thigh shattering the femur and the trochanter major. The resulting bone splinters—acting like organic shrapnel—had been driven into adjacent areas of the body and threatened to hamper healing should they become necrotic. Surgeons cleaned the wound and removed as many of the bone splinters and uniform fragments as they could, applying persulphate of iron in a compression to arrest the bleeding.

McClelland recovered sufficiently in five days to be removed by ambulance over ten miles of road to the Fair Grounds Hospital in Petersburg. The decision to send McClelland to the former Confederate hospital in Petersburg was based on his still-weakened condition. The larger, better equipped Union hospital at City Point, Virginia, would have required a longer, more arduous journey. Procedures to remove bone splinters from his wound continued at Fair Grounds Hospital during the following weeks.

Slowly McClelland seemed to be gaining strength. One of his company, Private Clarence Long, performed hospital orderly duties daily during this important recovery period.[7] On the morning of April 18, George McClelland was visited in his hospital tent by a Christian Commission representative, who announced, "Captain, you have a visitor." When the tent flap opened in response to the Christian Commission man's invitation to the visitor outside, McClelland's sister Annie entered. "The Indefatigable One"—as George had characterized her in some of his letters—had demonstrated the truth of that nickname. Based on sketchy details in an army telegram, Annie had taken passenger trains, a boat, an ambulance wagon, and a baggage train to find her wounded brother, and, despite challenging conditions, a paucity of information about her brother's whereabouts, and the assassination of the president having occurred during her travels, she found her brother and was able, with the help of Union surgeons, to nurse him back to stable health in the following weeks. It was an act of extraordinary devotion and love that George honored for the rest of his life.

In Her Own Words—The Letter of Annie McClelland

At breakfast they found out who I was. Said they had all seen George—"the beautiful Captain" they called him.

Fair Grounds Hospital
Two Miles from Petersburg, Virginia
April 18, 1865

My Dear Friends All,

I have found George thanks to a loving God. As you have already learned by his let-ter, he is doing well. I have been guided and guarded by angels in the shape of kind friends all along my journey. It just seems as if God took me by the hand and led me directly to George.

The telegram you know misled me. That mark "Pgh" meant Petersburg, not Pittsburgh as we supposed. [It] is [a] telegraphic error. As we know, Petersburg is not spelled with an "h." But before proceeding further, I must tell you that Father has not seen George yet. I suppose he has gone to Sutherland Station.

I have just been with George two hours and during that time he has looked up with his sweet face in wonderment and said: "Now I do wonder where Father is." Lieutenant Foster of the 155th who is stationed at the 5th Corps Hospital City Point told me that Father had been there about 6 days ago, but that he could not give him any information respecting George, but he thought Father had come to the Point in search of him.

Now I must begin at the beginning to tell you about my journey. I have before told you of my arrival at Washington. I will never forget the kind treatment I received at the hands of Mr. and Mrs. Jones when I took the boat for City Point. I met with hosts of kind friends, one in particular I must mention—a young man from Elizabethtown who knew nearly all the boys of George's Company. He came to me and said he wished me to consider myself under his special charge. That he would do everything in his power to assist me.

When we landed it was raining hard and such a horrid place I've never saw. I do not know what I should have done if my good friend had not been with me. We climbed the hill to the Provost Marshal's office, then went to the tavern. My friend hunted an ambu-lance going to the 5th Corps Hospital. The mud. The mud. I thought our wagon would be swamped.

We finally reached Lieutenant Foster's quarters. He was not there, but arrived in about an hour. Said he couldn't tell me where George was; that he had inquired and diligently searched for him in vain. I asked him if any of the Christian Commission agents were around. [He] said yes; he would take me over to their office. We went and found the agent who said: "I have heard from your Brother yesterday. He is doing well and I telegraphed the news to Mr. Weyman today at Pittsburgh."

You can imagine the load that was lifted off my heart when I heard such good news. He also said there were two delegates going up at 7 o'clock on the train and that I could go with them. My faithful friend, with Lieutenant Foster and the delegate, went with me to the car.

There was no passenger car attached to the train, only cars loaded with bags of sup-plies for the Army. They, however, fixed a nice place for me on or in the engine house. I was almost roasted.

I reached Petersburg at 9 o'clock at night. The streets were dark as a dungeon. The delegates took me to these rooms. (There is no scarcity of empty dwellings here.) It was a very fine house, but not furnished. In the parlor were about 20 ministers and delegates. Reverend Mr. Hall tried to make me comfortable as possible. Gave me the one cot in the house and had the darky serve me a cup of tea and biscuit. In the next room adjoining mine the twenty delegates stretched themselves on the bare floor, their cover a coarse army blanket. I slept soundly fearing no harm as I was with Christians.

At breakfast they found out who I was. Said they had all seen George—"the beautiful Captain" they called him. Well, two of them accompanied me to the hospital. One splendid old gentleman carried my traps. We reached the grounds in about twenty minutes walk. A lovely place—it is trees all around and birds singing sweetly. One of the friends said for me to wait outside the tent and he would apprise George of some one of his friend's arrival.

I did not wait long you may be sure. George was lying on a cot. He looked up in wonder and said: "Why, Sis, how in the world did you get here?" His cheeks were flushed and his forehead white as snow; his eyes brilliant. I thought it not strange they called him the "Beautiful Captain."

Since he came here he has been treated kindly, but it is shocking the treatment he had previously. Had it not been for a kind little Zouave of his Company who never left him, he might have died. His name is Clarence Long. He is with him now and stays by his side day and night. Another good man, Mr. Paige, is his constant friend.

He cannot be moved for some time the surgeon thinks, and if inflammation does not set in, George will recover. George is anxious about Father.

Well, I will close this scrawl and write again tomorrow. Direct letters as follows:
Fair Grounds Hospital near Petersburg, Virginia
C/o Sanitary Commission

Affectionately,
Annie McClelland

Chapter Sixteen

"What Will Become of All These Men?"

The Postwar Years—1865–1898

The Army of the Potomac

> It was a beautiful day, and the review was a stirring sight. Mr. Lincoln, sitting there with his hat off, head bent, and seemingly meditating, suddenly turned to me and said: "General Couch, what do you suppose will become of all these men when the war is over?" And it struck me as very pleasant that somebody had an idea that the war would sometime end.
>
> —Major General Darius N. Couch, April 1863, *Battles and Leaders of the Civil War*

The taste of victory after Appomattox was sweet for the Army of the Potomac, but the troops' daily routine changed little. They were doing camp chores and guarding stores until a demobilization plan could be developed by Union leadership. The army marched through Petersburg where the Fifth Corps made a small detour to pass in review for General Warren, now military commander of the "Cockade City" since his removal from command of the Fifth Corps at Five Forks. The army continued on to Richmond with two remaining corps—the Second and the Fifth. The Sixth Corps was assigned to the Danville Railroad to make sure that the surrender was being honored in North Carolina. The Ninth Corps was detached from the Army of the Potomac and sent to Alexandria, Virginia. The two remaining corps of the Army of the Potomac crossed the James River on a pontoon bridge and headed toward Hanover. Some of the men caught glimpses of the infamous Libby and Belle Isle Prisons as they passed through Richmond.

Traveling rapidly through the Virginia countryside on their forced march, the men covered some of the same ground they had fought over the year before. At one bivouac, the soldiers discovered remnants of gear, clothing, and bones of both Rebel and Federal soldiers hastily buried after battles during the Overland campaign. Their march took them past Hanover Court House, across the Pamunkey River, and on to a camp not far from the North Anna battlefield. As they passed Fredericksburg, some of the men took quick side trips to visit Marye's Heights where many had stormed the Rebel line two and a half years earlier. They trudged on, crossing the Rappahannock River and on to Aquia Creek, then finally to Dumfries where they camped for the night. The next day they continued their march over rough roads despite a driving rain. Some aspects of marching through Virginia, the men were reminded, did not change, war or peace. Many of the troops questioned why the army was being driven at such a punishing pace now that the hostilities were over. Some claimed that there was an economic reason for the haste; their commanding officers wanted to push them forward to muster out so that the expense of maintaining the army could be quickly reduced. By the morning of May 12, the army marched over Columbia Pike outside of Washington City and went into camp at Arlington Heights, the location of their encampment just prior to their march to Antietam in September 1862.

For a week and a half, the troops whiled away their time in camp waiting for the victory celebration—a Grand Review down Pennsylvania Avenue before Washington's political leadership, high-ranking military officers, and enthusiastic civilians. During this waiting period, resentment flared between the Army of the Potomac and Sherman's Western Army. Geographic differences and perceived slights by soldiers in both armies resulted in barroom brawls and rancor at all levels in the two organizations. Recognizing that the resentments could turn a joyous occasion into an ugly display of petty rivalries, Grant made sure that the two armies camped on opposite sides of the Potomac and marched through the streets of Washington on separate days: the Army of the Potomac on May 23; the Western Army on May 24. Grant's Solomon-like solution seemed to dampen even the most virulent antagonisms.

Tuesday, May 23, was a clear, sunny day in the nation's capital. The Army of the Potomac, marched, twelve men abreast, down Pennsylvania Avenue from the capitol under a cloudless, bright blue sky to the cheers of the citizens who lined the street. Flags flew at full staff, and black crepe was removed from public buildings for the first time since Lincoln's death six weeks earlier.

Before dignitaries on the reviewing stand, including President Johnson and General Grant, marched, in order: the headquarters staff of the Army of the Potomac; the cavalry corps; provost and engineering staff; the Ninth Corps (with a division of the Nineteenth Corps); the Fifth Corps; and the Second Corps. Officers and enlisted men agreed that their field uniforms—clean and neat, but without formal trappings such as sashes—would be the appropriate dress to make clear to the spectators that they were fighting units, not parade-ground dandies.

The army, marching in cadence, moved with the syncopated sound of boots on pavement while bayonets glimmered in the sunlight. Politicians, diplomats, and citizens alike watched in awe as the victorious Army of the Potomac passed in review. General Sherman, watching from the reviewing stand and mentally noting how his Western Army would stack up to the smart-looking Army of the Potomac, admitted to General Meade that his "poor tatter-demalion corps" would suffer in comparison. (Sherman's concern about his troops proved to be unwarranted. The Western Army marched "like the lords of the world," as one spectator noted later. Another in the crowd found Sherman's men "hardier, knottier" than their Army of the Potomac counterparts who had marched the day before.)

As he approached the reviewing stand, Joshua Lawrence Chamberlain thought of the one architect of the victory who was not present: "We miss the deep, sad eyes of Lincoln coming to review us . . . something is lacking to our hearts now—even in this supreme hour." Lincoln was not the only missing man whose specter hovered over the Grand Review. As Civil War historian Shelby Foote has written: "A total of just over 110,000 northern soldiers had died on the field of battle or from wounds received there; which means that, for every two men who marched up Pennsylvania Avenue on both days of the Grand Review, the ghost of a third marched with them."[1]

The Regiment—155th Pennsylvania Infantry

The 155th enlisted for the war, and was mustered out of the service because the war was ended. We wear its badge as the most honorable insignia that can be placed upon our breasts. We prize it more than coronet or garter, or ribbons of the far-famed Legion of Honor. We feel that while we live, the proudest title to which we can lay claim, and dying the richest legacy we can leave to our children and kindred is, that we were members of the One Hundred and Fifty-Fifth Regiment, Pennsylvania Veteran Volunteers.

—Sergeant John H. Kerr, rededication of the Pennsylvania State Monument, September 17, 1889

Amid the joy of celebrating the surrender of Lee and the end of hostilities came the news of Lincoln's death in Washington. The men of the 155th reflected on the endearing traits shown by the assassinated president when he had visited the Army of the Potomac in the field several times during the war, starting after the battle of Antietam and continuing up to his most recent visit to the army in early April 1865. For a man who had given so much to ensure the preservation of the Union, it seemed to the troops a cruel twist of fate that he was not there to savor the fruits of victory with them.

The regiment began the long march back to Washington, taking time to parade in review for their former Fifth Corps commander, Gouverneur Warren, when they passed through Petersburg. Joining Warren and his wife on the reviewing stand, General Griffin watched as the Fifth Corps marched in open order, saluting and cheering as they passed in review. Warren's old brigade of Zouave regiments, which included the 155th, paused at the reviewing stand, turned to face Warren, and cheered loudly for a prolonged period of time until their officers ordered them to resume their march. Warren was moved by the loyalty and respect the troops showed him that day, a bright ray of affirmation in a time of personal despair after being relieved of battlefield duty by Sheridan and Grant.

On May 7, the regiment marched through Richmond on its way to Washington. The men recalled the northern newspapers call "On to Richmond!" that had been their byword for nearly three years. Passing among the smoldering ruins of the former Confederate capital, the soldiers experienced a deep sense of anticlimax. The former prize was now a sad, ruined husk.

Returning to Washington, the 155th marched over ground where they had fought so fiercely during the past two years. The areas that had roared with artillery fire, been swarmed by men in mortal combat, and, finally, been strewn with the bodies of Rebels and Federals alike, were now strangely quiet and not unlike any other landscape of field, forest, and farm.

On May 12, the unfinished dome of the capitol came into view, and the men cheered, partly in acknowledgment that the war was truly over and also that their long, forced march through Virginia had been completed. They were close to transforming from soldiers back to civilians once again. After a week and a half in camp on Arlington Heights, the regiment participated in the Grand Review down Pennsylvania Avenue with the rest of the Army of the Potomac. Among the parading troops, the Zouave units were a bold splash of color and radiated a special élan. General Chamberlain singled out the regiment as the "brilliant 155th Zouaves" when he described the Grand Review in later accounts. His impression was shared by the parade-watchers that day as the 155th passed by garbed in their pantaloons, white leggings, smart blue jackets trimmed in yellow, and their red fezzes.

Several days later, the men of the Fifth Corps held an impromptu candlelight procession in their encampment. It was a solemn occasion bereft of most military overtones. Perhaps the men were contemplating the words of General George Meade's farewell address to them: "Let us honestly pray for strength and light to discharge our duties as citizens, as we have endeavored to discharge them as soldiers."

The 155th returned to Pittsburgh by train in early June to a warm reception by political leaders, clergy, and the general public. Short parades, a Zouave drill, and dinner for the returning veterans hosted by the City of Pittsburgh were all part of the celebratory welcome-home program from a grateful city. Upon their final muster out and disbandment, the regiment was down to two months and nine days before the original term of their enlistment would have expired. The final casualty count for the regiment in the war was 146 killed, 651 wounded (411 of those wounded were discharged due to the severity of their wounds), and 104 succumbed to disease. These casualties came from a total enrollment of 1,500 men. As a member of the 155th, the odds of not being killed, wounded, or falling fatally ill during a term of service were 2 out of 5.

After mustering out, the members of the 155th went back to the civilian world in a wide variety of occupations. Some returned to their rural roots by resuming farm work, while "city boys" filled the blue-collar ranks in Pittsburgh's steel mills and burgeoning local manufacturing industries. Others took paths that put them in leadership positions in such businesses as Carnegie Steel and American Steel in Pittsburgh, while still others ran successfully for state and local offices in Pennsylvania. Some came out of the war with calls to service. Several men went to medical school and became physicians. John Kribbs went to seminary and became a Lutheran pastor. James D. McDowell worked for the fledgling Red Cross in Washington under the leadership of Clara Barton. (Sergeant McDowell had helped take the wounded George McClelland to the field hospital at Five Forks and had remained with him through the night at Gravelly Run Church.) Charles F. McKenna went back to the practice of law and later was appointed a federal judge in Puerto Rico by President Theodore Roosevelt.

Other veterans of the 155th saw promise in the West and headed to Ohio, Iowa, Kansas, Montana, and California where they were businessmen, mining engineers, riverboat captains, and postmasters. David P. Allen went west and served as a justice of the peace in Nebraska. One 155th Regiment member who headed west, Jack Campbell, dropped from sight after the war. The regimental history reported: "Jack Campbell never attended reunions or communicated by letter. Whether scalped by Indians or 'dying with his boots on' in some Cowboy disturbances . . . or whether still in the land of the living, his surviving comrades never heard."

Many of the veterans of the 155th stayed in contact after the war and held reunions in 1875, 1886 (for the dedication of the 155th Regiment monument at Gettysburg), 1889 (for the rededication of the Pennsylvania monument at Gettysburg), 1894, and 1896. Then, their numbers much diminished in the twentieth century, survivors held reunions in 1903, 1905, 1906, 1907, and 1908 (for the dedication of General Humphreys's monument at Fredericksburg). In 1910, the Regimental Association published the 155th's history, *Under the Maltese Cross, Antietam to Appomattox, The Loyal Uprising in Western Pennsylvania 1861—1865.*

The final page of that history serves as an appropriate valediction for the 155th Pennsylvania:

> No words of the living can add to the simple grandeur of this record; where all were alike brave, and gave to their country "the last full measure of devotion." Their very heroism and sacrifice have lifted them to an equality of glory, to which we leave them.

The Citizen—George P. McClelland

> [T]he generation that carried on the war has been set apart by its experience . . . in our youth our hearts were touched with fire. . . . [W]e have seen with our own eyes, beyond and above the gold fields, the snowy heights of honor, and it is for us to bear the report to those who come after us.
> —Oliver Wendell Holmes, Jr., Memorial Day Speech, May 30, 1884

Thanks to his sister Annie's performing the roles of nurse and patient advocate with the attending physicians at Fair Grounds Hospital, George recovered well enough to be sent—via ambulance, train, and boat—to Washington City. There he could continue his recuperation at a general hospital under the care of a skilled medical staff. Annie returned to Pittsburgh to resume her occupation as a teacher and female head-of- household for the McClelland family home.

While he was in the hospital, McClelland was mustered out of service on June 2, 1865, along with the rest of his regiment. There were no parades or candlelight processions for the wounded captain; his days passed undergoing treatment for his wound. Examining surgeons concurred that the damage done to McClelland's left leg was severe—he could not adequately rotate the limb and the leg was approximately one inch shorter, due to bone loss, than his right leg. His disability was judged to be permanent. Because of the extent of his wound and the long-term prognosis, the physicians agreed that McClelland qualified for a three-quarters disability pension. He was, in their view, "three-fourths incapacitated for obtaining his subsistence by manual labor."

By August 1865, McClelland was back in the family home in Pittsburgh to continue his recovery. Despite the progress he was making and the close attention to his health paid by his sister Annie and his father, McClelland suffered a relapse due to infected splinters of bone still exfoliating from the wound. Physicians in Pittsburgh operated, removing dead tissue and bone splinters. (McClelland was examined periodically by government-authorized physicians to maintain his three-quarters disability pension. As late as 1878, the examining physician reported occasional discharge coming from the area of McClelland's wound.)

The next two years of George McClelland's life are obscure. The regimental history reported that he was "confined to his room" at the family home. His wound and the modest pension of fifteen dollars per month restricted what he could do in Pittsburgh both physically and economically. Annie and his father's presence were no doubt a positive aspect of his confinement after a three-year absence. Another bright ray was his appointment to brevet major[2] on August 22, 1865, by General Order 133. The appointment, recommended by General Joshua Chamberlain for "gallant and distinguished conduct" at Five Forks, was retroactive to the day of the battle, April 1, 1865.

No written record of McClelland's recovery period from 1865 to 1867 in Pittsburgh survives. Since he was recuperating in his hometown, we can assume that family and friends—especially members of the 155th Regiment who returned home to Pittsburgh—visited him often. McClelland's appetite for literature and current events, about which he wrote so frequently in his wartime letters, is strong evidence that he filled his days at home reading books, magazines, and newspapers to satisfy his intellectual curiosity. Whether his days were also filled with bouts of self-pity and melancholy is unknown. His Calvinism and history of self-discipline seem to argue against a prolonged period of darkness in his attitude about his past military life or his future civilian prospects.

By 1867, George had healed sufficiently and was restless for a change in his life. His brother Thomas, eleven years his senior, had established a successful sash, door, and blind factory in Davenport, Iowa, and the two brothers reached an agreement about employment. George would head west to Davenport, fill a clerical position in his brother's company that did not involve demanding physical work, and live with his brother, his sister-in-law, Anna, and his three nephews, Walter, George and Wilson, as he started this new phase of his life.

The oldest brother—perhaps initially motivated by a sense of sibling loyalty and charity for a wounded veteran—soon found the youngest brother had a talent for business. Customers who encountered "Major McClelland" found him a bright, enthusiastic young man with high integrity who radiated the aura of a war hero. Within three years, George was promoted to salesman at the T. W. McClelland Company. The war had been a boom time in Davenport, and the McClelland Company expanded its scope beyond manufacturing sashes and blinds and accepted contracting projects. Prior to George's arrival in Davenport, the company had helped build Camp McClellan, a Union army post, and a prisoner-of-war camp on Arsenal Island in the middle of the Mississippi River. Contracting work continued after George joined the organization. During the post-Civil War period, a library, a rooming house, and a city market were constructed by the company. In addition to commercial contracting work, the McClelland Company started building single-family housing, popularizing a two-story, three-bay, and front gable residence style in Davenport.

As the company grew so did George's responsibilities. He was promoted to higher-level positions in the company, eventually being named a vice president and sharing many of the executive decisions about running the company with his brother. If there had ever been any charitable aspect of bringing George into his company, Thomas changed his position. George had a perceptive, analytical mind; he was a trained leader of men; he exuded trustworthiness; and he had a developing level of business acumen. The youngest brother proved to be a valuable asset to the T. W. McClelland Company as it grew in the robust postwar Davenport economy.

As George McClelland began to feel a sense of professional promise and stability in his career at the company, he also underwent a personal change in his life. An occasional visitor from New Jersey, Juliet Snow—whose aunt, Helen Gifford, lived in Davenport—caught George's eye in the congregation of the First Presbyterian Church. Visits by Juliet from New Jersey began to occur more frequently and last longer. The feeling of interest was mutual. Juliet found George a handsome, well-mannered, confident, and cultured young man who was well respected in the Davenport community. George found Juliet an attractive, well-educated, and compassionate young woman who shared his interests in literature and culture. She was able to overlook their nine-year age difference—George being the senior—and did not see his disability, requiring him to walk with a crutch, as a negative. Juliet saw George as courageous not disabled.

Visits by Juliet over the course of two years led to a burgeoning relationship that resulted in George asking for Juliet's hand in marriage. In late September 1876, George traveled east to New Jersey to marry Juliet Snow and bring his new bride back to Iowa. The couple settled in a rented apartment. With members of both Juliet's and George's families already rooted in Davenport, it did not take the couple long to establish themselves in their adopted city where they took part in civic, cultural, and church activities.

One of the married couple's first civic activities was to participate in a meeting of the newly formed Davenport Library Association in July 1877. A group of interested citizens had been assembled to begin laying the groundwork for a free library. During the meeting, George McClelland suggested that they name Andrew Carnegie as an honorary member of the library committee. From his time in Pittsburgh after the war, George knew that Carnegie—who was amassing great wealth in the steel industry—was a strong advocate of the free-library system. The idea of an honorary membership for Carnegie on the committee bore fruit; he offered the library group fifty thousand dollars to establish a free library in Davenport. Later the Pittsburgh philanthropist increased the amount to seventy-five thousand.

George's interest in community endeavors was wide. In addition to his active participation in the First Presbyterian Church, he was a 32nd Degree Mason and a member of the Davenport Academy of Science. He also joined with a small group of Civil War veterans to get a long-promised soldiers' monument, honoring those who had fought with the Union, erected in the city. Bogged down by a lack of funds and direction, the monument project was revived by McClelland and eight other veterans who obtained funding, selected a site, and commissioned the base and statue in a year's time. By 1880 the monument was in place on a bluff on Main Street Davenport overlooking the city and the Mississippi River.

As a businessman with increasing stature in the community, McClelland was appointed a vice president of the Davenport Board of Trade and later president of the Davenport Loan, Building, and Savings Association. McClelland also joined the Union League Club in Chicago. His reputation as a Civil War veteran was well known in Davenport—including his role in helping put the soldiers' monument in place—but his involvement with the local Grand Army of the Republic (GAR) post was tardy. The Davenport organization—the August Wentz, Post Number 1—was established in the fall of 1881, but McClelland did not join the group until March 1887. Rather, McClelland gravitated toward another veteran's group: The Military Order of the Loyal Legion of the United States (MOLLUS.) He joined the State of Illinois chapter of MOLLUS in the 1870s and remained an active member until his death.

MOLLUS, formed just after Lincoln's assassination, was the more prestigious veteran's organization, composed exclusively of officers. Senior officers who were members included U. S. Grant, William T. Sherman, and Phillip Sheridan. Besides Grant, four other presidents were members of the organization: Rutherford B. Hayes, Chester A. Arthur, Benjamin Harrison, and William McKinley. At its peak, MOLLUS had 12,000 Civil War officer members.

The GAR was open to all Union Civil War veterans and had 490,000 members at its zenith.

One of McClelland's closest friends in Davenport was another Civil War veteran. William D. Middleton, two years younger than McClelland, had served in the 44th Iowa Regiment. After his discharge in 1865, Middleton went to medical school in New York City then returned to his hometown of Davenport to set up his practice. Dr. Middleton was a member of the First Presbyterian Church, along with the McClelland families, and by the 1870s had become George's physician. Middleton was called on to report on the progress of McClelland's wound for the periodic submissions to the Bureau of Pensions. Dr. Middleton greatly admired McClelland's fortitude and courage in dealing with his disabling wound as only a former soldier and physician could. The doctor was so impressed that he named his second child George McClelland Middleton in honor of his patient and friend. (George M. Middleton followed in his father's footsteps and studied medicine, also setting up his practice in Davenport.)

After George's father, Archibald, died, Annie was the only member of the immediate family left in Pittsburgh. Her siblings had all migrated west. George extended an invitation for Annie to join him and Juliet in the large home they had purchased in Davenport. Juliet welcomed her sister-in-law warmly, knowing that had it not been for Annie's persistence in finding George and nursing him back to health, that George might not have survived April 1865. Annie joined George and Juliet in their home in 1878. She was prepared to pursue her profession as a teacher when she arrived in Davenport, but she also let her brother and sister-in-law, married just two years, know that she would be pleased to be a helping hand for any new nieces or nephews that George and Juliet would add to the household.

On September 26, 1881, a son, Charles, was born to George and Juliet, but less than two weeks later, on October 7, the baby died of infant cholera. There would be no more children. George and Juliet began making plans, soon after Charles's death, to build a new house at the corner of Perry and Seventh Streets in Davenport. The architecture was a two-story, three-bay, front gable design being popularized by the T. W. McClelland Company for upper-income customers. George supervised the construction while Juliet directed the decoration of the house. It was a fresh start in a new home, leaving behind the sad memories associated with the old house.

> Year after year the comrades of the dead follow, with public honor, procession and commemorative flags and funeral march—honor and grief from us who stand almost alone, and have seen the best and noblest of our generation pass away. But grief is not the end of all. I seem to hear the funeral march be-

come a paean. I see beyond the forest the moving banners of a hidden column. Our dead brothers still live for us, and bid us think of life, not death—of life to which in their youth they lent the passion and joy of the spring. As I listen the great chorus of life and joy begins again, and amid the awful orchestra of seen and unseen powers and destinies of good and evil our trumpets sound once more a note of daring, hope and will.

—Oliver Wendell Holmes, Jr., Memorial Day Speech, May 30, 1884

Knowing as much as he did about his patient, Doctor Middleton surmised that McClelland's immune system had likely been compromised over the years because of his wound. He knew of cases reported in the medical journals of men who had recovered from significant wounds received during the war but later in life succumbed to various infections. Middleton counseled McClelland to take steps to ensure that he shielded himself from common sources of infection. There was little else that the doctor could do for his patient. (As the chair of surgery at the University of Iowa Medical School beginning in 1895, Dr. Middleton had access to the latest information regarding medical science available in the U.S. at the end of the nineteenth century.)

On Christmas Eve, 1898, George McClelland's health took a serious turn for the worse. By Christmas Day, his condition had worsened, and on the evening of December 26, Dr. Middleton and several of his physician colleagues came to the Perry Street house to examine McClelland. All the attending physicians concurred that George was in the final stages of pneumonia and that medical science could offer nothing to alter the inevitable decline of the patient. Juliet notified her brother-in-law Thomas of the latest report on George's condition, and then she and Annie alternated watching George in an all-night vigil.

At 1:30 p.m., on December 27, 1898, George Pressly McClelland died at his home on North Perry Street. The soldier, who had dodged death on so many battlefields during the war, succumbed in part to a wound received thirty-three years, eight months, and twenty-six days earlier. Every day since receiving the wound, McClelland had borne a constant, physical reminder of a war that he had entered as an untested boy and finished as a young man with a reputation for leadership, bravery, and endurance. Despite the physical limitations caused by the wound, he had led a productive civilian life, making contributions to his community, his business, and his family. In his eulogy for citizen-soldier McClelland, his minister succinctly summed up the man's winning attributes: "Step by step, he won his way by sheer merit and conspicuous gallantry."

Thursday, December 29, 1898, was cloudy and blustery when a horse-drawn hearse carried George McClelland's body over two and a half miles of city streets and country roads from North Perry Street to Oakdale Cemetery. Mourners gathered under the leafless white oaks and sugar maples at the crest of a rise to say their good-byes to the major at his "final bivouac."

George McClelland left a legacy with manifold beneficiaries. To his immediate family—Juliet, Annie, and several nephews and nieces—he left an estate that would be worth just over two million dollars in today's currency. To George McClelland Middleton, he left a substantial sum that allowed the young man to complete his medical studies and launch a career as a respected physician who served the residents of Davenport for the first half of the twentieth century. And, perhaps most enduring of all, McClelland left his letters to us who follow in the twenty-first century and beyond, letters that describe his selfless service to a cause that was essential and noble. Lincoln's simple but eloquent words to some of McClelland's brothers in arms best express our gratitude to McClelland:

> For the service you have done in this great struggle in which we are engaged I present you sincere thanks for myself and the country. . . . It is not merely for today, but for all time to come that we should perpetuate for our children's children this great and free government, which we have enjoyed all our lives.[3]

Notes

Preface
1. *Under the Maltese Cross*, 382, 383.
2. The exact words Chamberlain spoke that evening at the candlelight gathering were not recorded, but listeners called his speech "an eloquent address." The passage above is from *The Passing of the Armies* written by the general years after the war. It is, however, believed to accurately reflect Chamberlain's sentiments about the disbanding of the army in May 1865.

Chapter 1
1. Consumer Price Index, MeasuringWorth.com.

Chapter 2
1. David Donald, ed., *Inside Lincoln's Cabinet: The Civil War Diaries of Salmon P. Chase*, 121.
2. George B. McClellan, in *Battles and Leaders of the Civil War*, 2:552.
3. *Civil War Papers of George B. McClellan—Selected Correspondence 1860–1865*, 440.
4. James M. McPherson, *Battle Cry of Freedom*, 544.
5. The capitulation of over twelve thousand men at Harper's Ferry on September 15, 1862, was the largest in American history until the fall of the Philippines in World War II.
6. *Under the Maltese Cross*, 71.
7. D. P. Marshall, *Company "K" 155th Pa. Volunteer Zouaves*, 66, 67.
8. *Nil desperandum* translates to "Never give up hope."
9. Marshall, *Company "K,"* 67.

Chapter 3
1. McPherson, *Battle Cry of Freedom*, 570.
2. Marshall, *Company "K,"* 69.
3. John D. Billings, *Hardtack and Coffee: The Unwritten Story of Army Life*, 80.
4. Marshall, *Company "K,"* 71, 78.
5. Shelby Foote, *The Civil War—A Narrative,* 1:757.
6. *Under the Maltese Cross*, 89.
7. Billings, *Hardtack and Coffee*, 217–21.
8. *Under the Maltese Cross*, 91.

Chapter 4

1. James Longstreet, "The Battle of Fredericksburg," *in Battles and Leaders,* 3:79.
2. Francis Augustin O'Reilly, *The Fredericksburg Campaign,* 405.
3. Ibid., 401
4. *Under the Maltese Cross,* 95.
5. Longstreet, in *Battles and Leaders,* 3:82.

Chapter 5

1. *Battles and Leaders,* 3:119.
2. *U.S. Congress, Report of the Joint Committee on the Conduct of the War,* 37th Congress, 1863.
3. Marshall, *Company "K,"* 87.

Chapter 6

1. *Under the Maltese Cross,* 136–38.
2. Ibid., 140.
3. Foote, *Civil War,* 2:635.

Chapter 7

1. The shoes may have existed only in the imagination of Confederate division commander Major General Henry Heth.
2. Douglas Southall Freeman, *R. E. Lee: A Biography,* 3:58–59.
3. *Battles and Leaders of the Civil War,* 3:345.
4. Union losses exceeded 23,000; Rebel casualties, 28,000.
5. Jeff Shaara, *Civil War Battlefields: Discovering America's Hallowed Ground,* 104.
6. Roy P. Basler, ed., *The Collected Works of Abraham Lincoln,* 6:327.
7. *Under the Maltese Cross,* 150.
8. Ibid., 150, 151.
9. Ibid., 153.
10. An engineer on Warren's staff, he became the chief engineer for the construction of the Brooklyn Bridge after the war.
11. *Under the Maltese Cross,* 174.
12. Marshall, *Company "K,"* 112, 113.
13. McClelland says his belongings went "higher than Gilroy's Kite" in this letter. "Gilroy" is a derivation of the name "Gilderoy," a seventeenth-century Scots robber who, according to legend, was hanged so high at his execution that he resembled a kite in the air. The nineteenth-century expression to indicate extreme height was "higher than Gilderoy's—or Gilroy's—Kite."

Chapter 8

1. *Under the Maltese Cross,* 225–26.

Chapter 9

1. Foote, *Civil War,* 2:793.
2. T. Harry Williams, *Lincoln and His Generals,* 288.
3. Foote, *Civil War,* 2:876.
4. George Meade, *Life and Letters of George Gordon Meade,* 158.
5. Mason W. Tyler, *Recollections of the Civil War,* 127.
6. Marshall, *Company "K,"* 133.

Chapter 10

1. Under Lincoln's proclamation, those secessionists who took an oath of loyalty to the Union, supported the Emancipation Proclamation, and swore their allegiance with their signatures would be accepted back as U.S. citizens. When 10 percent of voters from a state accepted the amnesty requirements, the state would be recognized as a functioning body within the Union. Lincoln believed that secession was illegal and that the Confederate states had never left the Union; thus, the states would be returning to their proper relationship with the federal government, not being readmitted to the Union.

2. "Delightful Task! To rear the tender Thought

To teach the young idea how to shoot,

To pour the fresh Instruction o'er the Mind,

To breathe th' enlivening Spirit and to fix

The generous Purpose in the glowing Breast."

("Spring," by James Thomson, an eighteenth-century British poet)

Chapter 11

1. Marshall, *Company "K,"* 164.

2. *Under the Maltese Cross*, 248.

3. John D. Lentz's Report, *Official Records*, vol. 36, part 1, p. 556; and George T. Bowen diary, May 23, 1864, in Fredericksburg and Spotsylvania Military Park Library.

Chapter 12

1. Marshall, *Company "K,"* 190.

2. McPherson, *Battle Cry of Freedom,* 776.

3. *Under the Maltese Cross*, 312.

4. Ibid., 313.

5. Ibid., 32.

6. It is more likely that King was a dentist and that the regimental history reference to his being an M.D. is incorrect. Had he been an M.D., King would likely have been transferred to the medical corps, where his surgical skills would have been in high demand on the battlefield.

7. James M. McPherson, *For Cause and Comrades—Why Men Fought in the Civil War,* 82, 83.

8. Ibid., 131.

9. Marshall, *Company "K,"* 186.

10. McPherson, *Battle Cry of Freedom,* 804.

Chapter 13

1. Richard J. Sommers, *Richmond Redeemed–The Siege at Petersburg,* 251.

2. *Detroit Advertiser and Tribune*, October 20, 1864.

3. Private Frederick Rutert, captured December 11, 1864.

Chapter 14

1. McPherson, *Battle Cry of Freedom,* 844.

2. *Under the Maltese Cross*, 337.

3. Ibid., 341.

4. Official regimental records show 4 killed in the regiment, 2 from Company F; 16 wounded from the regiment, one of these from Company F; total casualties, 20.

5. "O for a lodge in some vast wilderness,
  Some boundless contiguity of shade,
  Where rumour of oppression and deceit,
  Of unsuccessful or successful war,
   Might never reach me more."

Chapter 15

1. "It was Bartlett's outstretched line in their rear, magnified by the magic lens of night into the semblance of the whole Fifth Corps right upon them, which induced them to withdraw from Sheridan's front and fall back upon Five Forks. So after all Bartlett had as good as fought a successful battle, by a movement which might have been praised as Napoleonic had other fortunes favored" (Joshua Lawrence Chamberlain, *The Passing of the Armies,* 77, 78).

2. Chris Calkins, *History and Tour Guide of the Battle of Five Forks,* 70.

3. Chamberlain, *Passing of the Armies,* 39, 40.

4. *Under the Maltese Cross,* 368.

5. Ibid., 457.

6. A reporter for the *New York World,* George Townsend, following the mortally wounded General Frederick Winthrop to Gravelly Run Church on the night of April 1, wrote of his experience there: "Gravelly Run Meeting House … a little frame church, planted among the pines and painted white with cool, green window shutters … I found its pews moved to the green plain over the threshold, and on its base floors the screaming wounded. Blood ran in little rills across the planks, and, human feet treading in them, had made indelible prints in every direction … Federal and Confederate lay together, the bitterness of noon assuaged in the common tribulation of the night, and all the while came in the dripping stretchers, to place in this Golgotha new recruits for death and sorrow."

7. Other Union soldiers receiving wounds similar to those of George McClelland were not as fortunate as the young captain. Of the six men who were wounded in the upper femur and trochanter major described in the *Medical and Surgical History of the War of Rebellion,* five died within a month's time. The sixth soldier survived but suffered from epileptic seizures for the remainder of his life.

Chapter 16

1. Foote, *Civil War,* 3:1,017.

2. An honorary promotion to a higher nominal rank due to exemplary battlefield performance.

3. Speech to 166th Ohio Regiment at Washington, D.C., August 22, 1864.

Bibliography

Acken, J. Gregory, ed. *Inside the Army of the Potomac: Captain Francis Adams Donaldson*. Mechanicsburg, PA: Stackpole Books, 1998.

Baptism Records of First Presbyterian Church, Davenport, Iowa, 1872–1895. Davenport Public Library.

Bates, Samuel P. *History of Pennsylvania Volunteers 1861–1865*. Harrisburg, PA: State Printer, 1869–1871.

Battles and Leaders of the Civil War. 4 vols. Robert Underwood Johnson and Clarence Clough Buel, eds. New York: Century, 1887–1888.

Bearss, Ed. *Fields of Honor*. Washington, DC: National Geographic, 2006.

Bearss, Ed, and Chris Calkins. *The Battle of Five Forks*. Lynchburg, VA: H. E. Howard Press, 1985

Billings, John D. *Hardtack and Coffee: The Unwritten Story of Army Life*. 1887. Reprint. Lincoln, NE: Bison Books, 1993.

Bryan, Charles, and Nelson Lankford, eds. *Eye of the Storm: Private Robert Knox Snowden*. New York: Touchstone Books, 2000.

Butko, Brian, and Nicolas P. Ciotola, eds. *Industry and Infantry–The Civil War in Western Pennsylvania*. Pittsburgh: Historical Society of Western Pennsylvania, 2003.

Calkins, Chris. "The Apple Jack Raid–'For This Barbarism There Was No Real Excuse' December 7–12, 1864." *Blue & Gray* (Summer 2005).

——. "The Battle of Weldon Railroad (or Globe Tavern) August 18–19 and 21, 1864." *Blue & Gray* (Winter 2007).

——. *History and Tour Guide of Five Forks*. Columbus, OH: Blue & Gray Enterprises, 2003.

Catton, Bruce. *The Coming Fury*. Garden City, NY: Doubleday & Company, 1961.

——. *Glory Road*. Garden City, NY: Doubleday & Company, 1952.

——. *Grant Takes Command*. Boston: Little Brown & Company, 1968.

——. *Mr. Lincoln's Army*. Garden City, NY: Doubleday & Company, 1951.

——. *Never Call Retreat*. Garden City, NY: Doubleday & Company, 1965.

——. *A Stillness at Appomattox*. Boston: Little Brown & Company, 1968

——. *Terrible Swift Sword*. Garden City, NY: Doubleday & Company, 1963.

——. *This Hallowed Ground*. Garden City, NY: Doubleday & Company, 1956.

Chamberlain, Joshua Lawrence. *The Passing of the Armies*. 1915. Reprint. New York: Barnes & Noble, 2004.

The Civil War Papers of George B. McClellan—Selected Correspondence 1860–1865. Stephen W. Sears, ed. New York: Ticknor & Fields, 1989.

The Collected Works of Abraham Lincoln. 9 vols. Roy P. Basler, ed. New Brunswick, NJ: Rutgers University Press, 1952–1955.

Collins, David, Rich Johnson, Mary Louise Speer, and John Willard. *Davenport—Jewel of the Mississippi*. Chicago: Arcadia Press, 2000.

Compiled Military Service File of George P. McClelland. National Archives and Records Administration, Washington, DC.

Crane, Stephen. *The Red Badge of Courage*. New York: D. A. Appleton & Company, 1895.

Davenport City Directories, 1868–1895. Davenport Public Library, Davenport, IA.

The Davenport Times, 1870–1898. Davenport Public Library, Davenport, IA.

Davenport Democrat and Leader, 1870–1952. Davenport Public Library, Davenport, IA.

Detroit Advertiser and Tribune, October 20, 1864. Detroit, MI.

Donald, David, ed. *Inside Lincoln's Cabinet: The Civil War Diaries of Salmon P. Chase*. New York: Longmans, Green & Co., 1954.

Dyer, Frederick H. *A Compendium of the War of the Rebellion*. Cedar Rapids, IA: Torch Press, 1908.

Faust, Drew Gilpin. *This Republic of Suffering: Death and the American Civil War. New York*: Alfred A. Knopf, 2008.

Foote, Shelby. *The Civil War—A Narrative*. 3 vols. New York: Random House, 1958–1974.

Freeman, Douglas Southall. *R. E. Lee: A Biography*. 4 vols. New York: Charles Scribner's Sons, 1934–1935.

Grant, Ulysses S. *Personal Memoirs of U. S. Grant*. New York: Charles L. Webster & Company, 1886.

Hall, Clark B. "Season of Change—The Winter Encampment of the Army of the Potomac, December 1, 1863–May 4, 1864." *Blue & Gray* (April 1991).

LaFantasie, Glenn W. *Twilight at Little Round Top: July 2, 1863–The Tide Turns at Gettysburg*. New York: Vintage Books, 2007.

Lorant, Stefan. *Pittsburgh—The Story of an American City*. Pittsburgh: Authors Edition, Inc., 1975.

Lord, Francis A. *Uniforms of the Civil War*. 1970. Reprint. Mineola, NY: Dover Publications, 2007.

Marshall, D. P. *Company "K" 155th Pa Volunteer Zouaves*. Reprint. Chicora, PA: Mechling Bookbindery, 1998.

McClelland, Annie. April 18, 1865, letter. Author's papers.

McClelland, George P. Forty-one letters, 1862–1865. Author's papers.

McPherson, James M. *Battle Cry of Freedom*. New York: Oxford University Press, 1988.

——. *Cross Roads of Freedom–Antietam*. New York: Oxford University Press, 2002.

——. *For Cause and Comrades–Why Men Fought in the Civil War*. New York: Oxford University Press, 1997.

——. *Hallowed Ground: A Walk at Gettysburg*. New York: Crown Publishers, 2003.

Meade, George. *Life and Letters of George Gordon Meade, Major-General United States Army*. New York: Charles Scribner's Sons, 1913.

Medical and Surgical History of the War of Rebellion 1861–1865. Surgeon General Joseph K. Barnes, ed. Washington, DC: U.S. Government Printing Office, 1870.

Medical Records of George P. McClelland. National Archives and Records Administration, Washington, DC.

Oakdale Cemetery, Records of Internments, and Burial Plat. Davenport, IA.

The Official Military Atlas of the Civil War. Major George B. Davis, Leslie Perry, and Joseph W. Kirkley, eds. 1891–1895. Reprint. New York: Barnes and Noble Books, 2003.

O'Reilly, Francis Augustin. *The Fredericksburg Campaign*. Baton Rouge: Louisiana State University Press, 2003.

Pension Records of George P. McClelland. National Archives and Records Administration, Washington, DC.

Pittsburgh City Directories, 1850, 1852, 1856, 1860, and 1862. Library Archives, Heinz History Center, Pittsburgh, PA.

Porter, Horace. *Campaigning with Grant*. New York: Century, 1897.

Rhea, Gordon. *The Battle of the Wilderness–May 5–6, 1864*. Baton Rouge: Louisiana State University Press, 1994.

——. *The Battles for Spotsylvania Court House and the Road to Yellow Tavern– May 7–12, 1864*. Baton Rouge: Louisiana State University Press, 1997.

——. *To the North Anna River–May 13–25, 1864*. Baton Rouge: Louisiana State University Press, 2000.

Rosenblatt, Emil, and Ruth Rosenblatt, eds. *Hard Marching Every Day– Letters of Private Wilbur Fisk*. Lawrence: University of Kansas Press, 1992.

Scott County, Iowa Probate Records, 1898 and 1899. Davenport Public Library, Davenport IA.

Sears, Stephen. *Gettysburg*. New York: Mariner Books, 2004.

Sears, Stephen, ed. *On Campaign with the Army of the Potomac–Civil War Journal of Theodore Ayrault Dodge*. New York: Cooper Square Press, 2003.

Shaara, Jeff. *Civil War Battlefields–Discovering America's Hallowed Ground*. New York: Ballantine Books, 2006.

Sommers, Richard J. *Richmond Redeemed–The Siege of Petersburg*. Garden City, NY: Doubleday & Company, 1981.

Svendsen, Marlys A., and Martha H. Bowers. *Davenport–Where the Mississippi Runs West*. Davenport, IA: City of Davenport, 1982.

Thomas, William G., and Alice E. Carter. *The Civil War on the Web–A Guide to the Very Best Sites*. Wilmington, DE: Scholarly Resources Books, 2001.

Tyler, Mason W. *Recollections of the Civil War*. New York: G. P. Putnam's Sons, 1912.

Uhl, Lauren and Tracy Coffing. *Pittsburgh's Strip District–Around the World in a Neighborhood*. Pittsburgh: Historical Society of Western Pennsylvania, 2003.

U.S. Congress. Report of the Joint Committee on the Conduct of the War, 37th Congress. Washington, DC, 1863.

United States Census, Iowa: 1870 and 1880. Davenport Public Library, Davenport, IA.

United States Census, Pittsburgh, Pennsylvania: 1850 and 1860. Carnegie Library, Pittsburgh, PA.

Under the Maltese Cross. Pittsburgh: The 155th Regimental Association, 1910.

The West Point Atlas of the American Civil War. Thomas E. Griess, ed. Garden City Park, NY: Square One Publishers, 2002.

Whitman, Walt. *Drum Taps*. New York: Library of America, 1982.

Williams, T. Harry. *Lincoln and His Generals*. New York: Alfred A. Knopf, 1952.

Index

1; and crossing of Rappahannock River by Union soldiers, 52; family property of, 9, 15; and fortifications for Fredericksburg, 39, 60; Grant's view of, 179-80, 184; health problems of, 187; and Hill, 187; intelligence for, 82-83, 100, 101, 102; Lincoln's military strategy on Richmond versus, 119, 145-46, 156, 158; in Maryland with Army of Northern Virginia, 8, 16, 19-20; on McClellan, 19, 41; and "mud march" in Virginia by Union soldiers, 67; photograph of, 139; plans for invasion of Pennsylvania by, 18, 20, 21, 96; and reinforcements for Carolina coast, 66; resignation offer by, refused, 105; retreat of, after Gettysburg battle, 104, 105, 111-12, 116, 119-20; retreat of, from Petersburg, 259-60; size of Confederate army under, 19, 39, 48, 84, 97, 98, 145-46, 148, 239, 240, 241; surrender of, 260, 261-62; tenacity and resolution of, to keep fighting, 32, 221, 239. *See also* Army of Northern Virginia
—battles: Antietam, 19-20, 23; Chancellorsville, 79-88, 95; Five Forks, 255, 257; Fort Stedman, 242; Fredericksburg, 52-55, 95; Gettysburg, 97-105; Hatcher's Run/Dabney's Mill engagement, 240-41, 241; Petersburg campaign, 207, 208, 209, 216, 222, 225-26; Rappahannock and Rapidan Rivers skirmishes (fall 1863), 146-50; Vicksburg campaign, 95-96; Wilderness, 181
Lee, William Henry Fitzhugh ("Rooney"), xxi, 216, 240, 241, 256, 258
Leesburg, 107
Leslie, Frank, 73
Letterman, Jonathan K., 74, 75
Letters to soldiers. *See* Mail service; McClelland, George Pressly; *and McClelland family members*
Lewis Farm, 255, 260
Libby Prison (Richmond), 90, 91, 268

Liberty, Md., 108
Lincoln, Abraham: amnesty proclamation of, 163, 165, 281n1; assassination of, 264, 268, 270; and Buell, 37; and "bull dog grip" approach to war, 240; and Burnside as commander of Army of the Potomac, 38, 50, 66, 68; and call for military recruits, 221; on Chancellorsville battle, 85; criticisms of, x, 13, 14; and Emancipation Proclamation, 37, 281n1; on "fiery trial" of Civil War, x; and Five Forks battle, 259; Gettysburg Address by, 158; and Gettysburg battle, 105; and Grant, 120, 166; gratitude to Union soldiers by, 278; and Hooker as commander of Army of the Potomac, 68, 80, 85, 96, 97; and Kilpatrick's plan for Richmond raid, 163; and McClellan as commander of Army of the Potomac, 17-18, 37-38, 50; McClelland on, x-xi, 13, 160, 161, 223, 233, 234; and Meade, 105, 119, 120, 145-46, 156, 163; and Navy, 223; peace overtures by, 239; and Petersburg campaign, 207; physical appearance of, 33; in Pittsburgh, 2; and presidential election of 1864, 186, 203, 208, 222, 223, 226, 233, 239; pro-Union graffiti of, 22; and public support for Civil War, 199; recruitment for Union army by, 3, 4, 5; rural analogies of, 120, 147; on secession as illegal, 281n1; secession of South following 1860 election of, 1-2; and Sharpsburg, Md., campaign, 23; strategy of, on Richmond versus Lee's army, 119, 145-46, 156, 158; visits to troops by, 33, 85, 270; on writing as communication, 10
Livestock, 27, 41, 44, 47, 86, 181, 192, 211, 228, 230, 231, 237. *See also* Foraging and raiding for food
Long, Clarence, 264, 266
Longstreet, James: and Alexander's artillery, 52, 53; on Antietam battle, 52, 61; and defense of Richmond, 38; in Georgia, 122; and Gettysburg battle,